CROSSROADS
OF FREEDOM

CROSSROADS
OF FREEDOM

Slaves and Freed People in Bahia,

Brazil, 1870–1910 **WALTER FRAGA**

TRANSLATED AND WITH AN INTRODUCTION BY Mary Ann Mahony
FOREWORD TO THE BRAZILIAN EDITION BY Robert W. Slenes

Duke University Press   Durham and London   2016

Designed by Courtney Leigh Baker
Typeset in Minion Pro by Westchester Publishing Services

Library of Congress Cataloging-in-Publication Data
Names: Fraga Filho, Walter, [date] author. | Mahony, Mary Ann, translator,
writer of introduction. | Slenes, Robert W., writer of foreword.
Title: Crossroads of freedom : slaves and freed people in Bahia, Brazil, 1870–1910 /
Walter Fraga ; translated and with an introduction by Mary Ann Mahony ;
foreword to the Brazilian edition by Robert W. Slenes.
Description: Durham : Duke University Press, 2016. | Includes bibliographical
references and index.
Identifiers: LCCN 2015041558|
ISBN 9780822360766 (hardcover) |
ISBN 9780822360902 (pbk.) |
ISBN 9780822374558 (e-book)
Subjects: LCSH: Slaves—Brazil—Bahia (State)—History—19th century. | Freedmen—
Brazil—Bahia (State)—History—19th century. | Slavery—Brazil—Bahia (State)—
History—19th century.
Classifica tion: LCC HT1129.B33 F5513 2016 | DDC 306.3/620981/42— dc23
LC record available ath ttp://lccn.loc.gov/2015041558

Cover art (leftt o right): Black women and canoe paddlers on the dock at
Cachoeira, 1930 (detail). Arthur Wischral / Public Archive of the State of Bahia.
Roceiros at the Market, Cachoeira, 1930. Arthur Wischral / Public Archive
of the State of Bahia. Black family, Cachoeira, 1911 (detail).

Contents

A Note about Currency and Orthography

Both before and after abolition and the fall of the Brazilian Empire, the basic unit of currency was the real (réis in the plural). One real would have been written Rs.$001. The sum of 100 réis was usually written Rs.$100. One mil-réis was equal to 1,000 réis and written Rs.1$000. Larger sums were counted in contos de réis, each one of which was equivalent to 1,000 mil-réis. One conto de réis was written Rs.1:000$000. (Adapted from Barickman, *Bahian Counterpoint*, n.p.)

Brazilian orthography has changed a great deal since the documents on which this book is based were produced. In keeping with current practice, spelling is modernized in the text but maintained in the original in the notes and bibliography.

MAP 1. The Recôncavo, Bahia, and Brazil in South America.

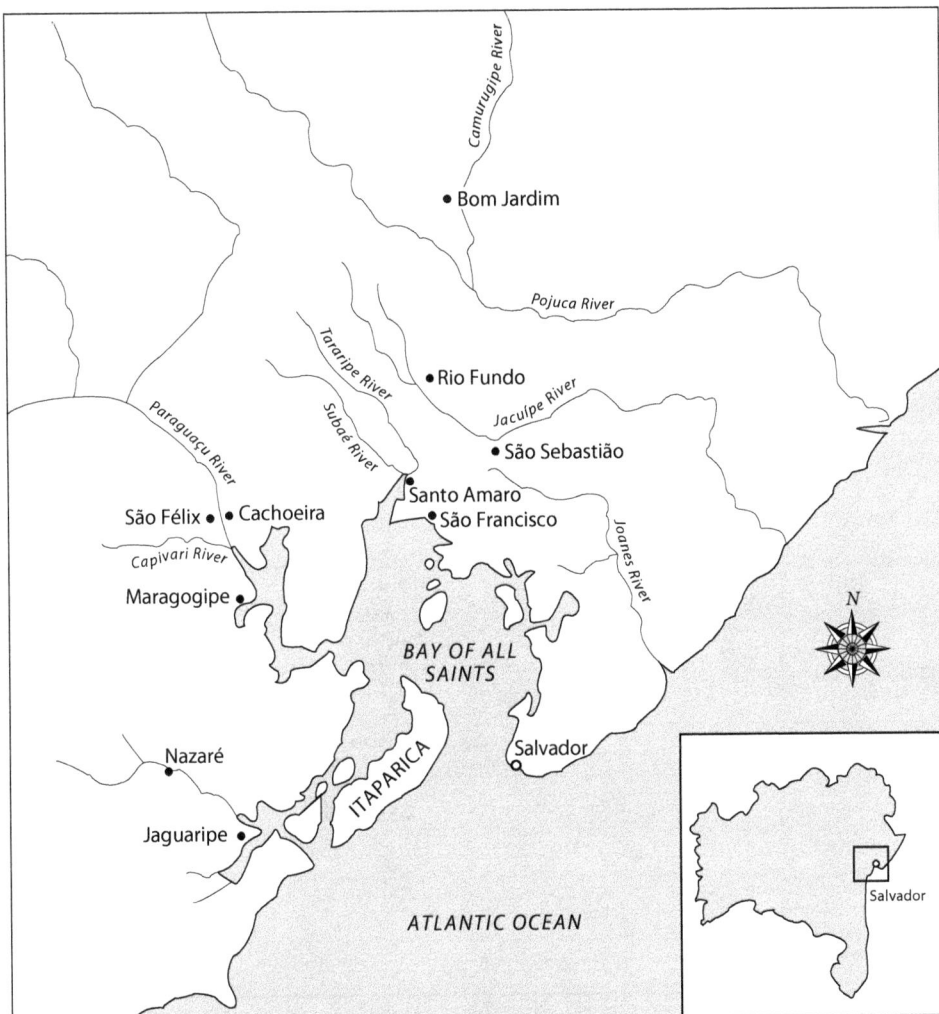

MAP 2. Cities and towns of the Bahian Recôncavo.

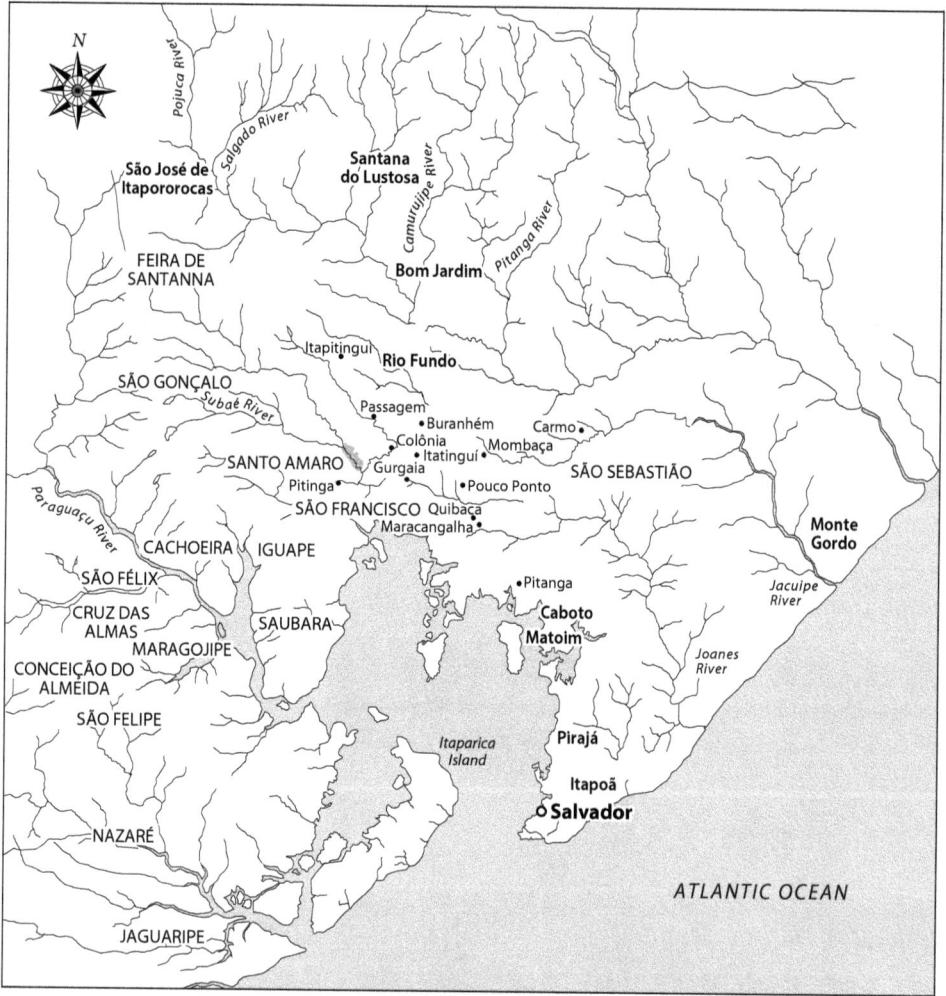

MAP 3. Principal plantations and rivers of the late nineteenth-century Recôncavo.

Introduction to the English-Language Edition
MARY ANN MAHONY

Slave traders transported more Africans to Brazil than to any other part of the Americas. Between about 1570 and 1857, slave ships disembarked some 4.5 million Africans in Brazilian ports.[1] Brazil was one of the first European colonies in the Americas in which enslaved Africans toiled on plantations and in mines, and it was the last place in the hemisphere to abolish slavery. The enslavement of Africans and their descendants, thus, marks Brazil strongly.

Nowhere is Brazil's African heritage clearer than in the northeastern state (formerly province) of Bahia. Enslaved African and Afro-descended laborers made Bahia one of the wealthiest plantation regions in the Americas as early as the sixteenth century. In 1870, when *Crossroads of Freedom* opens, between seventy thousand and eighty thousand Africans and their descendants lived and labored in Bahia's most important sugar-producing region, the Recôncavo. Indeed, as many as twenty-two thousand lived in the two largest Bahian sugar-producing municipalities alone—Santo Amaro and São Francisco do Conde. Although the number of enslaved laborers was shrinking in Brazil at the time because of the end of the slave trade and the passage of the Law of the Free Womb in 1871, slavery remained the dominant form of labor on Recôncavo sugar plantations until slavery ended on May 13, 1888. Even as abolition approached, these enslaved Africans and Afro-Bahians produced an average of 41,800 tons of cane sugar annually for some of the most important planters and political figures in nineteenth-century Brazil.[2] As Walter Fraga shows, when abolition was promulgated, ex-slaves ceased to work for the sugar planters under the old conditions. Their efforts to control their lives, exercise their newfound freedom, and change the terms of labor in the Recôncavo brought sugar production crashing down in 1888 and left planters struggling to cope financially and emotionally. *Crossroads of Freedom* tells this story.

History and Historiography of Slavery and Freedom in Brazil

Crossroads of Freedom is an important book that builds on recent developments in the historiography of slavery and freedom in Brazil and the Americas.[3] The study of the history of slavery in Brazil initially developed as an effort to understand whether slavery had been a benign or brutal institution in Brazil and to determine what role, if any, it may have had in the nation's trajectory.[4] These early scholars, whether arguing for a cruel or a paternalistic slavery, therefore, emphasized the impact of slavery as a system on the development of Brazil rather than the experience of the enslaved. Although Emília da Costa described various forms of slave protest in 1880s São Paulo, most scholars in these early generations saw abolition as something that primarily happened to slaves rather than an event that they helped to bring about.[5]

Similarly, as Fraga argues in his introduction, studies of the post-emancipation period in Brazil focused on the transition from slavery to free labor rather than on the experiences of former slaves themselves. The most influential contributions to this literature focused on the Southeast, where waves of European immigrants began to arrive in the 1880s, followed by Japanese immigrants when coffee planters found European workers unsatisfactory.[6] Only one study of the "transition" dealt directly with the Northeast.[7] Historians of the Northeast who studied the history of the first republican period (1889–1930) tended to address questions of rural oligarchies, messianic movements, bandits and export economies. Important as these topics were, in the North and Northeast, as in the Southeast, slaves, slavery, and slave owners disappeared into the mist of the past. The first republic was not studied as a post-emancipation period or a post-emancipation government. In some cases, the local history of slavery was denied.[8]

More recently, scholarship on slavery and freedom in Brazil has moved in new directions with significant new findings. Scholars influenced by microhistory and social history, as well as the linguistic turn in historical studies, have made slaves and freed people the subjects of history. Adopting a "history from below" approach, they argued that scholarship about slavery and freedom had treated slaves as things and denied the enslaved their humanity and agency. Jacob Gorender criticized them for making slavery seem less harsh than it actually was, but there can be no doubt that this scholarship turned the enslaved into thinking, breathing, calculating, dreaming, and planning people on the basis of previously unused archival materials. In this new direction of research, no one denies that slavery was based on coercion; rather, "both paternalism and violence are seen as complementary forms of slave control."[9]

As the social and cultural historians of slavery and freedom in Brazil began their research, they delved into police reports, criminal investigations, civil and criminal court transcripts, and ecclesiastical records, as well as other manuscript sources. They began to read documents compiled by elites "against the grain" for what they might tell us about the thoughts, feelings, and actions of subaltern subjects. They also began to pursue the oral history of subaltern groups, a methodology central to Latin American labor history but which scholars of slavery and abolition in Brazil had rarely used.[10]

These new historians of slavery and freedom put slaves and ex-slaves at the center of their work, but following individual and family groups of slaves, ex-slaves, and other nonelites through space and time to tease out the trajectories from slavery to freedom remained nearly impossible. Here and there, detailed documents allowed historians to reconstruct the complex experiences, sometimes over long periods of time, of individuals or small groups of ex-slaves, but not of large ones.[11] Most of the free and freed poor population was illiterate at abolition, and remained so well into the twentieth century. Consequently, they did not leave their own written records of their experiences. Nor were their memories recorded through a government program, as occurred in the United States.

Complicating this lacuna was the difficulty in locating ex-slaves in the records. Slave owners, of course, kept meticulous records of their property, but slaves rarely carried surnames. When they became free, some chose to adopt the ex-master's surname, but others did not. Still others began with one name and then changed it. Brazilian naming practices are not as standard as those in Spanish America, Europe, or the United States, and could vary significantly from generation to generation. Moreover, formal marriage was not necessarily common among the Afro-descended poor, and common law marriages were not officially recognized in the documents, especially at the birth of children. Add to this the fact that many freed people concealed their enslaved pasts after abolition, and it becomes clear that discovering how individuals and family groups actually experienced the end of slavery and beginning of freedom was not easy. Tracking them was impossible until the development of easily searchable spreadsheet and database software, but it is still difficult, as I know from personal experience. The process requires hundreds of hours of research and data entry.

Walter Fraga took up this challenge, using Carlo Ginzburg's historical method of nominative record linking, nicknamed "linking data" or "crossing data," to bring together the fragments of information about people found in multiple different types of documents in an effort to follow them and their families as they emerged from slavery into freedom.[12] In so doing, he brings slaves and ex-slaves out of the shadows to which the transition to free labor literature had condemned them, and he refutes the argument that slavery was so damaging and demoralizing that ex-slaves could not adapt to freedom. He does not argue that ex-slaves were necessarily successful after the end of slavery, but he shows clearly that they struggled to make their understanding of freedom real.

Crossroads of Freedom uses the methodology of microhistory, social history, and cultural history to break new ground, but it also builds on significant research on slavery and freedom in the Americas over the last several decades. A full discussion of that historiography is beyond the scope of this introduction, but a few additional words about the trends on which he builds, and to which he contributes, as they relate to Brazil, and particularly Bahia, are in order.

In 1977, when Stuart Schwartz's article "Resistance and Accommodation in Eighteenth-Century Brazil: The Slaves' View of Slavery" appeared, the notion that slaves might attempt to negotiate with their masters was controversial. The dominant view at the time considered slavery to be so brutal that the enslaved could not reproduce and mortality was extremely high. Constant surveillance, discipline, and violence were all required to keep slaves working.[13] Resistance took the form of massive escapes or violent backlashes against brutal masters. Schwartz had already begun revising our understanding of escaped slave communities, and the document on which the 1977 article was based, a treaty presented by fugitive slaves to their master in 1879, required historians to consider the possibility that negotiation was central to slavery. João José Reis's *Slave Rebellion in Brazil*, first published in Brazil in 1986, also argued for a more subtle understanding of slavery. *Slave Rebellion* examined the most important urban slave revolt in the Americas, but it also made clear that slaves could work with minimal supervision while still planning to overthrow the system that enslaved them. Reis showed that common work experiences and a common faith could form the basis of a common consciousness among African laborers of different backgrounds, although not necessarily between Africans and Afro-Brazilians.[14] In the following years, additional research on slave resistance revealed that both negotiation and conflict were central to maintaining slavery in Brazil.[15] Slavery was based on violence, but, as Silvia Lara argues, that violence was not indiscriminant. Rather, in day-to-day master-slave relations it was measured, corrective and exemplary, designed to "guarantee lucrative production, survival of the slave, and the maintenance of seignorial domination."[16]

When Schwartz published the fugitive slaves' document, the possibility that slaves might have access to land on which to grow subsistence crops and sell the excess in local markets was still a subject of debate in Brazil. Research on what is now termed the "internal economy of slavery" was in its infancy there, although it was well under way in the Caribbean and the southern United States. In Brazil, until 1994 when Barickman published a seminal article on the subject, there was no consensus that provision grounds existed, let alone on what they meant. Indeed, in "'A Bit of Land Which They Call a Roça,'" Barickman asserted that his first task was "simply to establish whether slaves on the engenhos [plantations] and cane farms of the Recôncavo often cultivated provision grounds."[17] His answer was a definitive yes they did, and he concluded that "although factors inside and outside plantation boundaries restricted the development of the economy Bahian slaves built for themselves, they were slaves who, within the limits imposed by slavery, 'negotiated.'"[18] Barickman's 1990 doctoral dissertation, revised and published in English in 1998 and in Portuguese in 2003, made clear that the economy of the Recôncavo was more complicated than previously thought. Slaves indeed had access to provision grounds, although they did not produce enough food to provide all of their needs or to make the sugar plantations self-sufficient.[19]

During this period, historians also began to challenge long-held assumptions that slavery was so violent and dehumanizing that slaves had been unable to form families. In the 1970s, using the methods of demography and new technologies, historians began to analyze demographic trends among the enslaved population of Brazil. Some were able to develop complex statistical portraits of communities but they tended not to discuss individuals. The issues related to names and formal marriage discussed above particularly inhibited efforts to tie together persons found in documents organized according to the masters' logic. Over time, however, historians digging in archives and building databases and genealogical charts have been able to demonstrate that enslaved men and women did form families as well as real or fictive kinship ties, although masters, the Brazilian government, and the Catholic Church did not necessarily recognize them. Some of those families now can be traced over multiple generations and studied to see how slaves worked toward the freedom of family members and planned, or tried to plan, for the day when they might eventually become free. Indeed, historians now see family ties as central to notions of freedom, and indeed, consider that they help to explain both certain forms of slave control and slave resistance.[20]

The new methodologies and the new focus on the experiences of slaves themselves also brought significant changes to the study of abolition in Brazil.

Until the 1990s, most historians did not see abolition there as a process in which slaves or ex-slaves participated significantly.[21] The turn to "history from below," however, uncovered a variety of forms of slave resistance to slavery, and an active effort on the part of slaves to advance the cause of abolition. By the 1870s and 1880s, slaves, ex-slaves, and the free adult children of slaves, as well as some members of the new middle classes, were making slavery very difficult and expensive for slave owners. From São Paulo to Rio de Janeiro to Bahia, slaves worked slowly; they fled (individually or in groups; temporarily or permanently); they complained to the authorities about harsh masters; they sued masters for their freedom or they punished them for transgressing the moral economy that had developed on Brazil's plantations. Their actions were central to the timing and character of abolition.[22]

The realization that slaves were pushing for abolition, and not just passive recipients of social change, required historians to take a new look at the post-emancipation period. The new direction, in combination with dialogue with scholars of slavery and freedom in the United States and the Caribbean, put freed people and the post-emancipation period at the center of one of the most important new directions of Brazilian historiography. Scholars of the period began trying to understand what freedom meant to people who had been captives. As they did, they found that making a firm dividing line in Brazilian history between the pre- and post-emancipation periods was inappropriate at best. New research is showing that the experiences of slavery shaped ex-slaves' understanding of both slavery and freedom, that slaves' strategies for freedom grew out of that understanding, and that, after abolition, they tried to put those plans into practice. Among other things, scholars are showing that ex-slaves attempted to establish themselves as free citizens.[23]

Despite the flourishing of literature on Brazil, and the increasing attention to both slavery and freedom in Bahia, in the mid-1980s, there remained no scholarly study of the end of slavery on Recôncavo sugar plantations from the perspective of the enslaved themselves.[24] In the following decade, Barickman demonstrated the attachment of Bahian sugar planters to slavery and the collapse of their sugar economy with abolition. Kim Butler compared the activities of free Afro-Brazilians in São Paulo and Salvador after abolition, and both Dale Graden and Jailton Brito studied abolition movements in Bahia. Others had shown that Bahian export agriculture diversified after abolition, but until 2004, no scholar had examined the end of slavery and the beginning of freedom on Recôncavo sugar plantations, from the perspective of the enslaved themselves.[25]

Crossroads of Freedom fills that gap while also breaking new ground by bringing us into the world of the enslaved men, women, and children who toiled on Bahia's sugar plantation in the last decades of slavery in Brazil. Fraga asks what they thought of slavery, what their plans were for freedom, how they struggled to bring their dreams to fruition, and what happened to them. He does not show these struggles in a vacuum. Rather, he contextualizes their trajectories by introducing us to once powerful sugar planters, bankrupted and traumatized by abolition, who may have lost their wits, their property, and some of their national standing, but whose families still retained significant influence locally and regionally.

Several conclusions emerge from Fraga's history. One is that the fight to obtain material and symbolic resources on the plantations during slavery shaped ex-slaves' expectations of freedom after abolition. In concrete terms, this meant that, when freedom came, ex-slaves did not expect to give up resources they had won with difficulty during slavery. Struggles over land, over time to work that land, and over the ability to live with family, begun under slavery, continued in the Recôncavo after slavery ended. Access to land, control over time, and family connections were central to ex-slaves efforts to establish themselves as citizens in the post-emancipation period. In this way, the efforts of the Recôncavo's ex-slaves seem much like those of their counterparts in the Caribbean and the U.S. South after slavery ended.[26]

Fraga's research lends credence to arguments by Silvia Lara and Barbara Weinstein, among others, that some of the boundaries that historians have erected between the study of slavery and the study of free labor, or between the history of people of African descent and those of indigenous people in the Americas are artificial.[27] *Crossroads of Freedom* can be profitably read by scholars of rural people throughout the Americas, whether descendants of Africans, of indigenous groups, or of mixed-race groups, peasants, proletarians, or semiproletarians.

Questions of Translation

Translating a work of this quality and complexity involves more than opening up a dictionary. Although the language of the original is superb, its Portuguese sentences could not simply be translated word for word into English and left to stand on their own. Retaining the flavor of Fraga's prose in translation required switching many sentences from passive to active voice, which in turn sometimes meant moving sentences around in paragraphs. Readers familiar with the original Portuguese will, therefore, find some slight differences between the two texts.

Readers will also find that some Brazilian terms and concepts, especially those related to race, agriculture, and labor, remain in Portuguese. Fraga and I had hoped to translate all terms and concepts into English to make the text more accessible to undergraduates, but several proved unwieldy or even problematic in English. This is, in part, because usage of terms for race, agricultural property, and agricultural labor were often fluid and ambiguous in post-emancipation Bahia. Planters and their ex-slaves did not use the same terms in the same way. And as ex-slaves tried to establish themselves as free citizens, they often tried to distance themselves from slavery and any label associated with it, while planters and their representatives continued to use the language of the past. Also some of the terms have false cognates in English. Consequently, we decided to leave some terms in Portuguese, while translating others. The key to the decision was whether or not the translated term helped to clarify the text.

The terms referring to slave origin, and skin color, are a case in point. Brazilians had (and have) multiple terms for skin color, many of which also reflected a judgment about the culture or status of the individual described. Such terms were fluid, and their usage changed over time.[28] In the nineteenth century, slaveowners used *africano(a)* or *crioulo(a)*, terms reflecting origin, as well as *preto(a)* and *negro(a)*, to describe dark-skinned people in Brazil. Unless modified by free or freed, *africano(a)* referred to a slave born in Africa, while *crioulo(a)* usually described a Brazilian-born slave. Prior to abolition, Fraga has found that *preto(a)* referred to black slaves regardless of origin, while *negro* usually referred to freed persons. After abolition, elites and their representatives used terms like *preto(a)* or *crioulo(a)* to cast a shadow of slavery over freed people. *Preto(a)*, in particular, was a pejorative after abolition.

Unlike in the United States, Brazilians did not lump all people of African descent into a single category of black. They had numerous terms for non-whites of mixed race, generally reflecting differences in skin tone. These included *mestiço(a)*, a generic term for a mixed-race person in Brazil; *mulato(a)*, a generic term referring to a person of mixed African and European ancestry; *pardo(a)*, another term for mixed race, literally meaning brown, usually modified by light or dark; *cabra*, referring to the child of a *preto(a)* or *negro(a)* and a *pardo(a)*; and *moreno(a)*, another term for brown.

Brazilian understanding of concepts of race and skin color were and are therefore quite different from those in the United States, and although English may contain analogous terms, they do not necessarily carry the same meaning. I have therefore kept the terms for origin and color in the original Portuguese with two exceptions: *negro(a)*, is translated to "black," to distinguish it from the similar term in English and from *preto(a)*; and *mestiço(a)* is translated to mixed race. The glossary provides specific definitions according to the usage of the period.

Readers may also note that these terms are sometimes used as nouns and sometimes as adjectives describing color. Portuguese is a romance language in which nouns and adjectives are not gender neutral. Thus, readers will see different endings for nouns and adjectives describing men and women. When the term refers to a woman, the feminine version appears; for men, the masculine appears. Since "côr," the word for color, is feminine in Portuguese, when the term "color" is used as an adjective, the feminine will appear.

Decisions also had to be made with regard to terms for agricultural property and professions, for which Brazilian Portuguese has a wide variety of options, reflecting the complexity of plantation agriculture. *Engenho* and *senhor do engenho*, terms respectively for "sugar mill" and the "lord of the sugar mill," were the most straightforward. Here I chose to use "plantation" and "planter," because at the time most Brazilian engenhos had extensive lands, cane fields, as well as processing plants. Their owners were, above all, planters and the owners of large estates with prestigious homes, many outbuildings, large numbers of slaves, and hundreds of acres of land. Where the text refers specifically to the millworks on the property, I have used the term plantation sugar mill. Such terminology distinguishes them from *usinas*, the fully industrialized central sugar mills introduced to the Recôncavo in the latter part of the nineteenth century.

Other agricultural terms have remained in Portuguese. The term *roça* often referred to the small plots of land that slaves were able to farm on plantation lands belonging to their owners before slavery, but the term continued to be used after slavery ended. Sometimes the original Portuguese remains in the text but is also translated as "provision grounds," "garden plots," or "small plots of land." *Roceiros*, which is sometimes translated as "peasants" in the literature, were farmers with roças. Fraga found that roceiros did not necessarily own the land on which their farms sat, but after abolition, they were not obliged to provide service on plantations and large farms, and therefore had a status different from, and higher than, someone who continued to work for the landowner. Roceiros paid rent of some sort when they did not own the land. Consequently, I have chosen to leave roceiro in Portuguese. *Morador(a)*, literally "resident," also remains in Portuguese. Its meaning has changed significantly over time. In the sixteenth century, according to Stuart Schwartz, the term could sometimes denote an independent farmer who grew cane. By the late eighteenth century, it referred to a "part time free laborer who lived on a fazenda [ranch/farm] or engenho [sugar plantation] and was quite distinct from the lavrador [farmer] who grew cane."[29] Rebecca Scott describes moradores as tenants who farmed land in exchange for working on a plantation, and who occupied a position between peasants and proletarians.[30] Fraga found that morador covered a wide variety of arrangements, from permanent worker resident on a plantation to sharecropper. Many, but not all, had access to roças, although they were not as independent as roceiros. Moradores, he found, were *always* required to work several days a week for the owner of the plantation on which they lived, in exchange for the privilege of living on and farming the land. Nevertheless, they, not the landowner, owned the crops they grew.

The meaning of the words *lavoura* and *lavrador* could also vary according to context. Lavoura could mean "farming," "agriculture," "agricultural sector," "husbandry," or a number of other terms. Sugar, for example, was *a grande lavoura* or the prestigious agricultural sector, while tobacco was nicknamed the *lavoura dos pobres*, or the harvest of the poor in late nineteenth century Bahia.[31] The documents frequently describe individuals as having the profession of lavoura, or farming or agriculture. Where that is the case, Fraga argues that these people were field hands and that is the term that I have used, if the context seemed appropriate. Other individuals are described in the documents as living from *suas lavouras*. In other words, they are clearly denoted as living from *their* crops or *their* harvest. This might mean that they were roceiros, in that the individuals in question cultivated only their own crops, but the documents often distinguish between roceiros and people who live from their crops, so I have done so as well. Finally, a lavrador, when used without a modifier such as *lavrador de cana* ("cane farmer"), could refer to anyone from a well-established farmer with slaves but no land of his or her own to a morador. Where the word is clearly used to refer to a well-established farmer, I have used "farmer," where it is unclear, I have left "lavrador."

References to consensual unions among enslaved or freed people also required decisions about translating into English. Some had to do with rendering the gendered language of nineteenth-century Brazil, which was profoundly patriarchal, appropriately in English. When this study begins, Brazilian law recognized only one form of marriage, that sanctified by the Catholic Church in a wedding ceremony. After 1891, civil marriage became the most important legal marriage, but marriage in the Catholic Church continued to be widely practiced. Throughout the period, however, large numbers of Brazilians, and probably the majority of enslaved and freed people, lived together in consensual unions of various durations, although in some areas formal marriage was clearly practiced by the enslaved and free poor alike. Brazilian authorities, whether secular or religious, looked down upon women involved in informal arrangements, and given the approach of the author, the practice raised questions for translation. The terms "husband and wife" or "marriage," used alone, in English, suggest a legal status that most of the relationships discussed in this book did not enjoy. *Amásio* or *amásia*, the words for male or female concubine, were the legal terms that officials often used to describe consensual unions, but they imply a prejudice that, at least in the analytical sections of the text, did not seem appropriate. Consequently, I have chosen to use the term "common law husband and wife," as well as "consensual union" to describe the partners and the relationships. Where amásia was used by the authorities, however, "concubine" appears.[32]

Terms for Brazilian administrative structures and legal institutions are also complex. To some degree, this was because Brazil's government organization and legal system were strongly influenced by continental European models, and the analogous terms in English were unwieldy. But Brazil also underwent significant changes to its political system, and therefore to its administrative structures, between 1870 and 1910. When the book opens, Brazil was a constitutional monarchy, led by Pedro II, a descendant of both the Portuguese and the Hapsburg royal families. Many wealthy Brazilian planters enjoyed titles of nobility, such as João Maurício Wanderley, the Baron of Cotegipe. Administratively, the empire was divided into provinces, which were administered by provincial presidents. The monarchy fell in 1889, replaced by the first Brazilian Republic. In 1891, a new Brazilian government signed into law a new constitution that reshaped Brazilian government institutions. The emperor gave way to a president; provinces became states; and provincial presidents became governors. Barons and counts lost their titles, and were officially referred to as mister or, in some cases, colonel, reflecting membership (often honorary) in the local National Guard battalion. The new constitution also established civil marriage and civil registries of births, deaths, and marriages, where previously only ecclesiastical registers of baptism, marriage, and the last rites had existed. Brazilians who read history are accustomed to these shifts, but they can be confusing for those accustomed to a different tradition. I have chosen to allow the administrative terms to reflect the change in government systems, to emphasize that Brazil moved from a centralized monarchy to a decentralized federal republic during the period under study.

Finally, decisions needed to be made about how to handle citations of English works translated into Portuguese or works translated from Portuguese to English. Our original thought was to transfer all possible citations to the English versions of books and articles for the facility of readers unfamiliar with Portuguese. This ultimately posed two problems, one practical and the other conceptual. First, English and Portuguese versions of a given book or article are not necessarily identical. The literature here contains two excellent examples of this: João José Reis's *Slave Rebellion in Brazil* is a revised and expanded version of the Brazilian original. On the other hand, B. J. Barickman's *A Bahian Counterpoint* does not contain all of the rich research and detail of his dissertation, but the Brazilian edition of his book does. Consequently, the two books are not strictly translations, but different editions. More to the point, Fraga used the Portuguese editions of most of the books in question and we decided that the bibliography should reflect that. We therefore left the citations used in the original Brazilian edition, but translated all titles for the convenience of readers unfamiliar with Portuguese.

Finally, a few acknowledgments. It is my pleasure to present this wonderful book by Brazilian scholar Walter Fraga to an English-speaking audience for the first time. Like many Brazilians and Brazilianists, we met while laboriously digging through precious nineteenth-century documents in the reading room of the Public Archive of the State of Bahia. In the twenty-five-plus years since I first made my way to the pink colonial building in Salvador's Baixa das Quintas, my life has been enriched in innumerable ways. I have met and worked with historians from many parts of the world. In the process I have learned more than I ever thought possible about Brazilian history, friendship, and collaboration. Thank you!

These acknowledgments would not be complete without recognition of the colleagues and friends who read pieces or all of this translation. They include Emília Viotti da Costa, Stuart Schwartz, João José Reis, Hendrik Kraay, Joan Meznar, Carla Silva Muhammad, and colleagues and students in the Department of History at Central Connecticut State University. My thanks also to Valerie Millholland, who had confidence in this project, and Gisela Fosado, who saw it to fruition.

Crossroads of Freedom is an important book: it explores the experiences of one of Brazil's largest groups of slaves just before and after abolition in a region with one of the longest and most intense histories of slavery in the Americas. It received the American Historical Association's 2011 Clarence H. Haring Prize, for the most outstanding book on Latin American history written by a Latin American author in the five years prior to its publication. I am therefore extremely pleased to present this translation to the English-speaking public. I trust that you will enjoy it.

Foreword to the Brazilian Edition
ROBERT W. SLENES

This book is at the crossroads of various paths in recent historiography.[1] Walter Fraga followed the trails of experience and self-reflection blazed by slaves, freed people, and masters, to understand conflicts and alliances in the Bahian Recôncavo (the bay on which Salvador is located, and its immediate agricultural hinterland) from the end of the nineteenth to the early twentieth century. In so doing, he abolished the radical dissociation between "slavery" and "freedom" which had led many scholars to see the end of bondage in 1888 as either the terminus of one historical road (and research agenda) or the beginning of another; for it became clear that strategies, customs, and identities were worked out before emancipation shaped subsequent tensions between subalterns and their superiors. Indeed, the focus on actual lives, lived and pondered, as a way to discover broader social logics, brought Professor Fraga to the path of microhistory, an approach that seeks "God" (evidence of larger processes of change and continuity) in the intricacy of "detail."[2] This option, in turn, took him to people's names—that is, to the method of nominative record linkage—as a strategy for tracking persons over time in order to trace individual and collective biographies. *Crossroads of Freedom: Slaves and Freed People in Bahia, Brazil, 1870–1910* is the point of encounter of these diverse but converging paths.

To say this, however, only weakly defines the book's qualities. The crossroads in this case are exceptionally charged with power—so much so that it is difficult to do justice to Fraga's method in a brief compass. How does one explain, for instance, the magic of chapter 2, in which the author employs detailed police documents and an exceptionally rich trial record to reconstruct the assassination, by slaves, of a priest-administrator on a sugar plantation of the Carmelite Order in 1882? Fraga analyzes and contextualizes the case so skillfully that it illuminates slave owners' theater of dominion and bonded workers' refusal to play their ascribed roles, at the precise moment when slavery as a labor system faced a profound crisis of legitimacy.

How does one describe, as well, the wizardry of chapter 5, in which Fraga uses very diverse sources—among them, lists of slaves in probate records, two criminal trial proceedings, and the correspondence of a sugar plantation owner—to follow a group of freedmen over time, before and after abolition, and "triangulate" their experiences from several points of view? The author looks first at an episode in June 1888 involving the "theft" (expropriation) and slaughter of seignorial cattle by a small group of freedmen still living on the property where they had recently been emancipated. He then turns to another event, equally well documented, in 1889, in which some of the same individuals can be seen participating in an association of freed people dedicated to the same end. The analysis of these cases lays bare the day-to-day conflicts between former masters and slaves over the latter group's "customary right to garden plots" (continually trampled upon by landowners' cattle) and, indeed, even reveals some of the symbolic resistance of freedmen to planter rule. (Upon reading the first version of this chapter, my colleague, Professor Sidney Chalhoub, suggested that it be titled "The Great Cattle Massacre," since it calls to mind historian Robert Darnton's attempt to uncover— also from a banal, but culture-revealing episode—the metaphorical arsenal that printers' apprentices in eighteenth-century France drew upon to take shots at their guild masters.)[3] Finally, to cite one more example among many, how might one characterize the enchantment of chapter 8, in which Fraga reconstructs the family ties of slaves and of people freed on May 13 (those liberated at abolition in 1888) on another sugar plantation, from varied sources—including an interview with a male centenarian who still remembered some of the people encountered in the written documents about the property and furnished details about their lives circa 1920?

It would not be surprising if many readers of these chapters, even those familiar with the historical method, are left with the impression that Fraga has a "strong Saint" (*santo forte*) as his counselor; after all, how else might one explain his serial discovery of so many marvelous sources, much less the uncanny skill (*feitiço*) in his analysis? In fact, however, *quem sabe faz a hora*; command of craft makes opportunity—including the possibility of "luck"— happen, and creatively puts order into the results. Professor Fraga is gifted with patience, meticulousness, and imagination to an extraordinary degree; he did not need help to open new paths (*abrir caminhos*).

And what paths they are! For the tracks and trails of this microhistory lead to new interpretive highways. The Orixás are indeed in the particular. The crisis of the slave system reveals itself here in all its complexity, on a specific ground that is "good for thinking." Recent studies on Brazil's Southeast have characterized the destruction of forced capitalized labor as an eminently political process. Manifesting itself in the countryside and on the streets, as well as in official places like Parliament and the courts, this process in the Southeast destabilized the "imaginary institution" of slavery, thereby drastically reducing the "futures market" in commodified people—that is, the expectations regarding the subsequent life of capitalized labor—as is evident in the crash of the purchase market in bonded workers, from 1881 on.[4] Fraga's book documents a similar history in Bahia, using the tools of the social historian. It also demonstrates the economic force of slave labor in sugar. (Sugar planters in the Recôncavo not only largely depended on bonded workers until the eve of abolition;[5] they also, for many years, were unable to attract or coerce a sufficient number of free laborers to maintain production at pre-1888 levels.) The study then shows that the crisis in the legitimacy of slavery in Bahia during the 1880s—occasioned in part by the opposition of common people to this labor system, as well as by movements of flight and rebellion among bondspeople—was broadly similar to the process occurring in São Paulo, Rio de Janeiro, and other places.

Fraga's book also blazes a trail into virtually unopened land: that is, into the labor systems and the experiences of workers in Bahia during the post-abolition period. It shows the relative bargaining power of freed people in this region; here, the former slaves were able to increase the number of days during the week that they could devote to their own garden plots on lands still owned by their previous masters, at least well into the 1890s. This was something that apparently lay beyond the reach of their counterparts in that other major sugar-producing region, the Zona da Mata of Pernambuco.[6] One also observes in this early post-abolition period a significant migration of freed people from the rural Recôncavo to cities and other agricultural areas (the cocoa region in southern Bahia, for instance), which confirms this analysis; evidently, many persons found that the best opportunities for work and income lay outside the Recôncavo—a situation that, for a certain time, must have increased the bargaining power of those who decided not to move.

Migration, in any case, brought to the towns and the manufacturing sector men and women who—as Fraga shows in detail—had created community and family ties, as well as common customs and traditions of contestation, during slavery. Indeed, perhaps the most promising trail this book opens for other researchers lies in the suggestion that the lived and pondered experiences of former slaves contributed to forming the sociability of urban workers. "It is not surprising," writes Fraga, "that thirty-one strikes broke out in Salvador and the [towns of the] Recôncavo between 1888 and 1896," nor that "on May 12, 1902, when calling upon the 'Bahian people' not to forget 'our emancipation,' . . . the labor leader and ex-abolitionist Ismael Ribeiro spoke out in the name of 'my ancestors.'"

In the epilogue, Professor Fraga recalls the "inexpressible melancholy" of the Afro-Brazilian engineer, André Rebouças, in 1895, on realizing that the conquest of full citizenship for people of color in Brazil "[was] still a long way, a very long way, off, in the centuries to come." Yet all of Fraga's analysis reveals that projects and hopes for reform in this direction were not lacking in turn-of-the-century Bahia. Indeed, such projects and sentiments were so in evidence that they provoked strong reactions from the elite—including the attempt, ultimately successful, to empty the annual celebrations of May 13 of that demand for additional rights which had characterized them immediately following 1888. Countering the amnesia produced by defeat, Fraga's study foregrounds struggles which did in fact exist and which could help inspire the opening of new roads toward citizenship today.

Crossroads of Freedom has its own history of converging paths. It was originally a doctoral dissertation in history at the Universidade Estadual de Campinas (Unicamp). It clearly reflects the theoretical and methodological concerns of professors and students associated with the Center for Research on the Social History of Culture (CECULT) at that university. But it also engages in dialogue with a recent international bibliography on the experiences of slaves and freed people in other historical contexts.[7] Then too it reflects the author's solid training in history as an undergraduate and master's student at the Federal University of Bahia and his close interaction with young and established Bahian scholars, some of them also with doctorates from Unicamp.[8] Indeed, at the crossroads of these and other paths, a new generation of historians is aborning in Bahia—or rather, is "taking the stage." (I play here on the expression *baiano não nasce, estreia*—"people from Bahia are not born, they premiere.") In this "show" of style and competence, Walter Fraga has a leading role.

—*Campinas, May 2006*

Acknowledgments

In writing this book, I have enjoyed the assistance and support of numerous people and institutions. Over the course of the two years in which I sat in the research room of the Public Archive of Bahia, I benefited from the good will and patience of the staff there, particularly Raymundo, Daniel, Edvaldo, Lázaro, and dona Maura, who located documents for me. I am immensely grateful to the employees of the *cartórios* of São Sebastião do Passé, Iguape, Rio Fundo, Lustosa and Santo Amaro, who zealously maintain the precious manuscripts in their care. Despite having other, more important concerns, the staff of the Santa Casa de Misericórdia Hospital in Santo Amaro, allowed me to examine their important documents.

A CAPES fellowship financed the research. The support of the State University of Bahia (UNEB) and particularly of the Department of Human Sciences of Campus V in Santo Antônio de Jesus was fundamental, allowing me time away from teaching to carry out research and writing.

Numerous individuals made important suggestions for the project or helped me to locate documents. Lígia Sampaio graciously recommended that I read several important sources and gave me access to her father's writings, pictures, and memoirs. João da Costa Pinto Victória helped me to locate private correspondence and photographs, and shared the research he had developed during his career. Constância Maria Borges de Souza read most of the chapters. Her comments led to important improvements. Neuracy de Azevedo Moreira helped me with the statistics.

I am grateful to Silvio Humberto Passos, Rosana Santos de Souza, Marilécia Oliveira Santos, Ericivaldo Veiga, Louise Blakeney Williams, Mark Rondeau, Paula Mahony, Marina Silva Santos, and my compadre Carlos Ailton, for the motivation to keep on going. I shared concerns and learned a great deal from the friendship and the research of Mary Ann Mahony and Hendrik

Kraay. I am further grateful to Mary Ann Mahony for this first-rate translation and for the sensitivity to confer beauty and elegance to the English text.

I am enormously grateful to João José Reis, Hebe Mattos, Maria Cristina Wissenback, and Silvia Lara—for their criticisms and suggestions. Silvia Lara and Sidney Chalhoub read the first version of this book and contributed a great deal to its improvement. João Reis put his library at my disposal and discussed several possible interpretations of my documentation with me. Rebecca Scott encouraged me and suggested a number of different options for developing the theme that this book addresses. Peter Beattie, Susan O'Donovan, Joseph C. Miller, Alejandro de la Fuente, and Joan Meznar read and commented on parts of the book, and for that I thank them. Robert Slenes accompanied this project from the beginning and pointed out various ways to bring it to a conclusion. Emília Viotti da Costa, Stuart Schwartz, and Hendrik Kraay read the entire volume and made excellent comments. Valerie Millholland of Duke University Press deserves special thanks for her generosity in putting this book at the disposition of the American public.

My cousin, Paulo Fraga, provided friendship and hospitality while I conducted research in Rio de Janeiro, and Manoel Ferreira (Manoelzinho) patiently recounted to me the details of his life on a Recôncavo sugar plantation.

Finally, I am grateful to my family, who have been my inseparable companions in this and several other ventures. My brothers and sisters, Rosa, Waltércio, Valdilene, Apollo, Ana Maria, Raimundo, and Galileu, always encouraged me. My children, Laís, Victor, and Isabel, followed this project every step of the way, cheering me on to the end. And finally, I dedicate this book to my parents, Domingas and Walter, who always believed in me.

CROSSROADS
OF FREEDOM

Introduction

This study examines the experiences of the slaves and ex-slaves who lived and labored in the Bahian Recôncavo, one of the oldest slave societies in the Americas, from the last two decades of slavery through the first twenty years after abolition on May 13, 1888. The Recôncavo was one of Brazil's most important slave-holding and sugar-producing regions, but sugar was not the Recôncavo's only crop, nor did all slaves work in sugar. Sugar was, however, the region's most important crop and most slaves there worked in sugar, even as abolition approached. Examining this history, therefore, reveals the implications of abolition and the consequences of the end of slavery for a significant sector of Brazil's black population.

Until quite recently, May 13, 1888, has primarily constituted a chronological divider between two distinct periods of Brazilian history. Abolition in 1888 and the installation of the Brazilian Republic in 1889 marked the end of one era and the beginning of another. Key to this new period were a number of new elements: free labor, massive growth in European immigration to southeastern Brazil, industrialization, and organized labor. With the new focus on these factors, the legacy of slavery and the men and women who had lived through slavery abruptly disappeared from Brazilian history.

This "disappearance" of the former slaves from the study of the post-emancipation period was, in some respects, ideological, in that it was a way to show that Brazil had done away with the legacies of slavery once and for all. This racialized discourse made it possible to discuss Brazil without reference to Africans or their descendants. In other words, it silenced them.

In the 1940s, in his classic study *História econômica do Brasil*, Caio Prado Júnior argued that free wage labor had "substituted" for enslaved labor in the last years of slavery. By substituted, he meant that the period saw the emergence of capitalist labor relations and labor movements, the principal actors in which were the European immigrants who had begun to arrive in great numbers in Brazil's Northeast in the 1880s.[1]

In the 1960s and 1970s, Prado's work inspired a number of studies in Brazil of what is conventionally called the "transition from slavery to free labor." The authors of these studies also understood the end of slavery as the point of departure for the development of capitalism in Brazil. Slavery, they argued, had so damaged the minds and bodies of ex-slaves and freed blacks that they were unprepared to respond to the demands of a society based on wage labor. From this perspective, blacks, whether ex-slaves or free, appear as "things" or parts of a macroeconomic machine that marginalized them from the most dynamic process of social transformation of the period.[2]

Toward the end of the 1980s, as the centennial of abolition in Brazil approached, a series of studies based in research in new archival manuscript sources brought about a profound revision in the historiography of slavery in Brazil. Challenging the idea of the slave or ex-slave as "thing," these studies began to explore enslaved agency in the most diverse aspects of their daily lives.[3] Previously unexplored documentary sources allowed Africans and their descendants to emerge in the historical literature as thinking beings capable of independent initiative and thoughts about how to live and resist slavery. And, above all, Africans and their descendants appeared as individuals who carried with them memories and understandings of the world learned in Africa.[4]

In Brazil, these revisionist interpretations of slavery have had significant consequences for students of the post-abolition period. Without discarding cultural and social contexts, these studies have attempted to reveal the daily experiences and the improvisation of slaves and freed people as they forged identities and developed survival strategies during and after slavery.[5]

In the 1990s, a number of studies reexamined the role of Africans and their descendants in the movements to end slavery in Brazil. Their deeper analysis of the tensions that marked the end of slavery and their connection to slaves' understanding of freedom began to reshape the historiography.[6] Hebe Mattos de Castro's study *Das cores do silêncio* (On the colors of silence) was an important contribution in this regard, as it examined the tense discussions about the meanings of freedom that took place in the days immediately after the abolition of slavery.[7]

In the 1990s, some historians also began to broach the temporal boundary of the end of slavery in 1888 to study more systematically the day-to-day experiences of the populations emerging from slavery. For Bahia, two historians from the United States pioneered the effort to analyze the black experience beyond the limits of abolition. In *Freedoms Given, Freedoms Won*, Kim Butler compared the post-emancipation experiences of Afro-Brazilians in two important Brazilian cities, Salvador and São Paulo. In *From Slavery to Freedom in Brasil*, published in 2006 but based on his 1991 PhD thesis, Dale Torston Graden brought a hemispheric perspective to Bahia's experiences in the post-emancipation period, especially as they related to local struggles for citizenship and access to land.[8] In this period, the historiography of the post-emancipation period also began to include studies of the daily life, the life histories, and the memories of ex-slaves.[9] Studies of the impact of racism and racial theories on the daily lives of Afro-Brazilians became especially important.[10]

This book is the heir of these historiographical debates, but it moves beyond them to explore the history of ex-slaves through their trajectories. My goal is to lift the curtain on significant historical transformations by exploring the trajectories of individuals, families, and communities. This exploration of trajectories allows us to see what those who emerged from slavery thought and felt about freedom.[11] They show us that the day-to-day experiences of slavery influenced choices, attitudes, expectations, and plans for freedom in the post-emancipation period in any number of ways.

Thus, this study does not examine the maintenance of, or breaks with, patterns of behavior developed in slavery. Such notions oversimplify the complex relationships and conflicts that developed in post-slavery Bahia. Rather, this study uses the dynamics of day-to-day relationships to reveal how past experiences could fuel aspirations or return as memories and recollections.

Nor does this study of trajectories aim to reveal the "behavior of the average" freed person in order to infer broader patterns of behavior or social relationships. I am not searching for models, nor do I believe that models can account for the wealth of lived experiences, the dynamics of the multiplicity of the choices that freed people made over the course of their lives. Rather, I explore how the people who emerged from slavery tried to shape the directions their lives would take in numerous creative ways despite the unforeseeable future and the limits placed on them by a society based on profound socioracial inequalities.

This study does not explore the "transition" from slavery to free labor either.[12] Aside from suggesting that the shift from slavery to freedom was a linear historical process, studies about transition focus primarily on the economic aspects of the substitution of slaves by free workers and rarely consider that most of the "free people" had once been slaves or were descended from them. Slavery was much more than an economic system; it molded behavior, it defined social and racial hierarchies, and it shaped feelings, values, and the etiquette of command and obedience. Sharp social tensions marked slavery's end, wherever it existed, as long-held demands were unleashed and, at the same time, freedom took on new meanings and expectations. The ex-masters of Bahian slaves understood that the period was dangerous, such that they tried to reduce its complexity to a question of the "substitution" or "transition" to free labor. This study aims to go beyond such notions to consider the attitudes and behaviors of the various social actors in a very specific context—the major plantations of Bahia's Recôncavo in the last years of slavery and first years of freedom.

For some time, historians and anthropologists have been exploring aspects of the history and culture of Bahia's black population in the post-abolition period. Focusing on African heritage and/or the reinvention of such heritage in Bahia, these studies have allowed us to accumulate immense knowledge about the religiosity, family, race relations, forms of resistance, and participation in the labor market of Bahian blacks.[13] But we know little about the destinies of ex-slaves, about their experiences and plans for freedom, their memories of enslavement, and the ways in which they related to their former owners and to the communities of which they were a part. Even the Recôncavo, which has been the subject of numerous historical studies, is still awaiting the systematic study of the populations that emerged from slavery there.

This study does not pretend to fill that void, but it does address various aspects of freed peoples' experience in the post-abolition period. Many of the questions discussed here grow out of a dialogue with the historiography about the rich and complex trajectory of the black populations after emancipation here in Bahia, in Brazil, and elsewhere in the Americas. Recent studies avoided dichotomies such as rupture and continuity or dependency and autonomy and, in so doing, broadened the possibilities for understanding the various meanings that ex-slaves attributed to freedom.[14]

In this study, I am trying to go beyond generalizations to perceive how the ex-slaves interacted with others—including ex-masters and members of the communities to which they belonged—as they went about their daily lives after emancipation. Doing so required building an empirical base that allowed me to see their post-emancipation trajectories. It was extremely complicated, given that the documentation produced in the years after abolition is nearly silent on the juridical status of people who emerged from slavery. Brazilian ex-slaves rarely left documents that they had written discussing their memories of slavery and their experiences of the first days after abolition, unlike their African-American counterparts, who left diaries and letters. Therefore, locating the men, women, and children who lived the last years of captivity on the plantations has been a formidable task.

To follow these people through time and space, I drew on many different kinds of documents—registers and lists of slaves attached to postmortem inventories, as well as certificates of baptism, birth, and death in local, state, and national archives as well as private collections. Using the methodology of nominative record linkage, nicknamed "crossing data," I was able to follow individuals and family groups over time by putting together data from lists of slaves attached to postmortem estate inventories with parish baptismal registers and the notarial registers created after the declaration of the Brazilian Republic in 1889.[15] The information about the locales in which they were born and lived, the names of the properties on which they worked, and the names and surnames of parents, grandparents, and godparents offered important directions for reconstructing individual trajectories and social networks alike.

Viewed in isolation, the notarial registries, for example, have little to say, either because the notaries did not take into account peoples' pre-abolition social conditions or because the freed people themselves hid such information. For ex-slaves, affirming freedom and the rights of citizenship did not encourage revealing their pasts in slavery. Only a few did as Juvenal when he registered the death of an elderly friend. He described himself as a "freedman" and a crioulo resident of the São Bento Plantation. He described Salomão, the deceased, as eighty years of age, single, and an "African Preto" "who had been a slave on that plantation and lived in an earlier period of labor service." He also stated that he did not know Salomão's "parentage or other circumstances because the deceased African had been very old."[16] Among hundreds of birth certificates in the Cartório of the Registro Civil of São Félix, I was able to find only one that mentioned previous slave status. In it, the notary recorded that Domingos Florêncio dos Santos had informed him that, at four o'clock in the morning of February 16, 1892, "his ex-slave" Maria Rita dos Santos gave birth to a "parda colored" baby boy called Porfírio, whose maternal grandmother was Rita Maria dos Anjos.[17]

Given this lacuna in the post-emancipation civil registries, documents produced prior to abolition were essential to reconstructing individual and family group trajectories for slaves and their descendants. For example: On July 17, 1889, the single seamstress and "Brazilian citizen," Ângela Muniz, who lived on the Mombaça Plantation in Monte Parish in the town of São Francisco, reported the birth of a daughter, baptized Gertrudes. Mother and daughter carried the same surname as their grandmother, Antônia Muniz. The list of slaves attached to the 1880 postmortem inventory of Mombaça's owner revealed that Gertrudes's mother and grandmother were two of the 119 slaves who lived on the plantation at the time. Both were labeled crioula field hands.[18]

On January 1, 1891, the birth of a "parda colored" girl named Marinha was registered in the notary's office of São Sebastião. The records indicate that she was the daughter of Maria de São Pedro and granddaughter of Rosalina, both of whom lived on land belonging to the former Carmo Plantation. Checking the list of slaves on the Carmo property in 1865 reveals that the little girl's grandmother, Rosalina, was enslaved there at the time. The girl's mother, Maria de São Pedro, seems to have been born after the 1865 list was compiled, since her name does not appear among the slave children belonging to the plantation. The reader will meet Rosalina again in chapter 2 of this book.[19]

Taken together, these documentary fragments reveal ex-slaves' struggles for freedom from slavery. On February 10, 1889, the twenty-year-old crioula ex-slave Etelvina Rego went to the notary's office in Rio Fundo a district of Santo Amaro, to register her son Antônio, who had been born a few days before. The father, Antônio do Rego, was the son of Serafina do Rego, and both lived on the Paranaguá Plantation. But the little boy's grandmother had also appeared on the list of slaves who fled Paranaguá in June 1882. A number of slaves had escaped together, claiming that they had completed the term of captivity determined in the will of their former owner, Antônio Honorato da Silva Rego. The new plantation owner, the Baroness of Monte Santo, published the names of all the fugitives in the region's newspapers. Among them was Serafina, a "crioula preta," the thirty-year-old mother of three children.[20] Clearly, Grandma Serafina had been a fugitive, and little Antônio's father had probably been among the three children that she took with her when she fled the plantation.

Such events were common and the snippets of peoples' experiences left behind in documents help us to reconstruct fascinating stories. This methodology allowed me to follow the lives of the slaves and freed people on the plantations, as the reader will observe throughout the book. By "microanalyzing" these documentary bits, I was able to see how the family ties and other relationships that developed among slaves of the same plantation during slavery were preserved and enhanced during the post-abolition period. I was also able to see the social and symbolic logic that shaped the choices that individuals and groups made before and after slavery ended. I argue that the material and symbolic resources of the communities forged under slavery were fundamental to their survival strategies after captivity ended, especially when they tried to expand the space available to them both on and off the old plantations.

Returning to the structure of the book, the first three chapters provide a general picture of the enslaved population on the Recôncavo's sugar plantations in the last years of slavery. They demonstrate that social tension existed on the large sugar estates at that time and continued into the post-abolition period, although with different meanings. Chapters 4, 5, and 6 reveal the conflicts, tensions, and negotiations over rights and resources on the plantations that emerged between former masters and ex-slaves shortly after May 13, 1888, the day that slavery ended in Brazil.

Chapters 7 and 8 analyze the tense relationships between the owners of sugar plantations and freed people who remained on their properties after abolition. Here we reveal the social consequences for freed people of remaining on the properties on which they had been born or on which they had served as slaves. Within communities formed during slavery, the freed people tried to modify relationships with their ex-masters, confirming traditional rights and expanding beyond them. Further, they gave new meaning to the ex-master's paternalist "protection" and used it on a daily basis to conquer and amplify their own space for survival.

Finally, the last chapter tackles the question of the challenges freed people faced when they left the places of their former enslavement after abolition. Ex-slaves made freedom real when they migrated, whether within or beyond the Recôncavo, whether to break ties to ex-masters or to look for work. Wherever they went, the men and women freed by Brazilian abolition on May 13, 1888, moved in the context of, and frequently in opposition to, the wishes of individuals and groups who hoped to control them.

ONE

SLAVES AND MASTERS ON SUGAR PLANTATIONS IN THE LAST DECADES OF SLAVERY

The World of the Sugar Plantations

In Portuguese, the word Recôncavo refers to any land circling a bay, but in Brazil it refers to the region bordering the Bay of All Saints, one of only two large bays on the Brazilian coast. The district measures roughly 10,400 square kilometers and boasts significant deposits of the clayed soil that Portuguese colonizers of Brazil learned was excellent for growing sugar.

The Recôncavo was the first region the Portuguese systematically occupied when they began to colonize the land that we now know as Brazil. In 1549, they founded Salvador—the capital of Bahia—as a fortified city to protect settlers of the interior. In the following decades, settlements moved inland, following the rivers that flowed into the bay—the Paraguaçu, the Jaguaripe, the Subaé, and the Sergimirim. In the lowlands along these rivers—especially in those stretches of river accessible to navigation, Portuguese settlers established villages that later became the towns of Cachoeira, São Félix, São Francisco do Conde, Maragojipe, Santo Amaro, Jaguaripe, and Nazaré das Farinhas.

At the time, the Recôncavo was home to numerous indigenous groups. For centuries before Europeans first claimed the territory, Tupinambá Indians had dominated the Paraguaçu River valley and Itaparica Island at the mouth of the Bay of All Saints. As the Portuguese settled the Atlantic coast, they forced the existing indigenous occupants deep into the Recôncavo. Those who resisted colonization and its associated conversion to Christianity soon discovered that the Portuguese would bring indigenous groups from other parts of Brazil to fight them. Those who surrendered to Portuguese occupation found themselves enslaved on the new sugar plantations that the Portuguese established along the coast.

As the Portuguese became disillusioned with indigenous labor, they began to import Africans into Bahia to work as slaves in the construction of Salvador and on the plantations producing sugar.[1] The first Africans who disembarked in Bahia were probably part of the colonizing expeditions that settled Salvador, but as their role in plantation agriculture began to grow in the 1570s, their numbers rose quickly. Over the course of the next three centuries, the Atlantic slave trade would bring some four million Africans to Brazil from culturally diverse parts of the continent. These included West-Central African peoples generically known in Brazil as Congos, Angolas, Cabindas, and Benguelas, as well as West African peoples, particularly groups originating in the hinterlands of the Bight of Benin; Yorubas (called Nagôs in Bahia); Hausas; Nupes (called Tapas in Bahia); and Fon, Mahi, Adja, and other Gbe speakers (called Jejes), as well as other small groups. In the Recôncavo, therefore, as in other parts of Brazil, peoples who would have had little contact in Africa lived and worked side by side, exchanging words, foods, customs, and religious practices. These interactions meant that Africans formed new alliances and established new cultural practices in the Recôncavo and that numerous African ethnicities contributed to the ways in which Africans and their descendants there lived and thought.

By 1822, Brazil had become independent from Portugal, and the Recôncavo had become the most important center of sugar production in Bahia, and one of the most important in Brazil. Approximately 90 percent of Bahia's sugar plantations lay in the rural parishes near Salvador and the Recôncavo towns of São Francisco do Conde, Santo Amaro, and Cachoeira.[2] Sugar estates dominated these districts, and land was concentrated in few hands: in Iguape, just outside of Salvador, for example, twelve property owners controlled 80 percent of the available land in the middle of the nineteenth century.[3]

Recôncavo planters grew more than sugarcane: a diversity of soil types on their properties allowed them to cultivate tobacco, manioc, beans, corn, and other crops in addition to sugar. Slaves and freed people also grew subsistence crops on land allowed them by the planters. The resulting harvests supplied the plantations' slaves as well as the free and enslaved urban populations of the rural towns and Salvador.[4]

Throughout the colonial period and for most of the nineteenth century, the Recôncavo was the most important economic region in Bahia, and sugar was its premier crop. But both the sugar industry and the region entered an economic decline in the 1870s from which they would not begin to recover until the end of the century. The problems originated in a deterioration of international prices for sugar, brought on, in part, by competition from beet sugar. To aggravate the situation, labor costs increased significantly. Sugar planters relied entirely upon enslaved labor to the final days of Brazilian slavery in 1888, despite the close of the African slave trade to Brazil in 1850, and the emancipatory laws passed by the Brazilian government in 1871 and 1885. Total abolition in 1888, therefore, hit them particularly hard.[5] All of these problems eventually brought about a precipitous drop in Bahian sugar exports and the associated revenue stream.

During this time the Recôncavo was also the most densely populated region of Bahia, and the area where the largest number of slaves were concentrated. According to the 1872 census, the region contained 35.7 percent of the provincial population. At the time, 165,403 slaves lived in Bahia, representing 12.8 percent of the provincial population as a whole. In 1887, the province's enslaved population had declined to 76,838, and nearly half of that decline (42 percent) had taken place in the previous three years. Despite the drop in population, Bahia remained the fourth-largest slave-holding province in Brazil.[6] Most of those slaves continued to live in the Recôncavo because sugar planters simply refused to let go of their last captives.

The demographics of the enslaved population changed over time. After 1850, when Brazilian law definitively abolished the African slave trade, the ethnic composition of the black communities on the sugar plantations changed rapidly.[7] Prior to the close of the slave trade, most Recôncavo plantation slaves had been born in Africa, but by the 1870s, most were Brazilian born. While

TABLE 1.1. African, Crioulo, Mixed-Race Slaves (a sample), 1870–1887

Color/origin	Number	Percent
African	80	10.2
Crioulo	514	65.3
Pardo (mixed race)	44	5.6
Cabra (mixed race)	149	18.9
Total	787	100.00

Source: Postmortem inventories, 3/1206/1675/1 (1869–1887); 8/3444/4 (1887–1891; 7/3212/6 (1868); 6/2586/3086/3 (1870–1889), APEB.

the Atlantic trade continued, men outnumbered women on sugar plantations by as much as two to one. By the last decades of Brazilian slavery, however, there were some properties with more enslaved women than enslaved men. According to Stuart Schwartz, Pitinga and Conde were two such plantations: on the former there were 60 enslaved men and 67 enslaved women; while on the latter there were 45 men and 60 women.[8]

These demographics are reflected in a sample of 798 enslaved laborers on Recôncavo sugar plantations, constructed from the slave lists in the postmortem estate inventories of ten planters who died between 1870 and 1887 and summarized in table 1.1. The sample includes 446 men and 352 women, indicating that male laborers were more numerous than female workers on most plantations at the time, but the gender disparity seems to have been much smaller than it had been at the beginning of the century. Strikingly, only 10.2 percent of the captives in the sample had been born in Africa. Crioulos, as Brazilian-born Africans were known, dominated the group numerically, totaling 65.3 percent of the labor force on the plantations studied. Pardos and cabras—in other words, slaves of mixed African and European ancestry—together made up another 24.5 percent of enslaved workers. Combining the groups of slaves categorized as mixed race with the group labeled crioulo reveals that nearly 90 percent of the workers in the sample had been born in Brazil. In other words, in the last decades of slavery, the enslaved population on Recôncavo sugar plantations was overwhelmingly Brazilian born.

By the 1870s, many of the enslaved workers on Recôncavo plantations belonged to family groups extending back generations. In our sample 35.6 percent of the slaves worked alongside at least one relative and lived and worked with two or three generations of their family. That means that some enslaved men and women had formed families and maintained stable relationships across generations, something once thought to have been impossible.[9]

These biological and fictive ties were solidified through baptisms, marriages, burials, and festivals held in plantation chapels or village parish churches. One study of slave baptisms in Recôncavo sugar parishes showed that when enslaved men and women chose godparents for their children, they often looked to captives enslaved on other plantations.[10] This interaction across properties was possible because the sugar plantations were fairly close to one another, in some cases sharing borders and owners. Over time, these biological and fictive ties allowed Africans and their descendants in the Recôncavo to devise collective strategies that would contribute to their material and cultural survival after abolition.

Table 1.2 makes clear that between 1870 and 1887, more than half (52.4 percent) of the labor force was between eleven and forty years of age. In other words, despite the end of the slave trade and the Brazilian legislature's gradual emancipation laws, a large contingent of enslaved workers of productive age still labored on the sugar plantations in the last two decades of slavery. Removing the children and those with no profession listed from the sample reveals that, as shown in table 1.3, 82.3 percent of the slaves on the plantations were field hands. In other words, the large majority of captives labored in the cane, the sector that traditionally employed the largest number of captives. At the same time, the plantations employed a large number of enslaved artisans—shoemakers, stonemasons, joiners, and blacksmiths. Many captives listed as field hands may also have had some artisanal skills. As we will see, after abolition, such artisanal skills allowed some ex-slaves to support themselves when they left the plantations.

The availability of such enslaved laborers explains why the plantations could operate without making major adjustments to the labor force as the nineteenth century progressed. Perhaps this was why the planters resisted abolition almost until May 13, 1888. In the 1880s, it seems that there were good reasons why Bahian abolitionists considered Recôncavo sugar planters the most intransigent slaveholders in the province.[11]

Although Recôncavo sugar planters retained large numbers of enslaved laborers and opposed abolition, whether they liked it or not, the end of the Atlantic slave trade, deaths, individual manumissions, flights, and gradual emancipation all combined to reduce the number of slaves available to them. Therefore, in the last two decades of slavery in Brazil, they had no choice but to find ways to cope with the shrinking captive population on their properties. The documents indicate that planters turned to a number of alternatives to cope with the increasing difficulties of obtaining enslaved laborers, including some involving master-slave relations themselves. Planters with multiple

TABLE 1.2. Age Profile of the Recôncavo Sugar Plantation Slaves, 1870–1887

Age groups	Number	Percent
0–10	161	20.3
11–20	139	17.5
21–30	142	18
31–40	133	16.8
41–50	105	13.3
51–60	75	9.5
60 and over	36	4.6
Total	791	100

Source: Postmortem Inventories, 3/1206/1675/1 (1869–1887); 8/3444/4 (1887–1891); 7/3212/6 (1868); 6/2586/3086/3 (1870–1889), APEB.

TABLE 1.3. Slave Occupations, 1870–1887

Professions	Number	Percent
Agriculture	459	82.3
Domestic	26	4.7
Artisan	22	3.9
Carter	22	3.9
Sailor/boatman	10	1.8
Sugar-mill worker	8	1.4
Cattle herder	4	0.8
Nurse	4	0.8
Overseer	2	0.4
Total	557	100

Source: Postmortem Inventories, 3/1206/1675/1 (1869–1887); 8/3444/4 (1887–1891; 7/3212/6 (1868); 6/2586/3086/3 (1870–1889), APEB.

properties sometimes moved captives around, concentrating laborers on their most profitable estates. Alternatively, they hired slaves from neighboring planters to supplement their own labor force, or rented out their own slaves when demands on their plantation allowed.

During the 1882 harvest, for example, the administrator of the Lagoa Plantation in Santo Amaro noted that he paid "some slaves" belonging to the property with a combination of cash and food to work on Sundays, normally a day of rest for slaves. He also hired free workers either by the day or by the task, paying them in food or cash as well. Among these free laborers were a number of skilled workers (machinists, carpenters, blacksmiths, and cauldron makers), as well as fifteen cane cutters, eight "hoe and sickle workers," and fourteen firewood carriers. The cane cutters included two women—probably freedwomen—who worked alongside the slaves. The manager also indicated that he had paid "some slaves" belonging to the plantation in cash and food to work on Sundays.[12]

Many planters engaged free laborers to supplement enslaved workers as abolition approached, but according to Barickman, they lacked a dependable supply of free workers. He found that, at the time, members of Recôncavo's free and freed population, most of which was black or mixed race, did not need to work in the sugarcane industry to support themselves.[13] This was why, as a wealthy planter from the Recôncavo reported in 1871, "those free people" could not be convinced to weed the plantation cane fields. They would only work in the plantation sugar mills, packing and hauling processed sugar. Clearing fields was the only agricultural work they would perform on the plantations.[14] As a result, the plantations hired migrant laborers from quite distant corners of Bahia to work the plantations, especially during the dry season. Planters considered these workers unreliable, however, because there was no way to force them to remain on the plantations once the seasonal rains began. This scarcity of free labor helps to explain why the planters depended upon slavery right up until the eve of abolition.

Surviving on the Plantations

In the last three decades of slavery, relationships between masters and slaves on large Recôncavo sugar plantations were complex. Many documents offer glimpses of these relations, but the account book of Francisco Moreira de Carvalho, the Count of Subaé (1825–1888), who owned three sugar plantations in Santo Amaro (Benfica, Água Boa, and Roçado), provides extraordinarily detailed information about activities—both the day-to-day and seasonal—involved in producing sugar.

According to the count's records, slaves received supplies both as a regular practice and as a reward. Plantation management distributed food—normally meat and manioc flour—throughout the year, but most intensively in August and September, when the harvest and grinding of cane began. At the beginning and end of the harvest, the slaves received cloth or ready-made clothing. On September 26, 1864, the planter noted: "I gave pants and a shirt to all the pretos [black slaves] at Palmeira and Alambique . . . , I gave clothing to the preta [black] slave women at Palmeira; homespun, cotton and cloth from the coast of Africa." On October 14, 1872, he noted the distribution of twelve pairs of pants and twelve shirts to the "pretos at the still." He also provided cloth for children's clothes, because on April 5 of that year he recorded the purchase of cotton yardage for the *moleques*, a term specifically referring to enslaved boys. Sometimes he seems to have rewarded individual slaves, perhaps for practicing some specialized craft, following a seignorial logic: for example, on September 1872 the count noted: "I gave pants and a shirt to Pedro Jeje."[15]

According to the count's records, planters sometimes rewarded enslaved laborers with money. For example, on January 30, 1870, the count paid Rs.30,000 to the preto João Nicolau. He also paid a few slaves to work on Sundays and holy days according to the records.[16] This practice reflected the growth in the opportunities for paid work in the sugar districts, as the number of slaves on the plantations began to fall in the last two to three decades of slavery. According to historian Robert Slenes, slaves valued this wage labor very highly.[17]

Some slaves participated in the sugar sector as small farmers who supplied cane for processing to the sugar mills on the plantations. In 1882, among the farmers who supplied the Lagoa Plantation sugar mill with cane were ten slaves. In payment, they received a share of the sugar that the mill produced, just as the free farmers did. On the other hand, they did not receive any of the cane syrup [mel]. As Lagoa's owner commented that year, free farmers received fourteen of the 70 barrels of cane syrup produced that year, but the rest remained with him, because "the slaves don't get cane syrup."[18]

Recôncavo slaves found ways to earn money other than working on the sugar plantations, as was the case in other parts of the Americas.[19] We know that many slaves raised animals, especially oxen, pigs, and chickens, for their own consumption or for sale. They primarily did so in a sharecropping relationship with their owners or neighboring planters. Among such slaves was Daniel, an enslaved African agricultural worker on the São Pedro Plantation in São Francisco who was accidentally shot in a cane field, as he made his way back from another plantation where he raised pigs in "partnership" with a woman named Virginia. To get the time off to make the trip, he had claimed to be sick so that he might be excused from work.[20] On the plantations near the bay, slaves gathered shellfish to supplement their diets and to sell. When slavery ended, many of them relied on these activities for support to avoid the cane fields.

These alternative economic activities also allowed captives to work toward freedom. On June 18, 1864, Petronila, a thirty-eight-year-old freed crioula woman who lived in the sugar district of Paramirim, was obliged to explain to the authorities of São Francisco do Conde how she earned her living. She had become the principal suspect in the theft of a wallet containing Rs.1,800,000, belonging to a relative of her former owner. The *subdelegado* suspected her because, several days after the money disappeared, she bought her freedom and purchased fabric and a silk skirt from a traveling salesman. Suspicion against her increased when her common law husband of six months, the free crioulo Joaquim Inácio Piranduba, was seen "parading" through town in store-bought shoes.[21]

Under interrogation, Petronila explained that, over the course of the previous four years, she had saved the money necessary to buy her freedom from "her business," making and selling porridge on the streets of Paramirim. She also said that she and her sister Durvalina owned cattle that they cared for in the pastures of nearby plantations. In other words, activities she had carried out while living as a slave had allowed her to save for her freedom. On the day she purchased her freedom, Piranduba had accompanied her to Paramirim and he counted out the money paid to her master.[22]

Petronila was versatile and very active: aside from laboring in her master's home, she sold porridge and raised cattle in a sharecropping arrangement on another property. Few slaves had the opportunity to engage in as many activities as Petronila, but like others, her actions all supported the goal of buying her freedom. And, as was the case with others, freedom was a family project: Petronila's common law husband and at least one sister, Durvalina, helped her to obtain it. We don't know if or how Petronila and Piranduba managed to free themselves from the charges, but their story illustrates the breadth, worth, and complexity of the internal economy of slavery. And it shows how suspicion could fall on slaves who engaged in economic activities outside of their master's purview.

The internal economy of slavery could also include the clandestine removal of crops or animals from the plantations. Masters considered such removals to be thefts and punished slaves whom they caught severely. On October 2, 1865, for example, the Count of Subaé "tied up Felipe and José de Santana on suspicion of being sneaky." As he commented in his diary, "if it's not one group, it's the other." The following day he sent the two men to his sugar plantation, the former for theft and the latter for sabotaging a machine.[23]

Slaves sometimes also supplied some of their subsistence needs by raising crops on land granted them by their owners. Toward the end of the eighteenth century, Luís dos Santos Vilhena reported that planters allowed some slaves to grow agricultural crops on Sundays and holy days on subsistence plots that they called roças, the produce of which slaves were expected to use to feed themselves.[24] In the middle of a series of slave revolts during the 1830s, Miguel Calmon du Pin e Almeida, one of imperial Brazil's most important analysts of agricultural management, recommended that Recôncavo sugar planters concede "some property" to slaves as a way to maintain order on the plantations. In his *Ensaio sobre o fabrico do açúcar* (Essay on the production of sugar), Calmon advised that access to subsistence plots

> is a powerful method of distracting [the slaves] from their sad condition, and inspires in them the desire to work and even to establish families. Convincing them to plant food crops, permitting them to raise some animals, or engage in some profession, will doubtless help them to be happy, improve their habits, and reduce their tendency to engage in disgraceful activities, which slavery generates and feeds.[25]

Recent studies emphasize that such independent agricultural activities reduced the costs of slave subsistence and maintenance to the planters, but that they also allowed the slaves some personal independence.[26] Over time, slaves developed the sense of having "rights" to these bits of land, and any owner who interfered with their access to such lands had problems.[27] Indeed, access to the subsistence plots became a permanent source of conflict between slaves and masters. Consequently, rather than cut off slave access to roças, masters tried to reduce the amount of "free time" that such slaves spent tending to them.

Selling their crops in local markets provided slaves with subsistence plots the opportunity to earn money and acquire goods that they could not otherwise obtain. Going to the market also allowed them to develop business ties and friendships with other slaves and freed people from neighboring plantations, with people from the surrounding towns, and with sailors who transported crops to the markets in Salvador, the capital and principal port. These relationships were helpful if slaves decided to question the legitimacy of their enslavement by fleeing their masters.

Attachment to roças was so strong among slaves that, in the decades prior to abolition, some remained on the plantations after they were manumitted. Among such freed slaves were several Africans who continued to cultivate small plots of land on the Itatinguí Plantation after they obtained their freedom. A conflict between two of them sheds light on the microeconomy of these freed people and on their sense of ownership of these cultivated lands, as well as the strength of the communities on the plantations.

On March 26, 1885, freed African João Gonçalves attacked another freed African, seventy-five-year-old widow Júlia Argolo, who "did not know her parents because she had come from the Coast of Africa at a young age" and who had taken the surname of her owners at manumission. As Argolo later told the *delegado*, she lived from "her little roça that barely produced enough to feed her."[28] The trouble broke out as she was leaving that subsistence plot and witnesses stated that, in the struggle, she dropped a straw basket containing cassava, okra, and bananas—in other words, produce from her subsistence plot—on the road. Apparently, she was on her way to the market to sell the surplus from her tiny farm.

According to Felipe Pontes, another "free African" who lived from "his roça," the fight between Gonçalves and Argolo grew out of a conflict over money. Gonçalves believed that Argolo should have asked him to hold money he believed she inherited from her common law husband because he was "an African of the same nation as the victim" or a "compatriot," but he suspected that she had entrusted her savings to outsiders instead. But Pontes also revealed that Gonçalves previously had tried "to move into the victim's house," and she had refused him. In other words, the quarrel actually grew out of personal, ethnic, and financial disagreements. Ethnic solidarity and belonging to a community of freed people were important aspects of day-to-day life on the plantations.[29]

Despite the conflict, the fact that ex-slaves were able to support themselves by cultivating small pieces of land, selling the surplus in local markets, and saving small amounts of money indicates that such freed people had managed to carve out a place for themselves within the plantation system. Clearly, as we will see throughout this book, access to subsistence plots and the development of other independent activities on the plantations while slavery still existed shaped ex-slaves' ideas about freedom. After the abolition of slavery, such notions of freedom led ex-slaves to struggle to maintain access to their subsistence plots and continue their other activities, just as they had before slavery ended.

To engage in such activities, slaves needed to convince masters to allow them "free time" beyond the Sundays and holidays they were normally allowed, either through negotiation or subterfuge. It is possible that doing so became easier in the 1870s and 1880s, especially during the cane harvest, because of the growing enslaved labor shortage. Some slaves spent that "free" time working away from the plantation on which they were enslaved, especially during the cane harvest.

Such extra time was usually paid with food (meat and manioc flour) and a bit of money. Planters and overseers understood the importance of such activities, which afforded slaves significant freedom of movement, and by the last decades of slavery punished "insubordinate" slaves by prohibiting them. Some of the conflict on the plantations, and particularly the rebelliousness of plantation slaves as the end of slavery approached, grew out of overseer efforts to impose such penalties.

The approaching end of slavery and the labor shortage appear to have led planters and overseers to increase workloads for slaves on the plantations. Doing so led slaves to resist in various ways. In the 1930s, an ex-slave named Argeu commented on his experiences as a slave on a Recôncavo plantation in the last days of slavery:

> I ran away on purpose. It was the only way to get some rest. It brought me a lot of trouble and a whipping, but a week in the stocks and having cachaça, salt and pepper put on my wounds was better than the punishment of working day and night.

Argeu also remembered that there were other ways of avoiding the planters' excessive labor demands. He said that, even though he was extremely healthy at that time—made of steel as he said—he would "pretend to be sick so that he wouldn't have to work. He [the master] would make me take herbs for cough and constipation when he thought I was trying to put one over on him." That may be why the Count of Subaé's diary contains so many references to escapes and "insubordination" during harvest season, exactly when cane cutting and grinding demanded the most work from the slaves.[30]

Conflict between planters, overseers, and slaves became more frequent as masters or overseers tried to extort more work from the captives, especially if that occurred during seasons customarily dedicated to rest. In 1870, on the Benfica Plantation belonging to the Count of Subaé, the slaves rebelled against the overseer after they were forced to clean a cane field during the rainy season. In a letter to the Count of Subaé, the overseer wrote that the moleques [enslaved boys] had time off during the dry season that year, but they refused to return to work when the rains came, and as a result, the cane fields were overrun with weeds. The captives had refused to obey the overseer's orders, alleging that they were not accustomed to weeding the cane fields in the winter. The overseer handed out the hoes on June 12, but very little was accomplished that day. The following day, a Saturday, he forced the slaves to work and personally went to check on their progress, ordering them to stop "fooling around." He later wrote that he gave two or three of them "a tastc of the whip" but it did not help. On Sunday, a day normally dedicated to rest on the plantations, the slaves did not appear for work. When they finally turned up on Monday, they brought with them a letter to the overseer from their master, the count. In his reply, the manager could not hide his fear at being one of only five free men on the property as he confessed that he had lost control of the slaves.[31]

In 1883, slaves of the São Bento Plantation rebelled after the overseer forced them to work on Sunday to finish a job that they had not completed the day before. One free plantation worker later said that the slaves worked half a day and then left to "get their rations" without waiting for the overseer to call them to do so. When ordered to return to the fields to work, they refused. That night, the slaves, carrying their tools, headed off to appeal to the owner. But before they could make it to the plantation house, the overseer intercepted them. In the confrontation that followed, a slave named Francelino was fatally shot. His companions—Anastácio, André, and Miguel—reacted by using the tools they carried to kill the overseer.[32]

In the two conflicts described above, the slaves looked to the plantation owner for help against the overseer. In other words, they questioned the overseers' orders, but they did not challenge the plantation hierarchy. They went through the appropriate channels for complaining about things they considered "unjust." But as the 1880s progressed, expectations of freedom upset these customary ways of doing things.

As expectations of freedom rose, the planters continued to rely on physical punishment for bad behavior or refusing to work—the traditional forms of control on Recôncavo sugar plantations. But this ran contrary to the slaves' expectations that slavery was about to be abolished. Unsurprisingly, therefore, during the 1870s and 1880s, the enslaved population was increasingly unwilling to tolerate the traditional forms of slave control, especially corporal punishment.

Consequently, in the 1870s and 1880s, efforts by masters or overseers to physically punish slaves exacerbated tensions on the plantations. On March 28, 1871, the crioulo slave Benedito seriously wounded the Cotegipe Plantation overseer. The slave later admitted that he hit the manager several times with a sickle because the man had threatened to beat him.[33] On March 6, 1879, Victor, an enslaved agricultural worker on the Estiva Grande Plantation in Conde, killed the overseer after being threatened with a beating.[34]

The slaves had enormous expectations of freedom and their masters feared the end of slavery during this period. To understand why requires consideration of what is known as the gradual abolition of slavery in Brazil. Beginning with the 1871 "Law of the Free Womb," the Brazilian imperial government signaled that slavery would eventually end in Brazil. The slaves learned of this and other measures, and saw them as legal weapons to improve their conditions within slavery and also to gain their freedom.[35] The next section describes the general political climate relating to slavery at the time and shows how it affected day-to-day relations on the plantations.

Escape and Ideas about Freedom

The Law of September 28, 1871, known as the Law of the Free Womb, had the most significant impact on slave-master relationships of all the emancipatory laws passed by the Brazilian imperial government in Rio de Janeiro prior to abolition.[36] First it liberated all children born to enslaved women after its passage and labeled them *ingênuos*. The law also required masters to register all of their slaves with the local authorities, in a measure designed to guarantee greater fiscal control over owners. Further, it instituted an emancipation fund aimed at freeing registered slaves with revenues derived from taxes on enslaved property, fines, the lottery, and allocations from public budgets. The authorities could free any slave who had not been registered without having to spend one cent.

As historians have long recognized, the Law of the Free Womb liberated enslaved women's reproductive organs. But, as Sidney Chalhoub argues, the law also formally recognized several rights that slaves had attained over the years, and which by 1871 were custom. In addition, it guaranteed slaves' rights to their savings and their right to free themselves for a price, and in so doing made more possible some of their hopes and dreams. Chalhoub was correct to highlight these aspects of the law, but in my view, the law most significantly allowed slaves to sue masters who refused to allow captives to purchase their freedom.[37]

Bahian plantation owners disliked the Law of the Free Womb. When the bill was initially introduced to the Brazilian legislature, one planter outlined the group's objections in a book published under the pen name "A Bahian farmer." The "farmer" argued that the law would destroy the family, encourage slaves to betray their masters, ruin the labor force, and infringe on private property. He argued that the planters would support emancipation as long as the government followed tradition—in other words, as long as masters could determine when freedom would be conceded, and who would and would not be freed. In his view, that was the only way Brazil could guarantee an orderly transition to freedom, and avoid the "bloody" conflicts that characterized the process in the United States.[38]

Despite resistance to it, bureaucratic difficulties in implementing it, and some fraudulent use of the emancipation fund, the Law of the Free Womb did open up avenues for slaves to use the legal system to obtain their freedom. In doing so, the law expanded the struggle for freedom from the plantations to the courts and drew judges, lawyers, court-appointed guardians, and trustees, as well as witnesses, into the fray. The law's passage provided slaves with new allies in their legal struggles for freedom.[39]

When lawsuits about freeing slaves reached the courts, members of large slave-owning families frequently found themselves on opposite sides. Seeking to retain some measure of control over the freedmen, sugar planters became involved in the liberation of slaves belonging to neighbors or disaffected relatives. In August 1879, for example, a disagreement within the Passos family led plantation owner Temístocles da Rocha Passos to appear in court as the guardian of the crioulo slave Teodoro, who was suing his owner, Balbina de Oliveira Passos, for his freedom.[40]

These legal disputes allowed freed and free people to bring the fight for the freedom of their enslaved relatives and friends to the halls of justice. For example, on September 21, 1880, Antônio José de Freitas brought suit to free his common law wife, Maria Cândida de Jesus, whose owner was about to sell her out of Bahia. When her owner petitioned for documents required for her to leave the province, the judge refused him, ruling that Maria Cândida should remain available to the court until the case was decided. Even the master's invention of false names (Arcanja or Arcanjela) to facilitate her sale did not succeed.[41]

Plantation slaves were aware of the rights granted them in these emancipatory laws. In January 1875, authorities in Salvador arrested the "preto" Raimundo who had escaped from the Laranjeiras Plantation in São Francisco. That October he sent a petition to the chief of police describing himself as Raimundo Bitencourt, cabra, blind in one eye and the slave of Joaquina de Bitencourt. He went on to say that he knew that his mistress had not registered him and he had fled to the city to "take care of his freedom." He also stated that he had paid 92 mil-réis in savings to a "guy named Malaguias José dos Reis for arranging his freedom."[42]

Toward the end of the 1870s, the slaves began to notice that although planters controlled the courts near the plantations, they enjoyed no such authority in Salvador. Many officers of the courts in the provincial capital actually sympathized with slaves: such individuals prohibited the sale to other provinces of slaves who were saving to buy their freedom; they granted freedom to slaves who were not in jail when they applied for liberty; and they established the price of freedom at values below those demanded by the masters. From then on, therefore, Recôncavo slaves who hoped to sue owners for their freedom increasingly fled to Salvador.[43]

Recôncavo plantation slaves also fled to Salvador to complain to the police about mistreatment, to seek police assistance in conflicts with their masters, to appeal for protection in legal disputes, or to block their relatives' sale out of Bahia. On October 19, 1881, the chief of police reported that the crioula slave Rosalina, who, with the "baby at her breast" had fled the Quingona Plantation in Santo Amaro, was at the Salvador Police Headquarters complaining of mistreatment. He ordered them held in the Bahian House of Corrections, and six days later, returned Rosalina and her son Eutrópio to their master. But, when he did so, the chief of police instructed the Santo Amaro delegado to tell the planter not to "punish his slaves as harshly as he had this unfortunate woman."[44]

As slaves fled to the police with greater frequency, the authorities interfered more intensively in master-slave relations on Recôncavo plantations. On February 12, 1881, the chief of police told the delegado of Mata de São João to inform the owner of the Pitanga Plantation that the enslaved man, José de Santana, described as a crioulo, was in Salvador to complain about the behavior of the plantation's overseer. According to the chief of police, the slave was "so old and decrepit that he could hardly walk." Given the elderly slave's weakness, the police chief recommended that he be freed and transferred to the Poor House.[45] On May 19, 1881, the chief of police instructed the delegado of São Francisco to tell Francisco Vicente Viana, the owner of the Macaco Plantation, to come and retrieve one of his slaves from prison. João, the man in question, had arrived at the police in such a state that he had been transferred to the Misericórdia Hospital.[46]

The increase in accusations of mistreatment in the 1880s does not mean that the planters were punishing slaves physically more frequently than in previous periods. Rather, slaves knew that they could count on the police and justice officials to interfere in their relationships with masters. Many complaints during the period concerned other forms of mistreatment. Arrested on October 20, 1879, the São José Plantation slave David, described as married, crioulo, over thirty, and the father of a child, alleged that he had fled his owner because "of the mistreatment he had received, being forced to work more than anyone could reasonably be expected to."[47] Like other slaves during that period, David had turned to the authorities in Salvador because he knew that he could count on them to support him in his struggles with his master.

In addition to denouncing mistreatment, the slaves also ran to the police to assert that they no longer wished to serve their masters. On March 29, 1879, the chief of police ordered the enslaved man Lourenço imprisoned. He was described as crioulo, thirty years old, and a fugitive from the Pindobas Plantation in São Francisco belonging to Antônio da Rocha Martins de Argolo, "whom he no longer wished to serve." On October 25, 1879, the authorities transferred the enslaved woman, Antônia, a crioula belonging to Pedro Celestino dos Santos, to the House of Corrections after she declared that she "no longer wished to serve him." On November 6, 1879, they imprisoned another slave named Antônia, this one an elderly mulata who had fled her mistress, after she "complained about mistreatment, because of which she no longer wished to serve her."[48] In February 1881, the enslaved woman Clementina, a crioula, fled the Cajaíba Plantation with her ten- to twelve-year-old daughter named Flaviana and presented herself at police headquarters. In her statement to authorities, Clementina alleged that she had fled her mistress, Clara Vianna de Argolo, for having lost the confidence that she "had always held" in her and therefore she no longer intended to serve her.[49]

On the night of March 3, 1883, the subdelegado of the Santana Parish in Salvador informed his superiors that Raimunda Porcina de Jesus, leader of a well-known local musical group called Chapada, had brought in a crioulo slave named Fiel, who had fled the Macaco Plantation in Santo Amaro. According to Porcina de Jesus, Fiel—whose name ironically means faithful in Portuguese—had sought her out in the capital and begged her to buy him. Fiel had apparently known of Porcina's group, composed of her slaves, and may have hoped to join it. According to the official report, Porcina de Jesus contacted Fiel's owner, Ana Gama Guimarães, and offered to buy him, but the mistress had refused to sell the slave. Fiel, in turn, refused to return to his owner, insisting that he preferred prison. Faced with this impasse, Porcina de Jesus decided to bring the slave to the chief of police, so that the official could decide what to do.[50]

In fleeing to police protection, denouncing mistreatment, or requesting a change of ownership, the captives challenged their owners' control over their lives. The authorities usually returned such slaves to their owners, but in such a way that they showed masters that their management of enslaved property was not immune to outside interference. In particular, masters learned that the authorities could and would check the veracity of accusations of mistreatment, even going so far as to enter private property to do so.

The slaves also became aware that the urban abolitionist movement was growing stronger by the day. The abolitionists publicized their cause at events and conferences where they also raised money to help free slaves. In addition, they provided the slaves with legal assistance, including negotiating conditions of freedom with masters, offering captives protection as they waited for the verdicts on their legal cases, examining the slave registers to check for omissions or carelessness on the part of masters, and rewriting petitions or appearing as attorneys in lawsuits against masters.

In the capital and in Recôncavo towns alike, abolitionist lawyers advertised their services in support of the cause in the newspapers. An announcement published in a Cachoeira newspaper in 1887 read:

> José Teodoro Pamponet offers his services in support of abolition in this city, . . . The enslaved who believe they have the right to their freedom, whether because of the Law of November 7, 1831, or because of some other law, may seek him out in this city, at the office of this newspaper.[51]

The notice reflected the increasing radicalization of the abolition movement in the 1880s. Some abolitionists began to provide refuge for fugitive slaves, prohibit the sale of slaves to other provinces, and make it more difficult to use enslaved labor in the city. They transferred slaves who had been beaten to Bahian properties belonging to abolitionist sympathizers where they could work for a salary or, if that was not possible, sent them to other provinces.[52]

By the 1880s, fugitives could anticipate that escape meant permanently breaking the ties of enslavement. By that time, the large black and mestiço population in Salvador, a significant percentage of which was free or freed, made it very difficult for the police to find fugitive slaves in the city.[53] Most of those who fled the plantations for Salvador, therefore, hoped to lose themselves among the thousands of black and mixed-race inhabitants of the capital. Fugitives from the plantations found work in the public construction projects that employed enormous numbers of free workers at the time. On February 17, 1876, the chief of police ordered the subdelegado of the Pilar Parish to help recapture Francisco and Felismino, two slaves, who belonged to an Iguape planter. He suspected that they had found work on the construction crew building the Dourado docks. When the subdelegado went to check the payroll, however, he was unable to locate the fugitives, who had probably changed their names before applying for work.[54]

Numerous other such cases appeared in the 1880s. In November 1880, an enslaved man named Manoel, described as preta, thirty-eight years of age, and away from his mistress for a long time, found a job building the railroad connecting the Recôncavo town of São Félix to the cattle raising town of Curralinho, to the north.[55] In July 1883, the chief of police ordered his subordinates to locate Boaventura, a man who had been conditionally freed, and who was suspected of working on the extension of the São Francisco railroad.[56]

The contracts between the provincial government and the companies that were building the railroads contained clauses that prohibited the hiring of captive laborers. In seeking work on such construction projects, the fugitive slaves probably assumed that the authorities would not be able to find them among the large number of free black people. But as we saw in the two cases above, at the beginning of the 1880s, the local authorities checked railroad construction sites when slaves were missing.[57]

In fleeing the plantations for the towns or the capital, the slaves activated kinship and friendship ties with free and freed people living in those urban centers, which masters revealed in newspaper advertisements aimed at locating their missing captives. In February 1882, the owner of the Cinco Rios Plantation in São Francisco stated that two slaves who had run away from him were "very humble," but that Thomas, described as a skinny, twenty-five-year-old cabra slave, of average height with scars on his face, and Félix, described as a crioulo slave of the same age with an injured leg, had "since they were kids" "a habit of running away and wandering around Santo Amaro, Alagoinhas and Salvador, where they had a lot of friends."[58] In June of that same year, a farmer from Feira de Santana announced that his missing slave Calisto, a crioulo man of about forty years of age and very little beard, had "relatives in the [village] of Bom Jardim."[59] This information, important in locating fugitive slaves also provides clear evidence of the networks of friendship and kinship that facilitated the escapes.

Urban centers were not the only destinations of slaves who fled the plantations. Some sought refuge on other plantations hoping to gain the protection of the owner. In doing so, the slaves were attempting to take advantage of the competition for labor that had developed in the Recôncavo as a result of the labor shortage. Sometimes they were successful. At the beginning of 1882, according to an ad in the Santo Amaro newspaper, thirty-eight enslaved men and women had fled Paranaguá Plantation belonging to the Baroness of Monte Santo. Subsequent events revealed that the slaves believed that they had completed the period of labor required in the will left by their deceased master Antônio Honorato da Silva Rego, who died in 1872.[60] The baroness then discovered that many of the fugitives had taken refuge on the Benfica

Plantation belonging to the Count of Subaé. In a letter to him, she wrote that she could not understand why the Paranaguá pretos should have taken refuge on the count's lands, and needled him saying:

> Now I wish that your Excellency would have the goodness to tell me why these fugitives from Paranaguá are still on your property unless it is true that you encouraged them to leave my plantation, as some of those fugitives who were recaptured said to me personally; do you think that is good that Your Excellency should go and capture people under my authority and bring them to your property?[61]

The competition among planters for access to laborers who obtained or tried to obtain their freedom, the emancipatory laws that increased the possibilities for manumission, and slavery's increasing illegitimacy, along with the growing influence of abolitionism, came together with the initiatives of the slaves themselves in various unexpected ways. This was the context in which the captives made choices and developed their own ideas about freedom.

TWO

TENSION AND CONFLICT ON A
RECÔNCAVO SUGAR PLANTATION

Each of the old Recôncavo sugar plantations, especially the oldest,
has its tale to tell. And all those estates, some of which date
from the seventeenth century, were the site of terrifying dramas and
tragedies. But some events contained no hint of tragedy or
drama and neither do the stories about them.

—JOÃO DA SILVA CAMPOS, *Tempo antigo, crônicas d'antanho,*
marcos do passado, histórias do Recôncavo

The oral tradition of the Bahian Recôncavo is replete with stories of evil and
vicious plantation owners who killed their slaves in the stocks or at the whipping post, threw their slaves into hot ovens or cauldrons of boiling cane juice,
or buried them alive. But that same tradition also retains references to slaves
who retaliated against plantation owners, killing them or leaving them im-
poverished.[1] One such tale is about a priest—the manager of the plantation
his religious order owned—who kept his slaves on a "short leash" and did not
hesitate to wield the lash whenever he was dissatisfied with their behavior.
One day, however, the slaves got together and put an end to their problematic

master, even if he was a priest. As the story goes, they cut up his body with pruning knives and machetes and stuck his head on a fence post; his remains had to be taken to the grave in a sack.

Bahian historian and folklorist João da Silva Campos documented this story toward the end of the 1920s, identifying the victim and detailing the circumstances of the murder. According to this collector of Bahian oral traditions, Carmelite friar João Lucas do Monte Carmelo was killed when his slaves took justice into their own hands. The murder occurred in the morning, while Friar João Lucas was inspecting the slaves' work in the cane fields. Supposedly, the slaves overpowered the priest so rapidly that he could not defend himself with either the whip he gripped in his fist or the knife and pistol stuck in his belt.

Silva Campos also recounted another story about Friar João Lucas, this one called "The Mysterious Carmelite Prisoner." According to Silva Campos, the priest kept a young white girl, filthy and in rags, hidden in the Carmelite monastery in Salvador, the headquarters of the Bahian division of his religious order. She was the urban victim of the priest's cruelty.

In the 1920s, when Silva Campos was collecting Bahia's oral traditions, it was still possible to locate people who had known the priest or who had witnessed the events in question. In researching each of these stories, therefore, Silva Campos interviewed a number of individuals who had known Friar João Lucas, including fellow priests and former students who had lived with him at the monastery, as well as at least one ex-slave.[2]

Jardilina de Santana Oliveira faced a different situation when she carried out her research on the oral traditions of the Recôncavo town of São Sebastião in the 1990s. By that time, everyone who had known Friar João Lucas was long since dead, but Oliveira heard the story of Friar João Lucas's murder as she gathered stories told by the "ancestors." That is probably because the Carmelite Plantation, where the crime took place, lay less than four miles from what is today the center of São Sebastião.[3]

Why Oliveira heard multiple versions of the story is less clear, even if we take into account the inevitable exaggerations that would have been introduced to the tale over the course of more than a century. Yet close examination reveals that, despite the passage of time, the differences in the stories that Oliveira heard are not arbitrary. All of the versions agree that slaves killed the priest; the differences lie in the description of the events leading up to the attack. In other words, the punishments that Friar João Lucas inflicted on the slaves and provoked them to attack him.

Archival research revealed that Father João Lucas really was murdered by his slaves, on the Carmo Plantation in São Sebastião, Bahia, in 1882, six years prior to abolition. This chapter examines the extant documents to reconstruct the crime. Especially important are the transcript of the criminal case against the slaves accused of the crime and the voluminous associated correspondence.[4] Devoting such attention to the murder of Friar João Lucas requires little justification. His killing was a violent crime against a master, an extremely serious offense in a slave society, especially when the victim was also a respected member of a prestigious religious order. But this murder also reflected the broader tensions and conflicts in the Bahian Recôncavo at the time. In other words, the incident was more than just fodder for frightening stories, as the folklorists treated it.[5] Indeed, the richly detailed documents reveal the nature of the relationships between masters and slaves on the sugar plantations of the Bahian Recôncavo and important aspects of the intimate lives of the enslaved in the last decade of Brazilian slavery.

This chapter also analyzes the stories about the murder that have come down to us, especially those about the priest's excessive cruelty. Doing so helps us to understand why this episode figured so prominently in the oral history of Recôncavo blacks. In exploring the stories about the murder, I seek to explore why black oral history emphasizes the priest's excessive cruelty. I hypothesize that the incorporation of these stories into local oral tradition reflects vestiges of the tensions and conflicts that marked the last years of slavery in the Bahian Recôncavo.

The Unforgettable Harvest of 1882

September 14, 1882, began like any other day on the Carmo Plantation, belonging to the Carmelite Order of Bahia, with the enslaved field hands heading out to the sugarcane fields as the sun rose. At that time of the year, work on a sugar plantation was normally intense, because the harvest was about to begin, although many other agricultural tasks were not yet finished. That day, Friar João Lucas had ordered the slaves to weed the sugarcane, by cutting unwanted undergrowth away from the cane stalks. "Cleaning," as Bahians called this activity, was an unpleasant and exhausting task that kept the slaves busy from dawn to dusk in the months leading up to the harvest.[6]

As the slaves toiled in the hot sun, the plantation's administrator, Carmelite friar João Lucas do Monte Carmelo, rode his burro up and down the rows of cane, supervising the slaves' activities, accompanied, as always, by his personal servant—a slave named Pedro. One free morador later recalled that Friar João Lucas (as he was called) was on edge that day, bellowing at the slaves frequently. That was not unusual, since the priest lost his temper whenever the slaves made a mistake or were insubordinate.

That day, however, the slaves seem to have lost patience with the priest. The trouble began only hours into the day's labors when the crioulo slave Silvestre carelessly left some weeds near a cane stalk. Manoel da Assunção, the enslaved "fieldworkers' foreman," ordered Silvestre to go back and clear away the weeds, commenting that "since they were slaves they were to obey orders and in this case that meant that he was to clean up that cane stalk immediately."[7] Silvestre didn't like the foreman's tone and began to mutter loudly enough for the priest to hear him. The priest forced Silvestre to clean the cane stalk and ordered him to shut up, but the slave kept on grumbling. The priest then instructed the foreman and a slave named Isidoro to remove Silvestre from the fields, take him back to the plantation headquarters, and lock him up.

Silvestre's behavior directly challenged his master, Friar João Lucas. The priest occupied the top administrative and religious positions on the Carmo Plantation. Although the estate belonged to the Carmelite Order, rather than to him personally, he carried out all of the activities of an owner: he decided what needed to be done, supervised the field hands, and, as we saw above, disciplined the slaves. In his religious capacity, he said Mass in the Chapel of Our Lady of Carmel, located at the edge of the plantation. There he also baptized the enslaved and free children born to residents of the plantation and the surrounding districts. The plantation's slaves considered him their master, although, as we will see, they understood that legally they belonged to the religious order rather than to him personally.

Friar João Lucas's decision to lock Silvestre up upset the slave's coworkers in the cane field. One of them, Silvestre's brother, Prudêncio, talked about the issue with some of the others—Tibúrcio, Félix, Saturnino, Higino, Balbino, Amâncio, Luís, Pedro Torquato, and Roberto—and they decided to confront Friar João Lucas. Later, members of the group gave at least two versions of the results of that discussion. In one, they insisted that they had planned to apologize to their master on Silvestre's behalf; in the other, as the crioulo Higino testified, they had decided to kill the priest almost as soon as he left the cane field with Silvestre and the foreman.[8] Whichever version we believe, clearly the decision was collective, as Silvestre's brother and his friends and coworkers decided to take action together. Ties of family and friendship bound these workers.

Before Friar João Lucas reached the plantation sugar mill, however, he had pardoned Silvestre, apparently in response to the foreman's appeals. The priest may have given in because he realized that punishing a slave so close to the harvest would only upset the other captives and make it more difficult to get the crop in. Thus, shortly after they left the cane fields, Friar João Lucas ordered Silvestre back to work, so that the cleaning could continue apace. The foreman later testified that he escorted Silvestre back to the cane fields with the priest and his aide, Pedro, following behind.

Arriving back at the cane field, Friar João Lucas noticed that some slaves were missing. Manoel da Assunção later remembered that, at the time, the priest said to "let them go . . . and then asked the rest of the slaves why the others had fled, [and] hearing that there wasn't any [reason], he went back to the house, leaving the foreman and the others to keep working." Silvestre later gave a slightly different version of what happened when the priest noticed the missing slaves. He claimed to have heard the priest say: "Let them go, they've got no reason [to leave], who owes God pays the Devil."[9]

The priest's statements suggest that he no longer considered physical punishment the most efficient and effective method of legitimizing his authority. Why else would he feel it necessary to justify himself to the remaining field hands by telling them that there was no reason for the absent slaves to flee? These interactions reflect the central problem of the legitimacy of the entire system of social relations based in slavery at the time.

After the priest left the cane field for the second time, the conflict escalated. On the way back, as he was passing through a gate in one of the plantation fences, he came face to face with the missing slaves, who had been looking for him. As the priest's servant, Pedro, closed the gate, he noticed that the slaves took off their hats to Friar João Lucas, in a gesture of deference. Some of those involved later stated that when they encountered the priest, they apologized for their imprisoned friend's behavior, but the priest responded that he had already pardoned Silvestre and that if they were looking for him they should go back to the cane fields. Then he threatened to punish them all. In response, the slaves attacked the priest with the tools they carried, including pruning knives and hoes. In a few seconds, Friar João Lucas was dead.

A few days after the crime, Pedro Torquato, one of the slaves involved, described the events in question as follows:

> They were working in the cane fields, in the presence of their master Friar João, when the foreman Manoel da Assunção bawled out the slave Silvestre for having left a bunch of weeds at the base of the cane

stalks that he was working on; at which point Silvestre told the overseer to quit complaining that the cane wasn't clean because the weeds weren't that bad. His master Friar João noticed the way Silvestre spoke to the foreman, and told the foreman and another slave named Isidoro to tie him [Silvestre] up and take him back to the plantation sugar mill, and his master accompanied them, riding on his burro. When the little group had gone some distance away, the respondent and his companions decided to go and ask for Silvestre's release, and so they headed back to the plantation headquarters by a different route than the one that the master and Silvestre had taken; since they didn't find him, they came back by the route that the master and his prisoner had taken and so they ran into the master also on his way back, accompanied only by Pedro [Celestino], [whom the slaves called] his lackey. At this point, their master asked where they were going and what they were doing, and they replied that they had come to ask that Silvestre be released, and the master responded that the request should have been made in the cane fields and not there and he began to swear at them; at which point they got angry and killed him.[10]

It is not difficult to imagine that, leaving the cane fields, the slaves intended to save Silvestre by any means necessary. Therefore, when they found the priest, they made a gesture of deference in hopes of reaching an agreement. Friar João Lucas, on the one hand, responded that he had already pardoned Silvestre, but then also showed his irritation that slaves should intercede on each other's behalf. To punish or not to punish was a privilege reserved to the master, and a decision for him to make without interference from the enslaved. That may have been why Friar João Lucas threatened to punish Silvestre's friends.

On the other hand, Tibúrcio, another slave involved, suggested that there were other reasons for the priest's reaction. According to him, during the confrontation the priest brought up previous transgressions, threatening that "one by one, they would have to pay for making him spend money to round them up whenever they fled the city."[11] That was what provoked the final unraveling of events.

During the interrogation, Silvestre told the authorities that "those ten slaves got together in a group and, when they arrived at the cane field where the others were working, they screamed—we killed the devil, you'll see him dead on the road."[12] The reference to the devil is significant, since the slaves were talking about a priest. Clearly, the workers in the cane did not consider the friar to be a "good" master.

As news of the priest's death spread, confusion reigned in the cane fields. Work came to a halt; children ran loose and women cried, desperately worried about what would happen to their men when the authorities discovered the murder. For a short time, there was actually an uprising on the plantation.

The testimony of José Rufino de Argolo, a fifty-year-old cowherd who lived on the Carmo Plantation, helps us to understand what happened after the priest's death. He told the authorities that as he was crossing the plantation he came across a "bunch" of slaves armed with sickles. They threatened him and forced him to go back the way he came. Later, however, he was able to get in touch with Vitorino Pires, a farmer who also resided on the plantation, and tell him that the Carmo Plantation's slaves had revolted. On hearing the news, Pires sent him to gather the neighbors, so that they could go as a group to investigate the situation and "prevent anything bad" from happening.[13]

To judge by Argolo's deposition, the plantation residents followed a preestablished plan for dealing with a slave revolt. The local free population had prepared for trouble with the slaves, because the Recôncavo had a large captive population with a history of unrest. Pires did not suggest to Argolo that they should go to the plantation alone. He said that they should raise the alarm and go in a group to find out what the slaves were doing. Their actions clearly reflect a preexisting agreement about maintaining order and preventing "anything bad" from happening.

Before Pires, Argolo and the others were ready to leave for the plantation; however, a "little black girl [negrinha]" arrived, sent by the Carmo Plantation's enslaved foreman, Manoel da Assunção, to inform Pires of the priest's death at the hands of his slaves. At that point, Pires went to the priest's home where he found Silvestre and the rest of the men involved in the crime, "all armed with sickles," and discussing their next move. Pires later reported that he then inquired about what had happened to Friar Lucas, and Tibúrcio responded, "What's done is done." Luís, on the other hand, replied: "It was a calamity!" Vitorino later recalled that the slave Pedro shouted at him: "What are you doing? Get out of here, or else there'll be a lot of dead men, and we've already done what we're going to do and now we should get out of here."[14] They were trying to protect the other plantation slaves from the repression that was sure to follow.

Thirty-eight-year-old José Pereira Mimoso, the "free overseer" on the Carmo Plantation, recalled that the "agricultural foreman" had sent the moleque João Antero to tell him that the "blacks" had killed the priest. Mimoso then left his home, gathered some of the plantation's other free moradores, and took off toward the cane fields, where he found the priest's body. He noticed that

Friar João Lucas's pockets were inside out, that two notes lay across his nude buttocks, and that a little box of snuff sat on his back. The slave Domingos handed him the keys to the barrels of meat and manioc flour that Friar João Lucas always carried in his pockets. It seems that, following the priest's death, the slaves had taken the keys and raided the usually well-protected plantation storehouses in search of things they otherwise almost never saw in their diet or, perhaps, could sell.

In their testimony, the plantation's free residents showed how the news of the priest's death circulated through the plantation and surrounding area. They made clear that, in the immediate aftermath of the crime, the enslaved overseer, Manoel da Assunção, sent a *negrinha* and the moleque to notify the neighbors of the trouble on the plantation. Thus, a "little black girl" and a "black boy" were the sources of the original accounts that made an indelible impression on the local population.

The inquest into the death of Friar João Lucas took place the day after the crime, in the presence of medical experts and witnesses. The experts noted that various parts of the corpse, including the head, the face, the thorax, and the legs, showed wounds, including contusions and abrasions. Neither they nor the witnesses, however, mentioned that the priest had been decapitated nor that he was armed when he was killed, as Silva Campos would later recount. The testimony clearly indicated that the death was violent, but over time, the oral tradition amplified that violence enormously, to compensate for the supposed excessive violence with which the priest punished his slaves.[15]

Mimoso testified that he came across the eleven fugitive slaves as he was on his way to telegraph the police and the Carmelites in the capital. He just had time to shout "Damn you, you killed the priest!" before they responded that they had already done what they intended to do. Then one of them told him that he should go and take care of his children, and that God had given him many more years of life for that purpose.[16] The message was clear: Mimoso should mind his own business if he did not want to suffer the same fate as the priest.

That same afternoon, the slaves left the plantation, but they didn't get very far or remain free for long. The authorities arrested them nearby the following day. Understanding their experiences requires a review of the history of the Carmo Plantation.

The Carmo Plantation, sometimes called Terra Nova, sat in the parish of São Sebastião das Cabeceiras do Passé, part of the town of São Francisco do Conde, in the heart of the Recôncavo.[17] According to Carlos Ott, the Carmelite Order acquired the plantation's land through a Portuguese royal land grant in 1679. Initially, the order used the "two square leagues" of land that they received to raise cattle and only later began to cultivate sugarcane. By the middle of the eighteenth century, however, Terra Nova was one of seven sugar plantations the order owned. According to Friar Felipe Barbosa da Cunha, in 1757, the plantations were occupied by large numbers of slaves and freedmen, and the largest settlements in the area.[18] According to Carlos Ott, the slaves who worked the plantations began to rebel against the Carmelites as early as 1730.[19]

In 1835, in addition to the property in São Sebastião, the Bahian Carmelites owned extensive properties, according to an inventory of the order's assets. In Salvador, their property included dozens of houses and plots of land; in the Recôncavo town of Cachoeira, it included a tobacco farm and cattle ranch; in the provinces of Sergipe and Pernambuco they owned two more plantations. Altogether, 255 captives lived and worked on these properties: 15 of them at the Salvador monastery; another 8 at the Cachoeira monastery; 88 on the Palmar Fazenda in Lagarto, Sergipe; and 64 at the Carmo Plantation in São Sebastião.[20]

Eleven years later, in 1846, Sales e Souza indicated that the order remained wealthy, basing his assessment on an inventory of the monastery's property sent to Bahia's provincial president. At that time, aside from the houses and lands that it rented out in Salvador, the order also owned a plantation with forty slaves in Pernambuco, managed by a leaseholder. In Cachoeira, Bahia, they owned the São João Fazenda with nine slaves. And they owned the Carmo Plantation, which Sales e Souza described as "a plantation called Terra Nova, situated in the village of S. Francisco, with functional water wheel and grinding stones, including 109 head of oxen, 71 horses and 147 slaves including the young and the old." Clearly, the captive population at the Carmelite Plantation had grown between 1835 and 1846, perhaps as the result of transfers from less profitable properties. In 1870, however, the number of slaves belonging to the Carmelites had dropped to 130.[21]

By 1882, the Carmelites had owned and managed lands and slaves in the Recôncavo for more than two centuries. They were not the only religious figures to do so. The Benedictines and the Jesuits (the latter to 1759) also owned large Recôncavo plantations worked by enslaved labor.[22]

Yet the Carmelites' extensive holdings did not necessarily assure their financial stability. In 1830, João Lucas do Monte Carmelo himself, at that time prior of the monastery, admitted that the order was in a difficult and embarrassing financial situation, due to debts incurred by his predecessors. To solve the problem, he requested permission to sell particularly burdensome properties, including the Camaçari sugar plantation in Pernambuco.[23] In 1848, the evidence suggests that debts exceeded the order's income.[24] The Terra Nova Plantation was, therefore, the Carmelite fathers' most important source of revenue.

Friar João Lucas do Monte Carmelo had been born in Porto, Portugal, and, following his ordination, rose quickly through the order's ranks.[25] By the 1830s, he was already prior, the second-highest leader in the Bahian order's hierarchy, subordinate only to the provincial.[26] He became master of novices in 1835 and from 1866 to 1874 served as both provincial and prior. Such responsibilities gave him authority over the young men preparing for the priesthood as well as some four dozen peers, divided between the Salvador monastery, the Cachoeira property, and other provinces. By the time he took over the administration of the Carmo Plantation, therefore, Friar João Lucas had a great deal of experience in managing the order's property, including the slaves.

One aspect of plantation management at that time involved deciding when and on what basis to free slaves. The priest's feelings about freedom had a significant impact on the order's slaves. On August 27, 1845, for example, Sales e Souza petitioned the provincial president to annul a grant of freedom awarded to a slave named Joana from the Terra Nova Plantation. According to the petition, Friar Manoel Joaquim de Santa Escolástica had liberated the slave "against our Constitution" to "relieve" the ex-administrator of the plantation, Friar João Lucas de Monte Carmelo. Yet Friar João Lucas did not wish the enslaved woman to be set free: attached to the petition was a letter in his own hand opposing the enslaved woman's freedom.

This incident indicates that by 1845, Friar João Lucas had already served as plantation administrator, only to step down, and then, at some unknown later point, resume the responsibility. Testifying before the jury in 1884, the enslaved man Higino stated that Friar João Lucas had been running the plantation for eighteen years; in other words, that he'd been managing the property since 1866. That seems likely since that was the year he became provincial.

Father João Lucas's tenure as provincial did not run smoothly. By the time of his death, he had been having discipline problems with the slaves since at least 1880. Runaways posed a particular challenge. In addition, he faced opposition from his peers, as the investigation that took place after his murder revealed. Such conflicts may have grown out of his management style or his treatment of the slaves and were significant enough that they surfaced in the investigation of his murder.[27]

When Friar João Lucas took over management of the Carmo Plantation, the order had just completed another inventory of their properties. This one, carried out in 1865, contains detailed information about the slaves belonging to the plantation at the time. According to the document, that year, the enslaved labor force numbered seventy-five adult slaves, including twenty-nine men and forty-six women. Among the forty-one enslaved children listed were Luís, Balbino, Silvestre, Prudêncio, Saturnino, Higino, Tibúrcio, Roberto, and Pedro Torquato, who as adult men would be accused of murdering the priest. Two more of the accused, Amâncio and Félix, appear in a different list—one enumerating the slaves who worked in the monastery in Salvador.[28] The order probably transferred these latter two slaves to the plantation at the end of the 1870s, when public criticism of religious orders owning slaves intensified.

Combining the data from the inventory with the information contained in the criminal case allows us to learn more about the slaves implicated in the priest's death. Table 2.1 reconstructs what we know about them. With the exception of Amâncio and Félix, all those involved in the crime had been born on the plantation. Indeed, with the exception of Amâncio, all of them were the sons of enslaved women belonging to the Carmelites, and most of them were between twenty and thirty-four years of age when the murder occurred. In other words, all but two of them had grown up together. All of them were field hands who worked in the cane and they shared a common work experience, which surely extended to other day-to-day aspects of their lives, such as where they lived, how they entertained themselves, and their concerns about their status as slaves. Only one among them had been married in church, but the references to mothers and brothers demonstrates that they came from families that had lived under Carmelite control for at least two generations. Belonging to a religious order with two centuries of stable control of the plantation had protected these enslaved families from separation.

Neither the 1865 list of slaves, nor the trial transcript, contains any reference to Africans. It may be, therefore, that all of the enslaved laborers on the plantation had been born in Brazil. Their description as cabra colored, or as second-generation crioulos, could indicate that the Carmelites had been substituting Brazilian-born slaves for Africans before the final prohibition of the African slave trade to Brazil in 1850.

TABLE 2.1. Slaves Involved in the Attack at the Carmo Plantation

Name	Origin	Age in 1882	Civil status	Ancestry	Color
Félix	Crioulo	34		Son of Rosalina, crioula, deceased	
Tibúrcio		26	Married	Son of Damásia, crioula, deceased	
Silvestre	Crioulo		Single	Son of Inês, deceased	Cabra
Saturnino	Crioulo		Single	Son of slave Maria	Cabra
Prudêncio		32	Single	Son of Inês (i.e., Silvestre's brother)	Parda
Higino	Crioulo	20	Single	Son of Damásia, crioula (i.e., Tibúrcio's brother)	
Balbino		25	Single	Son of Maria, cabra, deceased	Cabra
Amâncio		54	Single	Son of Efigênia, deceased	Cabra
Luís		20	Single	Son of Malfada, cabra	Cabra
Pedro Torquato	Crioulo	26	Single	Son of Maximiana, crioula, deceased	
Roberto	Crioulo	20	Single	Son of João Paulo and Felicidade	

Source: *Livro e inventário do Convento do Carmo da Bahia*, 1796–1935, ff. 125–27v, APCSE; *PC*, 22/757/01, 1884, APEB.

The men involved in the murder all belonged to a work crew, a common form of agricultural labor organization on sugar plantations at the time.[29] These gangs of laborers in the cane fields were entirely enslaved; those free men whom we know lived on the plantation tended cattle or grew their own crops. We do not know how the free men's work was managed, but the enslaved work crews were subject to an administrative hierarchy headed by the administrator, Friar João Lucas. Below him came the general manager or "free overseer," José Pereira Mimoso, and below him came the crew foreman, the enslaved man Manoel d'Assunção. The presence of this enslaved foreman should not surprise us: slaves held such positions of authority on many plantations in the Recôncavo. There were even cases of enslaved women exercising such roles and, by all indication, supervising other women. But slaves rarely became general managers, for obvious reasons.

The Carmelites' management strategy followed the model that had been common on Recôncavo sugar plantations since the middle of the nineteenth century. The crew foreman had more direct contact with the slaves, given that he oversaw the quantity and quality of the agricultural labor required to make the plantation produce. The general manager took care of slave discipline and imposed punishments on slaves. But from time to time owners or administrators such as Friar João Lucas dealt with these issues personally; when that happened on the Carmo Plantation, Mimoso, the general manager, didn't go to the fields. As we saw in the previous chapter, the presence of the general managers allowed the owners to maintain their authority by remaining aloof from day-to-day interactions with the slaves. Despite that, however, the growing tension produced by slave pressure on the managers was undermining the plantation hierarchy. At the Carmo Plantation, the priest wanted more effective control over the plantation slaves, but in the process of trying to get it, he placed himself in danger.[30]

Friar João Lucas did not live on the plantation in idle luxury, even though he was the provincial head of the order. He was intensely involved in all questions related to the Carmelite Order in Bahia and its properties. He divided his time between managing the plantation and handling his religious and administrative responsibilities in the capital. The court case contains references to various trips that he made to Salvador, usually accompanied by a number of slaves. According to the case record, he always went to Salvador on September 15 to participate in the Festival of Our Lord of Passos, near the Carmelite monastery. On the day he died, he must have been preparing for the journey to the city. He could not foresee that his life would take another path.[31]

When Errors Lead to Truth

The day after the crime, the citizens and soldiers of São Francisco do Conde joined together to search for the escaped slaves. They captured the fugitives that same day and sent them to jail in the capital, Salvador. In the following days, the gravity of the situation encouraged the authorities to move quickly. They opened two investigations: one carried out by the local delegado in São Francisco do Conde itself, and the other in Salvador, handled by the provincial authorities there. Each inquiry came to a different conclusion about the causes of Friar João Lucas's death, as well as the motives and intentions of the slaves. That was, in part, because two different teams carried out the investigations; but it was also because the investigators had different ideas about the crime and those ideas led to different conclusions.

In Salvador, Alfredo Devoto, delegado of the first district, led the investigation. On September 16, he interrogated the eleven slaves who had been captured and attempted to learn the authors of, motives for, and circumstances of the attack on the priest. Félix, Tibúrcio, Saturnino, Roberto, Pedro Torquato, Luís, Prudêncio, Higino, Balbino, and Amâncio all took complete responsibility for the crime. They all insisted that their other workmates were innocent, going so far as to say that no one could have stopped them. Tibúrcio specifically stated that the foreman Manoel da Assunção and the slave Isidoro, who were bringing Silvestre to the plantation sugar mill, could not have done anything, because they were already back in the cane fields when their master was killed. The "general manager" was at home, because "he didn't supervise" the slaves "when his master was on site." Then they reiterated that the decision [to kill their master] was collective and the action spur of the moment.[32]

The slaves gave different accounts of their motives and the circumstances of the murder. Félix said that he and his workmates had committed the crime because the priest refused to pardon Silvestre. Tibúrcio said that the priest had pardoned Silvestre, but shortly thereafter they had learned that he told the foreman to lock the slave up as soon as it got dark. The crioulo Roberto added something new when he said that the workmates had gotten together to put an end to the priest's life "so that they would be free of him because of the poor treatment that they received."[33]

According to Roberto, the master's decision to physically punish Silvestre set the events in motion. But Alfredo Devoto didn't pay much attention to this; he pursued other hypotheses and tried to drag evidence out of the slaves to prove them. He tried, for example, to establish how frequently the slaves came to the city and whether or not the priest accompanied them. In response to this line of questioning, the slave Félix said that Friar João Lucas usually only brought his lackey Pedro and another slave named Carolino with him when he went to the city, and that neither of those men had been involved in the crime.[34]

The delegado suspected that the slaves killed the priest in an attempt to obtain their freedom. He asked them if the slaves on the plantation had heard that they would be set free in the event that Friar Jõao Lucas died or was replaced by another administrator. Tibúrcio and Félix said they didn't know anything about freedom. The parda slave Prudêncio, quite prudently, stated that he didn't believe all the talk about freedom, although he admitted that many people talked about it on the plantation, as did "all sorts of individuals from the common people" in the city. Tibúrcio also reported that, on the plantation, many slaves talked about freedom, as did "all sorts of people here in the city." When it was his turn, Amâncio revealed that news about freedom "was being spread by local freed people."[35]

Pedro Torquato, who had accompanied the priest on a trip to Salvador two weeks earlier, added to the testimony about rumors of freedom. Like the others, he stated that "for some time everyone on the plantation had been talking about that," but he went on to say that he had "heard it here in the city from the students who lived in the Carmelite Monastery and from other people in the streets." These students, most of whom were young men and had come to the city from other parts of Bahia and the broader Northeast of Brazil to attend one of Salvador's schools, were boarding in the monastery. Most were studying at the Bahian Medical College, one of the most active centers of abolitionist activism in Bahia at the time.

Under questioning, Torquato and his workmates indicated that they knew quite a bit about happenings in the city: they were particularly attuned to the implications for their futures of talk about slavery in the streets and in the Carmelite monastery.[36] Basing their attitudes on the students living in the monastery and the rumors that they heard from the "people in the street," the slaves surmised that the antislavery sentiment and the enthusiasm for abolition in the city were quite strong.

Pedro Torquato also knew about the conflict within the order and what it might mean for the plantation slaves. He assured the police that, with the exception of Friar Inocêncio, none of the Carmelite priests at the monastery liked his master, although he claimed not to know why. He also stated that he did not know anything about any enemies that Friar João Lucas might have at the monastery, or the attitudes of the lay residents, although he admitted that he knew that another priest had once threatened Friar João Lucas at gunpoint.[37] In other words, the slave knew that even though Friar João Lucas occupied an important position in the Carmelite hierarchy, he did not enjoy much support from his peers.

Devoto's questions suggest that he suspected that enemies of Friar João Lucas beyond the plantation had influenced the slaves' behavior. He theorized that the slaves had been influenced by people who took advantage of their desperation. In other words, the slaves' hope of achieving freedom had encouraged them to attack the priest. Devoto, like the rest of the authorities at the time, underestimated the capacity of the slaves to hatch their own plots. He preferred to believe that they had been motivated by desperation or influenced by others.

Devoto was a man of the city with the strong preconceptions and prejudices about rural slaves common to urban dwellers. Yet his view is important;

through his investigation, he inadvertently revealed the complexities of what took place on the Carmo Plantation that September day. As he investigated possible connections between the priests' problems in the monastery and the crime on the plantation, he revealed that the divisions within the order reverberated beyond the monastery walls. He must have been frustrated at being unable to confirm his suspicions, but his questions and concerns got the slaves talking. Their responses, in turn, revealed important aspects of their lives: the tension with Friar João Lucas; the ways in which they understood the relationships between the priests of the Carmelite monastery; their flights and their comings and goings to Salvador.

Physical Punishments, Flights, and Penalties

The murder of Friar João Lucas reflected the final unraveling of the master-slave relationship on the Carmo Plantation. The murder investigation revealed that the conflict had been developing for some time and that the slaves had killed the priest because all possibility of negotiation between them had been exhausted.

Authorities from the Vila of São Francisco opened their investigation into the crime on September 18, 1882, under the direction of the subdelegado for the Passé Parish, Olímpio Antônio de Sá Barreto, himself a sugar-plantation owner. He pursued a different theory of the crime than Devoto, trying to establish other connections that would explain Friar João Lucas's death. Barreto's convictions about slave management led him to believe that the motive for the murder lay in the unreasonable way that the priest had punished his slaves.[38]

The slaves accused of the murder were still in Salvador when Barreto opened the investigation, so he began by interrogating the plantation's free residents. From the transcript, we get a glimpse of the way in which the free population on the Carmo Plantation viewed the relationship between Friar João Lucas and the slaves. The depositions make clear that the priest's treatment of his captives swung back and forth between generosity and harsh discipline. Vitorino Pires, described in the transcript as a "free farmer living on the plantation," stated that Friar Lucas "just got a bit irritated with their work habits." João Pereira Mimoso, general manager of the plantation, told Barreto that the priest was "just a bit irritated with those who didn't take their responsibilities seriously, and when someone was sick the priest himself took care of him, as, he, the witness, had seen many times."[39]

But mistreatment twice sent the slaves fleeing to Salvador: once to appeal to Friar João Lucas, who was at the Carmelite monastery at the time, and on

Orerm.ᵒ capitão de matto—Santos Cunha—cançado de deitar annuncios na Gazeta da _____ resolveu ir pessoalmente capturar os seus escravos

FIGURE 2.1. Criticism of members of the clergy who own slaves. "Priest slave catcher—Santos Cunha—tired of advertising in the Gazeta de _____ decided to personally recapture his slaves." *Jornal, O Faísca*, 1887.

the other occasion, to report abuse to the chief of police. From the slaves' testimony, it is clear that these flights were significant experiences. Higino confessed that in all the twenty years that he had been alive, he had only gone to the city twice, "on both occasions to flee with other companions to present themselves to the chief of police."[40] As we have seen, throughout the nineteenth century, the Carmelites and other plantation owners faced constant slave escapes. In his research into the history of the Carmo Plantation between 1808 and 1848, Carlos Ott came across various references to the Carmelites paying slave catchers to hunt fugitive enslaved men and women.[41] By the 1880s, however, the Carmelites were confronting a new type of escape: one in which the slaves ran to the authorities to denounce abuses by their master.

Another slave, Rufino do Carmo, admitted that, once, the slaves fled the plantation because of a "conflict" with the manager. He said that "the slaves behaved that way because, when something disappeared on the property, his master Friar João had ordered the manager to make them all work on Sundays until the thief confessed."[42] As we saw in chapter 1, Sunday work on the plantation meant that the slaves could not work their roças, or hire themselves out to work for someone else. Such Sunday work meant so much to the

Carmo slaves that they disobeyed [Friar João Lucas] and "went to work [that day] for 'old' Antônio Batista dos Santos," a sixty-some-odd-year-old free farmer who grew manioc on the Carmo Plantation. "In the afternoon when they came back," Rufino continued, "each one took his rations for the day and then they all left for the capital to go to the Carmelite Monastery to talk the situation over with their master Friar João Lucas, who gave them a few coins and sent them back to the plantation." Pedro Celestino, the friar's lackey who was with Friar João Lucas when the slaves appeared to protest, testified that "a group of slaves had appeared there complaining, but his master had placated them, telling them to go back to the plantation and giving each one of them a few pennies to do so."[43] In this particular case, the slaves had taken off because the punishment had prohibited them from hiring themselves out.

There is reason to believe, however, that the slaves received more than just a few cents when they complained to João Lucas: I suspect that they had also received a guarantee that they would regain their free Sundays and that the physical punishments would cease as well. That is why José Elias de Campos said that Friar João Lucas "for some time in the past had been very firm, but that after the slaves fled to the capital, he, Friar João, had gotten too soft."[44] This statement indicates that the masters' strategies for controlling their slaves were subject to change and that slaves could use flight to check their masters' wishes.

Given this history of negotiation over punishment with Friar João Lucas, the slaves may have interpreted the priest's order to have Silvestre locked up as a return to his old habits for dealing with his enslaved labor force. That was why they decided to kill him. Friar João Lucas, on the other hand, may have seen things differently: he may have interpreted sending Silvestre off to the plantation sugar mill and then pardoning him as a way of dramatizing his position as the almighty master, capable of punishing or pardoning offenses. In his deposition, Pedro, the priest's personal servant, revealed that just as Silvestre was being taken away, Friar João Lucas whispered to him: "tell Manoel that he should ask me to let Silvestre go—don't tell anyone but him." Pedro then went on to testify that "his master was a bit surprised when Manoel interceded on Silvestre's behalf before he, Pedro, had a chance to give him the message."[45] The priest's miscalculation cost him his life.

Barreto interrogated the accused slaves immediately on their return from Salvador to São Francisco on September 20. By that time, they had developed a more homogenous version of events than they demonstrated in their responses to questioning in Salvador. Silvestre told his interrogator that "his master didn't whip them, he used the *palmatória*, the stocks, and ropes [on them]." Félix said that "he put those he believed had eaten dirt in the stocks, hit them with the palmatória, or tied their hands up in a bag; but he didn't mistreat those he didn't suspect of such offenses and took care of them when they were sick."[46] From the evidence, it is clear that Friar João Lucas followed the seignorial management style common to planters in the area: for years he had mixed punishment and negotiation in his efforts to control his slaves, but as time passed he increasingly relied on punishment to resolve conflicts with them.[47]

Discipline meant more than forcing the captives to work. The priest was also doing his utmost to prohibit theft and other behavior on the plantation that he viewed as undesirable. The punishment for these transgressions was not necessarily physical: in taking away Sunday free time, the Carmelite had made it so that the slaves were incapable of earning wages though outside employment. He had put pressure on an essential element of the microeconomy of slavery.[48]

The priest attempted to control more personal areas of enslaved life as well. The enslaved Rufino do Carmo said that the priest "only punished those who had a habit of eating dirt."[49] A letter from Augusto de Araújo Santos, delegado of the first district of the capital, describes one such incident. Santos received orders from the city's police commissioner to check on the condition of a preta named Mafalda, reportedly being held in one of the cubicles of the Carmelite monastery. When he went to investigate, he found her in a monastery cell, and was able to examine her alone, with only the notary present to record his findings. When Santos arrived, Mafalda was prostrate on a large bench, surrounded by various home remedies and medicines. In response to questioning, she said that she had cut her foot in the plantation cane field and Santos verified that her foot was injured and terribly swollen. Taking his responsibilities seriously, the delegado asked how many times a day she was fed and whether or not she'd been beaten or placed in the stocks. Mafalda replied that "she ate three times a day and, some time ago she had suffered some raps to the hand and was in the stocks for having eaten dirt and some rags; but as soon as her master Friar João Lucas do Monte Carmelo discovered (on the plantation) that her foot was cut and inflamed, which until that time no one knew, he ordered her taken out of the stocks and treated, bringing her to the capital to better tend to her."[50] The delegado noted that Malfalda's hands did not carry the scars of the palmatória and her body did not show any signs of beatings. She was, on the other hand, very thin, her tongue was completely white and she had the symptoms of hookworm disease. He concluded that she was "addicted" to eating dirt.

When Santos finished questioning Mafalda, he went to interview others at the monastery, including the provincial and the student boarders. Friar João Lucas confirmed the slave's testimony. So did the students, who provided the same version of events as Mafalda and the priest, but added that the enslaved woman was under the care of a physician named Dr. José Luís do Almeida Couto.

The delegado seems to have convinced himself that the master was not responsible for the terrible state in which he found Mafalda. This story probably didn't end there though. The woman's presence must have caused quite a stir in the Carmelite community, given that all its members had taken vows of celibacy. The inquiry about her by a representative of the civil authorities, to which members of religious orders were not normally subject, must have also caused talk. It is possible, if not probable, that the story of the "Mysterious Prisoner of the Carmelites" which Silva Campos collected in the 1920s, was based on the presence of the preta Mafalda in the monastery. It may be that, to the delight of romantics, Mafalda—elderly, black, and enslaved—was transformed into a young white girl. The tale preserved, however, the information that she was emaciated and in very poor condition. Undoubtedly, she was kept isolated in a cubicle deep in the monastery, because women were forbidden from interacting with the members of that order, and, most important, she was a slave. Friar João Lucas tried to cover up her presence, but the rumors about it, possibly spread by students or disaffected priests, reached the ears of the police.[51] What connection Mafalda's treatment may have had to the priest's death is not clear, but we should remember that her son, the crioulo slave Luís, was one of the men accused of the killing.

We know that João Lucas was implacable with slaves who ate dirt. Research has shown that the enslaved consumed soil because of serious vitamin and mineral deficiencies in their diets, rather than because of "addiction," as was believed at the time. Mafalda's condition, therefore, undoubtedly grew out of the priest's tight control over access to supplies like meat and manioc on the plantation in São Sebastião.[52]

The São Francisco delegado closed his investigation into the murder on October 18 when the state's attorney charged the slaves with murder of their owner under Article 1 of the Law of June 10, 1835. This law outlined the punishments for crimes committed by slaves and was approved shortly after Salvador's most important slave revolt, the Muslim slave rebellion of 1835, known as the Malê revolt.[53] Article 1 required the death penalty for any slave found guilty of having killed his or her master, the master's wife and children, or the overseers. Throughout the nineteenth century, this legal weapon was the principal seignorial defense against slave attacks on their persons, families, and representatives.[54]

Four days prior to the close of the investigation, the Carmelite fathers, convinced of the "veracity of the facts," renounced their ownership of all the slaves who had been accused, with the exception of Silvestre, who had been absolved of responsibility for Father João Lucas's death. The Carmelites' actions acknowledged a new reality: they no longer had control of their enslaved property. From September 1882 to March 1884, the accused slaves remained imprisoned in the jail in São Francisco do Conde. While in jail, Saturnino died from "attacks of beri-beri." In March 1884, the others were transferred to the county seat in Santo Amaro for trial.

When the slaves' trial began in Santo Amaro on March 26, 1884, Rafael José Jambeiro, a fifth-year medical student, appeared for the defense. At the Bahian Medical College, abolitionism had become a popular political cause, and Jambeiro was among its supporters. Defending enslaved prisoners in the courts, whether in the city or the countryside, had become a way for militant abolitionists to push the cause of freedom. Jambeiro lost the case, but his fellow abolitionists followed the developments of the trial closely. After the judge sentenced the prisoners, an article appeared in the *Gazeta da Tarde* that blamed the verdict on the presence of "ignorant slavocrats" on the jury.[55]

During the trial, the authorities interrogated the slaves once again about the events of September 14, 1882. These depositions reveal significant aspects of the day-to-day lives of the slaves on the plantation, and, most important, the defense's strategy. The transcript of the case does not contain Jambeiro's arguments, but the depositions make clear that he tried to demonstrate that the slaves had been motivated by the excessive punishments that Friar João Lucas imposed on them. Thus, he attempted to convince the jury that the slaves had been the priest's victims rather than his executioners. Unquestionably, the crime fit perfectly into the abolitionists' view of reality.

We saw earlier, however, that Friar João Lucas was not excessively cruel for a slave owner, despite the way that he was described in the oral tradition about him. He behaved like his counterparts in the region, tempering repression with negotiation. He was not an especially "bad" master, even though the slaves described him that way at their trial. In their initial interviews in Salvador and São Francisco, the slaves even referred to the priest's willingness to negotiate: they mentioned his "pardon" of Silvestre as well as his gift of "a few . . . coins" when they went to him to complain about the general manager. But, master-slave relations were tense in the years prior to abolition and very little was required to upset their fragile equilibrium; explosions of rage on either side were easily provoked. It seems to me that the priest didn't measure his doses of punishment very well, especially given that slavery was rapidly losing its legitimacy in Brazil at the time and the slaves were harboring strong aspirations of freedom.

When they gave their statements to the authorities, the slaves emphasized physical punishment, but they revealed other elements of life they found oppressive, especially the loss of "free" Sundays and the poor diet. Perhaps that was the only way to justify themselves to their questioners and potential supporters. The slaves must have had a reason for attacking the priest other than the urgent need to protect one of their own from punishment. Because the fact is that these men, who probably believed in God and Our Lady of Carmel, killed a priest. Perhaps they were trying to justify their behavior to the master of the next world. The version of events that they constructed and that was incorporated into oral history about Friar João Lucas's excessive cruelty was possibly conceived as a way to convince God and man that the priest, aside from being a bad master, was a bad priest.

On March 27, 1884, the judge in Santo Amaro sentenced Tibúrcio, Pedro Torquato, Prudêncio, Higino, Roberto, and Balbino to life in prison at hard labor under Article 192 of the 1832 Criminal Code. The judge could have condemned them to death, but the jury decided on a more moderate penalty. Since the members of the jury understood that the five prisoners had been the primary authors of the injuries the friar suffered, their sentences were to be carried out immediately under Article 94 of the 1832 Code of Criminal Process as required in cases where the prisoners had confessed. In addition, Félix, Luís, and Amâncio each received prison sentences of twenty years at hard labor, under Article 192 of the Criminal Code. That article established a minimum penalty for those who participated in assassinations, but who had not delivered fatal blows.[56] The attorney appealed the sentences of those condemned to life at hard labor to the superior court, which forwarded the case on to the emperor for resolution. The documents do not reveal his decisions, but by all indications, the guilty men's fates had been sealed. Silva Campos believed they were pardoned a few days prior to abolition in 1888, but his information is not confirmed.[57]

The Moral of the Story

We must consider these events in their historical context, and, most important, as shaped by the social relations within slavery at the time. Studies of other Brazilian regions make clear that social tension and conflict increased throughout the country in the last days of slavery. In the last decades of the nineteenth century, slave disobedience was increasing all over Brazil. Slave ingenuity was undermining slaveocrat domination.[58]

The events that took place on the Carmo Plantation in September 1882 allow us to examine the resourcefulness of enslaved men and women in the Recôncavo at the beginning of the last decade of slavery there. This murder, and many other incidents of the period, call attention to the logic of the enslaved and to the meanings of their actions. Slave initiatives were centered on concrete aspects of the master-slave relationship: on questions of punishment; on the formation and protection of family and other affective ties; on the preservation of Sunday as a day of rest or work in subsistence plots; on the defense of values and attitudes; on safeguarding space and time to worship saints and gods; and principally, on obtaining freedom. It is true that these issues marked slavery all over the Americas; nonetheless, at a time when slavery was losing legitimacy in Brazil—the last nation in the Americas to abolish the institution—they acquired their own political meanings. As a result, slaves significantly changed their behaviors and their attitudes toward their masters, and especially in the ways they negotiated with and put pressure on those masters.

Escapes offer a good example of the redefinition of slave practices at this time. Through the 1870s, when slaves fled the Carmo Plantation, either as individuals or as members of a group, they aimed at leaving captivity. They were, in the the terms of the day, "running away." That was the case, for example, of the slave João who escaped the Carmo Plantation in early 1878 and was miles away when he was caught in August.[59] But beginning around 1880, the Carmo Plantation slaves, like their counterparts elsewhere, began to engage in another form of flight, one aimed at pressuring their master to reconsider his treatment of them.[60] On one occasion when they ran away, they went right to the chief of police to complain about the priest's punishments. They were not acting within the established rules of slavery and their behavior was shaking master-slave relations to their core.

These flights were significant events in the lives of the slaves involved. Escaping to the city allowed them to learn about the antislavery attitudes and opinions there, and possibly even come into contact with abolitionist thought and politics.[61] They may also have encountered abolitionist sympathizers among the Carmelites in Salvador. In the monastery itself, the slaves certainly heard student gossip to the effect that when Friar João Lucas died, the state would take over the order's property and they would be freed. This suggests that some people thought that slavery would end as a result of state intervention, particularly into the religious institutions.

All of this news made its way into the Carmo Plantation slave quarters, where the slaves analyzed it and debated it heatedly. It reinforced the slaves' conviction that certain seignorial prerogatives—punishments for example—could no longer be exercised. The slaves observed that support for abolition was undermining the pro-slavery consensus. Their references to "individuals from the common people" alert us to the antislavery agitation among popular groups in the city of Salvador. We know that urban dwellers were fundamental to organizing actions against masters opposed to freedom for their slaves and inhibiting police pursuit of those slaves who escaped. The Carmelites' slaves found it inspiring that all these people were saying that they would soon be free. Presumably, other slaves did as well.

The slaves may have begun to develop hopes about better days ahead when they heard from "outsiders" that they would soon be liberated. This suggests that Bahia's freedmen were not indifferent to the fate of friends and relatives still trapped in slavery. To awaken the hope of freedom in the hearts of captive workers was another way of pushing for the end of slavery. But the antislavery climate in the streets of Salvador and the promises of freedom by freedmen living there may have contrasted sharply with the inflexible posture of Friar João Lucas toward the enslaved people on his property. Beginning in the 1870s, some religious orders and even Carmelites in other parts of Brazil began to indicate that they would free their slaves eventually. In October 1871, the Benedictine fathers liberated all of their slaves and, in December of that same year, so did the Carmelites in Rio de Janeiro.[62] In this context, Friar João Lucas appears as the principal Carmelite defender of a conservative stance on slavery, explaining why the slaves did not consider him to be a good master or a good priest.

The slaves hoped to take advantage of antislavery sentiment in Salvador. At no point did they appeal to the authorities in nearby São Francisco, which plantation owners or their family members and friends thoroughly controlled. The slaves knew that no one there would take their pleas seriously. The authorities in Salvador, on the other hand, were more receptive to the slaves' demands, or at least public pressure on them to support the slaves was stronger. But that does not mean that the slaves could appeal to the police and other officials in Salvador successfully. In his trial in Santo Amaro, Tibúrcio lamented that when they fled to Salvador to complain to the police about their mistreatment, they were sent back to the plantation "without the Chief of Police having done anything about their complaints." Silva Campos, the folklorist who gathered the tales about Friar João Lucas in the 1920s, went further, arguing that the slaves were sent back to the plantation without ever having managed to speak to the chief.[63]

Despite the slaves' failure in Salvador, their actions seriously compromised the traditional foundations of seignorial dominion and authority on the Carmelite properties and elsewhere. To begin with, the tensions between the priest and the slaves crossed the boundaries of the plantation, entering the public domain and involving the police in the capital. Slaves were disputing the masters' right to take away privileges or to punish in other ways. The slaves' crimes took place exactly when masters and overseers were attempting to severely and violently enforce customary prerogatives.

In her study of crime in rural São Paulo, Maria Helena Machado provides convincing examples that many slave offenses against owners and overseers were not simply an explosion of instinctive rage against extreme oppression. Rather, she demonstrates that slaves were motivated by the their perception that their masters were suddenly breaking with the customary rhythms of labor and invoking unjust or exaggerated corporal punishments.[64] Nonetheless, the case that we have analyzed doesn't refer so much to a break with the past on the part of masters and their representatives so much as it suggests the slaves' rejection of such customary rules. The question of corporal punishment and the loss of Sunday rest sent the slaves of the Carmo Plantation collectively fleeing to the capital to report their master to the authorities. Those were also the issues that provoked them to end their master's life. The slaves were no longer prepared to tolerate punishments that their parents had suffered and that they themselves had, until that point, endured.

The slaves' behavior represented a new form of rebellion, one that emerged from the crisis of slavery's legitimacy in Brazil. They were not trying to force the priest to adhere to well-established norms for master-slave relations within slavery. They were trying to break with the past. In other words, their actions were "antisystemic" rather than accepting of the established rules. Recognizing that the slaves knew that they were on the brink of obtaining their freedom, that they were influenced by the abolitionist climate, that they were aware that the state could interfere in the relationship between master and slave, and that such intervention could disrupt Father João Lucas's monastic life reinforces the hypothesis that the slaves who killed the Carmelite were trying to break with the past rather than engage in a regenerative or a restorative rebellion.

In any event, what occurred on the Carmo Plantation was not an isolated incident. As we saw in the previous chapter, overseers' attempts to force the captives to work on Sundays motivated some of the conflicts that took place on Bahian plantations during this period. Depriving the slaves of Sunday rest was a traditional form of punishment for transgressions, but slaves were no longer prepared to tolerate such penalties. The frequency with which slaves protested efforts to restrict their Sunday activities in the 1880s worried planters in the region. A month after the priest's death, the *Echo Santamarense*, a Santo Amaro newspaper belonging to the Conservative Party that represented the political position of a significant number of local planters, editorialized about a crime wave against owners and overseers. Although the editorial did not directly mention the episode at the Carmo Plantation, it is evident that the author was thinking about what had happened there. In a bombastic tone, he began by stating that "a terrifying threat is hanging over our growers." Aside from criticizing the imperial government for its handling of the crisis in the sugarcane sector, and its failure to prohibit the spread of abolitionist propaganda on the plantations, he argued that slaves who attacked their masters enjoyed impunity. Then he recalled a time in which slaves who committed crimes were punished harshly: "In the past, it was a surprise to learn of 'unusual' acts carried out by individual slaves acting alone, and the outraged population summoned to pass judgment on the delinquent would unleash the sword of justice [on him], effectively executing the law."[65]

The author drew a lesson from the harsh punishments imposed on slaves in the past, stating that "the head that rolled down the steps of the gallows, offered a horrible spectacle . . . , but it intimidated the other malefactors" and "kept them from carrying out other planned assaults." He also pointed to a dangerous type of enslaved politicization in the crimes that were being carried out. While in the "good times" the slaves committed crimes individually and over "any old injustice," "today, it's not like that, if you think about it, now when ten or more slaves get together to plan something, they bring together all of the means at their disposal, and their attitudes show that they have no fear of corporal punishment for a crime that they'd successfully carried out." The author of the editorial concluded by complaining that "at that point in the 1880s," the "delinquents" behaved as though they were convinced that the emperor would absolve them of all sorts of crimes.

This criticism of Dom Pedro II grew out of his interest in emancipation and his efforts to substitute hard labor for death sentences. Newspaper articles such as these revealed that the planters and their representatives were panicking, as they envisioned themselves, their relatives, and their employees as potential victims of what they called the slaves' "ferocity." This fear provoked nostalgia for a time when they believed that their lives and properties had been protected by slaves' fear of the law. The slaveocrats were trying to legalize terror, which would carry terrible consequences not only for slaves but for the entire black population.

Masters and slaves alike may have spread the story of Friar João Lucas's death during this tense period as an example of slave reprisals against cruel and unjust masters. But the event took place at a time when slavery was equated with injustice and cruelty. Thus, it was very difficult to distinguish "just" from "unjust" enslavement. The story of the priest's savagery became part of black oral history at a time in which the slaves were attempting to affirm their right to freedom and, perhaps, to try to convince reticent masters that opposing abolition could cause them trouble. At the beginning of the 1880s, this story carried an aggressive message for supporters of slavery; it was a difficult and unforgettable lesson for all those involved in master-slave relations in Brazil.

THREE

CROSSROADS OF SLAVERY AND
FREEDOM, 1880–1888

In the final decades of slavery in Brazil, thousands of slaves fled Recôncavo sugar plantations for nearby towns and cities, especially Salvador. In doing so, the slaves took into account the growing interference of the police in master-slave relations, the sympathy toward slaves that some judges were showing, and the growth of the abolitionist movement. They also considered growing popular hostility toward slavery.

Several scholars studying abolition have analyzed the antislavery street protests that broke out in Brazil during this period, including in the towns and cities of Bahia.[1] This chapter traces the links between slaves on the sugar plantations and the participants—free, freed, and enslaved—in those urban antislavery demonstrations. In doing so, it reconstitutes social connections that developed out of the antislavery struggles and allows us to explore the repercussions of growing urban unrest for master-slave relations on the plantations.

In the 1880s, the sugar-producing districts formed part of a large transportation and commercial network that extended well beyond the Recôncavo. Most Recôncavo sugar plantations sat on the shores of the Bay of All Saints or along the rivers that crisscrossed the region. The largest plantations boasted their own river landings, canoes, skiffs, and launches, not to mention slaves skilled in river and maritime navigation. The railroad connected the newer sugar plantations that spread north away from the bay, especially toward Rio Fundo and Lustosa, to towns closer to the bay, as well as to the river and sea routes to Salvador. Muleteers, leading mule trains that included dozens of animals, hauled goods and provided transportation between railheads and ports and distant towns in the hinterlands.

All of this movement within the region led to the development of close ties between and among the residents of rural and urban areas that facilitated the spread of news. Slaves carried news as they rowed or sailed boats laden with merchandise from place to place. As Wanderley Pinho wrote in the 1880s: "Every boat that arrived [at the Freguesia Plantation] brought with it the news of the revolutionary tracts of [antislavery activist Eduardo] Carigé [1851–1905] or Antônio Bento da Bahia: slave flights, whippings of fugitives in the slave cabins, insolence and rebellion on the part of the slaves."[2] Railroad workers, passengers, and muleteers carried that news with them into the Bahian interior on trains and trails. When they returned to the railheads and river landings, they brought reports from distant ranches, plantations, and farms. Recôncavo slaves paid special attention to any report about slavery and abolition—in other words, to news that would affect their futures.

We also know that slaves gathered information from sources closer to home. As they carried out their duties in the plantation houses, domestic servants overheard masters discussing parliamentary debates and the growing abolitionist movement. As we saw in the previous chapter, slaves on the Carmo Plantation learned about events and debates about slavery from their contact with freedmen in the towns as they traveled to markets to sell the produce from their subsistence plots. All of this news wound up in the slave quarters.

In the 1880s, plantation slaves who found themselves in the Recôncavo's large towns (Santo Amaro, Nazaré, or Cachoeira) or the provincial capital (Salvador) noticed that individuals belonging to many different social groups were expressing antislavery sentiments. Free and freed people alike denounced owners who punished their captives too harshly. Sometimes they rescued fugitives from the police or interfered with owners' attempts to sell slaves away from Bahia. This urban assistance meant that masters found it increasingly difficult to recapture escaped slaves and increased the slaves' chances of using flight to break definitively with slavery. [3]

Support from the free and freed population allowed fugitives to blend into the urban laboring population and avoid notice by the authorities. In January 1884, the subdelegado of Mares reported that a crioula called Maria died in the Rua da Calçada. In the process of identifying her, the detective learned from the neighbors that she was a slave who had escaped from a plantation in Feira de Santana at least four years earlier.[4] Her neighbors had helped her to hide in plain sight. In those years, masters were finding it difficult to recover captives who fled.

Free and freed Africans and Afro-Bahians had many reasons to assist slaves who were attempting to escape slavery. One was that slavery complicated the lives of all people of African descent—free, freed, or enslaved. In particular, free or freed individuals could be confused with slaves and imprisoned on suspicion of being fugitives. In May 1876, for example, Manoel José Fortunato the delegado of Cachoeira, arrested Manoel Gouveia, an African he suspected of being an escaped slave. Gouveia insisted that he had been freed three years earlier and that he had moved to Cachoeira from the state capital to find work. He stated that, prior to his emancipation, he had been employed in agriculture, but when there was not much farm work, his master sent him to hire himself out [in the city] in order to "pay him for the week." The delegado became suspicious at the "nervous and shaky" way that the African answered questions and demanded Gouveia's emancipation document. The prisoner could not produce it, claiming that it was with a friend who lived on the Novo Plantation in Santo Amaro.[5] Similarly, in February 1877, a crioulo named Eleutério José da Mota was arrested in in Salvador, because "he was wandering about begging, making himself a suspect of being a slave, a deserter, or a vagrant." In April of that same year, in the Areia Preta Fazenda woods near Salvador, João da Silva, described as pardo, found himself about to be taken prisoner on suspicion of being a slave or a deserter. Da Silva assured the guards that he was a free man, employed as a sailor on a boat that hauled manioc flour up the coast from Valença to the capital.[6] In October 1877, the overseer of the Freguesia Plantation placed an African named Rodrigo, who claimed to be free, in the stocks on suspicion of being

Scenas da Escravidão na provincia da Bahia

O tigre do engenho-Bom-Successo—revestido de forma humana marcando as suas victimas com ferro em braza.

FIGURE 3.1. Scenes of slavery in the province of Bahia.
"The tiger of the Bom Successo Plantation—dressed as a man, brands his victims with a hot iron." *Jornal, O Faísca*, 1887.

a plantation slave, because he couldn't produce an emancipation certificate.[7] In April 1882, eighteen-year-old Jerônimo de Sousa was taken prisoner in the streets of Salvador under suspicion of being a fugitive slave, even though he insisted that he was free.[8]

Experiences like these in Salvador from the 1870s on contributed to the growth of popular indignation about corporal punishment and other mistreatments to which slaves were subjected. On many occasions, the public demanded that the authorities act against masters who physically punished captives or subjected them to degrading conditions. On May 4, 1874, the subdelegado of the Santana Parish, Salvador Aires de Almeida Ferreira, reported that he had learned—via both a "private" complaint and a story in the *O Alabama* newspaper—that José Nunes de Barros Leite had beaten a parda captive. Arriving at Leite's house, the subdelegado found the parda in question, a girl named Fausta, chained to a tree stump. Leite defended himself saying that

Fausta was "conditionally free." The investigator removed her from her master's control, but ironically sent her to the House of Corrections to "put an end to these sufferings."[9]

In April 1875, residents of the Pilar Parish complained to police that Portuguese immigrant Joaquim Augusto Leite Galvão was subjecting a "little parda girl" named Cândida to physical punishment. On examining her, the subdelegado verified that the girl showed signs of a beating and removed her from the owner's residence. The subdelegado reported that Cândida had denied being beaten, but seemed "intimidated" (or terrorized) during questioning. To gather more evidence and protect her from reprisals, the subdelegado decided to remove her from the master's control.[10]

During this period, collective action also interfered with masters' efforts to recapture fugitives or sell slaves away to other provinces. On May 1, 1877, a large group of urban poor people stopped the sale to southern Brazil of a slave named Joana. She had fled the Pericoara Plantation in the Vila of São Francisco some months previously. According to the police report, the "masses . . . encircled her and protected her" as she was being moved from the House of Corrections, where she was held after her recapture in January, to the ship that would take her south. The enslaved woman was pregnant and under pressure from her rescuers, the police took her to the Santa Casa da Misericórdia (Charity Hospital).[11] Her champions may have been relatives, or friends and neighbors who had come to know her during the time she was a fugitive.[12]

In the 1880s, antislavery attitudes among the popular classes and within the organized abolition movement tended to coincide. On April 13, 1883, the *Echo Santamarense* reported that a group made up of boat men and two individuals "high up in the abolitionist movement" prevented sugar plantation owner Francisco Antônio Pinto from loading the five slaves he had sold onto the ship that would take them into the interprovincial slave trade. In the article, the paper demanded that the chief of police do something to stop such incidents.[13] Engineer and essayist Teodoro Sampaio—a black man who was also the son of a slave—reported that, in the 1880s, the canoe paddlers who ferried people and goods between Cachoeira and São Félix announced that they would no longer carry slaves on their masters' business, but would convey fugitive slaves for free. In Salvador, the deaths of several slaves in a fire in the Commercial District shop in which they were being held pending embarkation to the South of Brazil, inspired the city's boatmen to even more aggressive action. Sampaio reported that members of the Clube Saveirista (the Boatmen's Club, an abolitionist organization) scaled the walls of Commercial District buildings that held slaves and rescued them.[14]

Such antislavery attitudes among the general population may have provided the local abolitionist movement with political power. In March 1886, the authorities tried to send an enslaved man named "Pichita" Salustiano by train from Salvador to Inhambupe, a town several hundred miles to the northwest. Salustiano's master had died and the authorities were attempting to hand the captive over to the man's heirs. As antislavery activists Eduardo Carigé and Panfilo de Santa Cruz tried to rescue the captive, word spread in the neighborhood and a large group of people turned out at Salvador's Calçada railroad station to help the abolitionists.[15] The crowd began to protest slavery and to try to prevent the police from putting the slave on the train. According to reports, the crowd was full of "people of the masses." Among them were canoe paddlers and other local residents who had been responsible for spreading the news about what was going on. They were also among the people who confronted the police officers as they brought Pichita from the police station to the train.[16]

Police reports contain several references to such incidents. On July 8, 1887, the subdelegado of Salvador's Conceição da Praia Parish reported that numerous people had protested his arrest of a "preta" woman, because he had no documentation proving that she was a slave. The commander of the Commercial District's police station resolved to refer the case to the chief of police. On being interrogated at police headquarters, the woman confirmed that she was the slave of sugar plantation owner José Araújo Aragão Bulcão and that she had come to the capital from Cachoeira with abolitionist Cesário Ribeiro Mendes.[17] On the night of September 21, 1887, on the Pitanga River on the outskirts of Cachoeira, abolitionists and free blacks and mulattos attacked slave catchers bringing a fugitive to the authorities. They managed to rescue the slave, but they wounded two of the slave catchers in the process.[18] On March 26, 1888, the subdelegado of Pirajá Parish, one of Salvador's suburbs, reported that the previous afternoon, more than three hundred people had accompanied three men and a woman who were thought to be fugitive slaves and their purported owners to the police station. The men who claimed to own the alleged fugitives could not produce any documents proving their rights to the captives. To avoid a lynching, the subdelegado sent the supposed owners to present their documents to the authorities in São Sebastião, because "the mass of the people was immense and it wanted to do away with these two men."[19]

Many members of the lower classes actively participated in the organized abolition movement. According to Teodoro Sampaio, many "members of the lower classes" joined the "Old Guard," a group connected to Salvador's

Gazeta da Tarde (Afternoon Gazette) newspaper. Among them, he recalled, was Tertuliano de Alcântara, nicknamed "Mr. Turkey," "an old white man, who aggressively defended against those who quibbled with the abolitionists and himself." Sampaio also mentioned that the freedman Manoel Benício dos Passos, "a bronze-colored man, of herculean stature, a fighter, and illiterate," nicknamed "Macaco Beleza," [was] "always ready to audaciously and intelligently challenge the opinions of those who disagreed with him."[20]

Sampaio also mentioned that a number of "articulate men" participated in the abolitionist meetings held in the bakeries, bookstores, pharmacies, and barbershops of Salvador. Among them he listed the crioulo Marcolino José Dias, "the hero of the Paraguayan Campaign," as well as Manoel da Cruz, Pedro Bala, Muniz Barreto, Jorge Saveirista, João Branco, and Tenente Olavo José de Almeida. He also mentioned sons of the lower classes, "including Pedro Augusto Deocleciano, Cândido Camurugipe, Domingos da Silva, Tibúrcio do Pelourinho, Dr. Sales de Sousa, and the 'popular orator' Roque Jacinto da Cruz, among others."[21]

Sampaio identified many of these lower-class abolitionists as black men. Among them he included Marcolino José Dias, Manoel Benício dos Passos [Macaco Beleza], Manoel Querino, and Salustiano Pedro, whom Panfilo and Carigé called the "fearless black man." Sampaio commented that "wherever he could be found" Salustiano Pedro was "occupied with the magnificent issue of Justice for his race." Salustiano enthusiastically praised the black man's heroism, calling attention to the valiant behavior of Henrique Dias in the army and Marcílio Dias in the navy.[22] In an article published a few months after the abolition of slavery, Eduardo Carigé revealed that "when he was still under the weight of enslavement," Salustiano Pedro helped to establish the Luís Gama Club, an abolitionist organization named after a one of Brazil's most important black advocates of freedom.[23] And, according to Sampaio, enslaved and freedmen participated in the demonstrations sponsored by the Bahian Liberation Society as musicians in the Barbeiros and Chapadista Marching Bands. Chapadista was composed of enslaved musicians belonging to Raimunda Porcina de Jesus.[24]

Journalist Eduardo Carigé, one of Bahia's most important abolitionist leaders, revealed in the pages of Salvador's newspapers that urban workers were involved in the movement. As he wrote, "I was able to state in the meetings that by the Second of July of this year there would be no more slaves in the capital" because the Luís Álvares Club was "assisting me to help the slaves escape." The society was "composed of wage earning slaves [*ganhadores*]," and the club "was divided into 11 sections, each one corresponding to a parish [in Salvador]." These sections corresponded to the work "cantos" or gangs concentrated near the docks, but present all over the city. The abolitionists' confidence in the effectiveness of the participation of the wage-earning slaves in the abolitionist movement lay in the essential roles that these workers played in the transportation of people and merchandise throughout all of Salvador's neighborhoods.[25]

As we saw previously, workers involved in the transport of people and goods between the Recôncavo and the capital, especially the canoe paddlers and boatmen, were at the forefront of the street demonstrations and all sorts of actions that facilitated slaves' efforts to escape captivity. To their group, we should add the railway workers, who used the railroad expansion projects to hide fugitive slaves. Abolitionist thinking spread forcibly among transportation workers. As Teodoro Sampaio later recalled, when he worked for the Bahia to São Francisco Railroad, he spread abolitionist propaganda throughout the interior of Bahia.[26]

As in other parts of Brazil, slavery had become a source of dissatisfaction among the urban popular classes.[27] Abolitionism was, probably, the most important formative political experience for those who would later become militants in other movements. That may have been the case of Ismael Ribeiro dos Santos, a tailor and one of the founders of the Centro Operario da Bahia (Bahian Workers' Center) in 1891, described as "of African origin and abolitionist."[28]

Popular participation was so fundamental to deciding the direction of events, that, a month after abolition, the Baron of Vila Viçosa was still complaining about the individuals who had incited the ire of the "ignorant classes" against the slave masters, in the last years of slavery. According to Vila Viçosa:

There were meetings everywhere, even in the streets of the capital, and in the middle of these unruly crowds, these orators of the taverns would rear up, vomiting blasphemy, and shouting insults at the planters, preaching the most subversive doctrines to the masses and advising the slaves even to steal and kill! This resulted in the almost total insubordination and vagrancy of the slaves, the legalization of escapes, and the disruption of agriculture.[29]

In the 1880s, the abolitionist movement turned its attention strongly against the sugar industry, the economic sector most resistant to slave emancipation. This development led to several confrontations between abolitionists and plantation owners. One of those conflicts took place on April 10,

Sr barão em perigo.

Hontem estavamos no engenho do Sr barão Muniz d' Aragão Elle celebrava suo anniversario. Tinhamos uma ricca et boad jantar, mas muito tarde. e nos voltaremos no noite pelas mare sensa desaventura Hoje muita chuva et todo dias em casa. —

FIGURE 3.2. The baron in danger. Julius Naeher, 1878.

1883, when abolitionists from Salvador rescued a "little pardo boy" from the clutches of the Baron of Cotegipe, one of the richest planters of the Recôncavo, a leader of the Conservative Party in the Brazilian Senate and well recognized as an opponent of abolition. At the time, Cotegipe was trying to load Lino Caboto, an eleven- or twelve-year-old boy who had served as his personal servant, onto a ship bound for Rio de Janeiro. As the baron, his servants, and the boy were in the process of boarding the vessel that would take them to Rio, a group of abolitionists led by Panfilo de Santa Cruz and Eduardo Carigé approached them on the pretext of verifying the boy's health. Once close to the group, they forcibly removed the boy from his captors and took him back to the city. "Outrage" spread among Cotegipe's supporters, violence erupted on the docks near the Companhia Baiana de Navegação, and the chief of police was obliged to interfere. Unsurprisingly, he forced the abolitionists to return the child to the ship. News reports of the incident called for the repression of this "anarchism" and lack of respect for private property. [30]

The following day, the conflicts on the docks continued when abolitionists and members of the lower classes prohibited yet another important Recôncavo sugar planter from embarking slaves to Rio de Janeiro. This case involved the Baron of Sauípe, three slaves, and an "ingenuo"—in other words, a child born free after the passage of the Law of the Free Womb in 1871. Once again, abolitionists arrived and intervened before the captives could be loaded onto the ship to take them to new masters. Several days later, all the slaves in question were shipped to their destinations, but these episodes taught masters that freely disposing of their human properties was no longer possible, or at least not easy.[31]

The Seignorial Response

The conflict between the planters and the abolitionists grew as the antislavery movement infiltrated the Recôncavo, the most important slave-owner stronghold in the province. Beginning in the early 1880s, masters complained that abolitionist propaganda was damaging slave discipline on the plantations. An editorial published in the *Echo Santamarense* on October 26, 1882, announced that agricultural property was being threatened "by an unmediated abolitionist propaganda and that the constant attacks on the lives of the planters were truly appalling."[32] In January of the following year, an article in the same newspaper complained that abolitionist propaganda was having noxious effects on property owners' interests. The writer condemned the "violent and virulent" language the abolitionist press used about slave owners and recommended that masters organize themselves against those who preached assassination and revolt.[33]

In the Recôncavo towns of Cachoeira and Santo Amaro, traditional strongholds of the sugar aristocracy, the sugar planters organized to confront the abolitionists. On August 29, 1884, the "agricultural and commercial class" met in the Santo Amaro town hall to take an "energetic position against the abolitionist ideas" that were being discussed in Parliament by the "upper administration of the government." Among those present at the meeting were several influential sugar planters, including Arthur Rios; the baron of Sergi, Francisco Lourenço de Araujo; and the Baron of Vila Viçosa.[34]

The following year, sugar planters and merchants from Cachoeira founded the Agricultural and Commercial Union.[35] When they represented themselves in the pages of the local newspapers, the members of the Cachoeira union did not openly defend slavery. By 1885, it was no longer possible to do so. Instead, they made a point of declaring that they were not "slaveocrats and that they supported the gradual extinction of slavery, without disturbing public order, revolutionary agitation or violations of the principles of law and justice." In other words, they argued for a gradual "transition" from slavery to free labor, under the control of the landowning class.

The members of the union took care to publicize any grants of emancipation that they made to their slaves. In doing so, they hoped to instill gratitude in the new freedmen and thus maintain their control over their former captives. At their meeting on March 29, 1885, the union liberated an enslaved girl named Honorina, described as fifteen years of age and "almost white." At the same meeting, they decided that local plantation owners should not allow free workers to farm any of their land.[36] They may have feared that access to land, in that climate, would make it more difficult to convince freedmen to look for work.

The planters responded to the local radical abolitionists by awarding grants of freedom to some slaves, and they transformed the award of these grants into solemn ceremonies. For example, on November 29, 1884, planter Francisco Muniz Barreto de Aragão awarded freedom to his slave, Luís, in what the O Guarany newspaper described as a "truly philanthropic" act. In a speech during the ceremony on the Vitória Plantation in the Iguape Parish, Barreto de Aragão described Luís to the spectators (which included some of his slaves) as an "extremely talented carpenter." After relating the reasons for his "liberal" act, he praised the slaves who, "deaf to the infamous advice of perverse advisers, with their eyes on God, tramp along the road of virtue, so full of thorns, but rewarded in the end." Referring to the abolitionists, the planter announced to the freedman that

> as of today, . . . you may present yourself to our fellow citizens more proudly than many whites or wealthy people, because you were always a man of character, probity and honor—qualities which many such people lack, especially those who, wishing to fish in turbulent waters, encourage slaves belonging to others to commit crime or to rebel against society, without exerting themselves in the slightest to bring about the liberty of so much as one slave.[37]

At the same time, the sugar planters began accusing the abolitionists of taking advantage of slaves and breaking the law in the name of freedom. On

March 11, 1885, the provincial president received a petition from seventy-seven "farmers and merchants" from the Muritiba District of Cachoeira, accusing the abolitionist Cesário Ribeiro Mendes and his companions of seducing away their slaves, preaching insurrection, and creating communities of escaped slaves (quilombos) in the area. The petitioners also accused the abolitionists of fraud, specifically of extorting the paltry savings of the slaves and obliging them to become the activists' servants. Furthermore, they charged the abolitionists with violating the regulations on freeing slaves contained in the Law of the Free Womb of September 28, 1871.[38] It is curious that the planters who previously had opposed the law were now defending it as essential to social control. As the document makes clear, the abolitionists had moved beyond writing newspaper articles to more daring activities, including providing safe haven for fugitive slaves.

The most spectacular confrontations between planters and abolitionists in the Recôncavo took place in Cachoeira. On April 21, 1887, the owner of the Novo Plantation in Iguape Parish, Joaquim Inácio de Siqueira Bulcão, accused one of Cachoeira's abolitionist leaders, Cesário Ribeiro Mendes, of hiding some of his slaves. According to Bulcão, Mendes "was making himself the scourge of planters in that area" by helping slaves to escape. The planter claimed that over the course of the previous two years, several captives had fled his property and that when he had tried to negotiate their return with Mendes, the abolitionist had refused to cooperate. Bulcão tried to transform his complaint into a generalized statement of the planter class's plight. He argued that if they were to end "this uproar that has peaceful property owners turning summersaults," such behavior required punishment.[39]

The jailing of abolitionist leader Cesário Mendes in July 1887 on a charge of concealing slaves fleeing Cachoeira's sugar plantations stirred the controversy even further. As Mendes was escorted to jail, such a large crowd developed that Delegado Joaquim Inácio Albenaz called for reinforcements to protect the jail from attack by the prisoner's "friends," since "as Your Excellency knows [he] has his followers and one must fear some effort on his behalf." On September 2, 1887, the delegado informed the chief of police that he had frustrated an attempt by Mendes to escape, aided by one of the prison guards, José Caiçara Mascarenhas.[40]

The Cachoeira abolitionists identified Delegado Albernaz as the local planters' loyal representative.[41] Throughout 1887, he ignored the complaints against planters for excessive punishment of their slaves.[42] In September 1887, the abolitionist newspaper O Asteróide criticized the delegado's behavior, accusing him of arbitrary arrests, particularly of people he suspected of being fugitives, and of "hurting" "people." In retaliation, on September 25, 1887, the delegado arrested João Ângelo Ferreira, while he was selling copies of the newspaper in Cachoeira.[43]

Events subsequently escalated. On the afternoon of October 4, Delegado Albernaz assaulted abolitionist Inácio José de Freitas, a man in his sixties, after an argument on a busy Cachoeira street. In response, Inácio's son, Henrique de Freitas, fired his musket at the delegado and took off running. Albernaz, in turn, shot at Henrique with his revolver and followed in hot pursuit through the streets of downtown Cachoeira. When Henrique was imprisoned, a large group of "people from the lower classes" gathered to protest his arrest, throwing rocks at the delegado and attacking the soldier who accompanied him. During the night, numerous people, many of whom belonged to the local abolitionist movement, threw rocks at or shot out the windows of the jail. The soldiers guarding the house where the jail was located shot back, and several people were wounded. The next day, the provincial president ordered the chief of police of Cachoeira to reestablish public order.[44] Within a few days, he had dismissed Albernaz.

By 1887, abolitionist activity and its repression had spread throughout Bahia. In Canavieiras, in extreme southern Bahia, on August 23, Maurício de Souza Prazeres was arrested after "numerous respectable persons" pointed him out as an "enticer" of slaves. A month later, on September 22, 1887, the delegado from the village of Camisão (today Ipirá) in the semiarid region to the west of the Recôncavo, accused abolitionist Pedro Alves Boaventura of hiding slaves and putting them to work on his properties.[45]

The Final Days

Disobedience and insubordination on the part of the enslaved grew during the 1880s until it shook the social order on the plantations. "Old" Francisco Félix reported constant conflicts with the slaves on his Outeiro Plantation during this period, as Isaías Alves, one of his descendants, learned while researching the family history. According to one report, a slave named Feliciano "asked him [Francisco Félix] insolent questions" when they encountered one another on the road.[46] Feeling affronted, Francisco ordered the slave punished. Alves did not say what had been "insolent" about the slave's words, but he considered that episode a sign of a "time of growing revolution." According to Alves, life on the plantations became insecure and "respect for masters diminished" during those years. Research into police records unearthed references to a slave named Feliciano, described as a crioulo, fifty years of age, belonging to Francisco Félix de Almeida Sampaio in Santo Antônio de Jesus. Feliciano came to the attention of authorities in 1882 when he fled to the capital and turned himself in to the police complaining that he had waited six years to be freed by the Emancipation Fund.[47]

Most of the planters believed that slaves like Feliciano behaved as they did because abolitionists were spreading propaganda on the plantations. Actually, the plantation slaves' behavior probably grew out of their awareness that debates about the future of slavery were taking place in the national and state capitals. By the mid-1880s, the emperor in Rio had indicated his interest in abolition, and proposals to end slavery were circulating in Parliament. Aristides Novis (1857?–1917?), a respected Bahian sugar exporter, later recalled that, at the time, the planters were divided on the question of emancipation and many consulted him about whether or not they should liberate their slaves.[48] Slaves heard this news from a variety of sources, analyzed it, and then developed plans, but it was difficult for planters to admit that. Slaves seem to have concluded that they could now openly question planter power, and that their masters were increasingly isolated. That is why conflicts with masters and overseers intensified in the second half of the 1880s.[49]

The behavior that masters perceived as disobedient and insubordinate reflected the growing refusal of enslaved men and women to tolerate slavery anymore. Toward the end of the 1880s, collective escapes from the plantations intensified. In February 1885, the owner of the Cachoeirinha Plantation, Inocêncio Teixeira Barbosa, reported that forty-five slaves had escaped his control, including twenty-five women, some of whom carried their ingênuo children with them.[50] In March 1885, Francisco Ribeiro Lopes complained that five enslaved women had fled his Pitanga Plantation. Among them were Catarina, Marcelina, Lourença, Rufina (with a daughter named Damiana), and Justina (with a son).[51] In June 1887, Rodrigo Antônio Falcão Brandão stated that six slaves had fled his Palma Plantation in Santo Amaro and that he knew that they were being held in the Salvador jail.[52] On March 3, 1887, the Count of Subaé wrote in his diary: "I received word that the pretos Firmino, Firmo, Antônio Luís, Juvêncio, Honorato, Pedro, Elias, Aprigio and Abraão had left the plantation."[53]

At the end of 1887, the planters began to make collective awards of freedom—some immediate, and some conditional. The newspapers attributed these awards to the planters' altruism and humanitarian spirit, but the planters were making calculated decisions about the present and future. Looking at current problems, they hoped to check slave discontent and avoid interruptions in agricultural production. Looking to the future, they aimed to instill "perennial gratitude" and respect in former slaves, and in so doing, guarantee a post-abolition labor force on the plantations.[54]

Not all of the planters agreed that collective grants of freedom were an appropriate response to the emerging crisis. According to Isaías Alves:

> Three months before the end, Uncle João Caetano had freed all of his slaves, which made many planters unhappy, because they thought he gave a bad example. Old Inácio Tosta advised freeing them, and at the same time inviting the slaves to stay and become free workers. Old Francisco Félix managed to keep several.[55]

Alves considered his ancestors' attitudes "enlightened," but he revealed that many planters opposed liberating slaves before being required to do so. At issue was the possibility that the imperial government would indemnify planters for their lost captive property at abolition. On July 11, 1888, almost two months after abolition, Cotegipe presented such a bill to the legislature. On that day, Recôncavo merchant and planter Aristides Novis recalled that, prior to abolition, the planters were divided on the question of emancipation. Many planters consulted him about whether or not they should liberate their slaves, but according to Novis, he had not shared his opinion on the subject. Novis himself did not grant freedom to his slaves prior to the abolition law, trusting in the possibility of indemnification.[56]

At the beginning of 1888, the abolitionists openly called for slaves to run away from the plantations where they were being held captive. In Cachoeira, the abolitionists actually distributed pro-emancipation leaflets in the slave quarters on the sugar plantations. Reflecting on the master-slave relationship on the plantations in such a situation, Wanderley Pinho wrote: "How could any work be done with the blacks so worked up by the demagoguery of the abolitionists, and [his Freguesia Plantation] so close to the capital, where the propaganda that refused to respect the institution of slavery was boiling."[57] On April 12, 1888, the Baron of Moniz Aragão, a major sugar planter in São Francisco do Conde, informed Cotegipe that abolitionist pamphlets had been distributed to the slaves on his Cassarangongo and Maracangalha plantations. In the document, abolitionists from São Félix and Cachoeira proclaimed that "slavery is theft" and urged captives to gather their relatives from the slave quarters and the masters' households and run away together to the cities. The pamphlet concluded with the words "Flee, Flee and you will be free."[58]

Less than a month before abolition, *O Tempo* predicted that large numbers of slaves fleeing to the city would have "terrifying" consequences for local commerce and public security. According to the article's author, the urban economy could not support the influx of slaves fleeing the plantations.[59]

At the same time, the abolitionists began to take advantage of seignorial fear. On April 17, 1888, the abolitionist newspaper *Gazeta da Tarde* reported that it had received a letter from Cachoeira, the writer of which reported that around eight hundred slaves had fled the plantations. On the same date, the newspaper informed its readers that slave escapes were having an effect throughout Cachoeira County. Abolitionist propaganda had caused all of the slaves in the Outeiro Redondo district of the county to abandon their masters, while in nearby Cruz das Almas master-slave relations had been devastated. As a result of this rural success, the paper also indicated that abolitionists in the capital had begun clamoring for slaves to flee. It went on to inform its readers that so many slaves in rural São Paulo, in south-central Brazil, had already fled that they had practically put an end to slavery in that province.[60]

On April 18, 1888, *O Tempo* returned to discussing abolitionism in the city. According to the writer, local farmers were freeing their slaves, inspired either by "humanitarian spirit" or anxiety that their slaves would be "seduced" "by speculators whose leaflets incite slaves to run away." The author predicted that these farmer actions would lead to serious consequences. He argued that, without coercive measures, the slaves would try to expand the definition of freedom, and in a short time, the farmers would find themselves without laborers for their farms. For this reason, he worried that freedom was being awarded without a law that would have required labor contracts to be signed between the parties. He reported that the planters were replacing slavery with either wage labor or sharecropping, but that neither labor system would work without coercive laws to oblige the workers to fulfill their obligations to planters.[61]

On that same day, *O Tempo* announced that an "abolitionist festival" had taken place at the parish church in Cruz das Almas, in Cachoeira County. On the occasion, 23 property owners freed 124 slaves. The ceremony began when Mass ended and Temístocles da Rocha Passos presented certificates of freedom to 54 of his slaves. Then, 22 other slaveowners followed his example and several citizens made speeches. According to *O Tempo*'s reporter:

> There was a touching scene in which freedmen went down on their knees at the feet of their ex-master and his family, weeping, and by their copious tears, showed how profoundly they recognized the generosity which they had received, and at the same time, demonstrated their gratitude for the humanitarian manner with which they were

treated during their captivity which, although not completely agreeable because of the nature of the condition, was nonetheless absent of bitterness and cruelty.[62]

The reporter emphasized the declarations of loyalty and fidelity that the freedmen made to their ex-masters during these ceremonies. "In light of such an imposing spectacle," the writer continued, "in view of the assurances that the freedmen gave in their bad Portuguese not to abandon their ex-master, so emotionally that they often broke down sobbing, no one could have avoided bursting into tears."[63]

On April 28, 1888, *O Tempo* reported on another freedom ceremony, this time on the Desterro Plantation, belonging to Pedro Viana, in the Iguape sugar district. Viana called together about one hundred slaves that he owned and announced

> that he had come to give them the documentation of their promised freedom; that this was another opportunity for him to thank them for being so good, so honorable and so worthy of appreciation and esteem; that he felt great pleasure in giving them freedom, not only for those reasons [already mentioned], but also because none of them had disappointed him by being "insolent or running away," although some of their friends had fled; finally that he didn't ask any of them to stay on his plantation, but neither would he prohibit anyone from remaining, and those who continued to be honorable and therefore his friends could count on his aid in misfortune.[64]

The article emphasized that the transition to free labor could take place in an orderly fashion and without compromising the social order.

According to the author, as he distributed the certificates, the speaker was interrupted several times by the copious tears and incessant sobs of the people in the audience, including the freedmen. Then Viana told the freedmen that he did not have the legal capacity to sign work contracts with them, but he asked what free-labor system they preferred. The freedmen replied that they could not decide the question themselves; they would leave the task of choosing the best way to organize their work to their "benefactor." This "happy reply" from the freedmen filled the planter with joy, and to commemorate the beginning of free labor on his plantation, he ordered a high Mass to be celebrated in the plantation chapel. During Mass, the master liberated another sixteen of his slaves.[65] Viana, and other planters like him, hoped that the transition would take place within parameters with which they could be comfortable.

Freedom ceremonies like this took place throughout the two weeks preceding abolition. The masters were anticipating the actions of the imperial government and trying to diminish the political impact of any law that would definitively abolish slavery. On May 2, 1888, the *Diário da Bahia* reported that the owner of the Orobó Plantation in Alagoinhas freed all of his captives, under the condition that they remain working for him until New Year's Eve. Then he allowed the ingênuos, officially his wards, to leave the property. The newspaper concluded that the owners' actions meant that he no longer believed slavery could survive. On May 4, 1888, that same newspaper announced that the Baron of São Francisco, a Recôncavo sugar plantation owner, liberated twenty-five of his slaves, thirteen of them on condition that they serve him until the cane had been harvested.[66]

This last-minute seignorial abolitionism could not stop the captives' push for freedom. On May 5, the *Diario* published a letter from João Vaz de Carvalho Sodré, owner of the Aratu Plantation, announcing that he had freed seventy-seven people. Sodré wrote that on April 30, 1888, he had granted unconditional emancipation to all of his slaves and had also given up the service of the ingênuos. He claimed he had planned to liberate them on Monday, April 25, to celebrate the birthday of a family member, and then to organize free labor on his plantation, but had been unable to do so because the slaves abandoned the property before he could announce his "act of generosity." He was surprised that most slaves had abandoned the plantation on Sunday, April 24, when he was absent, "in that way frustrating to a certain degree my plans." All the same, he tried to use the ceremony to prove that "I'm not one of those who are opposed to the requirements of progress and the necessities of our time."[67]

With only a few days left before abolition was to be announced, many masters recognized that trying to bind slaves to them with a "debt of gratitude" was pointless and that the old seignorial paternalism could not guarantee social order. They were unable to control the process of abolition: in the view of a prominent plantation owner from Santo Amaro, the country was falling to into anarchy, and "agriculture was being disrupted by . . . the insubordination and vagrancy of the slaves [and] the legalization of escapes," in combination with "the abnormality of the season and the miserable price of agricultural crops."[68] This was the context in which the Law of May 13 was enacted.

FOUR

MAY 13, 1888, AND
ITS IMMEDIATE AFTERMATH

On the 13th of May in Santo Amaro
The pretos [blacks] celebrated
In the Market Square
(Perhaps they are still doing so today)
The end of slavery
Of slavery
The end of Slavery.

—CAETANO VELOSO, "May 13,"
Noites do Norte, words and music by
Caetano Veloso, Nonesuch, 2001

On May 9, 1888, when the newspapers reported that a bill to abolish slavery had been introduced to the Brazilian legislature, everyone in the Bahian Recôncavo—enslaved and free—came to understand that the end of slavery was fast approaching. Local chronicler Isaías Alves later recalled that slaves gathered at the telegraph office in the Vargem Grande train station, near Santo Antônio, to await news about the approval of the law that would change their lives forever.[1] On many plantations, slaves stopped working in the cane fields, behaving as though they were already free. Many masters, as we saw in the previous chapter, liberated their slaves immediately, in hopes of stopping group flights and instilling gratitude in the ex-slaves. Others, however, continued to refuse to anticipate abolition, still hoping that the government would indemnify them for the loss of their captive workers.

On May 8, the streets of Salvador had filled with people anticipating abolition. Crowds flocked to the newspapers offices "with the intention of demonstrating the joy that possessed them." Later, when a large "popular throng" had gathered, the "Music of the Freedmen's" Brass Band (probably the former Chapadista Band) began to play, fireworks exploded in the sky, abolitionists made speeches, the crowd cheered the conservative politicians responsible for presenting the abolition bill to the legislature, and the lower classes paraded through the city streets.[2]

Celebrations also broke out in the towns and plantation slave quarters of the Recôncavo when the news reached them that slavery definitively ended in Brazil on May 13, 1888. Beginning that night, the delegado of São Francisco do Conde later reported, the freedmen celebrated with "noisy" sambas.[3] In other Recôncavo towns, men and women newly freed from the plantations joined the free poor in parties and parades sponsored by the abolitionist societies. A Cachoeira newspaper reported that on the night of May 13, "the people spilled out into the streets" accompanied by two brass bands. Residents of the houses that lined the parade routes made speeches and led cheers celebrating the great day from second-story windows. The following week, when the town council received the official declaration of abolition, about four thousand people paraded happily through the streets of Cachoeira and the neighboring town of São Felix.[4] Beginning on the thirteenth, abolitionist societies, students, the free poor, and ex-slaves also took to Salvador's streets, celebrating to the sound of brass bands. Night after night, there, fireworks lit up the façades of private homes and public buildings alike.

Several observers recorded the presence of ex-slaves in the streets of Salvador. Ex-slaves removed from storage the historic Bahian Independence Day floats of the *caboclo* (Indian man) and *cabocla* (Indian woman) defeating the serpent of Portuguese imperialism and carried them through the city's streets along the Bahian Independence Day parade route. The connection ex-slaves made between abolition and Bahia's Independence Day (July 2) by bringing out the floats suggests that the freedmen and women, as well as the free poor, believed that abolition finally completed the acquisition of freedom begun in 1823.[5] As one Bahian legislator observed:

> In the middle of that enormous wave of people, the black men, the ex-slaves stood out, basking, as they were, in the light of freedom, mixing with the crowd that received them with open arms. They looked like

people who had seen heaven . . . and with half open lips, they cried—Hurray for freedom![6]

The abolitionist, engineer, and historian Teodoro Sampaio (1855–1937), himself the son of an enslaved woman, remarked on how militant freedman and abolition activist Manoel Benício dos Passos (?–1898), whose nickname was Macaco Beleza, reacted to the news that slavery had ended. According to Sampaio,

> On May 13, 1888, the man was stunned into silence. In the middle of this enthusiastic crowd of citizens of all social classes, including the newly emancipated, with noise erupting from every neighborhood in the city, even the slums, while everyone else descended on the offices of the *Gazeta da Tarde* and the Libertadora Bahiana Abolitionist Society to recognize the roles they had played [in abolition], Manoel Benício wept. People noticed that he could not stop crying.[7]

In many parts of Bahia, the abolition celebrations continued for days. In the capital, a large "popular pilgrimage" made its way to the Bonfim Church to thank God for the liberation of the slaves on May 18.[8] On the morning of June 7, 1888, the freedmen and women of Santa Rita do Rio Preto celebrated when, in a "loud voice in the streets," town leaders followed the provincial president's orders and officially announced the abolition law. As the town council secretary walked the streets proclaiming something that everyone already knew, he was "met immediately and enthusiastically with fireworks and shouts of 'viva' by ex-slaves of both sexes."[9] Seven months after abolition, during the annual festivities of Salvador's Bonfim Parish, the chorus of the most popular samba was "Hey Massa Carigé, gimme here my freedom papers," referring to the abolitionist Eduardo Carigé and the slaves' efforts to acquire manumission in the last days of slavery.[10]

The evidence indicates that former slaves were active participants in these abolition celebrations. Their behavior, thus, requires that we consider the political implications of their involvement in the parades, in the procession to the Bonfim Church, and in other celebrations, such as, for example, the Masses offered by the Black Brotherhoods (Irmandades Negras). The freedmen's actions indicate that they knew they were experiencing a historic moment and suggest that they were using the abolition celebrations to exercise their new rights as citizens.

The celebrations of May 13 were a popular expression of the opposition to slavery in Bahia. The large numbers of people in the streets impressed contemporary observers. Two days after abolition, a reporter for the *Diário da Bahia* seemed impressed by the millions of "popular" people in the streets of Salvador. In one passage, he noted that "the masses demonstrated the most profound and enthusiastic joy that you could imagine." In another, he referred to the "enormously well-attended popular parade," to the "enormous multitude" and to the "large mass of the people" that wandered through the streets carrying the symbols of Bahian independence.[11]

Many feared the "masses" in the streets, a large part of which were composed of people coming out of slavery, and believed they foretold perilous future developments. Expressing those fears on May 14, one Bahian legislator protested against any reduction in the size of the province's police force, given the presence there of nearly eighty thousand people newly freed from slavery.[12] Indeed, such requests for increased police protection were common in Bahia at the time.

Sugar-plantation owner and merchant Aristides Novis was one powerful Bahian worried about the future. Three days after abolition, he wrote to his fellow planter and former prime minister, the Baron of Cotegipe, confiding his concerns about what took place in Salvador on May 13. "We are living in complete delirium!" he wrote. From the balcony of his home, he had heard ovations for Conselheiro Dantas, Rio Branco, Joaquim Nabuco, and other liberal leaders, but little praise for João Alfredo, Conservative Party leader of the imperial cabinet. He recognized that the partisan conflicts that had characterized all the discussions about slavery had reemerged in the celebrations of May 13. Nevertheless, he considered the presence of large numbers of ex-slaves in the street demonstrations more frightening than the near-total absence of recognition of the role of Conservative leaders in abolition.[13] Finally, he commented:

> Hurray for the 13th of May, hurray for immediate abolition without indemnification, they are the saviors of the Fatherland! Since the 13th of May we are living in complete delirium! Commerce was closed all day yesterday, marches in the streets, they went to find the Independence floats at Lapinha and they put them in the Palace Square; every night there is revelry; carnival, Independence day and the celebration of abolition all rolled into one! What an impact they've had, there are more than 3,000 pretos here who have come from the plantations. Just yesterday, speaking with the [Provincial] President and the Chief of Police, I requested that they make sure that these workers return to the plantations as soon as these celebrations are over. If [they do] not we will shortly be seeing an outbreak of thievery and murder.[14]

Novis considered the intermingling of thousands of freed people with the urban poor in the streets of the city to be very dangerous. To his despair, he recognized that the people had incorporated the scope and significance of the two most important popular festivals in Bahia—Carnaval and independence from Portugal—into their celebration of freedom in a potentially explosive combination.[15] The former slave owner found it intolerable to watch, at one and the same time, the inversion of order that was Carnaval and the glorification of independence that was the Dois de Julho (Second of July).[16] Behind this lay his larger fear that the celebrations would result in a serious threat to public order. Therefore, he did not hide his concern at the presence of more than three thousand pretos in the city streets and pushed the authorities to take repressive measures. In his letter, he even observed, "I only ask God that, after this display of patriotism is over, the government will provide us with laws that regulate labor and financial support for agriculture; if it does not, we will be in terrible shape."

In the same letter, Novis described his uncle's reactions to the ways in which the ex-slaves had thrown themselves into the celebration of freedom and how their behavior toward owners had changed after abolition. According to Novis, his uncle the Baron of Santiago—a major planter in the region— was "well, but perplexed, seeing the children he raised so carefully take to the streets, etc. etc."[17] It seems that losing his enslaved property shocked the elderly planter less than his sudden inability, on that historic day, to control the people he considered his "wards." The baron's confusion reflected the complete breakdown of the traditional forms of social control developed under slavery. The paternalism with which he had previously treated his "wards" did not help him to manage them on that first day of freedom.

For the ex-slaves and others who had supported and pushed for abolition, May 13, 1888, marked the beginning of a new era. It was in this climate of expectations that Cachoeira's mulato musician and militant abolitionist, Manoel Tranquilino Bastos, named his daughter Aurorina Maiotreze Bastos (Dawn May 13th Bastos), in honor of her birth on May 13, 1888.

A deeper analysis of the celebration of May 13, 1888, reveals the ex-slaves' expectations of and feelings about freedom. Their hopes and plans for liberty, engendered both during and after slavery, contributed to a series of changes in the patterns of behavior characteristic of slavery in the Recôncavo. This chapter reflects on the words and deeds through which the ex-slaves distanced themselves from their enslaved past. I argue that, in affirming their new condition, the freedmen confronted the material and symbolic limits of a freedom that had been born out of Brazilian slavery. Abolition had shattered the foundation for the day-to-day interactions between masters and ex-slaves on the plantations as well as elsewhere, but it did not fundamentally change the hierarchical social order of the Recôncavo.

In those first days of freedom, ex-slaves simply ignored their ex-masters' orders and openly questioned the hierarchical society in which they lived. It was a remarkable period in which the ex-slaves on and off the plantations tried to deepen the changes abolition brought to day-to-day power relations. The ex-masters, on the other hand, saw no deeper meaning in the freed people's behavior, only drunken excitement. Even so, the days following abolition were rich with significance as ex-slaves and ex-masters contested the limits of and the possibilities of freedom.

The Days following Abolition

To the unhappy surprise of many ex-masters, abolition brought changes in the speech and attitudes of the men and women who emerged from slavery. To confirm their freedom, the ex-slaves rejected roles central to their former conditions, seeking to distance themselves from an enslaved past. On many plantations, ex-slaves refused to accept the daily food ration, to work in the cane fields, or to work without pay. Many began to express themselves in ways that the ex-masters considered "bold" and "insolent." During that period, words and actions easily violated the parameters of what ex-masters understood as respectful and deferent behavior. Few masters could later avoid bitter memories of the manner in which their former captives began to behave.[18]

In 1933, Argeu described how the captives of the plantation where he had been enslaved celebrated the "day of liberty." He recalled:

> It was a terrible thing! Mr. Mata Pinto [the plantation owner] got everybody together, about 100 of us, for a samba; he broke open the wine and cane liquor, brought out tapioca pudding, and at dawn he says that everybody is free. What the devil! We already knew that, and the bonfire blazed all night.[19]

Here we see the master unsuccessfully trying to control the celebration of freedom, because the ex-slaves already knew that they were free. The morning after the party, the ex-master was even more disappointed to discover that his former slaves did not appear for work, since according to Argeu, "the following day nobody was left on the plantation." That morning the master's house was so quiet you could only hear "the noise of the flies; the devil had taken over that house."[20]

Years after abolition, Isaías Alves used family memories to try to reconstruct what happened in the "slaves' souls" on the day that they were all freed. According to him, music and bonfires filled his grandfather's plantation in Santo Antônio. One old family slave named Vitorino spent the night being "insolent and provoking," and proudly marching around shouting loudly "Long live equality." The ex-master was surprised at this behavior, since until that point Vitorino had always been respectful and "a good guy."[21] What most shocked the ex-master was the possibility that dangerous ideas of freedom and equality were mixing in Vitorino's head, as well as those of other freedmen. Such a combination was potentially explosive in a society based on social and racial inequality. Without realizing it, Alves was revealing how frightened the former owners were of their newly freed ex-slaves.

Alves also described the reaction of the ex-slave Januário, his grandfather's trusted cook, who,

> all stirred up, shouting about abolition, let a pot of rice burn on the stove. In a quite masculine voice, Aunt Heliodora shouted: "I know that you are all free, but go take care of my lunch, not to mention my pot of rice that you let burn!" The ex-slave, laughing, went back to the kitchen and never left his ex-master, who arranged a "hut" for him, which allowed him to marry Geralda, the slave of Misael Lopes, who was a splendid mulata and much lighter skinned than he.[22]

The author certainly intended that story to demonstrate the "warm relations" between former masters and ex-slaves, but he accidentally wound up revealing how much that day had changed day-to-day relations between freedmen and ex-masters. The slave could now laugh at a verbal reprimand by the mistress, an act that previously might have led to some form of punishment.

One of the basic conditions of seignorial authority—the ability to issue orders that slaves would obey—disappeared in the days following May 13, 1888. It was not an accident that one commentator suggested that abolition did away with "tradition" in the cane industry.[23] According to Alves, on the morning of May 14 on his grandfather's plantation,

> after hearing the news [about abolition], one [ex-slave] turned up with his head bandaged, another informed us that he was sick, and, when asked why the others [ex-slaves] hadn't come to work, he replied that they had been set free. The old man [the master] at being informed of all this, didn't get angry, just sad and worried.[24]

For the freedmen, such behaviors demonstrated that the ex-masters no longer controlled them. The former owners surely found the abolition of slavery to be traumatic.

In stating that they "had been set free," the freedmen on the Outeiro Plantation attempted to say that they no longer felt obliged to observe daily labor routines. Possibly, they understood working in the cane as a "continuation of slavery" and that was why they refused to bend their backs in agricultural labor or to take part in any other activity on the sugar plantation. That is certainly why, at dawn on May 14, they refused to respond to the call to the daily grind in the cane fields.

Many owners became frightened when they realized that neither paternalism nor threats would force their ex-slaves to work in the days after abolition, but some actually lost their will to live. Isaías Alves wrote that after the news of "the big event," "there were planters who committed suicide: some drowned themselves and others poisoned themselves, and others went crazy." On January 26, 1889, the *Diário do Povo* announced the suicide of a "major planter" from Conceição do Almeida Parish, in the area where Alves did his research. According to the newspaper, the planter's forty slaves had been liberated by the law of the thirteenth of May, and "crushed by this fact and even more by the circumstance of having the freedmen abandon their work, his mental faculties began to suffer, until at dawn on the 23rd of the current month he put an end to his existence."[25]

Antônio Joaquim Pires de Carvalho e Albuquerque, Baron of Vila Viçosa (1841–1915), a plantation owner from Santo Amaro, commented in the Bahian press on those early days of freedom.[26] On January 24, 1889, he wrote that after the announcement of the Law of May 13, flights and "demoralization" were provoking "general agitation in the [sugar industry]." At the news that "all Brazilian hearts should fill with joy," "reflective spirits" were, nonetheless, overcome with apprehension about the province's economy. After their initial excitement about the passage of the law, planters became depressed about the loss of workers and their lack of resources to pay salaries. "Since the 13th of May, labor has become completely disordered. The ex-slaves don't do anything except drift about, dancing and getting drunk." According to him, most of them abandoned the plantations and went to the city of Santo Amaro, but the "laziest" of them stayed at home and provided no service whatsoever.[27] In the baron's view, the behavior of the freedmen grew out of unthinking desires and the enjoyment of sloth, vagrancy, and drunkenness. He believed that the freedmen were neither prepared for freedom nor capable of reflective action, a view he shared with others of his class.

In the article, Vila Viçosa related his own bitter experiences on the day after abolition and could not hide his annoyance at his loss of moral authority over people who earlier had obeyed him. He wrote that

> when I left [the plantation] for Santo Amaro by train on May 12, the plantation's sugar mill was functioning, but when I returned on the 14th I had no way to continue grinding the cane; but that didn't surprise me, because I'd come from the city without my servant—he had been drinking since the 13th, and couldn't move; he only showed up the next day, all embarrassed, to tell me that he doesn't want to be my servant anymore and that he was going to look for another way to make a living.[28]

The baron contradicted himself when he described his servant's reason for leaving, because he acknowledged that the man had been motivated by a desire for "another way of making his living," rather than sloth. Even so, the baron believed that the servant's decision had resulted from the happiness and excitement about May 13. Vila Viçosa tried to imagine the ex-slaves' logic: "If we had to work every day when we were slaves, now that we are freedmen, we shouldn't have to work anymore." He imagined that they obeyed "only the habits of indolence and the temptations of vice and passion." To complete his portrait of the moral degeneration that abolition had unleashed, Vila Viçosa further commented that the cities had become "overrun by black women throwing themselves into prostitution." In his article, the Baron tried to demonstrate that slavery had served as a moral constraint on people who he believed were "naturally" inclined toward laziness, idleness, "vice," and "passion."[29]

Vila Viçosa was a harsh critic of the way in which the government had implemented the law of the thirteenth of May. He had advocated government indemnification of planters for the loss of their enslaved laborers, and it was in his interest to demonstrate that ex-masters were facing the confiscation of their human property, as well as disobedience and flight from the plantations. His comments make clear that he was dissatisfied at his inability to control the people who had belonged to him.

Many planters used words like "excitement," "dazed," and "drunk with joy" to describe the mood of the freedmen at the time. According to one observer, "The first impression was . . . of those guys (the ex-planters) holding back out of fear or wounded sensibilities, and these guys (the freedmen) carried away by an awareness of their own power . . . with no restraints on their aspirations."[30]

On another occasion, the author stated, "although it did not fundamentally change the hierarchical social order of the Recôncavo, redemption of the captives, caused the depression of some and the unruliness of others." The class accustomed to access to enslaved labor had difficulty believing that the black population, once it had been released from slavery, could live without the controls and limits imposed by slavery or that ex-slaves might have their own hopes and dreams for freedom.

The comments Vila Viçosa and the other observers left behind make clear that they saw abolition as more than just a law that cost them their enslaved laborers; to them, abolition had also destroyed a way of life based on patterns and etiquettes of command and obedience. Beyond that, it had dangerously threatened to invert the "places" that individuals occupied in the social hierarchy. That was why the Baron of Vila Viçosa deplored the day in which "mothers of quality" (read, white women and ladies of the manor) were obliged to work in the kitchen and their children went without breast milk.[31] Truly, the language expressed the laments of the planters at the destruction of the hierarchical rules and values from which they had benefited for centuries.

The trauma that Bahian masters experienced at the end of slavery even appeared in the pages of novels. In 1908, two decades after abolition, novelist Anna Ribeiro de Góes Bittencourt (1843–1930), herself the daughter of a large Recôncavo planter, explored the contrary feelings of the old slave owners at the loss of their captive labor forces in *Letícia*. The plot follows the matrimonial misadventures of the only child of a rich Recôncavo planter, set against the abolition of slavery, the fall of the Brazilian Empire, and the proclamation of the republic, crucial events with which the author illustrated the changes taking place in the private lives of the "sugar aristocracy. Written by a woman who lived through abolition and its aftermath, the novel explores the personal dramas of the planters whose wealth vanished when their enslaved laborers were freed. In many ways, it serves as the testimony of a person who experienced the end of slavery from the heights of the plantation mansions.

In one part of the novel, the author reproduces the speech of Letícia's father, Travassos, at what he defines as the "disordering of labor" growing out of the end of slavery:

It is impossible to live like this! I never thought that our slaves would leave us without a thought given how well we treated them. I always heard tell that slavery brought villainy, but many times, I responded to this noxious attitude by quoting *Uncle Tom's Cabin*: "Treat them like dogs and they will behave like dogs; treat them like men and they will behave like men." But look what happened! . . . When I told them that they were free, I said to them: Those who don't want to remain with me can leave: I won't hold it against you; I only ask you that you let me know in advance so that I can organize the work to be done. They all insisted that they would not leave me; some even added, "Even if my master throws me out, I won't leave; I'm going to die here. We didn't have a master, but a father."[32]

The passage expresses the master's surprise at the change in the ex-slaves' behavior and the ineffectiveness of his traditional forms of seignorial order. He interprets the freedmen's behavior through a paternalist lens, such that he sees their departure as a sign of "ingratitude."

So, I set a day to grind the cane, I let everybody know, the crates are full of cane, I get to the mill and some people are missing; where are they? They left without giving me the least satisfaction. Could anyone suffer this patiently? Madness, lies, it is like a plan to make me crazy.[33]

Bittencourt accurately re-created the masters' trauma at losing the services of their enslaved men and women. In one scene, Travassos's family and guests—among them several planters—gather around the antique table in the manor house's huge formal dining room. After serving the first course, Travassos's wife and Letícia's aunt, Dona Henriqueta, begs "her guests' pardon for the flaws in the dinner service because of the servants' rebelliousness." "Under slavery," she continues, "no house enjoyed better service than this one." Her comments unchain a vociferous debate among the diners about the best ways to deal with workers emerging from slavery. Sampaio, the hardline planter, criticizes the government harshly for letting the freedmen "drift about and insult their masters" and congratulates himself for always having treated his slaves firmly; for that reason, he says, "they are almost all with me." But later he finishes: "Just yesterday I gave a good beating to a guy I had put in the stocks." Another planter, named Cândido, comments that he believed it better to treat slaves less aggressively, since he could not depend on the government [to protect him against them].[34]

In this scene, the novelist seems to suggest that ex-masters disagreed about how to deal with the ex-slaves. Travassos himself appears as the archetype of the "good master," the one who had treated his captives generously. But all the planters were affected by abolition and even Travassos was subject to the "ingratitude" of his former captives. Dona Henriqueta, the plantation's matriarch, represents the white chatelaines of the manor houses who suddenly saw themselves deprived of enslaved workers, especially the domestics who cooked and waited at table. In one scene Dona Henriqueta deplores being obliged to prepare meals: "What alternative do I have but to take care of everything!" Eurico, Letícia's husband, responds ironically that he cannot complain about abolition; he does not miss the slaves. "That's because you're not in my place!" retorts Dona Henriqueta. "It's not just their absence; it's their audacity, the insults!" Later, she continues: "Who wouldn't consider them ungrateful? I raised many of them; I was a mother to them more than a mistress."[35]

Against her husband's wishes, Letícia decides to remain on the plantation to care for her father, principally because

> we are going through a terrible crisis, especially the ex-masters who live in the countryside. A bit of skill and tactical thinking is what is necessary to get work out of the ex-slaves. That is what my aunt [Dona Henriqueta] lacks. If I stay here a few more days, they will see that they need my help in the most insignificant aspects of running the house. Poor thing! She cries, she despairs, they [the ex-slaves] play the worst tricks on her. . . . I am proud to say that I still have some moral force with these people; they will see how they obey me.[36]

Despite Letícia's efforts, the plantation collapses in the crisis that hit the sugar industry after abolition. The loss of his enslaved property shocks Travassos, and Bittencourt suggests that is the principal source of the illness that causes his death shortly after the proclamation of the republic on November 15, 1889.

In this fictional account, as in their prose, the ex-masters described the freedmen's actions as unpremeditated, as simple refusals to work or a rejection of seignorial authority that did not reach the level of "skills and tactics." In the planters' view, this was one more problem with an abolition law that had abruptly liberated those whom they considered unprepared for freedom. Even so, the seignorial discourse poorly hid planter fears that the freedmen threatened the social order. Rarely in Bahian history had the practices and symbols of power and planter command been so profoundly challenged. The ex-slaves' initiatives shattered the planters' conviction that after abolition, they could control their subordinates just as they had during slavery.

The historian and folklorist João da Silva Campos included a local tradition in his 1942 collection that revealed the planters' nightmares in the days after May 13. In "O misterioso pilão de Pouco Ponto" (The mysterious case of Pouco Ponto), he explained that one morning three or four days after abolition, near Santo Amaro, a total stranger mounted on horseback rode up to the manor house of the Pouco Ponto Plantation, belonging to the Garcia

Pires family. After dismounting, he climbed the front staircase and entered the dining room to find the owner and his relatives at the table. The stranger pulled up a chair, and, without invitation, sat down and began to speak. He announced that he had been sent by God to take revenge for all of the cruelties, injustices, and crimes of the past. Sometimes he seemed to talk to himself, and then he demanded food, all of which he consumed voraciously. When he had eaten his fill, he left the house, mounted his horse, and took off down the road. No one on the plantation recognized him. Silva Campos offered two explanations for the mysterious visitor: either he was some "crazy guy," or he was someone who had "gone crazy as a result of the new Law of the 13th of May." The folklorist ended his narrative stating that Garcia Pires was a "firm abolitionist" and that, prior to abolition, he had already set free all of his slaves.[37]

The tale helps us to understand the planters' fears in the days following abolition, and identifies some of the symbols of the social order under threat. The apparition—Silva Campos insinuates that we are dealing with a slave owner who has lost his mind—came into the home of Pouco Ponto's owner and, breaking with all of the rituals of respect and deference observed in Bahia, made himself comfortable at the dinner table without invitation. The visitor identified himself as a messenger of God sent to require the planter to make amends for all of the injustices and "crimes of the past," in an allusion to slavery, by then abolished. The story reflected the crisis of conscience that haunted those who had previously owned slaves, even those like Garcia Pires, who had been an abolitionist of conviction according to Silva Campos.

In slave owners' memoirs, novels, and stories, abolition constituted a decisive break in the etiquette and values established under slavery. The planters had both political and ideological interests in portraying abolition this way. The notion that abolition was a serious rupture in social relations supported the political position that the imperial government had treated masters unfairly when it abolished slavery. Central to that position was the reality that the law had neither mandated indemnification of planters for lost laborers nor granted them any control over the freedmen. In the 1890s, the sugar planters blamed these imperial actions for the decline of the sugar industry and used them to justify their requests to the new republican government for agricultural credit, low-interest loans, and financial assistance in modernizing the plantation sugar mills. They argued that abolition had destroyed a lifestyle constructed on a solid hierarchical foundation, but as we have seen, social relations on the sugar plantation actually had been tense.[38]

Ex-masters continued to complain about abolition without indemnification for decades. In *As voltas da estrada* (The turns in the road), a novel published in 1930, Xavier Marques captured the planters' thinking about the aftermath of the end of slavery. In the fictitious city of Our Lady of Amparo, center of the "sugar aristocracy," in 1900, twelve years after slavery ended, the transformation brought by abolition still challenged the planters. Life was "very strange for the few remaining elderly ex-slaveowners, who had known a regime that they had believed to be the definitive and the only legitimate form of social organization. For them, life no longer held any glory. Everything was sadness, shame and decadence." The seignorial class no longer enjoyed their former titles of nobility and struggled to hide their economic decline. Essentially, "the master and mistress of a plantation who were basically unemployed and spendthrift potentates with hordes of underlings and retainers, were now anachronisms."[39]

Fully understanding this seignorial discourse requires reading such texts against the grain. Doing so reveals that the slaves had made plans for freedom while still enslaved and, after abolition set them free, worked to distance themselves from slavery based on those ideas. Seignorial discourse silenced this important aspect of the post-abolition clashes.

A "Badly Managed Freedom"

The letters and newspaper articles that the authorities and ex–slave owners wrote after abolition allow us to reflect on what they thought in the days and weeks after slavery ended. Taken at face value, they reveal the planters' efforts to show that the "disobedience" and disorder that seriously threatened the social order after May 13, 1888, grew out of the way that the government handled the "servile element." They also indicate that planters hoped to force the government to pass legislation guaranteeing them some measure of control over the freedmen. Read against the grain, these sources reveal important clues about ex-slaves' expectations for freedom. Among these long-held hopes and dreams were access to land and distancing themselves from the "subjugation" inherent in slavery. These insights help us to analyze letters from a prominent Recôncavo planter to the head of the province of Bahia.

Six days after May 13, Egas Moniz Barreto de Aragão, Baron of Moniz Aragão (1841–1898), one of the Recôncavo's most important planters and local leaders, expressed his concern about events in a long letter to the provincial president. While young, Moniz Aragão had studied law in Germany and pursued a diplomatic career. Later, he had returned to the Recôncavo to manage his several sugar plantations. On May 13, 1888, he was president of the town council of São Francisco do Conde. He reported that he had received the Ministry of Agriculture's announcement instructing the town council to publish the news of the Golden Law (the Abolition Law), but that he had not managed to call a meeting of the town council because the weather was harsh and the members were "taking care of their own interests" on their plantations. Moniz Aragão himself was at his Mataripe Plantation, trying to reestablish order.[40] Unsurprisingly, in the face of abolition, personal interest had taken precedence over civic responsibility.

Moniz Aragão also informed the provincial president that before they knew that slavery was officially abolished, almost all of the slave owners in the community had unconditionally freed their slaves and ingênuos—the children born free under the 1871 Law of the Free Womb—in an attempt to avoid a "mass flight" to the provincial capital. As I argued in the previous chapter, planters had been anticipating abolition and tried to avoid having slaves abandon the plantations. According to Moniz Aragão, only two planters—José Joaquim de Teive e Argolo and Town Councilman Constâncio José de Queirós—had remained firmly in possession of their slaves until May 13. He tried to demonstrate his own altruism by revealing that on May 7, in honor of his son's birthday, he had freed 346 adult slaves and another 143 ingênuos from his Cassarangongo, Mataripe, and Maracangalha plantations, "where a considerable number of longtime 'resident workers' and freedmen lived who formerly belonged to my wife and me."[41]

The manumissions at Maracangalha Plantation, discussed in detail in the next chapter, sought to contain disorder and insubordination and were not an act of generosity on the part of the baron. Starting in March, as was the case on other regional plantations, the Maracangalha slaves had refused to work in the cane fields. Clearly, the freedmen had heard about the parliamentary debates and the pressure to end slavery by the abolitionist movement. The refusal to work may have been the slaves' way of forcing the baron to award them freedom, something that, as we know, masters had been doing in response to group escapes and the resulting total paralysis of the plantations. Despite the arguments of the masters and the memorialists, such actions on the part of slaves and of freedmen did not reflect delirium.

The decree granting immediate abolition to Brazil's slaves did not take Moniz Aragão or his counterparts by surprise, since "the owners did not delude themselves into believing that the law would include a waiting period, while the slaves did not anticipate a Legislative solution." On the other hand, the behavior of the newly freed people in the months prior to abolition did surprise the baron. According to him, "Anarchy erupted everywhere beforehand and everything continues to be in a complete uproar." He noted that on thc "more ordered plantations, among which I count mine, there is what I would call respectful inertia." He wrote:

> In the last two weeks none of them has done any work, none of them understands what is good for them, nor do any of them know what to do. Here there is no delirious joy at being liberated; here there is simply a disposition to live from what falls from heaven, in the form of meat and cassava flour, without working, and from what they can steal from their neighbor.

The "respectful inertia" that Moniz Aragão noticed on his properties might mean that some owners still maintained some moral authority over their freedmen, but that it was not enough to allow the plantations to function effectively.[42]

Moniz Aragão wrote that the freedmen were throwing themselves into "vagrancy" and "audacious" theft of the herds in the pastures. According to him, the planters had been preparing "appropriate proposals [to resolve the situation]; but everything is all suspense and oratory; only by traveling about can you see the naked and cruel truth of the horrible and dangerous state into which this community has fallen." His concerns indicate that, on the thirteenth of May, refusing to work acquired a different meaning for the freedmen. Possibly, ex-slaves refused to work on the old terms of slavery which they saw as a "continuation of captivity." On the other hand, Moniz Aragão, like planters we saw earlier in the chapter, interpreted that behavior as the vagrancy and laziness on the part of ex-slaves.

Moniz Aragão's correspondence demonstrates that the freedmen in the region had expectations that went far beyond the rupture of the ties of slavery. That was why he feared the return of ex-slaves who had gone to Salvador in the days just before abolition. He expected that they would return and demand "to remain on the property, without working or paying rent or making any other arrangement with the plantation owner, simply because abolition had been promised and they were taking advantage of liberation." Perhaps he thought that this behavior would have been encouraged by contact with the abolitionist agitation in Salvador. That may have been why the baron deplored the failure of the authorities to prepare to repress "intrusions" or "rebellion" by the freedmen. The baron's statements suggest that his greatest concern involved the freedmen who remained on the properties but refused to work for their ex-owners under conditions of captivity. As he stated, a few planters were able to take advantage of some "moral force," but aside from this "paradigm" there was no way to contain the "vagrancy and the crime."[43]

In the baron's view, the freedmen's "theft" of livestock from the plantation pastures and their expectation of land represented a fundamental challenge to private property as well as a serious threat to the social order. The ex-slaves, on the other hand, seem to have seen their demands as part of a struggle for what they believed "justly" belonged to them as free men.

In a letter dated July 10, 1888, Moniz Aragão once again reported that he had not been able to hold a meeting of the local councilmen, because of the "disorganization of society and of labor" to which the community had been subjected since the beginning of the year. According to him, the councilmen, most of whom were plantation owners, could not leave their properties because they felt threatened by the "base instincts of the vagabonds who in their delirious joy were taking advantage of this badly managed freedom." His statements suggest that the planter-councilmen could not maintain order on their properties by their presence alone and that the "respectful inertia" and the "absence of excitement" that had characterized ex-slave attitudes in early May were giving way to "delirious joy." Like Vila Viçosa, he preferred to believe that the freedmen's behavior grew out of "base instincts" or "delirious joy" than to consider that former slaves had dreamt and planned of their days as free people.[44]

That same day, Moniz Aragão clarified his concerns in another letter to the provincial president, this one marked confidential. He reported that after receiving the notification from the Ministry of Agriculture proclaiming the approval of the Law of May 13, he had ordered the legislative decision published in a public notice. But after this,

> to our unhappiness, the great majority of the recently freed men in the community have not shown themselves deserving of the title of citizen that has been conferred on them; everyone knows that one found the best treated and best behaved members of the "Servile Element of the Province in this Recôncavo"; even so it is impossible to reorganize service, either in agriculture or in the home; everything is disorganized and in appalling confusion.[45]

He warned the provincial president that the refusal to work in the cane fields threatened sugar production, since, even if they could cut fresh canes to make sugar and molasses in the approaching harvest, there would only be old cane available for the next one. After that, he swore that the plantation sugar mills would have to shut down, because no one had planted new cane or prepared the fields for any other kind of crop. He predicted destitution and hunger for 1889 and 1890.

Then Moniz Aragão returned to the topic of "badly managed freedom" and "delirious joy." According to him, the recently freed men "imagined that the property owners had the power to grant them ownership of their subsistence plots, but did not want to so; the freedmen wanted us to carry out this Imperial Order, that is to say, turn over to them our lands for free without any compensation on their part."[46]

According to Moniz Aragão, the freedmen sought to require the planters to comply with a supposed imperial order instructing owners to provide land to those emerging from slavery. In his view, the ex-slaves misunderstood a sentence in the circular from the Ministry of Agriculture that ordered the announcement of the law of the thirteenth of May. The passage read that "converted into the pride of the nation, the land would no longer represent for him forced and unpaid labor, but the common good." For our baron, the "miserable freedman" mistakenly read "communism" in the statement. Moniz Aragão underestimated the freedmen's capacity for comprehension, since he believed that the desire to own land could only be the fruit of a misunderstanding or of a "badly managed freedom."

Moniz Aragão's worry also had to do with the way in which ex-slaves tried to disconnect access to their subsistence plots from their former obligation to work their ex-owners' land. Still, it is possible that, in those early days after abolition, rumors that the freedmen had the right to land circulated in the Recôncavo's slave cabins. Descendants of slaves in the region retain oral traditions that suggest that was the case. One granddaughter of ex-slaves named Faustina, currently resident on land formerly belonging to a plantation near São Sebastião do Passé, recounted that her grandfather, João do Ouro de Sena, used to describe the "day of liberty" saying that

> he was with the kids looking on the ground for some sticks to play with when he saw this huge brouhaha . . . all this shouting, lots of drums playing, men and women dancing samba. So when his father came home, he asked him: hey Papa, what's all that brouhaha? And his father answered: it is freedom; it is freedom my son. And then my grandfather asked: what's freedom? And his father answered: now we're going to work for ourselves, we're not going to work for the "man" any more, no siree. Now, each one of us can plant our own fields.[47]

Faustina's great-grandfather saw having a farm as a basic condition of life without subjugation. In other words, he believed that land freed ex-slaves from working for the "man."[48]

Unsurprisingly, the freed people's hopes appear to have been limited by fears that slavery might return. Faustina remembered hearing her grandfather tell her that

> after slavery everybody felt like they were free, but they still worried. They were afraid that they could once again live their lives as slaves. . . . . My grandfather told us that he kept working, but feared that someone would come along and tell him to go back to working as a slave. That's why people continued to be worried after slavery was over.

The ex-slaves' fears were not completely unfounded. In the months after abolition, the Recôncavo authorities demanded reinforcements to help contain what they referred to as the freedmen's insubordination. This attitude was inspired by the old fear that, with the constraints of slavery gone, the ex-slaves would turn to crime, and rob and ransack the plantations. These appeals also revealed that the freedmen's actions terrified the authorities. On July 6, 1888, Manoel Rodrigues Lima, subdelegado of Palame, wrote to the chief of police, saying:

> It seems that pernicious ideas like communism want to raise their heads here in this district since the Golden Law of 13 May. The ignorance that weighs on so many of our residents taken on a large scale [is] pernicious to individual security and to the right to property; and Your Excellency knows that the stability of these rights depends on the force with which it is maintained and guaranteed.[49]

The subdelegado ended his report affirming that, in his district, respect for authority had declined and "threats are directed at me and at anyone else who has even a tiny bit of land."[50]

On May 28, 1888, the delegado of Inhambupe, Bahia, wrote to the police chief complaining that he had found it necessary to increase the police force there, principally after May 13. He said that the town had seen a continuing increase in conflicts provoked by "insubordinate" individuals, many of them freedmen, "who abused their freedom, which is only natural; especially in the early days." The large number of freedmen in Campo Largo also worried Delegado Benvenuto José Aguiar. On July 7, 1888, he stated that their number "is reason enough to explain the anarchy, perhaps in the near future they'll start stealing, and before this happens, I want to and plan to take serious and energetic preventative measures." In July 1889, the delegado of Vila Viçosa, in extreme southern Bahia, displayed the same fear at the large number of freedmen there. He reported that "the town is exceedingly troubled, especially the Leopoldina Colony, where there are 2,000 13th of May freedmen."[51]

The anxious tone of the letters from Moniz Aragão and the other provincial authorities reveals the owners' fear about the unpredictable twists and turns of the process of abolition. For them, the most troubling aspect of abolition was that the former captives made clear they expected to break the ties that had bound them to masters during captivity. The meanings that ex-slaves gave to freedom, including ownership of land, convinced many masters that social order, as they understood it, was under serious threat.

The Historical Conjuncture

Understanding the hopes and fears of freedmen and ex-masters in the days after abolition requires reconstructing the economic conjuncture of the years 1888 and 1889. Abolition coincided with a deepening of the economic crises that had been plaguing the Bahian sugarcane sector since the 1870s. Competition from Caribbean producers and a decline in world market prices for sugar challenged the sugar sector throughout the last decades of slavery and complicated the planters' ability to address the challenges abolition brought. In particular, planters lacked access to capital, making it difficult to pay debts or salaries to newly freed workers. Consequently, many planters were obliged to stop production or break up properties.

The drop in sugar prices, the reduction in credit, the drought, and the social tensions on the plantations in 1888 and 1889 combined to bring down the sugar economy immediately. The Baron of Vila Viçosa, the prominent sugar planter from Santo Amaro, described the crisis in an article on August 14, 1888. He wrote that the Recôncavo was in ruins: in Santo Amaro and São Francisco do Conde, towns with the state's largest and most productive sugar estates, the plantations were abandoned, and cattle were overrunning the fields of those still in production because the fences had not been repaired.[52]

In another article published in February 1889, the baron argued that the problems caused by low sugar prices had been complicated by a serious labor shortage. Indeed, he blamed abolition for the loss of more than half of the 1888 sugar harvest. He charged that, with abolition, the planters lost their most important source of collateral—the enslaved laborers—and the need for cash increased with the necessity of paying salaries. The merchants who had provided the planters with the credit they needed to meet expenses between harvests withdrew their financial support, since the planters no longer owned the preferred guarantees—slaves. As Vila Viçosa understood things, the merchants who had financed the harvest were "filled with understandable doubt," and, therefore, refused to take sugar on commission or to approve new credit.[53]

According to Vila Viçosa, in the middle of 1888, the cane fields and the slaves' small farm plots were abandoned, broken fences remained unrepaired, and the cane grinding apparatus had not been maintained. With the sugar mills paralyzed, the cane fields were taken over by weeds and invaded by cattle. To survive, the owners sold their breeding cattle as well as the oxen that pulled the cane carts, for very low prices. And the "blacks" consumed the chickens, the pigs, the lambs—essentially, the last bit of property that they owned. This was how freed people and former owners spent the winter of 1888.[54]

Vila Viçosa predicted that the rest of 1889 would be no better. The central sugar mills could not find more than fifteen days' worth of cane to grind. The mill at Iguape manufactured only ten thousand arrobas of raw sugar, and the one at Rio Fundo was reducing raw sugar to juice to get it through the machines. Vila Viçosa was doing the same at his mill (the former Passagem Plantation) and he managed to produce a little more than five thousand arrobas of sugar in his two plantation mills; but things were very uncertain for the following year. He believed that after having spent their meager resources in "drifting about," the freedmen no longer had any means to earn a living because no one had any way to pay them.[55] In other words, the sugar mills were idle because the owners lacked capital to pay salaries for harvesting and making sugar or arranging for the planting of new crops.

On January 6, 1889, "a correspondent" from São Francisco reported that the "profound disorganization of labor after abolition" had aggravated the problems in the agricultural sector. Drought destroyed the new sugarcane shoots that the "most diligent and careful" had managed to plant after the law passed on May 13. Problems obtaining labor meant that plantation fences did not get repaired and hungry and thirsty cattle wandered into the cane fields as well as the manioc plots, aggravating the situation. Depression spread among the planters given that what little they had accomplished had been lost; plantations were shutting down and expectations were growing for famine in 1889.[56] On January 11, 1889, Cotegipe received a letter from Novis describing the situation:

> I am well, thank God, fighting against this terrible crisis, not to mention the drought. It's all over! here are no more fences on the plantations, everything's turned into general pasture—the price of refined sugar [in

the export market] is a disgrace, let me just say that molasses gets better prices at the *cachaça distillery.*[57]

Sugar production really did decline precipitously in 1888 and 1889. The majority of the plantations drastically reduced their production, and many did not plant or harvest so much as an acre of cane. In 1889, the *Diário da Bahia* published a list of the amount of cultivated land on Recôncavo plantations. In São Francisco, the location of the largest properties in the Recôncavo, nineteen out of seventy-four plantations were completely shut down and thirty-nine had cultivated fewer than one hundred *tarefas* (about forty-four hectares or about 109 acres) of cane.[58] Many plantations could cultivate only a small percentage of the sugarcane they had grown prior to abolition.

The terrible performance of Bahian sugar exports in 1889 reflected the decline in sugarcane cultivation. According to Bert Barickman, that year, Bahia exported only 1,685 tons of sugar, an amount equivalent to 3 percent of the average of sugar exports for the first half of the 1850s. Exports improved between 1891 and 1910, but Bahia still only shipped, on average, 8,483 tons of sugar each year, about 20 percent of the annual average from 1855 to 1888. This export performance was well below that of the neighboring sugar-producing provinces, especially Pernambuco, which doubled its sugar exports from 1850 to the middle of the 1890s. Bahian sugar-plantation owners appear to have had much more difficulty in adapting to abolition than did their counterparts in Pernambuco.[59]

The drought and its ramifications—ruined crops, scarce and high-priced food, especially manioc flour, and unemployment—had dramatic consequences for ex-slaves and for all of the Recôncavo's poor. In those years, hundreds of refugees from the province's dry backlands flooded the Recôncavo's cities and towns. On May 12, 1889, almost exactly a year after abolition, the delegado of Santo Amaro reported that the streets were filled with beggars going house to house pleading for assistance. Shortages sent food prices spiraling upward, and the hospital was unable to handle the large number of people in need of treatment.[60]

The situation was also desperate in São Francisco do Conde. On September 20, 1889, the family court judge described the "extreme poverty" in which the majority of the population was living, due to problems in subsistence agriculture, which high food prices aggravated.[61] A Salvador newspaper reported that "unemployed men sit around twiddling their thumbs because there is absolutely no work. Huge numbers of beggars plead for public charity every day, and the place hasn't experienced the slightest economic growth because almost all of the inhabitants of this lousy place are completely broke."[62] In July 1889, the delegado of Cachoeira requested additional police officers to help contain the three hundred or so drought refugees living in the city.[63]

The evidence suggests that difficulties with subsistence diminished the freedmen's bargaining power in their negotiations with the plantation owners. We should remember that, until mid-1888, Novis insisted that the freedmen's "heads were spinning" and they openly refused to accept the working conditions offered by the ex-masters. Perhaps ex-slaves retained some room for movement and so could refuse to accept working conditions they did not consider just. The articles by Vila Viçosa imply that, by early 1889, the situation had changed and many freedmen could neither support themselves nor find anyone to hire them. Their meager savings from agricultural production had been consumed during the winter and drought had destroyed their manioc farms.

On October 9, 1889, the inspector of public lands, Dionísio Gonçalves Martins, was asked about the absence of work and the large number of "unemployed Brazilians." He responded that, since May 13, thousands of individuals coming out of slavery had been living without a permanent address. Without the promise of land on which to cultivate their own crops, "seeing that the old owners would not give them any for that purpose," those workers refused the paid employment offered by their former masters.[64] The inspector made clear that salaried work was not sufficient to retain or attract individuals coming out of slavery. Ex-slaves were interested in land.

In Martin's view, the freedmen had initially thrown themselves into "the intoxication of events" and refused to work in the cane fields. When this "moment of fascination" was over, they tried to protect themselves against misery and hunger, which resulted in a huge demand for work. At the same time, they abandoned their old jobs, "which reminded them of so many physical and emotional hardships," and even though other properties paid lower salaries than they wanted, the freedmen continued to search for "stable employment," and therefore, they continued to face high unemployment. The drought refugees added to the group, and he observed that "the latter, less demanding than the former, because of their recent experiences, more readily accepted whatever salary they were offered, and often wound up with the jobs that the freedmen, tormented by the memories of slavery, would not accept." To judge by what the inspector said, the "memory of slavery" was still affecting the freed people's choices. The freedmen faced a dramatic situation as, on the one hand, they suffered from hunger, and on the other, from working conditions that still reminded them of slavery.

Some ex-slaves who abandoned the cane fields immediately after abolition may have returned to the old plantations in their struggle to survive, but even so, they were determined to change their working conditions. As one descendant of plantation owners from Pernambuco complained, the "return to their native field could no longer correct the economic chaos of the first hours of the Golden Law."[65]

Fire, Fear, and Repression

Undoubtedly, 1888 and 1889 were tense and significant years in the Recôncavo. Beginning in mid-1888, plantation-owner complaints about fires in the cane fields intensified. Many did not hesitate to link fires to the Law of May 13. In a letter on November 20, 1888, the Baron of Cotegipe wrote to Araújo Pinho: "I know that you suffered a fire at one of your plantations: problems don't come in isolation. What's going on at the others?"[66] He suspected that the fire had been set as a result of the insubordination that spread throughout the Recôncavo after abolition.

On December 4, 1888, Salvador's *Diário de Notícias* published a letter sent by a reader from the Vila de São Francisco demanding that measures be taken to contain the fires that were constantly starting in the Recôncavo. According to the writer, he had thought that they had been caused by the drought, but he changed his mind when he saw how frequent they were. Instead, he was convinced that they resulted from deliberate actions, by "criminal hands with links to the capital." In other words, they were the work of freedmen returning from the capital, after celebrating May 13 there.[67]

In São Francisco do Conde, the letter writer continued, no plantation or farm had escaped serious fire damage. "From the S[ão]. Paulo Plantation belonging to Captain Bandeira, near the capital, to the Piquara and Nazaré plantations, and wherever else you look, you can see the disastrous effects of burning." The report stated that sixteen large plantations had suffered fires, including Mataripe and Maracangalha, belonging to our friend the Baron of Moniz Aragão. It is, therefore, worthwhile, to look at the damages to some of the properties.

> Lately they burned more than forty tarefas of *cana de rego* belonging to the Baron of Moniz Aragão; belonging to Colonel José Joaquim de Teive and Argolo, some fifty tarefas in S. Lourenço e Almas; all the pastures of the Santo Estevão Plantation belonging to Joaquim de Carvalho, where they did six contos de réis worth of damage to the fences;

on the Tanque Plantation, belonging to the Baron of Rio de Contas; at Bomba and Pitanga belonging to Captain Ribeiro Lopes, it was a horror; at São Lourenço, belonging to Major José Maria Gouveia Portugal, nearly twenty tarefas of cane and an enormous amount of fencing disappeared because of the fire that was set; in Pouco Pondo, belonging to Mr. and Mrs. Pirajá; on the Barra Plantation belonging to Lieutenant Teófilo; Laranjeiras belonging to Captain Olympio; at Pinheiro, belonging to Antônio Barbosa de Andrade, the director of the Caixa Hipotecária when it was functioning, the fires were simply terrifying."[68]

The letter writer demanded action to protect their property. The writer criticized the courts for not having treated the problem sufficiently seriously and concluded by demanding that the provincial president pay more attention to Santo Amaro, where, he asserted, the problems were intensifying. Ultimately, he called on property owners to stop waiting for the government to save them and to take matters into their own hands. The owner of the Colônia Plantation, João Gualberto de Freitas, had already taken "energetic measures" to protect himself from major losses. Other documents tell us that Freitas put several freedmen in the stocks of his plantation and had others arrested for "insubordination," or involvement in thefts and arson.[69]

On December 16, 1888, the delegado of Vila de São Francisco, Luís de Oliveira Mendes, confirmed the accusations in a confidential letter to the state's chief of police. According to his account, all the property owners were demanding protection from the "terrifying scourge called fire in the cane fields." He reported that that arsonists were responsible for starting the fires, although drought made them worse. He then complained that it was legally impossible to keep prisoners accused of arson in jail for any length of time, since they were numerous and they had the right of habeas corpus. He concluded by asking the police chief for permission to skip the formal legalities and send the accused immediately to prison in the capital. He believed that such measures would reestablish order in the area. Without waiting for a reply, he sent two freedmen, Lázaro and Eusébio, to jail in Salvador with the messenger who carried his letter. The owner of the Monte Plantation, João Gualberto de Freitas, had turned them over to the police for "insubordination" and for setting fires in the cane fields.[70] The chief of police, however, refused to imprison the freedmen without trial and sent them back to São Francisco with instructions for the authorities to follow the law.

Accusations continued against the freedmen. On December 17, 1999, a resident of Vila do São Francisco reported that the fires, which he claimed had spread to all the plantations, principally destroyed fences and cane fields. He blamed the freedmen for many of the fires, alleging that they had been "purposely set by the freedmen who were so given over to vagrancy that they were a lost race."[71] On January 14, 1889, an article in the *Diário da Bahia*, entitled "Desperate Crisis," tied the fires to the freedmen and the crisis in agriculture. In it, the author revealed that the drought and the labor shortage were annihilating Bahian agriculture. The author explained that the few remaining resident workers were abandoning the plantations where they worked, and the author blamed government inaction for the problem. Then the writer observed: "We would never impugn the most important act of justice that the nation experienced [the thirteenth of May], but scoundrels, in combination with the drought, are provoking the abandonment of the plantations, and turning the fields into one big charred space." He went on to charge that "vagabonds" who hoped to steal plantation cattle were burning the fences and setting the fires in the cane fields and pastures.[72] The author of the report, certainly a former slave owner, defined the fires, the abandonment of the properties, and the theft of cattle as components of what he termed the freedmen's "insubordination."

Not everyone agreed that the freedmen were setting the fires. In a letter to the provincial president on December 17, 1888, the public prosecutor of Santo Amaro, João José de Oliveira Junqueira, admitted that burning cane fields was a constant and very nasty problem. It was true that "not . . . even one plantation or farm . . . has not been the victim of the flames." He insisted, however, that the drought caused the fires, and strong winds fanned the flames, and therefore he would not act against people who, because of negligence or "perversity," were accused of setting the fires.[73]

It is possible that the conflicts between ex-slaves and ex-masters on the sugar plantations contributed to the fires. The list of damages published in the newspapers confirms that the fires principally attacked property belonging to the masters: fences, cane fields, forests, and pastures. Prior to abolition, slaves had burned cane fields or forests to sabotage owners. Perhaps the practice continued after abolition. Resentment and social tension were certainly growing to a dangerously explosive level as planters' wandering cattle destroyed ex-slaves' subsistence plots and the ex-masters tried to punish ex-slaves who refused to work in the cane fields.

Plantation owners also hoped to gain political advantage from these events. Reporting terrifying news stories in the press allowed planters to demand that the imperial and provincial governments provide financial support to the sugar sector and reestablish planter control over the ex-slaves. They insisted upon repressing vagrancy, arson, and theft from the plantations.

All through 1888, the plantation owners appealed to the police for permission to punish insolent freedmen and anyone who refused employment in the cane fields. At the same time, they advocated that since free citizens could not be imprisoned easily for vagrancy, men and boys who refused employment be forcibly recruited into the armed forces. Such planter pressure on the authorities carried serious consequences for the freed people. On December 12, 1888, the subdelegado of the parish of Rio Fundo in Santo Amaro arrested a young man named Fabiano who allegedly "purposely" set fire to forty tarefas of cane on the Papagaio Plantation and sent him to the military as a recruit. In his report about the matter, the subdelegado observed: "It is a terrifying scene, a spectacle truly sad that this parish and Bom Jardim offer, reduced to ashes by the horrible fires that have daily devastated what little is left of this ridiculous harvest."[74]

Plantation owners and rural authorities attempted to rid the region of anyone who refused to work in the cane fields as well as workers they considered insolent or insubordinate. Throughout 1888 and 1889, Recôncavo delegados transferred numerous individuals accused of vagrancy to the capital for military service. For example, on December 11, 1888, the Santo Amaro delegado sent Malaquias Ferreira, "a vagrant with the worst sort of behavior," and José dos Santos, a vagrant who "had no way to support himself and no interest in finding one" to Salvador as recruits for the army. Vagrants were principally individuals who refused to work in the sugar industry, or those who sought some way of supporting themselves that did not involve labor on the sugar plantations.

Arrests for vagrancy were the most common way that the powerful dealt with individuals they considered "insubordinate" or unwilling to accept the master's authority.[75] The ex-owners feared losing control over the freed people, especially if they decided that they would no longer work in the cane fields or at other tasks traditionally reserved for them. This is why the plantation owners began to press the government for harsher measures against vagrancy and vagabondage. Truly, it was an attempt to limit the freedom of those emerging from slavery to choose where and when they would work and whether they would travel to find other means of supporting themselves.

Imprisonments of freedmen for "insubordination" intensified after abolition. In the sugar districts, the police arrested freedmen without following the law. The police records indicate how the authorities described these events. On October 25, 1888, the delegado of Santo Amaro sent Mauro Mendes to the capital because, wrote the delegado, he was a "vagabond, without any family connections and very ill-behaved, he was involved in stealing, especially targeting rural properties, and this was the only means of support that he had." In the same letter, the delegado reported that he was employing all of his forces to locate the thieves who stole the horses belonging to the Guaíba Plantation.[76] On November 18, 1888, the same delegado sent freedman Severiano Cardoso to prison in Salvador because he was a "lowlife without means of supporting himself, living only from robbing rural plantations."[77] On November 27, 1888, the delegado of the Vila do São Francisco informed prison authorities that a guy named Inocêncio and another man had been caught stealing saddle horses from João Gualberto de Freitas, the owner of the Colônia Plantation.[78] On December 18, 1888, the delegado of Vila de São Francisco sent Olímpio, a criolo, to the chief of police, indicating that the prisoner had been turned over to authorities for being "insubordinate."[79]

These measures against supposed vagrants and insubordinates were not restricted to the sugar-plantation districts. On January 25, 1889, the delegado of the backlands town of Curralinho sent "ex-slave" Benedito to the chief of police, recommending that he be sent to the military. Benedito was accused of being "a complete idler, living from whatever, stealing, drinking, creating disorder; becoming the scourge of the peaceful and orderly citizens." Obviously, the authorities had no scruples about interfering with the freedmen. Toward the end of that same year, the delegado of Santarém, informed the chief of police that he was worried about the presence in his community of large numbers of people freed by the thirteenth of May law. He asked his superior whether it would be possible to send them all into the army, as that was the only way that he could imagine coping with what he referred to as their scandalous behavior.[80]

Throughout 1888 and 1889, the violence against freedmen escalated in the Recôncavo. Many plantation owners began to act on their own, capturing people accused of setting fires or other crimes against property, and then administering corporal punishments and/or putting them in the stocks, just as they would have done during slavery. Some hired for their plantations private guards, instructed to intimidate or expel those freedmen who refused to work in the cane fields.

The Bahian authorities attempted to manage the conflicts in the Recôncavo. In December 1889, they sent eight police battalions to the region with instructions to arrest the "rural guards" working for the plantation owners and to help the town councils organize rural settlements that would "provide work for the vagabonds and the lazy bums who are being expelled from neighboring towns, and force each freed person to sign a labor contract."[81] The documents do not record how these police forces behaved on the plantations, but the measure demonstrates that the new state government intended to disarm the private armies and establish control over the population emerging from slavery as well.

On February 21, 1890, Governor Manoel Vitorino proposed establishing a rural police code.[82] In October, the *Jornal de Notícias* reported that the proposed code would assist the farmers in their struggle against the "lack of energy and the laziness of our workers." The proposed policy dealt harshly with any worker who did not fulfill a labor contract, sentencing transgressors to forced labor in public works. Such measures were necessary, the editorialist argued, because, since abolition, agricultural labor had become "uncertain, disorganized, and impossible" due to "inherited vices and educational shortcomings" in the sugar districts. People would only work two days a week—the amount of time necessary to purchase enough food and drink to last the rest of the week. According to the author, these new regulations would resolve the problem of vagrancy among rural workers, especially those who had just come out of slavery.[83]

The government never put the code into practice, but the fact that the governor proposed it reveals that in the tense conjuncture of 1888–1889, the authorities anticipated interfering in the daily lives of the recently freed population. The evidence suggests, on the other hand, that once that period had passed, the authorities became convinced that vagrancy laws would not bring social peace nor solve the planters' labor problems. In the new circumstances, the plantations needed temporary, rather than permanent, labor, which implied dislocating workers from the interior to the coast, something such laws would make more difficult. Moreover, the police feared that the freedmen would use the courts to denounce them for acting outside the law. Ultimately, the plantation owners came to understand that they must negotiate new working conditions with the ex-slaves. Understanding these new circumstances requires exploring the struggles between freedmen and ex-masters over rights and property on the plantations. Those conflicts deepened in 1888 and 1889, the most critical phase of the abolition process in the Recôncavo.

FIVE

HEADS SPINNING WITH FREEDOM

> Whoever owns an ox
> Should keep it fenced in
> I'm not planting crops
> For some ox to steal! . . .
> Whoever owns an ox
> Should surround it with sturdy fences
> I'm not planting crops
> For some thieving ox!

Shortly after May 13, conflict broke out between ex-slaves and sugar-plantation owners in the Recôncavo. This chapter examines those disputes to see how freed people and former masters negotiated the first exciting days without slavery. A cursory glance at the evidence demonstrates that freedom meant very different things to the two groups; a deeper look shows that the men and women who emerged from slavery were struggling to retain and even expand upon the customary rights and privileges they had acquired during the long fight against slavery. Doing so meant resisting planter efforts to manage their daily lives, to control their movements, to dictate work rhythms, or to impose punishments. Freedmen and freedwomen were struggling to survive outside the old plantation system, and in doing so, they clashed with ex-masters who hoped to turn them into dependent laborers. These disputes signaled a deeper struggle to define the limits and possibilities of freedom in the post-abolition period.[1]

For many former plantation slaves, freedom meant retaining their customary rights to subsistence plots, called, as we have seen, roças in Bahia. Such rights also implied access to plantation resources or the ability to carry out activities at the margins of the large sugar plantations. Defending such rights figured prominently in ex-slaves' survival strategies as they struggled to find alternatives to plantation labor in the period after May 13. The following pages explore those efforts.

Now That Freedom Has Arrived

Little more than a month after the abolition of slavery, on the afternoon of June 26, 1888, recently freed moradores on the Maracangalha Plantation beat up José Rodrigues da Cerveira, the thirty-two-year-old widower and resident manager of the Sapucaia Plantation belonging to the Baron of Cotegipe. Cerveira was hurt badly enough that, the following day, he needed a friend to write up the complaint he sent to Ernesto Alves Rigaud, subdelegado of the town of São Francisco do Conde. In response to the complaint, the next day two physicians visited the victim to examine him. They verified that the manager had suffered multiple contusions to his body.[2]

According to the police report, the injured manager informed the police that he had gone to the Maracangalha Plantation on June 26 to ask the overseer there—a man named Latino who had been freed on May 13—why some Maracangalha workers had killed one of the oxen on another of Cotegipe's plantations, Quibaca, and wounded others. He went on to tell the authorities that Latino had refused to answer the question and insulted him, and that the exchange had deteriorated into a shouting match. Shortly thereafter, several Maracangalha moradores had "barbarically" attacked him with hoes, cattle prods, sticks, and rocks.[3]

Because of the police report, Subdelegado Rigaud opened a formal investigation into the conflict. He began by interviewing the witnesses whom Cerveira had identified. Firmino Wanderley, a thirty-year-old carpenter, formerly enslaved to Cotegipe, said that he had seen the events in question, because he had gone to Maracangalha with the injured manager to discover who had hurt or stolen oxen from Quibaca. According to him, Cerveira had gotten upset when Latino greeted him in an "insulting way." After an exchange of insults, a number of Maracangalha's resident workers "barbarically" attacked the manager. He identified those involved in the assault as the freedmen Odorico, Germano, Onofre, Ismael, Rufo, Floriano, João Anastácio, Jacinto, Gentil, and Cosme.[4]

Other local residents provided further details. José Moreira de Pinho, the manager and morador at Quibaca, reported that he was at home when he heard Firmino shouting for the district's moradores to come to Cerveira's defense. He immediately headed to Maracangalha where he found a "really riled up" group of twenty or thirty freedmen armed with all sorts of tools. When he asked them where Cerveira was, he reported, the Maracangalha freedmen claimed not to know. So Pinho went in search of Latino, the Maracangalha overseer, who explained that the fight had broken out because some of the freed workers on the plantation had injured some Quibaca oxen. Another witness, Custódio José de Santana, a forty-one-year-old "artisan," said that he had seen two groups of free workers posted on either side of the road to Maracangalha. When he asked Latino about Cerveira, the overseer from Maracangalha had replied in an "aggressive and rude way" that "Himself" had left.[5]

Two witnesses reported trying to help Cerveira. A fifty-year-old "artisan" named João Tomé da Silva stated that he started gathering free workers from the Cabochi Plantation to go and defend Cerveira but stopped once he learned that the manager had returned home. Joaquim do Patrocínio Rosa, a thirty-five-year-old lavrador, also gave up the rescue effort when he learned that Cerveira was safe—bedridden and complaining, but at home.[6]

These witnesses saw Cerveira as the victim of ex-slave violence. Some of them had good reasons for siding with him, given that they all administered plantations for absentee owners. Their references to Latino's "aggressive and rude" behavior reveal how such managers interpreted ex-slaves' language and attitudes in the days and months after abolition: they were clearly appalled that ex-slaves no longer followed the norms established under slavery.

Despite their antagonism toward the ex-slaves, José Moreira and Custódio José revealed some important elements of the freedmen's behavior during and after the fight. Their testimony made clear that the ex-slaves acted collectively, both in trying to defend Latino against any potential threats and in warding off reprisals afterward. After the conflict was over, they refused to discuss it, leaving Latino to describe the event. Their behavior suggests, and subsequent evidence will confirm, that Latino was a leader among the freed slaves living and working on Maracangalha.

On June 30, Subdelegado Rigaud wrote to the chief of police in Salvador describing recent events in the parish. In the letter, he accused Maracangalha's moradores of obstructing justice and of threatening the court clerk who deposed them about the fight with Cerveira. According to the subdelegado,

> the place where the fight took place is currently home to a bunch of idlers, troublemakers, and thieves who have no respect for authority, who know no law other than their own, who mock everything and everybody, and who tell anyone who challenges them that no one will force them to leave. First, they make a mockery of my efforts to conduct the investigation that I mentioned, and then boldly armed with all kinds of weapons, they swear to resist any threats against them, even ones required to allow justice to be served, as in the present case.[7]

Rigaud ended his report with a plea for reinforcements to help him confront the "troublemakers." The subdelegado's letter reflected the emotional state of the police, the owners, and the managers of the region's plantations after a month without slavery. Rigaud tried to discredit the freed slaves, calling them "troublemakers," "idlers," and "thieves." In his view, the basis of the social order was under attack. The freed slaves refused to work and trespassed on private property; they no longer respected the authorities or the law.

Meanwhile, on July 6, the freed slaves involved in the incident—Odorico, Rufo, Ismael, João de Deus (John of God), Clemente, Germano, João Anastácio, Onofre, Jacinto, Arlindo, and Floriano—went to the delegado's office in São Francisco do Conde to complain that the manager of the Sapucaia Plantation had threatened them and then attacked them. The freed slave Ismael insisted that he had committed no crime but "that if he had he wouldn't say so."[8] The ex-slaves were behaving like free citizens who believed that they had the right to legal protection. However, the subdelegado did not share their understanding of their new position in society and immediately arrested them. Later that day, he telegraphed the chief of police and announced the capture of the eleven men involved in the conflict, asking permission to transfer the prisoners to the capital and justifying his request by claiming that the local jail lacked security.[9] By that point, the freedmen must have come to understand that the freedom granted them on May 13 was quite tenuous.

The authorities interrogated the imprisoned ex-slaves, and the resulting depositions are fundamental to our efforts to discover the roots of the conflict. Moreover, the freedmen's testimony helps us to better understand the repercussions of the Law of May 13 in their daily lives and the ways in which they attempted to support themselves after abolition. Odorico, a carpenter who had lived on Maracangalha for many years, told the authorities about the events of June 26:

The Quibaca cattle were constantly destroying the subsistence plots they had planted on the Maracangalha Plantation, and [so he and] some coworkers had butchered some cattle that they had found in their plot, including a dead cow, and eight days later, on a Tuesday, June 26, he'd been at home tying up a bundle of firewood, when he saw a group of guys near the Maracangalha Plantation headquarters, and so gathering up his bundle and [putting his] machete at his waist, he went to see what was going on and learned from his co-workers that José Rodrigues de Cerveira had hit Latino, Maragangalha's crioulo overseer, with "the flat side of a machete" and that the plantation freedmen, along with the witness, had taken revenge by beating José Rodrigues with clubs and sickles, breaking one of his arms, and hurting him in several other ways.[10]

In other words, according to Odorico, the freedmen beat Cerveira because he had mistreated Latino, their overseer, but the argument grew out of the Maracangalha freedmen's decision to punish the Quibaca cattle for trampling their subsistence plots.

Odorico mentioned another important detail in his deposition. He explained that when he and the others were interrogated about the incident, they had made a point of emphasizing that the Law of May 13 had freed them. In doing so, they revealed that they understood the significance of abolition in their lives, and they expected the delegado to treat them as free people. They were attempting to establish a clear division between their old status as slaves and their new status as free men.

Another of the freedmen, a twenty-five-year-old stonemason named Onofre, confirmed Odorico's version of events. He also described the damage the cattle had done to their crops and added that, on various occasions, he and his workmates had told the Quibaca manager and "Dr. Joãozinho" (Dr. Johnny, as they called Cotegipe) that the plantation fences needed fixing. Moreover, before taking "matters into their own hands," he said that the freedmen attempted to work with the manager and Cotegipe, the owner, to solve the problem, but the fences remained unrepaired and the cattle continued to trample their crops. As a last resort, they organized themselves to guard their crops from the animals, even though it doubled their work. Armed with scythes, the freedmen turned the wandering animals away from the subsistence plots, but in the process, several animals were cut with their tools. Coincidentally, around the same time, an old cow died near the manioc fields in question. That was why Cerveira, "who liked to boast that he wasn't afraid of anything," and Firmino, a servant of Dr. Johnny's, came to "get satisfaction" for what happened.[11]

The problem was not new.[12] For decades, the damage that cattle did to crops had provoked conflict in the Recôncavo—among planters, or between planters and the free poor. The law obliged owners to fence their cattle, but poorly maintained fences and wandering cattle were a constant source of tension between plantation owners and slaves with subsistence plots long before abolition. More than one hundred years previously, toward the end of the eighteenth century, Vilhena recommended that plantation owners should maintain their fences to prohibit cattle from trampling the manioc and other crops that the slaves grew. So doing, he advised, would improve slaves' living conditions.[13] Owners and managers were not accustomed, however, to freedmen themselves demanding that the fences on a neighboring plantation be repaired.

The conflict broke out at the end of the day, just when the freedmen—many of whom were concerned about the cattle damaging their crops—were returning from their subsistence plots carrying their tools, including scythes and cattle prods. João Anastácio, the only one who declared himself to be a "free man," later stated that, around five in the evening, as he was coming back from his fields, he heard "freedwoman" Nicoleta yelling for the other moradores to come running because Latino, the overseer, was being beaten up. That was how José Anastácio, Odorico, Germano, Arlindo, Onofre, Jacinto, Floriano, and Firmino wound up going to Latino's defense armed with scythes and cattle prods.[14]

In his lengthy statement to authorities, a twenty-two-year-old stonemason named Rufo added details about the altercation. The deposition reads:

> That the witness, a freedman from the Maracangalha Plantation, who together with his *companheiros* customarily planted crops only to see them destroyed by cattle from the Quibaca Plantation, went with Latino, the overseer at Maracangalha, to ask the overseer at Quibaca to deal with the situation but that manager did nothing so Latino went to the owner, who promised to have something done, but the cattle still continued to ruin the witness's fields as well as those of his companheiros so he, Odorico, Onofre, Germano, Floriano, João Anastácio, João de Deus and Firmino sliced up a cow; several days later José Rodrigues de Cerveira [the Quibaca manager] came to the big house at the Maracangalha Plantation and asked for the owner, but he wasn't at home; when Latino, the property's manager appeared, José Rodrigues asked

him who had cut one Quibaca cow and eaten another one? Latino answered that he didn't know, and José Rodrigues retorted that Latino was being disrespectful, and then Latino replied that the disrespectful guy was José Rodrigues, at which point José Rodrigues hit Latino several times with the flat side of his machete and Ismael could testify to that because he saw it happen and called some other guys to come and protect Latino from José Rodrigues, but Rodrigues refused to calm down and lashed out at them with the machete, and cut Ismael's forehead, and then he [the witness] and the others arrived with clubs and scythes, and tried to get the machete away from José Rodrigues, and Ismael managed to give his fist a good whack, which made him drop the machete, and he, the witness, grabbed it and broke it into three pieces . . . , and shortly thereafter things calmed down.[15]

While Odorico and Onofre insisted that the harm to the cattle had been accidental, Rufo stated that they had been hurt intentionally, in retaliation against the planter who refused to maintain his fences. Either way, the freedmen were defending their fields from the cattle, based on customary rights that they had negotiated over the years. Germano, a forty-five-year-old "agricultural worker," explained that he and the other freedmen had subsistence plots "since they were slaves of that plantation."[16]

As Hebe Mattos observed, prior to abolition, Brazilian plantation slaves always saw access to subsistence plots as central to the meaning of freedom. After abolition, they continued to demand access to subsistence plots as a condition of freedom. Studies of the post-emancipation period in other parts of the Americas have shown that ex-slaves also saw cultivating subsistence crops as essential to their struggles to develop autonomy from former masters.[17] Freed people knew that access to such lands allowed them to choose where, when, and how they would work. The small farm fields provided a viable alternative to laboring in the cane, which they had been required to do during slavery, and enabled them to work for themselves and for their families.[18] But in evoking "customary rights" to subsistence plots after abolition, the freedmen tried to carry gains that they had made during slavery over to the post-emancipation period.

The events at Maracangalha illuminate significant aspects of the freedmen's post-emancipation thinking and behavior. Although the freedmen were trying to assert their new status as citizens, they also recognized the plantation hierarchy and tried to follow the chain of command. To resolve the problem with the Maracangalha fences, they did not go directly to the manager of the neighboring Quibaca Plantation about his wandering cattle. First, they spoke to the Maracangalha overseer and left him to speak to his counterpart on the neighboring property. When that didn't work, the overseer went to the Quibaca owner. Only when their formal appeals were unsuccessful did the ex-slaves take matters into their own hands.

In acting collectively against Cerveira, however, they followed the pattern of behavior exhibited by slaves who took action against overseers: to avoid punishment of any specific individual, they all claimed to have beaten Cerveira. They also seemed to be trying to force Cerveira to make amends for mistreating their friends and acquaintances under slavery. João Anastácio stated that Cerveira and his brothers were "accustomed" to provoking fights, especially in the neighboring village of Candeias. On one occasion, he attacked a young girl named Liberta (Freewoman) who later died as a result. On another, he whipped a man named João de Freitas; beat up Olímpio, the master of a boat on a local river; and killed the boatman's wife.[19]

The witness statements indicate that the freedmen struggled to affirm their new condition, which required distancing themselves from behavior patterns inherent to slavery. Odorico revealed that he attempted to make Cerveira recognize him as a free man that day at Maracangalha: he said that after the fight, Cerveira mounted his horse, but his hat remained on the ground. The manager then ordered Odorico to pick the hat up and hand it to him. Odorico refused, saying "that José Rodrigues himself should pick it up, because he didn't own any slaves."[20]

Data on the freedmen contained in the criminal case against them and summarized in table 5.1 sheds light on the backgrounds of those involved in the fight. Although the authorities eventually charged seventeen freedmen with attacking the Quibaca manager, most of the data in the case involves twelve individuals. Of them, only four had been born on Maracangalha. The others had been transferred there from neighboring properties. The 1872 slave list for Maracangalha confirms that information, indicating that cabra Clemente and the crioulos Floriano, Firmino, and João de Deus had been born on the plantation. In other words, they lived on the plantation when it belonged to the Viscount of Passé and lived through the transfer, first, to his father, and then to Moniz Aragão, who acquired it in 1878. We can also add three others to the group who had been born at Maracangalha—crioulos Cosme, Vicente, and Henrique—who are not included in table 5.1, but were eventually charged. We also know that some of the men belonged to families that had been enslaved at Maracangalha for at least two generations. That was the case with Floriano, for example, whose mother Melânia was listed as a sixty-

_TABLE 5.1. Freedmen Involved in the Maracangalha Conflict, 1888

Name	Parents	Age	Place of birth	Period of residence (Years)	Occupation	Notes
Odorico	—	—	Cassarangongo Plantation	—	Carpenter	Lives from farming
Rufo	Adélia (crioula)	22	Cassarangongo Plantation	8	Stonemason	Lives from farming
Germano	Pomposa (crioula)	24	Cassarangongo Plantation	10	Field hand	Lives from farming
Onofre	Pomposa (crioula)	25	Cassarangongo Plantation	10	Stonemason	Lives from farming
Arlindo	Lethra (crioula)	24	Cassarangongo Plantation	10	Field hand	Lives from farming
João Anastácio	—	40	Passé Parish	10	Field hand	Lives from farming
Jacinto	Leocádia (cabra)		Madruga Plantation	10	Blacksmith	Lives from farming
Ismael	Josefa	25	Socorro Parish	12	Carpenter	Lives from farming
João de Deus	Maria Secundina	20	Maracangalha Plantation	20	Distiller	Lives from farming
Clemente	Josefa (deceased)	45	Juazeiro	—	Cowhand	Lives from farming
Firmino	Clara (African)	25+	Maracangalha Plantation	More than 25	Carter	Lives from farming
Floriano	Melânia (African)	30+	Maracangalha Plantation	More than 30	Carter	Lives from farming

Source: Criminal case, 29/1032/04, APEB.

five-year-old African field hand in 1872. His sister, twenty-year-old crioula Theresa, was also on the plantation. João de Deus's mother also worked on the plantation in 1872: the list described her as a forty-year-old cabra field hand named Maria Secundina.[21]

At least six additional men had lived at Maracangalha since they were very young, although they had been born elsewhere. Of this group, four referred to themselves as "sons of Cassarangongo," in other words, men who had been born on the Cassarangongo Plantation. Odorico was also born on that plantation and may have been transferred to Maracangalha at the same time as the others, but the evidence is not clear. The evidence suggests that

Latino, the Maracangalha overseer, also arrived at the plantation, although his absence from table 5.1 is conspicuous. The criminal case contains no information about his age or family ties, although one deponent stated that he was crioulo. On the other hand, the documents do record his proud demeanor and his leadership of the other men. That leadership, which predated abolition, explains why Maracangalha's owner, Moniz Aragão, made him overseer shortly before slavery ended.

Interestingly, in his record of their depositions, the notary noted that all the freedmen supported themselves with the proceeds of "their subsistence plots," although nine of the twelve had other professions from their time as slaves. This phrase certainly reflects the freedmen's actual words and indicates that they had a sense of ownership of their small plots. That is, the group emerged from slavery with notions of private property, which they applied to the plots that they cultivated on their former masters' lands. Recognizing this attitude is fundamental to understanding the freedmen's aspirations and the decisions that they made when slavery ended. The professions that they had learned during slavery corresponded to the needs and demands of the plantation, but it was as "roceiros," subsistence farmers that they planned to live in freedom.

On June 12, 1888, the prosecutor charged sixteen freedmen—Latino, Ismael, Rufo, Floriano, Odorico, João Anastácio, Jacinto, Germano, Gentil, Cosme, Onofre, Arlindo, Firmino, Plínio, Vicente, and Henrique—with assault. His summary of the charges stated that the misunderstanding between Latino and Cerveira grew out of a "small exchange of words" that did not justify the ex-slaves' reaction. After jailing eleven of those charged, the authorities made no effort to bring the case to trial, and the freedmen sat in jail. Six months later, on January 14, 1889, the municipal judge accepted the charges, explaining in his written opinion that the freedmen had assaulted the victim with "injurious words" and "with outrageous and phenomenal cannibalism . . . in a bloody, disproportional and horrifying fight." He then ordered the arrest of the five slaves charged earlier who were not yet jailed—Latino, Tirso, Gentil, Cosme, Vicente, and Henrique—and added another slave, named Tirso, to the group under arrest. These additional six joined the original eleven men rotting in jail.[22]

The case went to trial on September 26, 1889. Members of the jury included some of the area's most important plantation owners: Antônio da Rocha Moniz de Argolo, João de Araújo Aragão Balcão, Frutuoso Vicente Vianna, and José Rodrigues Bandeira. The presence of these planters suggests that the Baron of Moniz Aragão did not try to "protect" his former captives.

After all, they had been challenging his authority when the fight took place. On the other hand, Moniz Aragão's adversaries may have: planter Joaquim Alves da Cruz Rios, a long time enemy of Moniz Aragão, represented the defendants. The freedmen must have hoped to play on the rivalry between the two planters when they sought the assistance of their ex-master's enemy.[23]

The jury acquitted the ex-slaves of the charges that same day. It is curious that a jury composed primarily of influential members of the region's master class should decide in favor of the freedmen. Perhaps, by that point, the masters no longer felt the fear that gripped them in the first days after abolition or they were satisfied with the punishment already imposed—fourteen months in jail. Perhaps most of them were political opponents of Moniz Aragão and Cotegipe and they acquitted the freedmen to get back at the noblemen. Reviewing the last years of slavery at Maracangalha can help us to understand the meaning of these events more fully.

Maracangalha in Slavery and Freedom

In 1857, according to the Ecclesiastical Land Register for the parish of Our Lady of Monte, Maracangalha belonged to the widow Catarina Josefa de Araújo Pita, who had inherited it from her son, Cristóvão da Rocha Barbalho Moniz Barreto. Catarina did not administer the property herself: that year, her nephew and son-in-law, Francisco Antônio da Rocha Pita e Argolo, the Viscount of Passé, handled the day-to-day plantation business. According to the land register, Maracangalha bordered six other plantations, Cinco Rios, Pindobas, Sapucaia, Pinheiro, Cassarangongo, and Quibaca, the last of which also belonged to the widow.[24] Although each of the properties was enormous, one could see the headquarters of Cassarangongo, Sapucaia, and Quibaca from Maracangalha. It is not surprising, therefore, that news traveled quickly among them and what happened on one of the four plantations soon had repercussions on the others.

When Catarina died, her daughter and son-in-law, the Viscount and Viscountess of Passé, inherited Quibaca and Maracangalha. They already owned two of the other plantations that bordered Maracangalha—Cinco Rios and Pindobas—as well as three others—São Paulo, Feliz União (also known as Cobé), and Pinheiro. The viscount died in 1871, drowning in debt. It fell to the executor, Egas Moniz Barreto de Aragão, the Baron of Moniz Aragão, to arrange payment and settle the estate. The inventory of the viscount's property that Moniz Aragão prepared allows us to catch a glimpse of Maracangalha sixteen years before abolition.

When the viscount died, Maracangalha was a well-established sugar plantation. According to the inventory, the property consisted of more than 1,342 tarefas of land, of which 1,151 were the excellent sugar-growing *massapê* soils. In addition to cane fields, the property boasted a sugar mill for refining sugar, as well as 95 oxen for hauling and another 150 for breeding. Forty-five *senzalas*, "constructed of poorly-made supports, with mud walls, covered with thatch, with the doors in ruins" housed the slaves.[25]

An enslaved labor force of ninety-five people staffed the plantation. Among them were slightly more men (forty-nine) than women (forty-six, a minority (twenty-eight) of whom were Africans. Most of the slaves were adults or adolescents, but twenty-two were children between the ages of one and twelve. More than half of the slaves (fifty-nine) were the descendants of Africans, described as crioulos (fifty-one) or cabras (seven). Only one young girl was as a mulata, suggesting very little mixing with Europeans on the property. In other words, Brazilian-born people of African descent, the majority of whom were crioulos, dominated the plantation's work force.

Under normal circumstances, the viscount's share of the communal property would have passed to his legitimate children under Brazil's forced partible inheritance laws. But when the dust settled the viscount's father, Antônio Bernardino da Rocha Pita, the Count of Passé, who had cosigned many of his son's loans, owned much of the property, including Maracangalha.[26] The older man was no longer strong enough to manage his holdings, so he turned the day-to-day supervision of all his properties, including Maracangalha, to Cotegipe, his son-in-law. That meant that Moniz Aragão and Cotegipe had been making decisions about the people on Maracangalha for nearly two decades prior to abolition. In other words, Cotegipe, Moniz Aragão, and the freedmen of Maracangalha had crossed paths before.

Four years later, the elderly Count of Passé died, and although he was one of the most important property owners in the Recôncavo, he too was deeply indebted. Maracangalha was inventoried again, but conditions had changed. The enslaved labor force had been reduced by only a little more than 10 percent: it now included forty-four men and thirty-nine women. Strikingly, fewer than half of the Africans present in 1872 (twenty-four) were still on the property. The oxen herd, on the other hand, had shrunk by more than half—to only 118 head.[27] The Passé family appears to have been in decline financially.

In 1878, Moniz Aragão purchased Maracangalha from the Count of Passé's heirs. The plantation's new owner was one of Brazil's "great men." He was a German-educated attorney who had represented Brazil diplomatically in

London and Berlin. On his return to Bahia, he was elected to the Salvador City Council and the presidency of the town council of São Francisco do Conde, serving during the tense years of 1888 and 1889. During his lifetime he accumulated numerous honors, including Knight of the Casa Imperial, Commander da Rosa, and Knight of the Order of Nossa Senhora da Conceição of Vila Viçosa in Portugal. He died in Rio de Janeiro in 1898.[28]

The men who had controlled Maracangalha for much of the second half of the nineteenth century—Moniz Aragão, the two Passés, and Cotegipe—belonged to the same extended family. The elder Passé's wife was a Moniz Barreto de Aragão, and simultaneously both Cotegipe's aunt and mother-in-law. The younger Passé was his wife's cousin as well as her husband, and he was also Cotegipe's brother-in-law. Indeed, Cotegipe, his wife, his brother-in-law, and his sister-in-law were all either cousins or siblings.

Such complex family relationships were common among the Brazilian elite, who intermarried to subvert equal partible inheritance laws and keep property within the family.[29] This was how well-to-do Brazilian families avoided breaking up their estates and amassed political power over the course of centuries. It also helps to explain why, when the elder Passé died, two of his most productive plantations wound up belonging to Cotegipe and Moniz Aragão, although the latter purchased Maracangalha.[30]

As we will see, Moniz Aragão's acquisition of Maracangalha did not go smoothly. His reputation must have preceded him, because the slaves revolted at the news that they now belonged to him. On the evening of November 26, Moniz Aragão wrote a long letter to his friend, confidant, and relative by marriage, Cotegipe, describing what happened at Maracangalha the day he took control of the plantation. According to the letter, when Moniz Aragão reached the Recôncavo from Salvador, he ordered Favila—the plantation administrator—to gather the slaves at the plantation headquarters the following morning for his inspection, before they went to work in the cane. When he arrived at the plantation, he found the slaves gathered, "respectfully, like always with me." Then, like all Bahian planters who had just acquired a number of new "pieces," he began calling each one forward by name, recording their presence and condition, giving them a new set of clothing and a bit of money, and ordering them to gather up the oxen and brand them with his mark. And finally, he wrote,

> [Yesterday,] I made a little speech to the slaves and then I gave them the rest of the day off; I went to dinner at Pindobas and when I returned to the plantation at the end of the day, some slaves greeted me;

I checked with Favila about the work to be done today in the event of rain, and I went off to the house at Cassarangongo Plantation, where my mother and grandmother were waiting to congratulate me on my new acquisition.[31]

We can see here that Moniz Aragão was engaging the symbols and rituals of seignorial power in his acquisition of the Maracangalha Plantation. He knew that the slaves' recognition of that power was essential to the success of his new undertaking. To him, the Maracangalha captives' deferential behavior indicated that they would accept him as their master. Therefore, as he traveled the few miles back to the Cassarangongo Plantation, he was apparently convinced that his purchase of Maracangalha would go smoothly.

Moniz Aragão was wrong, however, because, as he wrote to Cotegipe, just before dawn he received a note from the Maracangalha Plantation manager informing him that the slaves had gathered in the *bagaceira* (bagasse shed) and were refusing to work for or to obey their new owner. He tried to calm the administrator, Favila, telling him to inform the slaves that he would arrive to take care of the problem after lunch. He recalled that, the previous day, he had been warned that "Rios and Company" were planning a "party" with fireworks at the Maracangalha gate, because one of them was overheard claiming that if Moniz Aragão took over the plantation, the slaves would not work for him. "Even then I did not pay much attention to anything but the way the slaves initially received me, just as the news this morning did not scare me." The Cruz Rios family owned land and slaves near Maracangalha and had been disputing ownership of the plantation for many years; the slaves' refusal to work for Moniz Aragão seemed to this rival family to be an important step toward achieving their goals.

That afternoon, Moniz Aragão headed to Maracangalha on horseback with "our" Prediliano, an enslaved personal servant. As they saw the new owner approach, the slaves came out of the sugar mill led by the overseer, also a slave. Only then did Moniz Aragão realize that the overseer was involved and that tipping the supervisor 5 mil-réis the previous day had not guaranteed his loyalty. In his letter to Cotegipe, the baron's detailed description of the meeting that followed shows that the slaves skillfully combined deference with a firm refusal to be transferred to their new owner. He said that they formed a line, greeted him, "and some fell to their knees in front of the horse that he rode." And then he said,

I asked them calmly: what was the meaning of this, my people? They all responded in one voice: We want to be sold, sir—Everyone? Yes, sir. But weren't you just sold to me? Yes, sir, but we cannot serve our master. Why? Because we only want to serve the children of Ioiozinho or Iaia [as the Viscount and Viscountess of Passé were called]. But what if they don't want you and they prefer that I should be your owner? They responded that if they can't belong to Ioiozinho or Your Excellency then they preferred not to remain on the property, they want to be sold away. The entire discussion was useless and I called them into the shade in the woodshed where they repeated the same things insisting that they would not work for me. I told them, still calmly, that they were being ridiculous, because if they did not want to recognize me as their owner, then I could present myself as your representative, and Zinho would be there to help me with that, and he would make them work and they would work where I wanted them to work; but as a sign of respect for Your Excellency, while we waited for your answer, they would have to do what I told them, under Zinho's supervision.[32]

All through the exchange, Moniz Aragão tried to convince the captives that he would retain his power over them, whether as their master or as the representative of Passé's heirs. The slaves must have known his temperament and his management style reasonably well, but they were probably bluffing when they said that they preferred to be sold away into the domestic slave trade rather than become the baron's property. Certainly, becoming the property of a new owner was problematic; whoever took over the plantation was going to try to make it produce to the maximum, and this took time; to the slaves, this could have meant that manumission was further away than ever. They may have believed that they were more likely to be freed if they remained with the viscountess, since several had been freed when her husband, their former owner, died. By the end of the discussion, Moniz Aragão had suffered a reverse, because the slaves continued to refuse to work for him and only agreed to work for one of Passé's heirs. Before leaving, however, Moniz Aragão took the names of those who did not want to serve him, as well as the "few who had taken the better part—in other words, who had remained calm." The slaves were not unanimous in opposing the new master's authority, but only a minority agreed to accept it.

Reservedly, Moniz Aragão confessed to Cotegipe that he had been so afraid during the embarrassing situation that he had dinner at Maracangalha and then left to spend the night at Cassarangongo, "because I was more comfortable there and to reassure my mother." Note that the micropolitics of slave rule were permeated with detailed reflections and small actions calculated to control the slaves. He said that given the slaves' attitude it would be prudent to proceed calmly and with "studied indifference toward these recalcitrants, rather than to deal with them more forcefully which would only make the instigators happy." He continued:

> So, I asked them whether or not they wanted to keep the money that I had given them; they didn't even insult me by refusing it—seeing that they asked me for money many times and I gave it to them; but I did say that they had to return the clothing that I gave them, and that each one of them cost money, and they would have to wait for Your Excellency to give me others or I would have to purchase others. I told them that also to make clear that the land mattered more to me than the slaves.[33]

The owner of Maracangalha tried to convince the slaves that he did not need them. At the same time, he tried to gain their confidence, reminding them that he had paid the overseer and distributed clothing and money among the rest of them. The baron ended his letter asking Cotegipe for help in finding a solution to his problem, "because I can't keep slaves who tell me to my face that they don't want to serve me; nor can I tell the banks that I don't want anything to do with the property anymore without coordinating something with you first."

Those events kept our baron tossing and turning all night, because at four thirty the next morning he began to write another letter to his confidant. He proposed that if Cotegipe could not easily replace the "recalcitrant slaves," he could assure the Caixa Econômica and the Sociedade do Comércio—the institutions that had financed his purchase of the plantation—that the difficult ones were worth Rs.30:300$000 while the respectful ones, including little Tertuliana who was listed among the first group by mistake, were worth Rs.8:450$000. He thought that he could sell the problematic slaves for the inflated sum he had mentioned and keep only those who were "under control or unable to work."[34]

We do not know what strategy Moniz Aragão used in the end to get around that embarrassing situation. No documents have yet turned up that might tell us whether the "recalcitrant" slaves were sold or obliged to submit to the baron's authority. According to table 5.1, he purchased "people" from other plantations for Maracangalha in the next few years, certainly because of his difficulties with the slaves when he acquired the property. At least half of the freedmen involved in Cerveira's beating had arrived at Maracangalha as slaves after Moniz Aragão acquired the property. During the decade or more that they spent on Maracangalha before abolition, however, they learned skills, formed families, and forged links to the existing Maracangalha community. In some cases, they also earned the right to their own subsistence plots. These factors mattered a great deal after May 13, 1888, when they decided to confront their master and refuse to abandon the property. We should not be surprised, then, that over the course of the decade they became the new "recalcitrant" ones.

In 1879, Moniz Aragão celebrated the proceeds derived from his new plantation. The sale of sugar that year earned him Rs.5:814$215 and the *mel* (sugarcane juice), Rs.7:074$215. In other words, the income from that year's harvest was worth almost half of the value of the "recalcitrant slaves."[35] In the following years, Moniz Aragão invested in improvements to the Maracangalha sugar mill: he updated the sugar-making equipment, purchasing a "vacuum machine" and caldrons, centrifugal turbines, and a small still. In 1880, he hired an English mechanic to install the new machines and make sure that they were running properly. In April 1882, he changed the plantation management, replacing the old overseer with a man named Manual Joaquim Alvares de Castro.[36] But maintaining slavery on his properties remained challenging. On the night of July 13 of that year, the pretos on his Pindobas Plantation shot at the plantation overseer, who was lucky to escape with his life. In trying to reproduce the captives' words about the event, Moniz Aragão emphasized the following expression: "Nobody saw nothing."[37]

After this and other disturbances, Moniz Aragão began to promote slaves to supervisory positions, offering them manumission and other favors in exchange for good service. He was trying to maintain order and increase cooperation on the part of the laborers, whether still enslaved or newly freed.[38] However, he did not achieve his goals. In an October 23, 1883, letter to Cotegipe, the baron stated that he faced a great deal of work and many difficulties. Before that year's harvest, he had been obliged to remove his ex-slave Ismael from the position of overseer, for "having abused his trust"; at the same time, he replaced another freedman, Jaime, as *caixa* at Cassarangongo. His reflections on the reasons for his problems with the freedmen who played supervisory roles are interesting. He wrote:

These people don't appreciate or feel grateful for their ex-owners' expressions of affection; either they consider themselves indispensable or they think they're big shots; sometimes, superior to the owners themselves; they begin with the ambition to run the place and later they begin to covet what doesn't belong to them. When they're not stealing, they are quite reverent and friendly; before you know it they're pretending that they're free. And that's the verdict on these days! This behavior on the part of the freedmen and the salaried workers doesn't bother me: I'm accustomed to work and to be treated ungratefully.[39]

In complaining about "ungratefulness," the baron exposed the fragility of the paternalist manner of dealing with slaves and freedmen, at a time when abolition was a topic of intense discussion. We can see, then, that beginning in the 1880s, Moniz Aragão had been experiencing problems with enslaved overseers, those men who mediated between him and the other slaves. And as we saw, an overseer led the slaves' resistance to the baron's acquisition of Maracangalha.

On November 7, 1883, Moniz Aragão returned to the topic of "disorder" on his plantations. He was taking "administrative measures," he wrote, to resolve problems on his properties: these included firing the freedmen Ismael and Jaime, and letting go Prediliano, the personal servant who had been with him when he confronted the "recalcitrant" slaves in 1878. He observed that "they began with a great deal of ambition to lead, but became communists and neglected their responsibilities. Since I'm not one to do things by half measures, I put things in order and now everything is running smoothly."[40] By claiming that they "became communists," he may have meant that the slaves and the recently freed men in whom Moniz Aragão had placed his trust were trying to amplify their personal independence at a time in which the end of slavery was being debated. Perhaps the slaves and freedmen were trying to increase their access to the plantation's property and resources. Certainly, their conflicts with the administrators suggest that the slaves had been pushing the limits of the system of slave control.

On October 3, 1887, Moniz Aragão observed that the slaves were even using his birthday to get out of work. He wrote:

Given that "Holy" Sunday followed the day on which we celebrated my appearance in this world of vagrants, these enslaved Brothers in Christ gave themselves a present, and even took half of Friday to prepare for the Masses, the sermon and the Baptisms, that were taking place here by special dispensation of the Archbishop. With each passing year, we become holy men and resigned to the evils that surround us, with no outlet except to reach for heaven.... Pagode, vagrancy and communism! These are the saviors of our ridiculous Nation![41]

As we saw in the previous chapter, throughout 1887 and the first part of 1888, tension ruled in the Recôncavo, including at Maracangalha, as the last days of slavery witnessed regular escapes and insubordination. In early April 1887, abolitionist pamphlets encouraging slaves to flee circulated through the Maracangalha's slave quarters. In hopes of controlling the situation, on March 7, 1888, Moniz Aragão had already freed 346 slaves from three plantations, Cassarangongo, Mataripe, and Maracangalha. Then, a few days before abolition, the baron went to stay at his Mataripe Plantation, from where he planned to coordinate the "transition" to free labor on his properties. He was not alone: all the members of the São Francisco Town Council had left town to reestablish order on their plantations, as he informed the provincial president on May 19, 1888.[42]

In making these changes, the baron hoped to stem insubordination on his plantations, but, as we can see, he was unsuccessful. His absence from Maracangalha encouraged the freedmen to break free of their enslaved bonds in anticipation of abolition. Beginning in March, a little more than two months prior to abolition, the slaves stopped appearing in the cane fields and began to dedicate themselves completely to their subsistence plots. Another look at the letters that the baron sent to the provincial president just after abolition, discussed in chapter 4, indicates that he could not have called Maracangalha among the "most well-ordered" properties in the region, unless the situation elsewhere was even worse. Otherwise he would never have described the behavior of the ex-slaves on Maracangalha as "respectful inertia."

After the announcement of the abolition law of May 13, the freedmen began to express their new condition in straightforward language that seemed "insolent" and "insubordinate" to ex-masters and overseers, and the Recôncavo seemed out of control. In a deposition taken by the São Francisco delegado, the Quibaca Plantation manager, José Moreira de Pinho, revealed that "when freedom came, the Baron of Moniz Aragão, the ex-master of the accused, called them to Cassarangongo from Maracangalha, and was told in reply it was as far from Maracangalha to Cassarangongo as from this place to that one."[43] In other words, the ex-slaves instructed their master to come to them should he need to speak to them.

Moreira de Pinho intended to show that the freedmen were insubordinate, but his comments also reveal the ex-slaves' firm intention to remain on the plantation, regardless of the ex-master's orders to the contrary. As far as they were concerned, any transfer represented the loss of access to their subsistence plots, which meant loosing freedom as they understood it. Clearly, their reply was a way of saying that that were no longer "things" that their ex-master, the baron, could move from place to place.

In the days following abolition, the freedmen of Maracangalha felt the sweet sensation of living without an owner. In those brief moments, they could freely sell the produce of their farm plots in the local markets, and no one could make them work in the cane fields. When Cerveira threatened Latino, some freedmen were in the manioc fields; others were making manioc flower or gathering firewood. Possibly more freedmen expected to be able to cultivate their own farm plots. Perhaps they understood that, from then on, access to a piece of land no longer depended upon paternalistic concessions by owners to reward certain workers. Certainly, in those first heady days, Latino, the overseer at abolition, managed the estate in the interests of his fellow ex-slaves, giving "permission" to participate in subsistence agriculture to any who requested it.[44]

As the case wound through the court system, the freedmen never mentioned working in the cane fields. We can see, therefore, why the subdelegado Rigaud referred to Maracangalha as a place full of "vagrants, hooligans and thieves." In his comments, he, like other plantation owners, confused the refusal to work in the cane fields with vagrancy. Where owners saw vagrancy, however, the ex-slaves saw an opportunity to improve their material and subjective conditions.

In other words, on Maracangalha, the process of making viable small farms out of subsistence plots acquired during slavery resulted from a vision for the future that—if it were to become generalized throughout the Recôncavo—could frustrate landowner efforts to reestablish control over the freedmen. In the eyes of the ex-owners, the possibility of ex-slaves "living on their own" or "supporting themselves" was dangerous because it placed the sugar industry in jeopardy. At the heart of all of these incidents lay efforts on the part of both ex-masters and ex-slaves to define the material conditions of subsistence. While, for the ex-masters, guaranteeing the future of the sugar industry was essential, for the freedman, strengthening and expanding access to small plots opened new possibilities for survival with more independence.

Consequently, the broken fences on Maracangalha and the neighboring plantation were probably not a simple case of owner negligence. Perhaps the voracity with which the cattle satisfied their hunger in the ex-slaves' farm fields coincided with the ex-masters' goals of reasserting control over labor. The ex-masters perceived the presence of ex-slaves "surviving on their own" at Maracangalha as a horrible example for recently freed workers on the neighboring plantations.

Such attitudes may explain why, according to the freedman Ismael, since they became free, Cerveira and others had begun taking "preventative measures" against them and "since his ex-master the Baron of Moniz de Aragão, was spending all his time at the Mataripe Plantation and ignoring them, José

Rodrigues [da Cerveira] decided to take his revenge."[45] In court, the freed-men declared themselves "persecuted" by the Baron of Cotegipe. They ac-cused him of instructing the people who lived on his lands to testify against them and "protect" Cerveira despite his violent behavior. As we will see in the following pages, the defense of the right of access to farm plots, the struggle to expand access to their own subsistence plots, and the affirmation of their free condition were not the only ingredients in the conflicts that occurred after abolition on Maracangalha and neighboring properties.

The Delights of Freedom

Police documents indicate that thefts and robberies increased on Recôncavo plantations shortly after abolition. The authorities attributed some of the change to the drought and famine that afflicted the region and its population between 1888 and 1889. During those years, hundreds of refugees left rural Bahia for the coastal cities, provoking shortages, unemployment, and an in-crease in food prices. In several parts of the region, property owners com-plained that bands of hungry people stole their crops and animals. When arrested on the night of April 14, 1889, six men caught stealing cattle from the pasture of the São João Plantation in Santo Amaro pleaded for clemency, stating, "they had been driven to this by hunger."[46]

Aside from these thefts motivated by unemployment and hunger, the authorities also reported that the freedmen were stealing from the planta-tion cane fields and pastures. Many masters blamed this development on the imperial government for abruptly removing from their tutelage and control individuals whom they claimed had no other alternative but crime. The issue requires closer examination.

The evidence suggests that, at the time, groups of ex-slaves were wander-ing all over the sugar districts of the Recôncavo. One such group had been operating in São Francisco do Conde under the leadership of an ex-slave named Marinho since May 9, 1888, a point at which everyone knew that the final abolition of slavery was close. According to the documents, the group of seven men had raided plantations and subsistence plots on the Ilha dos Frades (Monks' Island): at the Loreto Fazenda, they stole several items from the home of a Mr. Socrates; they carried off sails and tools from the boats belonging to the owner of the Enseada Fazenda; and they robbed the other freedmen living on the plantation of their money, clothing, and tools.[47]

These incidents were not restricted to the Recôncavo. The subdelegado in the southern Bahian town of Canavieiras reported that "after the cry of liberty, groups of [armed] blacks" attacked several plantations there.[48] Overall, these actions may reflect efforts on the part of ex-slaves to settle accounts with their former owners before abandoning the properties where they had suffered slavery.

We must be very careful, however, with how we interpret accusations by the sugar districts' authorities of freedmen stealing from ex-masters. Shortly after abolition, there was a great deal of conflict among freedmen and ex-masters about property rights and usufruct of land and other resources on the plantations. It is quite possible that what the masters defined as theft, the freedmen considered payment for services rendered or reparations as they passed from slavery into freedom.[49] Finally, the intensification of the supposed thefts on the days that followed abolition suggests that, for the freedmen, freedom brought the promise of greater participation in what was produced on the plantations or access to material resources, independent of the traditional power relations of slavery.

In addition, many thefts and robberies attributed to the freedmen appear to have reflected efforts to recover resources and defend customary rights acquired during slavery. Many owners believed that the end of slavery also meant the end of the "rights" and resources the freedmen had struggled to obtain. Perhaps prohibiting access to the subsistence plots became a form of seignorial punishment of freedmen who refused to work in the cane fields under the old conditions. Some disputes of this type reached the authorities. On June 6, 1889, forty-five-year-old field hand Tomás de Aquino was arrested for removing seed cane from the Passagem Plantation fields in broad daylight. We know that he was expelled from the plantation toward the end of 1888 and, according to witnesses, left a plot of cane behind. Sometime later, Tomás returned to Passagem to cut some seed cane, perhaps so that he could plant a new crop on the land of the Recreio Plantation where he now lived. Passagem's owner characterized Tomás's actions as theft, but the public prosecutor of Santo Amaro concluded that the ex-slave had been collecting cane based on his "rights" to it and not stealing.[50]

These considerations are fundamental to understanding the waves of theft of cattle and other property on Recôncavo plantations in 1888 and 1889. During that period, plantation owners in several locales complained that freedmen were attacking their cattle, sometimes surreptitiously, sometimes openly. The example of these supposed thefts in the sugar parish of Nossa Senhora do Monte, where Maracangalha was located, reveals a variety of motives for such episodes, from the desire to take reparations for services rendered during slavery, to efforts to defend and expand access to plantation resources.

The evidence reveals a connection on Maracangalha between the theft of cattle and the defense of farm plots, since many of the animals slaughtered had destroyed freed peoples' crops. As we saw, "stealing" cattle could be a freedman's reprisal against a master who did not fence his animals. In the following pages, we will encounter some of the ex-slaves involved in that incident again, because their efforts to survive in the post-emancipation period brought them to the attention of local authorities more than once.

Cattle were an important factor of production on the plantations: they fed the slaves; they transported people and cane and, on some properties, moved the cane grinders in the mill. The planters distinguished between the cattle raised for slaughter and the oxen employed in heavy agricultural labor, showering their prized animals with attention and care. Reflecting that interest, they often named favored animals.[51]

On February 11, 1889, Roberto Moreira da Silva, the owner of Pindobas Plantation, accused two "ex-slaves from Maracangalha," a cabra cowboy named Clemente and a crioulo carter named Antônio, of stealing his cattle. He claimed that they had herded the animals to Maracangalha, slaughtered them, and divided the meat among the moradores of several neighboring plantations. The delegado's investigation turned up a rope and the skins, bones, and other signs of slaughtered cattle on the riverbank near Maracangalha fences.

On further questioning, the plantation owner revealed more about the thefts. According to Moreira da Silva, one night in January, Clemente and Antônio drove a Hereford calf into the brush on Maracangalha, killed it, and divided the meat among their various companions. A few days later, a bull belonging to a neighbor turned up in his pasture with a leather cord wrapped around its hooves. He determined that the cord belonged to Clemente, who confessed that he had sold it to Pôncio, an ex-slave of the Viscount of Paraguaçu. The suspects admitted conspiring with others, including Luís Barbosa, a crioulo who lived on Quibaca; Gordiano and his brother Agripino, both crioulos who had belonged to Paraguaçu; Félix, an ex-slave of Cotegipe; and several others. Ex-slaves of several ex-owners were involved in the so-called thefts.[52]

The witnesses' testimony is quite interesting, since it reveals the ways that these events affected the day-to-day functioning of the plantations and the ex-slave masters' attitudes. Aurelino Ribero Sanches, a forty-year-old morador on the Pindobas Plantation, reported that after the disappearance of the "completely brown calf," Moreira da Silva ordered the plantation workers to find the animal. After searching the area, they found evidence that the thieves were "people from around Maracangalha." Antônio Henrique Bandeira Chagas, a thirty-five-year-old property owner who lived on the Paciência Plantation, declared that Dr. Robert was "very put out" with the theft of his prized calf. He suspected the "moradores of Maracangalha; because those people were unruly and had been causing problems for their master and his neighbors since obtaining their freedom."[53]

Other witnesses made clear that the ex-masters and freedmen had very different ideas about the meaning of the behavior in question. Bandeira Chagas declared that he was impressed that Clemente and Antônio bragged about having stolen the calf, how little weight they gave to the crime, and how they openly stated that they had "partners" on several nearby plantations. Manoel da Silva Elesbão, a forty-two-year-old "property owner" in Passé also found it strange that the ex-slaves showed "not the least inhibition" in confessing to having eaten cattle belonging to their ex-master and his neighbors, and insisted that "this had been customary." Clearly, what was a crime for the owners was "custom" or tradition for the freedmen.[54]

Emílio Augusto Bandeira Chagas, a forty-three-year-old "property owner" living on Paciência Plantation, who must have been a relative of the previous witness, revealed that when he was arrested, Clemente said:

> Since they had been freed, they had only eaten four of his ex-master's oxen from Maracangalha but they had also eaten some prior to freedom because all of the overseers, including Latino, participated in the "pig out," and . . . he shouldn't have to be the one who revealed what the guys in the plantation headquarters did wrong; he couldn't say how many of the neighbor's [oxen] he had eaten, because the same kind of thievery was well established in local society.[55]

Clemente was saying that the practice of stealing cattle was not restricted to Maracangalha; it had spread through all the neighboring plantations, principally "after freedom."

The freedmen were probably taking advantage of the fact that some masters had essentially abandoned their properties to appropriate their goods and resources. We know that Moniz Aragão was living on the Mataripe Plantation and, in view of the freedmen, essentially left supervision of Maracangalha to Latino, the overseer there. Thus, the freedmen at Maracangalha had been working under an overseer who was himself an ex-slave. The baron's prolonged absence from Maracangalha may have made the plantation a place where freedmen from many other places could gather, bringing with them the animals that they had taken from their ex-masters' pastures.

On February 15, 1889, in a long and detailed deposition at the delegado's home, Clemente confessed to the thefts, apparently in the hopes that "repentance" would mitigate punishment. On the other hand, his "repentance" may have resulted from several days spent in the stocks. A month later, the *Gazeta da Tarde*, one of the newspapers in the provincial capital, reported that the freedmen Amâncio, Lino, and Clemente had been beaten and imprisoned in the Pindobas Plantation stocks. When the chief of police asked the subdelegado to respond to the accusation, he would only say that the freedmen had been caught in the act of skinning several heads of stolen plantation cattle.[56]

Clemente's detailed deposition revealed that, to ex-slaves, the end of slavery signaled better days ahead. He described himself as the son of the Josefa, now deceased, more than sixty years of age, single, a cowhand and a field hand who had lived at Maracangalha for around forty years. That information makes it clear that he is the Clemente implicated in the 1888 beating of Cerveira discussed earlier in this chapter, even though his name was not among those who went to trial. He revealed that "once in a while the former slaves and moradores of that plantation (Maracangalha), in combination with those of neighboring properties, stole, killed and ate cattle from one or another sugar plantation, but that they had eaten most cattle in the months since March of the previous year." Elsewhere he said that he did not know exactly how many head of cattle they had slaughtered in the previous year, but the "partnership" had eaten many, "because shortly after Easter and after freedom, the [planter] negligence was enormous."

The deponent made clear that the thefts intensified between March and May 1888, a time in which the restrictions on slaves loosened with the absence of masters and, after, because of the expectations created by the passage of the law that finally definitively abolished slavery in Brazil. During that period, Latino, the ex-slave overseer, was the only representative of authority present on the plantation, and "he had also been a slave of the baron, [although] he had been overseer for more than a year."[57] If the "slaughter" of animals increased during that time, it might mean that the freedmen expected that the end of slavery would bring access to a greater share of plantation resources or an increase in their ability to negotiate with ex-masters and overseers.[58]

When asked about the butchered cattle, Clemente remembered four belonging to his "young master," one belonging to Dr. João Wanderley [Cotegipe], and four others belonging to plantation tenants. Those tenants included Firmino Vanderlei, an ex-slave of Cotegipe, who had accompanied Cerveira in his inauspicious 1888 visit to Maracangalha, discussed at the beginning of this chapter. As Clemente made clear, it was this incident "in the month of São João [June]" "that instigated the brawl . . . with the Administrator José Rodrigues who had come to make Latino take responsibility [for the thefts] and wound up being beaten up by the people from Maracangalha."[59] Throughout his statement, Clemente referred to the group in question as a "partnership," indicating that the invasions of the master's pastures had been organized and had involved freedmen from different plantations.

Clemente accused the overseer Latino of being a member of the "partnership" and "constantly deceiving the baron." In describing Latino's participation in the group, Clemente inadvertently revealed the way in which the overseer—an ex-slave himself—tried to give meaning to his personal freedom. He said that, one afternoon in August, Moniz Aragão had turned up at Maracangalha to prepare the sugar mill for grinding and was amazed to discover the overseer absent. The previous day, Latino had alerted everyone that the baron was coming, ordered the people in the "big house" to prepare a meal for the next day, and boasted about having received clothing from the city, 10 mil-réis and a russet horse from his ex-master. Then, the overseer, like someone who already considered himself free of "supervision," disappeared that same night "without giving any satisfaction to anyone."[60]

We can see that the ex-master and the freedman had different strategies for the changes that were coming. The former owner was attempting to control the freedman, offering incentives and presenting him with goods that may have marked their relationship under slavery. In exchange, he expected the freedman to run the plantation effectively, at a time when production was falling apart all over the Recôncavo. Moniz Aragão treated Latino in the same way that he behaved with all of his most qualified slaves, including those in positions of authority on his plantations, but his efforts were not successful. The freedman apparently agreed to work for him, but he also attempted to affirm his personal freedom, leaving the property without asking the baron's permission.

Clemente's deposition revealed that the ex-slaves primarily directed their efforts toward their ex-masters' cattle. He recalled that they had butchered and divided up a spotted calf named "Pano-Fino" belonging to his "young master," in other words, the baron's son, Martin Moniz, right there on the Santo Antônio plantation. And he reported that the freedman Antônio had taken the skin to cure into leather. He went on to say that the baron had offered a 10-mil-réis reward for the calf's return, but "no one wanted to help him." The refusal of the plantation moradores to cooperate with their ex-owner suggests that the ex-slaves' clandestine activities depended upon the complicity and the silence of the parish's free residents. During the interrogation, the subdelegado showed Clemente a skin, and he confirmed that it belonged to "Pano-Fino," since he recognized the brand with which he had marked the animal. Asked what had happened to the black calf belonging to João Campos, he admitted that the "partnership" had eaten it too.

Clemente went into detail about the way in which the freedmen captured the animals. He recalled that the calf belonging to Roberto Moreira da Silva was very gentle, so they had no difficulty in lassoing it as it lay in the bagasse shed of the Pindobas Plantation. Clemente, Pôncio, Gordiano, Luís Barbosa, Felipe, Jacinto, and Antônio drove it into the brush along the Macaco River, "where they normally killed the cattle, because it was a spot where no one came without a particular reason, and there they waited for the other members of the partnership." Asked by Moreira da Silva how they found their way during the night, Clemente revealed special knowledge, when he answered, "They found their way very well by the stars." After they skinned and butchered the calf, Antônio took part of the animal to divide among the "partners" from Maracangalha; Luís Barbosa and Jacinto brought another part to Quibaca; Felipe, Pôncio, Gordiano, Miguel, Félix, and others took the rest.[61]

Normally Clemente kept the animals' skins for curing, but they buried the skin of Roberto Moreira da Silva's calf in the Macaco River. The freedmen knew that sugar-plantation owner Moreira da Silva would make a huge "fuss" as soon as he noticed that his favorite animal was gone. They even placed a small cross on the spot where they buried the skin. The butchering always took place in remote areas of the plantations, either in the brush called the Dark Corner or along the banks of the Macaco River, and every killing seems to have been dedicated to the owner of the animals. Therefore, when they slaughtered the calf belonging to Moreira da Silva, they called it "Dr. Robert's killing." The "killings" and "pig outs" occurred in the middle of the celebration of the end of slavery. The slaughter of animals appears to have allowed the freedmen to enact festively a symbolic killing of their ex-masters. It is possible that is why they put the cross above the remains of Moreira da Silva's calf.[62] The notion that the end of slavery meant the death of seignorial authority seems to be present in a number of the ex-slaves' actions. Moreover, on making banquets out of their ex-masters most esteemed animals, they found a way to irritate and make fun of the people who had once owned them and controlled their lives.[63]

We can see that the so-called killing appears to have been followed by certain rituals of division and distribution of the stolen beef. It is possible that the division of the meat followed a tradition of the banquets at local festivals. Indeed, some of the verses of the old samba sung in the *bumba-meu-boi* festivals on Maracangalha in the 1950s quoted in the epigraph at the beginning of this chapter reflected the conflicts taking place there after abolition. According to the samba, the ox was butchered and eaten after being surprised eating the crops in the roças. In reprimanding the animal's owners, the refrain makes clear that whoever owned the ox should keep him fenced or walled in, since "I didn't plant a roça for any thieving ox to eat." Then the butchers distributed the various parts of the animal's body among the roceiros. [64]

Clemente made clear that the "partnership" included "lots of people from all over the district," but he only revealed names after the authorities guaranteed that they would protect him after he was released from prison. The information that he offered about members of the "partnership" is important and allows us to develop a tentative profile of the group. He confessed that the following people participated: Antônio, described in the document as a crioulo from Maracangalha (arrested along with Clemente); the crioulo Pôncio; the brothers Gordiano and Agripino; Félix and Miguel, ex-slaves of the Cabochi Plantation, but living on Cassarangongo; Luís Barbosa, crioulo, and Jacinto, cabra, both moradores of Quibaca; Odorico Mota, crioulo and Felipe, a mulato, longtime cowhand at Maracangalha and Pindobas, also moradores on the São José Plantation; Caetano, cabra; Gentil mulato; the crioulos Silvino, Eleutério, Cosme, and Manoel Joaquim (Antônio's brother); and Laurindo, crioulo, who had belonged to Pindobas but who had moved to Maracangalha to live with the crioula Júlia; Latino, the crioulo overseer, turned up just as Dr. Roberto's calf was being butchered and "took his piece"; Vicente, a crioulo, and Frederico, who came from the Cinco Rios Plantation to live with the crioula Laurinda; Ângela, cabra; Maria do Espírito Santo, Antônio's common law wife; "Eleutério's Nicoleta" and "Latino's Olímpia."[65]

Clemente suggested that the list could have been longer, given that "others from there and the surrounding area didn't always have the courage to come and take a cow, but always were the first to demand their piece of meat when an animal was slaughtered and butchered." According to Clemente's information, he, Antônio, Pôncio, Gordiano, Félix, and Firmino actually captured, killed, and dressed the animals. Other freedmen and women protected them by keeping their secrets but, in exchange, expected to participate in the fruits of what had been taken from the ex-masters. The wider freed community seems to have approved of their actions and supported them as a way of obtaining reparations from their ex-masters.[66]

The documents show that everyone on the list had some connection to Maracangalha. Antônio, Clemente, Eleutério, Cosme, Manoel Joaquim, Vicente, Laurinda, Ângela, and Maria do Espírito Santo may have been born thcrc; they certainly had all lived on the plantation since it belonged to the Viscount of Passé. The others had lived there for a shorter period, in some cases just since abolition.

The references to freedmen's changes in residence reveal their movements from plantation to plantation after abolition. Laurindo, for example, had been a slave on the Pindobas Plantation, but with abolition moved to Maracangalha to share a home with his lover Júlia. Vicente and Frederico, two ex-slaves from Cinco Rios who moved into Laurinda's house on Maracangalha, may also have done so because of some family connection. In his deposition, Roberto Moreira da Silva revealed that Pôncio, the ex-slave of the Viscount of Paraguaçu, moved from Cassarangongo Plantation to Maracangalha after abolition. His information suggests that in those first heady days of freedom, Maracangalha became a point of convergence for the ex-slaves of several area plantations, perhaps attracted by the possibility of obtaining roças or participating in the "banquets." Some settled there, but others only appeared on the plantation occasionally—to experience the sensation of living without a master.

We can also see that large numbers of women participated in the "slaughters" and the "banquets." According to Clemente, ex-slaves Maria do Espírito Santo, Nicoleta, and Olímpia participated in the company of their common law husbands. A look at the baptismal register for Monte Parish indicates that Ângela, a cabra, whom Clemente cited as a participant in the "banquets," was the godmother of Germano, who had a roça and had participated in Cerveira's beating. Germano witnessed the baptism of Ângela's two "ingênua" daughters in the early 1880s.[67] The women may have helped to prepare the meat, but it also seems as though they hosted relatives or friends who came from other plantations, thereby providing them with cover. Their presence also suggests that these clandestine operations in search of cattle involved entire family groups. Certainly, the partnership included several members of ex-slave Antônio's family, including his brother Manoel Joaquim, and his common law wife, Maria do Espírito Santo.

We also see that Clemente, Latino, Gentil, Cosme, and Vicente—men who were implicated in Cerveira's beating—appeared in this second case as cattle "thieves." Their presence clearly ties the clandestine butchering to the defense of the manioc roças. In butchering and consuming cattle that invaded their farm plots, the freedmen, at one at the same time, freed themselves from undesirable visitors and retaliated against masters who left animals free to ruin their crops.

The data about the ex-slaves' involvement in these two episodes indicates that the freedmen emerged from slavery in a variety of economic and professional situations, which must have influenced their options and choices after abolition. Those differences must also have determined their aspirations and their strategies for survival. Access to subsistence plots, holding a position as overseer, possessing a skill, and owning a riding or breeding animal were the marks of difference among the ex-slaves. Individuals who came out of slavery with privileges or goods behaved differently from those who, at emancipation, had nothing more than the strength of their arms.

Considering these observations, we can see the number of these actions increased and their quality changed over the weeks and months after abolition. Everything indicates that things began to go wrong when the freedmen, by mistake or in a tactical error, began to butcher animals that belonged to plantation tenants of modest means, some of them ex-slaves themselves. Remember that the freedmen of Maracangalha had slaughtered an animal belonging to Firmino Wanderley, one of Cotegipe's ex-slaves. They clearly did so, at least in part, because Firmino accompanied Cerveira to Maracangalha to find out why the Quibaca cattle were disappearing. These events must have begun to break down the code of silence that protected the freedmen. The situation became more complicated when they tried to take cattle from the pastures of the Pindobas Plantation. It was a clear, moonlit night when the group lassoed an ox, but the animal resisted, became enraged, and fled with Pôncio's rope around his neck. Early in the morning the following day, the freedmen tried to recover the rope by pretending to search for cart oxen in the Pindobas pasture, but they were too late. The animal was already being driven to the corral carrying the evidence of their crime with him.

Aurelino Ribeiro Sanches, a morador on Pindobas, was surprised to see the animal in question with a cowhand's lasso around his neck and wounds on his hooves, especially because it had not been selected for plantation service. The intimate relationships among the ex-slaves on the plantations helped to identify the "thieves." Panfilo, a crioulo carter who worked on Pindobas, "shouted right away that the lasso belonged to Clemente." He said that he recognized it because "they had both been slaves of the Baron of Moniz Aragão on the Maracangalha Plantation."[68] Shortly thereafter, Roberto Moreira da Silva went to Maracangalha to interview the moradores there about the attempted theft and then to Cassarangongo Plantation to insist that Moniz Aragão take measures to resolve the situation. When the latter learned what had happened, he sent for another carter, ex-slave Desidério, who also identified the lasso as belonging to Clemente. Pôncio, Gordiano, Agripino, Félix, Silvino, Gentil, and Manoel Joaquim overheard the conversation between ex-master and ex-slave and had time to flee. Clemente and Antônio did not have the same opportunity. They were hauling cane and did not immediately hcar that the owners had discovered their activities. When they found out, Antônio still tried to flee, leaving the cane-laden cart at the sugar mill and running down the road. As he ran, he ran into someone he knew—José Rodrigues da Cerveira—who forced him back to the plantation at gun point.[69]

In April 1889, the case went to the public prosecutor. He prepared charges, but never brought the case to trial. Perhaps it was lost or closed because of some agreement between the authorities and the plantation owners. But the documents that remain make clear that the clandestine intrusions seeking cattle and the maintenance of the rights of access to the subsistence plots constituted hopes for freedom. In one part of the investigation, the subdelegado wanted to know if the freedmen were continuing to receive the daily rations provided by the ex-master. The references to slavery were still fresh in his mind and that is why he wanted to discover possible connections between the freedmen's behavior and the rupture of the seignorial compact to provide subsistence to former slaves. Clemente explained that right up until the end of slavery and even after the "law," they had received food, clothing, and tools. When the meat arrived, he was the person who cut it up and gave it to the carter to distribute it among the others. He further affirmed that shortly "after liberty," with Latino's permission, his partners "boldly grabbed whatever they needed to make manioc flour, which they sold in Paramirim at thirty réis a liter and sometimes a little less."[70] We can see, therefore, that shortly after abolition, the ex-slaves seem to have supported themselves by cultivating manioc and processing it into the flour known locally as the bread of the poor, for sale in local markets. We can also get a glimpse of the overseer's leadership, since Latino himself gave the other freedmen "permission" to take what they needed.

It is clear that, in addition to increasing their customary rights to the roças, the freedmen were also trying to make it possible to support themselves now that freedom had arrived, principally by establishing free access to local markets. And not only that: from then on, they could put whatever price they wanted on the crops that they cultivated in their farm plots. Clemente insisted that over the course of four or five weeks after abolition they had received food from the ex-master, "but in the end, we didn't want to do anything else [for him] and we even rejected our rations." He made clear that this behavior had nothing do with the quality of the rations but rather that

> everybody was bewitched and their heads were spinning; they were making money off the plantation's manioc and almost all of them said

that they didn't need to work for the plantation anymore, because they didn't want to be subjugated anymore and they didn't want to go and get their rations from the manager either, but if he wanted to send them rations, he could send them, but if he didn't want to, he could keep them.[71]

Once again, the abolition of slavery appears in the freedmen's discourse as a watershed in his personal trajectory as well as that of his mates in the slave quarters. The references to being "bewitched" and to "spinning heads" revealed that the freedmen had decided to create the conditions necessary for survival so that they would no longer have to live under "subjugation." To have their own roça meant to envision the possibility of distancing themselves from the enslaved past and establishing their own space in the plantation world. For those freedmen, continuing to accept the rations provided by the masters meant having to continue to work in the cane, something that they were not disposed to do on the ex-masters' terms.

To them, making freedom viable depended upon increasing the production of their farm plots and establishing free access to the local farmers' markets. Fundamentally, the incidents involving freedmen and ex-masters were an expression of the different and conflicting projects they had for defining the material conditions of survival in a region dedicated to plantation agriculture. While the ex-masters were trying to guarantee the survival of the sugar industry by reabsorbing the ex-slaves into the labor force as dependent workers, the freedmen saw their roças as the guarantee of both their own subsistence and access to local markets, independent of planter control. Clearly, the ex-masters' assumptions that the freedmen were unprepared for freedom had no foundation.

"I'm going to Maracangalha . . ."

In the 1950s, Bahian musician Dorival Caymmi immortalized the village that developed around the Maracangalha Plantation and the neighboring Cinco Rios Industrial Sugar Mill in a song that treated them as a sort of promised land in the Recôncavo.[72] Although he had never seen the place that inspired him, Caymmi caught Maracangalha's mystique. The song's protagonist is determined to go to Maracangalha, "in a white suit and a straw hat," with or without Anália. His unwavering decision seems to recall, from some corner of popular memory, that at some point in the past, despite slavery and the hard work in the cane fields and in the sugar mills, at Maracangalha it was possible to envision freedom. If that were the case, it would not be absurd for us to hear in the song's lyrics the echoes and whispers of those rowdy days in which freedmen from nearby plantations headed to Maracangalha to plant roças or to experience the pleasant sensation of living without "subjugation."

The incidents that took place on the Maracangalha Plantation were not isolated or unusual. Throughout Bahia, ex-slaves demonstrated the desire to establish themselves independently from the sugar industry. In southern Bahia, ex-slaves applied to the government for permission to settle several areas of virgin forest. On May 24, 1888, the imperial land agent (*juiz commissário*) for Ilhéus, Teodoro Augusto Cardoso, telegraphed the minister of agriculture in Rio de Janeiro, explaining, "A large number of freedmen, who don't want to take on salaried labor, have requested permission to settle public lands, where they intend to grow cacao, the only agricultural activity to which the people of this rich and fertile county dedicate themselves." The judge said that he had denied the requests, based on the ministry's instructions on handling public lands, but he had promised the freedmen to ask for clarification, "given the large number of applicants and their impatience." According to Cardoso, "The interest of these people in the land and its ownership, and their abhorrence of wage labor is clear. They tell me that some, whose applications have been stymied, have begun to clear the forests and burn the land." On June 15, 1888, the minister of agriculture recommended that the provincial president provide the freedmen with alternative forms of labor so that they would not destroy the forests, "as I am told they are already doing."[73]

On January 21, 1889, the land agent made his opposition to such concessions clear in his response to a request made by a man named José Ricardo Floresta do Bonfim to harvest piassava palm fronds in the southern Bahian forests. As far as the public employee was concerned, the occupation of the public lands annihilated the future of those regions, "above all today when the ideas for colonization seem to have seriously quieted the public spirit."[74]

In the period right after abolition, the provincial authorities tried to prohibit the freedmen from having access to certain resources and economic alternatives. They saw defining the freedmen's "place" in the social division of labor and maintaining them as a workforce available to plantation agriculture as imperative. The sugar planters therefore moved to prohibit the freedmen's access to resources and activities that might guarantee them some independence from the sugar industry. In November 1888, there was a serious conflict on Misericórdia Plantation land in São Roque Parish, when several individuals, probably freedmen, tried to collect piassava palm fronds in the plantation forests. According to eyewitnesses, as punishment, the plantation owner whipped some of those responsible and imprisoned others in the stocks.[75]

In the Recôncavo, many ex-slaves planted crops on the land of abandoned plantations. On June 16, 1888, the delegado of the Vila of São Francisco informed the police chief that "vagrants, vagabonds and disorderly persons" had established themselves on the Bomba and the São Paulo plantations, and in the surrounding area. The delegado accused them of arousing fear in the local population and indicated that their numbers was tending to increase, "in view of the large quantity of freedmen who, not wanting to subject themselves to work, had abandoned the plantations." He claimed that he could do nothing about the problem, since he only had a staff of three officers, and he requested an increase in his police force. He closed by alerting his superior that the number of disorderly incidents was increasing in town because of the accumulation of "vagrant freedmen who hold noisy sambas every night."[76]

The evidence suggests that these freedmen's settlements survived for months, but that the plantation owners in the region eventually destroyed them. On March 28, 1889, the *Diário da Bahia* reported that, the previous Saturday night, a group of armed men, led by plantation managers working for Moniz Aragão, José Ramos, and our friend José Rodrigues (da Cerveira), set fire to the workers' houses on the Bomba Plantation in the Vila of São Francisco belonging to Captain Francisco Ribeiro Lopes.[77] In the process, they captured some workers, tied them up, and transported them to the Mataripe Plantation, where they were imprisoned. This may have been another example of reprisals against the ex-slaves who left Moniz Aragão's plantation.[78] Alternatively, these incidents may have been connected to disputes among ex-masters and freedmen over public lands or land abandoned by bankrupt plantation owners.

On April 6, 1889, the paper published another story signed by "The Victims" that charged the barons of Rio de Contas and Moniz Aragão with failing to enclose their properties properly and allowing their cattle to invade neighboring farms and ruin crops in the fields. The authors stated that the Bomba Plantation workers had suffered the most significant losses, since the plantation's owners were trying to clear the property to make way for cattle. The complainant also referred to the March 16 incident, stating that armed men led by Ramos and Cerveira had invaded the property, circled the workers' houses, broken down the doors, and tied up everyone they managed to capture. Then they confiscated the workers' money and belongings, including pigs, chickens, tools, and equipment for making manioc flour. The list of the stolen items makes clear that the ex-slaves' domestic economy included raising animals, growing manioc, and making manioc flour.

According to the report, the manager-led group torched the workers' houses and took the captured workers to the Mataripe and Tanque plantations of the barons of Moniz Aragão and Rio de Contas, respectively. There, the captives were placed in the stocks and beaten until Captain Francisco Ribeiro Lopes, "employer and ex-master," ordered their release.[79] The raid was clearly designed to break up the small communities of freed persons that were developing in the Recôncavo, within which might live the ex-slaves of the planters who had ordered the houses to be destroyed.

The author of the newspaper article, probably Captain Ribeiro Lopes himself, connected the events in the Recôncavo to what he referred to as the logical outcome of the law that abolished slavery. According to him, "the grandee who is deprived of living from the sweat of the miserable black cannot see them happy anywhere: [for him] jailing them or forcing them to work without pay—is the only question." He also accused the overseers and managers of the plantations in the area of behaving as a private police force when dealing with the freedmen. According to him, the freedmen were neither criminals nor vagrants, but "simply victims of ferocious persecution because they were prohibiting certain feudal lords from turning their plantations into cattle ranches."[80] The whistleblower revealed that the freedmen's farm plots might have been obstacles to the ex-masters' efforts to increase the amount of pasture on their plantations.

These earlier considerations allow us to reflect a bit more about what was happening in the Monte Parish shortly after abolition. While the freedmen were trying to find ways to support themselves outside of the plantations, the ex-masters were sensing danger. There was no other reason that they should begin to push to dismantle the "disorder" and "disorganization of labor" that they claimed to see in the Recôncavo at the time. Persecution and repression of the freedmen's efforts to engage in activities that offered them more independence from labor in sugar-plantation agriculture followed shortly thereafter. Possibly, we should also see the technological modernization that the masters began to engage in as part of their project to find a place for the freedmen in the sugar industry as dependent workers. On January 5, 1889, Moniz Aragão celebrated the receipt of a loan of 400,000 contos de réis from the provincial government to establish an industrial sugar mill at Maracangalha. According to the contract, farmers (lavradores) interested in furnishing the mill with cane would receive 10 percent of the capital, but those who had recently emerged from slavery were not eligible.[81] Moreover, at no point did the contract mention the existence of roças belonging to former slaves, let alone ex-slaves' rights to them.

These episodes demonstrate that the ex-slaves' struggles to affirm themselves as free persons and to support themselves in the post-abolition period grew out of their lived experience of slavery. To increase their access to land meant distancing themselves from dependence on the planters and the plantations. As Dale Tomich observed in his study of Martinique, the reconstruction of plantation agriculture after abolition was not a unilateral process or a function of a simple "transition" to a more rational "capitalist" system. It was a violent process, in which the former masters attempted to recapture the labor force and sought to submit them to new ties of dependence.[82]

SIX

AFTER ABOLITION: TENSION AND CONFLICT
ON RECÔNCAVO SUGAR PLANTATIONS

Freed people and ex-masters had different expectations about how they would relate to each other after abolition. These differences created tension as well as conflict in the Recôncavo's sugar districts in 1888 and 1889, as both groups attempted to define the boundaries of freedom. This chapter examines the ways that the ex-slaves struggled to create the conditions that would allow them to live without "subjugation," as they refused to abide by the work rhythms and the forms of authority established under slavery. Perhaps that is why ex-masters considered one of emancipation's most significant changes to be their inability to manage the population emerging from slavery in the same way as they had prior to abolition. The end of slavery unleashed decisive and irreversible changes in daily social relationships on the plantations.

The end of captivity placed the labor question at the center of debates about the "transition" to free labor in the Recôncavo. In the second half of the nineteenth century, the free population was able to maintain a certain amount of independence from the sugar sector. According to Bert Barickman, during that time, "a significantly large contingent of free workers was not incorporated into the labor force in the best-established and most traditional cane-growing districts of the Bahian Recôncavo,"[1] and therefore, sugar planters continued to rely primarily on slave labor until the eve of abolition. He found that the free population could avoid permanent wage labor and semiwage labor on the region's plantations by producing tobacco, coffee, and manioc flour. The economy also offered free and freedmen and women, most of whom were black or mestiço, other alternatives to permanent employment in the cane fields. They could find work in the cigar factories of Cachoeira, São Félix, and Maragojipe or in the textile industry that emerged in Salvador in the second half of the nineteenth century. Given these alternatives, the plantation owners could not count on a cheap, abundant, and stable free labor force prior to 1888. That is why they continued to depend on enslaved labor until the last days of slavery.

When the imperial government decreed the abolition of slavery, the plantation owners and their allies protested that the law brought change too rapidly and contained no clause allowing them to force the freedmen to continue to work in sugar. In response, they proposed that the government should stimulate immigration, arguing that European or Asian immigrants could solve the problem of labor scarcity. At the same time, many advocated the passage of antivagrancy laws to force "national labor" to continue to work in sugar. Immigration never took off in Bahia, so planters there had to continue to rely on domestic labor, most of whom had recently emerged from slavery.

Most of this domestic labor had been enslaved prior to abolition, and the laborers' experience of slavery defined the contours of the relationships that they developed with the plantation owners when free. In other words, what the freedmen understood as "just" and acceptable grew out of their understanding of slavery. They were particularly concerned that their working conditions on the plantations after abolition be compatible with their new condition as free people. That was why they refused to do things that they considered reminiscent of an enslaved past or that they believed would increase planter control over their lives.

When the ex-masters complained that plantation labor was disorganized after abolition, they were referring to their former captives' refusal to submit to the time-honored ways of running the sugar plantations, especially working long hours. The ex-masters accused their former captives of working only as much as was required for immediate subsistence and even of refusing to toil in the cane at all. But what the ex-masters saw as sloth and vagrancy, the ex-slaves saw as creating alternative forms of subsistence both on and off the plantations. These differences constituted the battlefield on which former masters and ex-slaves confronted each other in the year after abolition.

Tension and Negotiation

The two previous chapters make clear that after abolition relationships between ex-masters and freedmen became quite tense on Recôncavo plantations. The two groups could not agree on the new rules that would now regulate day-to-day social relations, and especially working conditions. Many ex-masters were humiliated at being required to negotiate labor relations with men and women who had been their captives. Their feelings were so strong that the experiences of that period became embedded in the memories of the ex-masters and the traditions of their families. Remembering important moments in his family history, Gastão Sampaio wrote that, in Nazaré on the day of abolition,

> in the middle of the fireworks and other celebrations, my grandfather rang the bell at the main house to call the slaves together, so that he could speak to them and he said: "You are free and, as far as I'm concerned, you can go off and make your fortunes to the extent that you can, without any hard feelings." Right away, the blacks got together in the kitchen with my grandmother, Mrs. Sinhá, whom they adored. After that, on their behalf she asked her husband to find a way to allow them to stay, since they insisted, "he'd have to kill them to get them to leave." That was how one of the first labor negotiations in Nazaré took place. All the workers became free, but, seriously, they only left the house when they died as old men and women.[2]

The ex-master's reference to "no hard feelings" seems to have actually meant exactly the opposite. It also appears that the ex-masters expected paternalism to define the contours of the transition from slavery to free labor.

Freed people also expected paternalism to continue to be somewhat important, but not in the same way it was prior to abolition. On Wednesday,

May 23, 1888, *O Tempo* published a report called "Demonstration of Appreciation," in which the author informed the readers that on the previous Saturday, six days after abolition, the Baron of Belém, president of the Cachoeira Town Council, received a "splendid" demonstration of affection on the part of the ex-slaves on his Calolé Plantation, in Iguape. According to the newspaper, the freedmen went to the home of their ex-master, covered him in flowers, thanked him for the "humane way" that he had treated them during slavery, and begged to be allowed to continue to work for him. Similar stories appeared in that newspaper during May 1888, certainly to demonstrate that slaves could become free laborers without disrupting the social order and leaving planter authority intact.

The Baron of Belém replied to his ex-slaves with a mask of magnanimousness. After thanking the ex-slaves for their "sincerity," he said that he would accept them as free laborers, as long as they were prepared to work,

> that he owed them only friendship and gratitude; that they made it possible for him to continue growing sugar; that if they intended to abandon him in the future they should tell him so now, because he would adopt a different way of life; but if, on the contrary, as they said, they intended to remain with him, he would give them the property and all of the tools necessary for them to work with him, and he would retain only a small portion of the resulting produce. When he allowed the freedmen to reply, they accepted his proposal and each one fought to demonstrate their happiness and gratitude by being the one to carry him on their shoulders.

The reporter finished his story enthusiastically stating that a large number of freedmen from other regional plantations and farms were heading to the baron's estate.[3]

The former master hoped to retain the ex-slaves on his properties because of what he referred to as a "debt of gratitude." The reporter did not realize, and Belém also failed to understand, that the freedmen were using the symbols of paternalism for their own purposes when they showed their appreciation. Similarly, the way in which events unfolded after May 13, combined with the expectations of the freedmen about emancipation, frustrated the masters' plans to use the traditional forms of control to manage the newly free population. Two months after abolition, a report on the condition of the sugar industry in a provincial-capital newspaper argued that, up until abolition, the sugar planters could liberate their slaves and try to "use gratitude to hold them on the plantations," but that full and immediate emancipation had frustrated those efforts, resulting in the most "complete chaos."[4] As the days went by, newspapers throughout the region devoted extensive space to the planters' complaints, openly protesting the way in which the imperial government had carried out the "transition" to free labor. To them, the government had implemented the abolition law precipitously, provoking insubordination and a breakdown of seignorial authority in the sugar industry. Moreover, the government had failed to adopt measures that would require the freedmen to work the sugar plantations.

In an article published on July 25, 1888, someone who signed himself as "Epaminondas," certainly a local sugar plantation owner, wrote describing the most recent events that had resulted from the Law of May 13:

> The plantations and farms that produce less prestigious crops [TR: in Bahia principally coffee, cacao, tobacco, and manioc flour at that time] have been almost entirely paralyzed by a shortage of freed workers, who have abandoned their labors because they saw that, even though a few freedmen remained because of the gratitude that they feel for their ex-masters, the establishments are almost completely inactive, and without hope of prospering because of the chaos and shortage of dependable labor that they are suffering, results that could have been prevented by our legislators who should understand that laziness is a congenital defect of those who work because they are forced to do so.

According to the reporter, the freedmen now refused to work as field hands unless the planters paid them a wage, and they abandoned the plantations if owners refused. As a result, freedmen had been flooding into the towns and cities to find work as casual laborers,[5] loading ships, hauling produce, carrying people, and selling food, "employment that carries no guaranteed salary, makes them lazy and encourages them to plan crimes against property and personal security."[6] The article's reference to the freedmen's "failure to work dependably" indicates that the ex-slaves who remained on the sugar plantations had decided to work less intensively in the cane. It also shows that the ex-slaves were using the threat of leaving, formerly considered escape, to pressure the ex-masters to give in to their demands, among which was payment for services.

Correspondence between Aristides Novis and the Baron of Cotegipe throughout 1888 gives us a better idea of what had been happening in the sugar industry. As a respected sugar exporter in Salvador, Novis financed harvests and lent money to the Recôncavo's large sugar plantation owners, among whom were Cotegipe. As an agent of the planters, he saw the financial situation of the sugar industry up close. He eventually became a sugar-plantation owner himself, acquiring several of his rural properties from indebted sugar planters.[7] That was how he came to own the Brito Plantation in Santo Amaro, and, in Iguape, the Praia and Campina plantations. At abolition, aside from administering his own properties, Novis was also running one of his uncle's plantations, the Ponta Plantation, in Iguape Parish. That uncle was another member of the Brazilian Empire's aristocracy, the Baron of Santiago.

After abolition, Novis traveled throughout the parishes of Rio Fundo and Iguape negotiating new labor terms with the freedmen on his own and others' plantations. The letters that he wrote to Cotegipe during his travels aimed, as he wrote in one, to keep his correspondent abreast of "our misfortunes." The letters are extremely valuable, as they reflect the impressions of someone who was directly involved in the first agreements with the ex-slaves. They reveal in detail the points of tension, the disagreements, and the impasses that divided the ex-owners and freedmen in the period immediately after abolition.

Through his letters, Novis was clearly trying to influence the positions that Cotegipe would take in the Brazilian Parliament, as the question of the indemnification of the planters for the loss of their enslaved property on May 13 was being taken up. It was, therefore, no accident that he should emphasize the shortage of capital, one of the most common planter justifications for their demands. On this point, he spoke as much for the planters as for the merchants who had provided the credit for the upcoming harvest. He also advocated measures for the control of laborers coming out of slavery. His recommendations largely took the form of laws that would oblige the freedmen to sign labor contracts with planters.

According to Novis, upholding order on the plantations became complicated several months prior to abolition. On March 7, 1888, he wrote to Cotegipe complaining about the decline in sugar prices and the summer rains that were making it impossible to grind the cane. As though these problems were not enough, on the plantations he encountered what he defined as "a terrifying number of escapes and a bad attitude on the part of the slaves who don't want to work."[8] The slaves were anticipating abolition and breaking the ties of enslavement two months prior to the end of captivity.

Novis was in Salvador on the day that the Golden Law of May 13 was declared. Three days later he shared his concerns about recent events in a long letter to Cotegipe. In that letter, as we saw in chapter 4, he related his fears about the celebrations of abolition in the capital. He also admitted to other worries, among which were the work contracts he was about to negotiate with ex-slaves on the plantations that he managed. "On Saturday, I'm going to Iguape to work out contracts for service, etc., etc., that law was passed in too much of a hurry! What a mess!"[9]

The reference to the "law passed in too much of a hurry" reflects the embarrassment the ex-master felt at having to negotiate working conditions with the recently freed slaves, especially because from the beginning of 1888, they had been refusing to work and many had fled the plantations entirely. Novis's unexpected trip to his plantations shows how necessary it was to come to an agreement with the ex-slaves to get the sugar mills going again. In the view of Novis and his counterparts, immediate and unconditional freedom put the freedmen in a position to negotiate for better working conditions. But, as we will see below, the freedmen's expectations went well beyond redefining working relationships. Abolition had raised the possibility of increasing their independence and improving their living conditions.

On May 18, the night before he was to leave for Iguape, Novis confided to Cotegipe that he felt at "a complete loss" about the sharp drop in sugar prices, which were shifting between Rs.1,000 and Rs.1,200 per arroba, which he believed to be too low to allow him to negotiate contracts.[10] Several days later, Novis himself perceived that the problem was more complex than he had thought and did not involve simply a lack of capital. On May 30, 1888, in a letter written after his first conversations with the freedmen, he vented:

> I am healthy, thank God, but in bad shape otherwise, given that I've been traveling constantly since May 13th, first to Iguape, then to Santo Amaro, and the result is pretty doubtful, because the freedmen are still agitated, and refuse to come to any firm agreement. In Iguape, on old Santiago's plantations, no one left, so I managed to start the following negotiation: they would all stay as lavradores and when the plantation required their service, they would work for Rs.500$ a day. . . . They formally refused to accept their rations because they said that would mean they continued to be slaves—but even so, I left orders that the elderly and the ingênuo children should be fed—obliging each worker to work according to his ability, but I tell you frankly, that I have no faith in the stability of these laborers.[11]

We can see that the population coming out of slavery was trying to exercise its freedom politically, rejecting arrangements that the ex-slaves judged to be incompatible with their new condition. Novis doubted the results of his first negotiations, since the freedmen were "agitated" and would not come to a firm agreement. Novis's words merit consideration, given that such comments appeared frequently in the planters' discourse as they tried to describe the emotional state in which they found the freedmen after abolition. Their observations reflected the ex-slaves' rejection of the conditions placed on them by the ex-masters, as well as the freedmen's firm decision to fend off attitudes and practices inherent in the slave order, so recently abolished.

From then on, the distribution of daily rations became a point of tension between ex-slaves and former masters. According to Schwartz, the methods of maintaining slaves could vary significantly on colonial plantations. "The slaves depended exclusively, or almost exclusively, on rations provided by the plantation owners on some properties. On others, they were allowed to grow their own food, using holy days and free time provided by masters. A combination of both forms of support existed on some plantations."[12] Rations were normally limited and the slaves were obliged to do double duty, on Sundays and holidays, to diversify their diets.[13] Robert Slenes showed that, during slavery, captives looked for ways to create and expand the alternatives available to them to diversity their diets and to be less dependent upon the rations the masters provided.[14]

After abolition, for ex-slaves on Recôncavo sugar plantations, the continuation of the rations meant the prolongation of dependency upon their former owners. In refusing to accept the daily rations, they were trying to say that they were working for money; perhaps their refusal also allowed them to feel more like free people.[15] Aside from that, they considered that they should bring home food that they choose, and not something chosen by their ex-masters. Alternatively, on some properties, the ex-slaves agreed to accept the rations on those days that they were working for the plantation but insisted on reserving part of the week for growing their own food. On other properties, the freedmen received the customary rations, in combination with money. But even so, these diverse seignorial solutions to the problem of feeding the slaves were not enough to make the ex-slaves continue to work in the cane fields. As Aristide Novis remarked,

> In Santo Amaro, on some plantations, they stay because of the rations, giving four days in the week to payment, and the other three they apply themselves to their fields, etc., etc. On the plantations along the Cotegipe River, the fallout has been worse. On Aratu, Mapele, Freguesia, Água Comprida, [and] Baixo, etc., etc., they all quit; on Jacaracanga they are working for the normal ration and a further gratification of

Rs.200$ each as I proposed, although I learned in the letter that I received from Chiquinho at Freguesia, that they are working at a snail's pace and are threatening to leave.[16]

The ex-slaves were also fighting to maintain guarantees that they had obtained during slavery, from which the planters were trying to disentangle themselves, citing the logic of wage labor. On May 21, 1888, the overseer at Freguesia Plantation informed Novis that, prior to abolition, slaves had received three or four days off and "Sunday's ration" when they became sick. After May 13, the slaves continued to request help, arguing that the wages they received were too low. The overseer interpreted these requests as a polite form of theft.[17]

Novis made various proposals about working conditions to the ex-slaves on his properties, and some included access to the roças. Nevertheless, along with the concession of plots of land, he insisted that the workers provide service in the cane fields under different conditions. On the plantations in Iguape, he allowed the freedmen to work their own fields, and he paid a daily wage of Rs.500$ for working in the cane. On the plantations in Santo Amaro, he gave the freedmen three days per week to tend their fields and required them to work for the plantation on the other four, which meant laboring on Saturdays and Sundays to make progress with their own fields. At the Jacarancanga Plantation, belonging to Cotegipe, Novis suggested that the ex-slaves work with the daily rations and Rs.200$ per day. Problems arose as Novis attempted to define the amount of time that the workers should dedicate to the fields of their ex-master and the time they should dedicate to their own, leading to impasse.

The freedmen showed their displeasure with the ex-masters' proposals about working arrangements in a number of ways, demonstrating that their expectations were much different from those of their employers. On some properties, they worked "very sluggishly" and threatened to paralyze the harvest, while they completely abandoned other estates. The freedmen were falling back on old ways of pressuring their ex-masters; what masters now called quitting or abandonment had been flight prior to abolition.

On June 20, Novis wrote to Cotegipe about the situation in Iguape, which he called critical. "Labor is, in general, disorganized, the lavradores who have the resources to do so, are more or less managing to function, but most of the sugar mills are completely shut down." He believed that the planters' major problem was in acquiring sufficient capital to pay the freedmen. Even so, he wrote indignantly, Inocêncio Gomes, a member of one of the most established planter families, had distributed a flyer opposing indemnification. Novis reiterated his support for government indemnification of planters' lost slaves, since most of the sugar planters were broke, including the Baron of Camaçari, who no longer had any "people." He hoped that government action could furnish the necessary capital to initiate the next harvest. Of course, here he was speaking as a merchant as well as a planter—he was hoping to get back the capital that he had lent to bankrupt planters.[18]

If only those planters and lavradores with capital were able to keep their property "more or less" functioning, it was because the planters had to deal with one of the freedmen's basic demands: payment for services rendered. The freedmen refused to work without pay, because they understood that to be "a continuation of captivity." In a letter dated July 11, Novis expressed his anxiety at this situation when he wrote:

> Finding myself in dire straits, on the one hand, funds to advance to the planters so that they could pay the salaries of their workers, etc., etc., on the other, the credit that they requested, the banks are completely exhausted and out of the market, imagine what a terrible situation! Those who owe me money are ready to turn their plantations over to me, since they don't have the funds to work them, etc., etc.,—after all, if we don't have banks and indemnification, we are lost. . . . Labor is in complete chaos, there are no workers for the plantations—they [the ex-slaves] only want money and, when they work a lot, they work for three days a week which is what they require to buy meat and manioc flour.[19]

The freedmen's interest in receiving cash wages grew out of their expectation of expanding the choices open to them in their daily lives. Payment for services meant having money in their pocket, which in turn meant freedom to choose their food for daily meals, or the ability to buy a train ticket or a steamship passage to somewhere else.

The freedmen also wanted more "free time." Under slavery, the struggle for the control over the amount of time they labored in the fields was a constant source of conflict between slaves and planters, through which the captives contested the conditions of domination and exploitation. For the slaves, free time represented a social space to be protected, and, if possible, expanded.[20] The tension that existed during slavery between masters who wanted to extract the most labor possible from their slaves, and slaves who struggled to expand the margins of their free time, emerged forcefully in the first days of freedom.[21]

Under slavery, captives worked five days a week, having only Saturdays, Sundays, and, eventually, Holy Days of Obligation to themselves. Only by fleeing, sabotage, or some other such action could they get other days to themselves. After abolition, the demand to work for the plantations on three days indicates that the ex-slaves were trying to redefine the weekly division of labor on the plantations. This, perhaps, was the most sensitive point of the negotiations taking place with the planters. That was why Novis and the others complained that the freedmen would only work the number of days required for them to pay for their basic necessities. From the perspective of the ex-slaves, reducing the number of days that they worked in the cane meant expanding the time dedicated to their own crops, or developing other alternatives off the plantations. Working fewer days on the large cane plantations was essential to their new condition as free men.

The end of August brought the period of most intense activity on the plantation—grinding cane. Novis did not believe he could depend upon the freedmen for grinding, "because if they come for the 'cleanup' or planting, they only want to work three days a week, which is enough to allow them to buy a little meat and manioc flour, then when the work gets harder and requires more diligence, will they be of any use? That is the big problem that we have to resolve."[22]

The "cleanup"—or weeding—meant the periodic removal of the weeds that grew in the cane fields. It was tiring and kept the workers busy from planting to harvest. Of all the tasks involved in cane growing, it was the lightest, but also the most disagreeable. Unlike other duties on the plantations, assigned on the basis of quotas or by the task, weeding was continuous—from sun up to sun down.[23] During slavery, the workers were obliged to spend long hours in the sun weeding throughout the year, even in the intervals between other activities. The slaves' efforts to try to reduce the number of days they worked in the cane fields conflicted directly with the planters' needs for weeding those same fields.

Grinding cane for sugar began between August and September and extended into March of the following year. It was the period of most intense activity on the plantations. In those months, workers harvested the cane, transported it to the mill, ground it up, and then made it into sugar. Work never stopped; if necessary, it could extend well into the night. Normally, the grinding stones operated for eighteen to twenty hours a day, to guarantee that the sugar-making process could continue. Keeping the sugar mill running required maximum productivity from the workers, and coordination by management of the cane harvest, cane grinding, and the operations in the sugar mill.[24] During that period, successful sugar making required the worker to submit to the implacable rhythm of production. In their few free hours, the slaves tried to sleep or to look for food. According to Novis, after abolition, the freedmen refused to agree to the intense, long work days of the grinding season.

According to our correspondent, in the middle of the 1888–1889 grinding season, most of the Recôncavo's sugar mills were shut down and certainly damaged; cattle were invading the cane fields, and freedmen were stealing cattle from the plantations and selling them in the local markets. In São Francisco, only three sugar mills were functioning; on the others, the freedmen had "crossed their arms." In Iguape and Santo Amaro, sugar-making activities had come to a complete halt. In the parish of Bom Jardim, "the freedmen had abandoned the cane and only wanted to plant tobacco and manioc." Therefore, the refusal to work in the sugar mills and cane fields was connected to the freedmen's efforts to develop some sort of alternative form of subsistence. The tobacco harvest also began in September, exactly in the period of the most intense activity on the sugar plantations.[25] Certainly, the freedmen who had access to roças were determined to work most intensively on their own tobacco and manioc fields, to the detriment of the cane crop.

As 1888 came to a close, Novis had not managed to find a satisfactory solution for the impasse in which he found himself with the ex-slaves who lived on the plantations under his administration. On October 6, 1888, he wrote:

> Around here things are proceeding in the worst way, nothing's gotten done!! The grinding season began and most of the sugar mills are shut down!! The freedmen will not do this work, not even on another plantation that is functioning . . . and putting up with the constant demands, and they are only working half of what is normal because as soon as it gets to be 3:00 in the afternoon, they want to quit, because they say that they should not work at night.[26]

In this letter, Novis complained about the increase in theft on the properties. He wrote:

> Robbery is developing on a large scale! And the authorities are doing nothing! Stealing horses from the plantations is no problem! Nor is stealing oxen and driving them to market; yesterday I heard that they took four horses from the Guaíba Plantation belonging to the Baron de São Francisco, and two from his son, and three head of cattle from the Brito Plantation!! Now they are attacking and robbing our homes

like they did on the Baron's d'Água Plantation, and they took china, etc., etc., etc., on the Baron of Sauípe's plantation.[27]

Once again, supposed "thefts" contributed to the tensions between the freedmen and the ex-masters. Cattle were an important form of exchange and also of payment for services rendered in the rural economy. The evidence suggests that the freedmen considered the supposed thefts to be a way of imposing a "just" wage for their services on the plantations at a time when the plantation owners found themselves without capital. Novis was surprised at how openly, in the middle of the day, the freedmen would appear in the markets near the plantations. According to him, "the audacity of the thieves got to the point where they even tried to sell animals that they did not yet have: they agreed upon a price and then went to steal them afterwards from their masters' properties."[28] The invasions of the plantation "main houses"— the symbol of seignorial power—also terrified him. From what Novis said, the freedmen were only taking items of day-to-day use, especially the highly valued china. Thus, what the planters considered theft, the freedmen considered remuneration for services rendered.

In several parts of the Recôncavo, the tension between plantation owners and ex-slaves grew into serious conflicts. On August 1, 1888, *O Tempo* published an article evaluating the condition of agriculture in Cachoeira:

The current state of affairs is desperate. The planters are seeing their properties deserted, and their fields without crops, because they cannot find anyone to do that kind of work. We are in the middle of the planting season and not one single property owner has planted one third of what he would have done in previous years. Everyone is depressed and, we anticipate that, to judge by all of the parishes in this district, a horrible calamity will overtake this country, if a complete halt is not put to the march of such dire events.

About the planters' unsuccessful efforts to negotiate with their ex-slaves, he had this to say:

There is absolutely no agreement about work that the freedmen will consider advantageous and agreeable; and even when they have agreed to their ex-masters' proposals, they break them without any explanation, or they don't fulfill them, because there is no law in place that guarantees labor, there is no obligation on their part to do anything. There is only one thing in which they believe and that they want: wage labor; but, at the moment, that is a utopia on the agricultural properties in this district.[29]

In a letter on October 6, Novis wrote that some planters had suspended the grinding so as not to have to deal with the freedmen's demands. "Some property owners ordered the sugar mill caldrons to be fired up, but then they took out all the fuel because nobody turned up to work, even if they were paid punctually!!! Your Excellency can see what a deplorable state we are in!"[30] It is clear here that some planters suspended the grinding so as not to have to accede to the freedmen's demands. A planter who did not require his ex-slaves to work for him did not feel obliged to allow them to live on his property or let them farm roças on his land. The closing of the sugar mills could mean the end of the old arrangements that had regulated relations between landowners and tenants.

On December 19, 1888, *O Tempo* reported that the ex-slaves on a plantation in São Félix had rebelled. According to the newspaper, after abolition "most of the freedmen were ungrateful and, since they considered themselves free, thought that they could absent themselves from the work that they had contracted to do, and they revolted in various parts of this country, awakening everyone's indignation and stupefaction with this shabby and repulsive behavior." The "call for revolt" arrived at the Natividade Plantation, belonging to Colonel Francisco Vieira Tosta. The reporter did not go into detail about the reasons for the conflict, but the evidence suggests that the freedmen had rejected labor arrangements that reminded them of slavery. The informant, citing paternalistic notions like "ingratitude," let loose all of his seignorial ire about the freedmen's behavior:

> The workers that just a short time ago because of the law's grace left behind the work gangs in which they labored like some vermin seeking refuge from the difficulties of a fruitless future. Ungrateful for the goodness and tolerance Mr. Coronel Vieira Tosta displayed despite the negligence and the bad taste with which, as contractors, they have tilled the land that belongs to him, today they armed themselves against the only benefactor who has treated them with recognized generosity, in this way, giving other freedmen an example of incomparable corruption.[31]

According to the reporter, Vieira Tosta immediately reported his problems to the delegado in town, but before the police could arrive, the "seditious ones" had fled.

In the days after abolition, many ex-masters expelled freedmen from their land for acts of insubordination and "ingratitude." The masters adopted drastic measures in an effort to force the ex-slaves to submit to the old forms of "subjugation" and deprive them of long-term rights of access to roças.

Work and Daily Life after Abolition

Despite the growing tension, the drought, the loss of productive capacity, and the difficult economic conjuncture, most of the Recôncavo sugar plantations functioned in 1888 and 1889, although they did not enjoy the positive performance of previous years. Exploring the day-to-day labor relations that were established in this period of upheaval is fundamental for understanding how the ex-slaves related to the sugar industry. The experience of slavery and the expectations of freedom were decisive for the freedmen as they struggled to define the boundaries of their new condition.

According to Wanderley Pinho, the plantation owners never liked to keep written documents of any kind, much less payroll records or notes about the harvests. Many of them preferred to rely on their memories for data about prices, the weather, good or bad results from grinding cane, and so forth. Unfortunately, very few record books from the plantations have survived the ravages of time. Luckily, one "draft" account book from the Freguesia Plantation survives, and it contains the administrator's notes from 1889 to 1901.[32] Those notes include numerous pieces of information about daily life on the plantation, weeding the fields, grinding, transportation of sugar, and, most important, payment of the recently freed workers. The information in this account book shows the workers coming out of slavery participated in the productive life of the plantation after abolition.

Freguesia Plantation belonged to Cotegipe and was located in the parish of Matoim, in Vila de São Francisco do Conde. This property was also one of those Aristides Novis visited during his travels through the Recôncavo after the declaration of the Law of May 13. According to him, Freguesia was not immune from the conflicts that followed abolition, since that was one of the plantations that the freedmen "abandoned."[33] The manager's notes about the 1888 and 1889 harvests, however, indicate that the sugar mill kept running throughout this period, although changes had been made because of the end of slavery, and signs of crisis were obvious.

At least sixteen of the seventy-four slaves living on the plantation in 1887 were on the plantation payroll as free workers in the months after abolition. The payroll records include details about the tasks that workers performed to maintain the property, including repairs to the roof, cleaning the plantation house, repairing fences, washing the boat,[34] supplying firewood, and other such activities. The records also contain the names of each worker who carried out these activities, what was done, and the amount paid in wages. Unfortunately, the manager did not keep careful notes about planting and cutting cane, the activities that engaged most of the ex-slaves. For example, on August 26, 1889, he noted only "the pretos of Caboto, 3 tarefas and 10 braças of big cane." His use of the term "pretos" for black clearly indicates that he was referring to workers who had recently come out of slavery.[35]

Despite the lacuna, the registers offer revealing details about the forms of payment adopted on the plantation in the days after abolition. In 1889, for example, a few specialized workers were paid by the day or month for their labor, but most were paid "by the task," in other words, the planter decided what needed to be done and negotiated with the freedman over the amount to be paid. Therefore, on May 19 of that year, ex-slaves Atanásio and Cláudio received Rs.1$500 each for "washing the boat." On June 20, the administrator paid twenty-three workers he described as "pieces" to bundle up and burn four tarefas of weeds; on that same day, he paid another forty-three "pieces" to cut seeds. Like "pretos," "pieces" was a common way of referring to slaves who labored in gangs prior to abolition, and his use of the terms indicates that he had not yet abandoned the vocabulary of slavery. In April, the administrator paid ex-slave Marcelina to sew eighty-nine sacks of sugar, and Samuel to carry four cartloads of firewood. That same month, he determined that clearing a tarefa of land with a hoe was worth Rs.6$000, and paid Martiliano Rs.25$500 for having cleared a little more than four tarefas of flat land.[36]

Payments to the freedmen were based on the forms of payment to free workers common during slavery. On the colonial plantations, it was customary to pay free workers by the task or by the day. The planters paid for the cutting of so many loads of cane, or for the planting of so much land.[37] According to Bert Barickman, prior to abolition specialized free workers, like seamstresses, carpenters, blacksmiths, joiners, cabinetmakers, and other artisans, were usually paid by the task, or by the number of days worked. Free workers in the cane fields received either a daily wage or a payment based on the amount cut. Both forms of payment continued after abolition, and freedmen liked them because they were cash payments.

The accounting records of the Freguesia Plantation between 1889 and 1898 show that some ex-slaves remained among the plantation's laborers throughout that period. Freguesia was not an isolated case. The Benfica Plantation payroll records for 1913 show some ex-slaves still on that property, even twenty-five years after abolition. Among those who were receiving weekly payments, were José Quirino, Tertuliano, José de Santana, José Banha, Lourenço, José Batista, Alexandre, Rufino, Salu, Paulinho de Jesus, José Vitorino, Felipe Santiago, and Zacarias, all of whom were ex-slaves of the now-deceased Count of Subaé. Except for the carpenter, José Vitorino, all of the men planted cane, corn, tobacco, and hay or repaired fences and cared for the cattle.[38]

Recall that the population that emerged from slavery was complex. The ownership of a few items of personal property, the right to a bit of land, professional expertise or employment as an overseer, established differences among the members of the enslaved labor force, defined choices, and influenced the amount of bargaining power a worker enjoyed with the ex-masters. Specialized workers, especially those involved in the grinding and processing of sugar, were in a better position to bargain for access to property and resources on the plantations that were other workers. These differences also influenced their decisions about the directions their lives would take when abolition freed them.

The planters tried various strategies to hold on to the workers coming out of slavery. Writing about the relationships that developed in the Recôncavo after abolition, German traveler Maurício Lamberg asserted that many landowners tried to attract tenant farmers, many of whom were ex-slaves, by offering them a piece of land on which to grow cane that would be ground in the planter's sugar mill and the result divided between the two.[39] According to Lamberg, after slavery ended, a class of small farmers developed, composed, in part, by the former plantation slaves. They were not property owners, but rather *colonos*, or sharecroppers, who divided their production with their former owners. Aside from this, they had access to pieces of land to plant subsistence crops, as well as the ability to graze a few head of cattle on common pastureland. He also observed that given the crisis in the sugar industry, many planters ceased to plant cane themselves and, instead, began to support themselves from the income that they earned from these sharecroppers. The system did not function well on every property, according to Lamberg, because, among other reasons, the pretos did not trust the planters, "previously their owners and masters."[40]

Some planters were granting small amounts of land to freedmen who wished to plant subsistence crops, in exchange for work in the cane fields. He also mentioned others who were establishing a sharecropping system with their ex-slaves. Other ex-owners offered material incentives in addition to land. On January 15, 1895, a newspaper from the capital announced that the proprietor of the São Paulo Plantation in São Francisco do Conde was supplying plows and oxen "for free" to farmers who would settle on their property.[41]

We know that leasing properties was quite common in the Recôncavo through the middle of the twentieth century. Planters gave usufruct to a piece of land to a tenant who would cultivate subsistence crops or raise animals. Part of whatever was produced could be sold in the local markets. The renter could also plant export crops, particularly tobacco or cane, but in exchange, he had to pay for the land he occupied in cash or weekly work on the large plantations. Payment in labor was called "paying back the profits,"[42] and the number of days a week that the tenant was obliged to work for the landowner varied considerably.[43] In this period of crisis in the sugar industry, leasing lands became a source of additional income for many ex–slave owners. The record book that Pinho Júnior, the owner of the Benfica Plantation, kept indicates that, for example, in April 1911, he received Rs.270$000 réis for "renting the lands of Passo da Pedra," being used for the planting of tobacco.[44]

Despite the seignorial efforts to develop dependency, the ex-slaves could negotiate with ex-owners about living conditions on the old plantations. Morador covered a wide variety of labor relations. Commonly, a morador was a worker who lived on the plantation as a condition of working in the cane some number of days a week. Many moradores had access to plots of land on which they grew the crops for their own subsistence. Others cultivated small parcels of land and then paid their rent in cash. These resident workers were perhaps the ones most independent from the owners, and they tried to distinguish themselves from the others by calling themselves "roceiros," or small farmers. It is also possible that the plantations were operating with "rented [or temporary] workers," who stayed on the plantations only as long as necessary to complete the tasks that they were hired to perform. Most agricultural slaves probably became "rented" workers after abolition.

Planters had to provide material incentives to retain domestic workers or freedmen and women with special skills on the plantations. That was why, when he prepared his will on June 8, 1888, the Count of Subaé, owner of the Benfica Plantation, left legacies to his "servants": Benedito Borges Moreira; José Pardo, "my traveling companion"; Fernando the cook; Rufina, the cook's assistant; and to the "distinguished" Jacob, the African, "in gratitude for the good treatment that they provided to me."[45] It is possible that the freedmen connected to important productive sectors also received cash incentives and access to certain resources on the properties. The ex-slaves who had important supervisory positions on the plantations also received rewards.

On June 4, 1893, old Araújo Pinho, the heir of the Count of Subaé, informed his son that he spent an entire week on the Benfica Plantation, "putting things in better order." He confided that "today managing collective labor on an agricultural property demands, on the part of the administration, a prodigious amount of patience and other rare qualities."[46] Araújo Pinho did not clarify what he meant by "rare qualities" nor the reasons why "managing collective labor" on the plantations was so complicated. On the other hand, his correspondence with the Benfica administrator offers some valuable insights about the points of tension between the planters and the ex-slaves and their descendants. The freedmen's demands and expectations continued to have repercussions in the day-to-day relationships on the plantations several years after slavery had been abolished.

Toward the end of the 1910s, when old Araújo Pinho's son finally took over the management of the Benfica Plantation, he may have come up against what his father had called the difficulties of "managing collective labor on the agricultural properties." On July 12, 1927, the administrator tried to explain why he had not finished work on the fence around the yard of the plantation manor by saying that "the folks who have tobacco farms don't want to work, so I called some other folks from Passo da Pedra who built a little of it last week." The following week, the administrator wrote that "they've only worked a little, the workers who have tobacco fields don't want to come when called. Your Excellency should come here in the near future because you are missed." August arrived, and the administrator's troubles continued: "It's difficult to get the folks with tobacco fields to work."[47]

We can see that the administrator could not convince the moradores to carry out the tasks required to run the plantation because the price of tobacco was so attractive. The reference to the plural "folks" shows that the workers who had come out of slavery had found that collective action was their strongest tool in negotiating with planters and administrators. Perhaps because of this, they had managed to inhibit the exercise of violence against them in day-to-day labor relations, so much so that when he was unable to convince them to come to work, the administrator was obliged to appeal to the planter to use his moral authority.[48]

Some ex-slaves managed to expand their options in cultivating their roças, even planting export crops like tobacco.[49] Possibly, tensions were increasing between the old sugar export economy, long considered a "noble" activity, and the "internal economy" of the ex-slaves. Tobacco could be harvested throughout the year, which caused problems for the sugar plantation owners when tobacco prices were higher than sugar prices or when there was intense demand for labor on the part of the local tobacco industry.[50] The concerns of the administrator at Benfica show how the ex-slaves' independent activities could conflict with their ex-masters' interests. Thus, the price of tobacco or manioc could determine the labor supply for the cane fields.

For all these reasons, acquiring workers for the labor gangs necessary to make the sugar plantations function required constant negotiation to reconcile the needs of the plantations with the alternative activities that the ex-slaves and their descendants had developed. Aside from this, it was necessary to negotiate with the workers over the payment for services that they expected. On July 15, 1930, the administrator José Antônio de Santana wrote that "the folks are not satisfied with the price that I gave them of Rs.9$000 per tarefa for turning the more heavily overgrown areas" into pasture.[51] The possibility of higher wages in the tobacco fields may have made it difficult to recruit sugar workers. On July 29, 1930, the administrator wrote that "the plowing is a bit behind schedule, the folks with tobacco fields haven't turned up." At the beginning of the following month, he wrote again that "the plowing is a bit behind schedule because the folks are taking care of the last of the tobacco crop."[52]

The ex-slaves and their descendants also showed the political ability to negotiate or benefit from their new condition of freedom, managing to bargain for better payments. On February 1, 1928, the administrator of Benfica wrote that the cane harvest was under way, but the work in the pasture was behind schedule because "the folks left and are working outside the plantation because they want me to increase the price." The following week, he repeated that the "folks" were unsatisfied with their weekly wage and were disposed to look for work off the plantation.[53] We can see that the freedmen and their descendants were using "absenteeism" from the plantation on which they lived as a way of pushing for better wages.[54] During certain times of year, especially the harvest, absenteeism could result in important gains for members of the work gangs.

The letters of Aristides Novis made it clear that the people coming out of slavery were trying to change the rhythm and the duration of their labor in the cane. The freedmen were trying to take part of the week that they worked for the planters in intensive workdays for themselves. They created what we might define as a "divided week" that involved working a few days a week for the ex-master and taking care of their own needs the rest of the week.[55] In the days immediately after abolition, Novis said that the freedmen only agreed to work for three days a week, and the evidence suggests that was the rule on most of the plantations in the Recôncavo all through the first decades of the twentieth century. Francisco Ambrósio, who had been born to slaves on the Europa Plantation in the Lustosa District, said that, at the beginning of that century, he and his relatives—some of whom were ex-slaves—cultivated their farm plots two days a week (Monday and Tuesday) and only thereafter would they work in the cane fields belonging to their ex-owners. Francisco demonstrated that he was aware of the implications of that labor system for him and his relatives when he emphasized that their lives were now different from those of "slavery times," when they were obliged to work solely for their masters.[56]

Nevertheless, the way the workweek was divided could vary significantly, according to the kind of work that the ex-slaves engaged in, as well as their professional specialty, or the kinds of negotiations that they established with their former owners. At the beginning of the twentieth century, on some cattle ranches near Feira de Santana, the tenant was required to spend only one day a week working for the landowner, and the rest of the week he was able to care for his own fields or his animals.[57] These combinations could vary significantly, but it is important to emphasize that the ex-slaves and their descendants managed to pull several days a week out of their ex-masters. There can be no question that the divided workweek was a freedman's achievement.

In the view of the ex-masters, this demand on the part of the freedmen was nothing but "a tendency to idleness." That was the argument that the sugar elite made when they included the freedmen's refusal to work more than four days a week among the reasons for the collapse of Bahia's sugar mills. What the planters saw as time devoted to idleness, the ex-slaves considered the "free time" that could be dedicated to the production of their own subsistence, alternative activities carried out off the plantations, or even recreation.[58]

Perhaps the reference to the "labor shortage" that planters constantly mentioned after abolition was related to this refusal on the part of the freedmen to work more than they considered just or appropriate to their new condition as freed persons.[59] In the eyes of the ex-masters, the workers coming out of slavery were becoming too demanding, as they were always ready to reject working conditions that reminded them of slavery. According to Mariana da Costa Pinto Vitória Filha, who experienced the Carapiá Plantation as a fully functioning sugar plantation as a child, around the 1930s groups of people composed of more than twenty relatives "came down from the backlands" to cut cane. She observed that these people did not mind taking shelter in a huge tile-covered shed called a "senzala," or slave quarters, in which the oldest tenants of the plantation—many of them descendants of slaves—refused to live.[60]

Over the years that followed abolition, the freedmen tried to increase activity that was independent of the sugar estates, cultivating subsistence crops on their farm plots and selling the excess in local markets, reducing the rhythm of labor, negotiating better wages, and forging living conditions that were quite different from those lived under slavery. We can interpret their initiatives as local manifestations of what one historian of the post-abolition period in the United States called "testing the limits of freedom."[61] In addition, these initiatives represented one element of the struggles of the freedmen to avoid the "subjugation" of slavery returning under other forms.

The resources that the freedmen managed to drag out of their ex-owners in the first two decades after abolition was quite different from what they hoped they would achieve with freedom. Most of the productive resources of the plantations continued to be concentrated in the hands of the owners, and access to land depended to a large degree on relations of dependency. In addition, freedmen's achievements were constantly under threat. In the areas where sugar production was modernized, as in rural Santo Amaro, the landowners pushed to end the divided workweek. All through the first decades of the twentieth century, the mill owners complained about the work habits of rural laborers and pressed for legal measures that would oblige those laborers to work a full week in the cane fields. All through this long period, the ex-slaves and their descendants were locked in a bloody battle to defend the divided week from those who wanted to turn them into wage laborers.

Similarly, beginning in the 1890s, changes to land use in the Recôncavo constantly threatened the farm plots. Among them were the expansion of the cane fields belonging to the new industrial central sugar mills and planter decisions to convert plantation farmland to pastureland for cattle. These latter changes came about because ex–plantation owners began to invest in cattle rather than sugar, which implied turning the spaces previously devoted to the farm plots into pasture. For the descendants of slaves in the countryside, that meant fewer options for surviving.

As will become clear in the next chapter, the freedmen anticipated that the end of slavery would transform their lives. They expected to be able to improve the conditions under which they and their families labored, whether for someone else or for their own subsistence. And they hoped that freedom would bring a change in the way they and their families were treated.

SEVEN

TRAJECTORIES OF SLAVES AND FREED PEOPLE
ON RECÔNCAVO SUGAR PLANTATIONS

Some descendants of Bahian sugar-plantation owners remembered the ex-slaves who remained on their properties many years after abolition. In his memoirs, historian Pedro Calmon recalled that his grandfather asked his niece to support "old Lisardo," a preto from Mataripe, for the rest of his life. "He was one of the plantation slaves, uncouth but respectable" wrote Calmon. He had saved the baron from a revolt organized by free workers known as *colonos* on his Canavieiras Plantation, presumably after abolition.[1] Lisardo's situation seems like that of many elderly slaves when slavery ended. They had no choice but to live under the "protection" of their former owners.

Another grandson of sugar planters, Isaías Alves, visited several planta-tions that still employed workers who had once been enslaved during a "sen-timental journey" that he made to the rural districts of Santo Antônio and Nazaré, around the turn of the century. On the Outeiro Plantation, formerly belonging to his grandfather, Alves spoke with an ex-slave named Benvinda who still remembered the difficult times of "her enslavement," including the day she arrived at the plantation. She recalled: "I was in a wicker basket hang-ing on the side of a mule, and so was Belisário; Graciléia walked in the middle of the gang that was yoked together. When I arrived, I started to cry, and old Sampaio sent the girls to take me out for some fun to make me feel better.[2]

Memoirs like those written by Calmon and Alves emphasize the old mas-ters' good qualities, especially generosity to their ex-slaves, or attest to the supposedly benign nature of the patriarchal relations that reigned in the Recôncavo's sugar districts. Taken together, these documents offer impor-tant insights into the complexities of and the variations in the relationships that developed after abolition. They suggest that some ex-slaves continued to reside in the locales in which they had been born or in which they had served as slaves.[3] They also show that many ex-slaves continued to be connected to the sugar industry. They may have left the properties in which they lived as captives, but they had found employment on other plantations.

This chapter examines the experiences of the freedmen who remained connected to the cane industry, many of whom continued to live on the properties where they were born or on which they had served as slaves.[4] It looks at how and to what degree such ex-slaves tried to modify relationships with their former owners. And it shows how the meanings of freedom for ex-slaves changed the patterns of their social relationships, particularly those with former owners. The decision to remain on the plantations was a strate-gic choice for survival in the post-abolition period, rather than an inability to adapt to freedom.[5] In their day-to-day interactions with ex-owners and their representatives, ex-slaves tried to set limits and to make clear the differences between their past in slavery and their present in freedom.[6]

Abolishing Slavery in Daily Life

The records of the Hospital da Santa Casa de Santo Amaro (the Santo Amaro Charity Hospital) between 1906 and 1913 reveal that most of the hospital's pa-tients lived and worked on properties on which they had been born. Among the 232 patients described as blacks (pretos and crioulos) and mestiços (par-dos, cabras, and morenos) were many ex-slaves or the descendants of slaves still living on the plantations. Of that total, 189 (80.6 percent) lived on the estates on which they had been born. The 43 others lived on other agricultural properties or in one of the Recôncavo's towns and villages. The data makes clear that ex-slaves and their descendants tended to remain on the estates where they had been born, although there was significant mobility among the population resident on the plantations.[7]

Comparing the Santa Casa Hospital records with pre-abolition slave lists reveals details about the enslaved past of several patients. On August 23, 1910, ex-slave José Eduardo de Jesus was hospitalized with anthrax. Described in the documents as a sixty-eight-year-old preto, child of unwed parents, José Eduardo worked as a carter on the Pouco Ponto Plantation where he had been a slave until 1887.[8] On July 7, 1913, fifty-year-old Simão so-and-so (de tal), also described as a single preto child of unmarried parents, was a morador on the São Miguel Plantation where he supported himself from farming his roça. The 1871 list of the slaves from that plantation, at the time belonging to the Baron of Pirajá, includes an entry for a sixteen-year-old crioulo agricultural slave named Simão. Simão probably obtained his freedom prior to May 13, 1888, because his name is not on a list of that plantation's slaves in 1887.[9]

Hospital records contain a great deal of information about patients' professions. According to the documents, 42.8 percent of the people who remained on the plantations described themselves as "living from farming" while another 31.6 percent indicated that they were roceiros, or small farmers. Domestics made up the third-most-numerous group, with twenty-four women, or 12.8 percent of those hospitalized. The rest of the group was composed of skilled and semiskilled artisans and professionals connected to the process of sugar making: carters (7); stonemasons (4); joiners (2); blacksmiths (2); carpenters (2); a shoemaker (1), and a wagon driver (1). Among these skilled workers were a machinist and a turbine tender, whose work reflected the modernization of the plantations and the sugar industry. Four day laborers, two valets, two servants, and a fisherman also required medical attention.[10]

The civil birth registers of the parishes of Rio Fundo and Santana de Lustosa, two sugar-producing districts of the important Recôncavo sugar county of Santo Amaro, also indicate that between 1889 and 1892 most plantation laborers still lived where they had been born. I was able to identify the birthplace of eighty-nine of the parents of the seventy-three children born in the Rio Fundo Parish in Santo Amaro between 1889 and 1890. I was also able to identify the origins of fifty-six people mentioned in the records of the fifty-four Santana do Lustosa children whose births were registered between 1889 and 1892. Of them, 67.3 percent of the fathers and mothers of Rio Fundo

FIGURE 7.1. Vitória Plantation, in Cachoeira, 1930.
Arthur Wischral / Public Archive of the State of Bahia.

FIGURE 7.2. Black workers in the cane, 1930.
Arthur Wischral / Public Archive of the State of Bahia.

children had been born in the village of Rio Fundo or on the plantations on which they worked. The other 32.7 percent came from nearby parishes. On the other hand, in Santana do Lustosa, 85.7 percent had been born in the parish and only 14.3 percent had been born elsewhere.[11] The larger percentage of migrants in Rio Fundo may reflect the construction of a modern, industrial sugar mill there, but the data is not conclusive on the permanence or mobility of plantation workers. The evidence about Rio Fundo and Lustosa makes clear, however, that the plantations continued to operate on the basis of a local labor force, a good part of which had come out of slavery.

Research on the Europa Plantation in Santana de Lustosa, belonging to the Costa Pinto family, indicates that between 1889 and 1900, thirty-one children were born to families living on the plantation. Most of the fifty-one parents and grandparents of those children had also been born in Santana de Lustosa. Nineteen of those adults carried the Costa Pinto surname, a clear sign of an enslaved past. An African woman named Lucara da Costa Pinto, a man named Romão da Costa Pinto, and their children—Margarida, Maria Romana, Micaela, and Helena da Costa Pinto—all still lived on the property. During these years, Lucara and Romão's four children appeared at the notary's office to register their children. This detailed data allowed us to locate one of Lucara's grandchildren, a man named Francisco Ambrósio, born on the Europa Plantation in 1906 to Lucara's daughter, Helena da Costa Pinto, and Ambrósio de Jesus. Mr. Ambrósio still lived in the village of Lustosa and was one of the informants for this project. He recalled that as a child on the plantation he met his Nagô grandmother, who spoke a "strange language," and he remembered his uncles and aunts, all of whom had once been slaves and worked in the cane fields.[12]

Many factors encouraged freed people to remain on the plantations where they been enslaved. In the years immediately after abolition, neither the weather nor social and economic conditions favored those who wished to leave the area. Drought devastated Bahia in the second half of 1889 and all of 1890. In addition, after slavery ended, discrimination against ex-slaves, as well as police repression of individuals who had once been slaves, increased. All freed people faced a generalized suspicion that they were potential criminals. An ex-slave far from his place of birth could easily be viewed as a dangerous outsider and imprisoned as a "suspicious person," a drifter or a vagrant. On New Year's Day 1889, a Cachoeira newspaper report about the theft of horses said, "When animals disappear they say: look to the gypsies and the freedmen."[13] Together with unemployment, the shortage of foodstuffs, and the drought, discrimination may have discouraged migration out of the Recôncavo to other parts of the province.

The desire to end dependency on former masters did not necessarily lead ex-slaves to migrate to other places. For many, remaining on the plantations where they had been enslaved may have been tied to expectations of sustaining and expanding alternative spaces for survival on those same plantations or in the areas in which they had been born to slavery. Moving could mean starting over, a difficult process for those who had managed to accumulate a few goods and "rights" during a long life in slavery. Ownership of an animal or the usufruct of some piece of land on which to grow subsistence crops made a huge difference in the lives of the families coming out of plantation slavery. For ex-slaves, remaining on the property of their former owner meant the possibility of access to the material and symbolic resources that they acquired while enslaved. Maintaining access to such resources, which guaranteed the ex-slaves survival after abolition, might have fed their hopes of opening up other alternatives both on and off the plantations where they lived. Such considerations were important factors in decisions to stay. Choosing to remain on the plantations where they had been enslaved followed a logic different from the one that their former owners anticipated.

The Recôncavo sugar plantations were the locus of black communities with deep roots. The community and family ties forged during slavery were fundamental to the survival of the freed black population and an important factor in ex-slaves' decisions about where to live. The protection provided by family, fellow workers, and neighbors helped in the struggle for survival. Each community had accumulated historical experience in dealing with the plantation owners and with other sectors of the free population in the locale.[14]

These considerations are important for understanding the choices that the freedmen made within the context of the possibilities available to them after slavery. For slaves who had acquired the "right" to own roças, abolition must have promised the strengthening of such rights. We cannot forget that defending customary access to the manioc fields brought the ex-slaves of the Maracangalha Plantation to resist the ex-master's decision to remove them from the property after abolition. On that occasion, the freedmen also defended their free access to the local markets and the right to determine the price that they would charge for the manioc flour produced on their roças. For this reason, we cannot disconnect freed people's efforts to remain on the plantations from their expectations about their new condition as free people and, in particular, their redefinition of the strategies employed to expand their own spaces.

Yet remaining on the plantations was not only connected to the material requirements of survival; religious practice also helps to explain why many men and women remained in the places where they had spent a good part of their lives in slavery. The world of the plantations not only retained memories of the difficulties of slavery; it was also testimony to insistent efforts to conquer space in which to honor African gods and saints. In São Félix, for example, the son of African parents and Candomblé priest (*babalorixá*) Anacleto Urbano da Natividade received the right to organize "discreet" celebrations of the rituals dedicated to Obaluaiê from the Tosta family, owners of the Nossa Senhora da Natividade Plantation. Obaluaiê, also known as Omolu, was "the Gege-Nagô god of sickness and disease who often bestowed upon his initiates the ability to heal."[15] During the smallpox epidemic of 1888–1889, Anacleto prescribed herbal remedies to the ill residents of São Félix and neighboring Cachoeira who sought his aid. According to oral tradition, the curer even treated members of the plantation owner's family. After the epidemic was over, he received permission to construct a Candomblé temple (*terreiro*) on plantation lands. Research shows that his religious leadership grew stronger after abolition, when his temple attracted devotees from other area plantations.[16]

Remaining on the old plantations required that the individuals coming out of slavery confront issues about working conditions and the labor discipline common during slavery. One of the greatest challenges for ex-slaves who stayed on the plantations may have been the struggle against forms of power characteristic of slavery. Here it is important to explore the strategies that ex-slaves followed, the ways in which they mobilized resources and created situations designed to reduce the likelihood that ex-masters could rely on forms of domination that had been common under slavery.[17]

As discussed in the previous chapter, some ex-masters tried to negotiate the conditions under which the former slaves would remain on the plantations. In trying to create dependent workers, ex-masters strove to maintain some control over the workforce that had emerged from slavery. It was no accident that the ex-masters continued to cultivate an image as the "protectors" of their former captives and their descendants. That is why some of the symbols of seignorial power and authority survived the end of slavery. Among them was a language of slavery: ex-masters continued to refer to the resident workers and informal tenants on their properties as "my people" or "my moradores," as though these people still belonged to them.

The correspondence between plantation owner Araújo Pinho and his administrator shows the degree to which the sugar planters remained important figures in the Recôncavo at the beginning of the twentieth century. The letters allow us to see that Araújo Pinho still enjoyed a great deal of power over "his" resident workers. The administrator kept him informed about the workers' behavior and always called upon the owner to mediate any conflicts he had with the ex-slaves. In addition, the planter was asked to resolve differences among neighbors, intercede on behalf of his moradores in conflicts outside the property, obtain the release of workers who had committed crimes, resolve judicial disputes, take care of the ill, bury indigents, and do various other things. He was the person who lent local farmers the money to plant and cut cane.

For reasons such as these, during the period that we are studying, many ex-planters continued to play prominent roles in the daily lives of the ex-slaves and their descendants. On June 26, 1892, when ex-slaves Valério and Etelvina Dutra were married in the Cruz Plantation chapel, the priest noted that the ceremony took place "in the presence" of the ex-owners Luís Rodrigues and his wife, Amélia Rodrigues Pereira Dutra. On June 30, 1894, "dona" Amélia sent a representative to the wedding of ex-slaves Afonso Dutra and Emília Avelina in the parish church at Iguape. It may be that the decision to adopt the surnames of their former owners represented a strategy on the part of the freedmen to remain close to the Dutras, in an effort to maintain and amplify "rights."[18] Throughout the three centuries of Brazilian slavery, the freedmen gained experience in the best ways to interact with seignorial power and to take advantage of seignorial paternalism.

Therefore, remaining on the plantations did not mean that the ex-slaves were indifferent to or ignorant of the implications of freedom in their lives. Indeed, May 13 was celebrated on Bahian sugar plantations many years after abolition, in a clear indication of the importance of emancipation to Recôncavo sugar workers. One former resident of the Cruz Plantation later revealed that no one ever went to work on that day. The plantation moradores, many of whom were ex-slaves or their descendants, got together in the plantation's Candomblé temple to sing, dance, play capoeira, and to commemorate what they called "the day of liberty." On May 12, 1912, on the eve of the anniversary of the passage of the Golden Law, sugar planter Pinho Júnior took refuge on his Benfica Plantation, perhaps to avoid the noisy celebrations that would take over the streets of the town of Santo Amaro, where he normally lived, the following day. But he could not even escape the revelry on his own plantation. And there, he had to contribute Rs.4$000 "for the day's celebrations."[19]

Every day, the freedmen made it a point to distance themselves from the slavery that they had left behind. In the early 1930s, ex-slave Argeu warded off painful memories of slavery, especially those involving punishment and control over his life, by shouting, "to hell with you, you devil!" as though the expression would prohibit the return of slavery to his life.[20]

Freedmen may have sought the "protection" of a powerful ex-master to survive in a world dominated by whites. The dependent relationship with the ex-master was the price to be paid for continued access to the bit of land required to survive and support a family. But "protection" was a field of negotiation and conflict between ex-slaves and former masters. The ex-slave might consent to becoming one of the ex-owner's "protected" people as long as the protector accepted certain responsibilities and acknowledged that the worker was free. In the post-emancipation period, ex-slaves insisted upon freedom from unpaid or excessive labor and physical punishment in their day-to-day work lives.

Some ex-slaves accepted ex-owners' "protection" as long as doing so guaranteed spaces for survival both on and off the plantations, as well as the ability to expand those spaces. When ex-slaves found themselves in difficult situations, or in conflict, with other powerful and abusive individuals, they could call upon the paternalism of the former masters for assistance. On May 6, 1903, Higino Froes, ex-slave and resident on the Catacumba Plantation in Santo Amaro, turned to his "old ex-master and protector," Colonel Américo Froes, when armed men threatened his son and stole cattle that he was raising in his ex-master's pastures. Inheritance questions unleashed the events in question, but all the witnesses said that the oxen were Higino's. One of those witnesses was Pacífico Pires, a man who had been born on the Passagem Plantation, and was now a "rural worker" living on Catacumba. The evidence suggests that he was an ex-slave.[21]

To some extent, the freedmen's affirmation of freedom implied the destruction of seignorial authority or, at least, a different basis for exercising it. In a novel by Xavier Marques, published twelve years after abolition, a former plantation slave exclaimed, triumphantly, "There are no more masters. These are different times. Today everybody is one. Everybody is as good as everybody else."[22] In reality, the question was more complicated, since racism infused daily life. Reflecting on the decline of the Bahian sugar industry, German traveler Maurício Lamberg blamed owners, who were unable to adapt to the idea that their workers were no longer slaves, but free men with the right to be paid for their labor, to claim their new condition, and above all, "to be treated with dignity."[23]

To avoid interference from ex-masters, many freedmen tried to distance themselves physically from the plantation headquarters. On some plantations, the ex-slaves deliberately moved as far away from the master's house as they could while still remaining on the property, as a way of limiting their former owners' interference in their lives. In his memoirs, Gastão Sampaio recalled a black community on the Paus Altos Fazenda in Umburanas in the 1920s called "Blacks of São Joaquim," occupying a hill by the same name. "Many of the plantation tenants lived there, including a group of Blacks who built shacks there, had their fields there, and supported themselves there, away from everyone." According to Sampaio, they appeared at the plantation head-quarters on the days that they were required to pay rent and one or two others days when their labor was required. "I don't know if it was by coincidence, but the few that I met were very quiet, short and strong. They were quite isolated—real country hicks. They left home only to go to the churchyard on holy days and at the end of the year." According to Sampaio, they performed the services required of them, but otherwise avoided the plantation head-quarters. Such communities could be found on other Recôncavo plantations as well. According to one elderly informant, at the beginning of the twentieth century, there was a place called Baixa Grande on the Cruz Plantation where several black families lived in almost complete isolation. According to him, the plantation owners had a great deal of difficulty in getting them to work on the plantation.[24]

In refusing to accept the old work discipline, in affirming their freedom to seek out better wages elsewhere, and, most important, in rejecting physical punishment, the ex-slaves were seeking to expand the options for survival available to them. Truthfully, these questions marked the field on which the ex-slaves who remained on the sugar plantations would struggle with the for-mer masters. The criminal cases that we will analyze below carry the marks of these tensions and conflicts.

To begin, ex-slaves frequently had to insist that they were free people and to fight against the presumption that they could still be treated like slaves. On June 15, 1891, Maurício José de Santana, a man who described himself as "des-titute," appeared at the police station in São Gonçalo Parish to accuse An-tônio Ferreira Portela Júnior, owner of the Buranhém Plantation, of having physically attacked him. Given Maurício's condition, he was probably an ex-slave. A medical examination revealed that Maurício was a fifty-five-year-old crioulo, who used crutches because one of his legs had been amputated. The experts verified that he exhibited bruising on his throat and on his face, consistent with the charges that he had made. Maurício told them that as he was passing in front of the Buranhém Plantation gate, he exchanged words with Portela, the owner, about some timber that had been taken from the

FIGURE 7.3. Ex-slave and daughter of the ex-master, at Rumo Fazenda. Feira de Santana, 1930. Private collection of Lígia Sampaio.

Itatinguí Plantation, where he lived and where he was responsible for guarding the forests. Right away, Portela went at Maurício, dragging him down off his horse, taking his crutches, and beginning to beat him. When the owner started to threaten to put Maurício in the stocks, some of the Buranhém Plantation workers intervened and broke up the fight.[25] Maurício's complaint and the Buranhém workers' refusal to obey the owner and put a free man in the stocks indicate that the recently freed population did not approve of physical punishment.

Conflict frequently broke out when former owners or their relatives tried to control the behavior of their former captives, especially if discipline was involved. In the village of Muritiba, Jerônimo Vieira Tosta, brother of planter Joaquim Vieira Tosta, ran into trouble when he admonished his brother's ex-slave, Pedro, for "behaving very poorly." Tosta did not stop at a reprimand, however, but also punished Pedro physically, creating a "fuss" or "misunderstanding" that several tenants in the area said that they had seen. Pedro considered this treatment inappropriate to his new condition as a free man and decided to take revenge. Perhaps Jerônimo Tosta hadn't been thinking about the changing times and was not expecting any reaction, so he behaved in a way that he considered normal, because Pedro had been a "servant in the home of the defendant's brother" since he was a child.

Nevertheless, on March 1, 1892, between eleven o'clock in the morning and noon, on the Ilha Fazenda, Pedro beat his ex-owner's brother with a piece of wood and hit him several times with the flat side of a machete, a practice normally reserved for disciplining children. One witness testified that shortly after the incident Pedro arrived home with a wild expression on his face saying that he had "given Yoyô Jerônimo a few whacks and the guy had run off." Augusta Francisca do Amor Divino, a twenty-five-year-old, single lavradora, remembered that she was in the home of Jerônimo's brother Joaquim Vieira Tosta making manioc flour when "Pedro, an ex-slave of Mr. Joaquim" arrived, grabbed his hat from the potter's wheel, and "as he hurriedly disappeared inside the house" said, "Now I'm getting my revenge." At his trial, the ex-slave evoked faithfulness and deference to his former owner, as well as an understanding of the way the members of the jury thought, by signing his name as Pedro Vieira Tosta. He was trying to convince the jury that the persecution by his former master's brother is what motivated him rather than antagonism toward the entire family.[26]

The village of Muritiba was also the stage for other similar conflicts. On February 22, 1896, Roque, an ex-slave of José Vicente de Almeida, was arrested in the village at about eleven at night because Marcelino José de Almeida, a relative of his ex-master, did not like the "look" that the ex-slave gave him. Roque was described as a man of about forty years of age, the son of Maria, deceased, who had also been "the ex-slave of José Vicente." Marcelino stated that Roque had long-standing "troubles" with his father, and therefore, he and his brother had decided to pick him up, because they were afraid of being attacked by the "tough" and the "criminal." When he heard that the two boys were planning to arrest him, Roque took out his guns and fired at both of them, wounding them. Manoel Pedro Cavalcante, who testified in the criminal case against Roque, had no problem in labeling the prisoner "preto," the socioracial term for black that was used during slavery to identify slaves, when he stated that he saw Roque leaning against a wall, armed with a machete.[27]

Many conflicts took place because ex-masters interfered in the lives of freedmen or the members of their families. On March 19, 1893, Francisco de Assis Queirós, from São Sebastião do Passé Parish, who made a living with his "manioc fields," complained that planter Manoel Maria de Bitencourt had whipped him and then placed him in the stocks. Bitencourt became upset when he learned that his tenant had taken some posts to build a fence around his manioc field without permission. Francisco de Assis said that, once imprisoned in the stocks, Bitencourt threatened to hit him with the palmatória, a tool designed to allow masters to strike slaves on the hands, and that the only reason the planter did not carry through on his threat was that his wife appealed to him on the ex-slave's behalf. The worker accused the planter of using violence to keep his family in "subjugation."[28]

Ex-slaves defined freedom according to the forms of treatment that they experienced prior to the Law of May 13. In 1933, the ex-slave Argeu said that shortly after abolition he left the plantation on which he had served and justified his decision by saying, "I drive the cane carts when I want, nobody hits me, you joke with me, Iaiá gives me money for tobacco, the captain jokes with me too. I just don't work in the rain."[29] Being "well treated," defined as not being punished and setting their own work rhythms, seems to have been the ex-slaves' basic requirement for freedom.

In his memoirs, Brazilian novelist José Lins do Rego recounted many stories about his childhood on a northeastern Brazilian sugar plantation. Although the plantation was in Paraiba rather than Bahia, Lins do Rego's stories document the efforts of ex-slaves and their descendants to resist treatment they associated with slavery. One story recounted the disappearance of a key to the dispensary, where food and other supplies were kept. A black domestic servant named Pia was blamed for the theft, and offended by the unjust accusation, she attempted to commit suicide. Before she could carry out her plans, however, she was discovered. Old Albuquerque hit her twice with the palmatória that he had used "during slavery times." Several days later, Pia disappeared from the plantation and no one ever heard from her again.[30] Many ex-slaves who were physically punished would simply leave.

The ex-masters learned that the ex-slaves might leave if they felt abused as free people. Ex-masters who insulted or maltreated ex-slaves came to know that they ran the risk of losing their workers, especially if they were skilled. One of the characters in José Lins do Rego's novel *Menino de engenho* (Plantation boy) made sure that his employer knew that he would leave if he was unhappy. In the novel, the character Cândido was the sugar master at the Corredor Plantation. He had "come out of slavery" and threatened to leave the property whenever he became upset at the way that he was treated. According to the narrator, "He did not flinch like the others did when my grandfather yelled. I would hear him shouting: 'I'm leaving for Dr. Lourenço's Gameleira Plantation!'"[31] The freed people also referred to slavery to limit the ways their labor could be exploited. Lins do Rego recalled old Generosa, an ex-slave who worked in the plantation house kitchen, who reprimanded anyone who imposed upon her, even the "living room people" with the phrase "Slavery's over."[32]

Ex-slaves did not always adopt strategies that brought them closer to their former masters. Some of them stayed on the plantation land, but well away from the plantation headquarters, and sought to avoid labor in the cane by finding alternatives. In 1917, Professor Pedro Celestino da Silva observed that most of the people from the old sugar parish of Iguape lived on the shores of the Bay of All Saints and made their living fishing and gathering shellfish in the bay's mangrove swamps. Their rejection of routine work discipline offended the Bahian scholar's notions of "economic progress." "It is obvious that life is so easy for the less fortunate classes, who are the most numerous members of the population, that around here, they only worry about getting food when their stomachs are empty." Later, he concluded: "Shortsightedness drains their ambition to work and allows a nauseating indolence to prevail, so prejudicial to the people who live near our rivers."[33] The professor's economic rationalism did not take into account that, for the Iguape fishermen, many of whom were ex-slaves and their descendants, the "demands of their stomachs" should be supplied by work that they themselves controlled. The following section takes up these questions again, exploring the options for survival, the attitudes, and the goals of the ex-slaves who continued to live on one particular Recôncavo plantation after slavery ended.

The news about abolition thrilled the slaves at the Cruz Plantation in Iguape, and they all stopped working for three days as soon as they heard it. According to oral tradition, over the course of the next few days, some people left the property and migrated to Cachoeira or to Salvador. Inácio Rodrigues Pereira Dutra (1802–1888), the Baron of Iguape, watched in horror as slavery disintegrated on his plantation. He could not accept that "disorder" and "disobedience" had taken over his domain. In an unexpected response, he brought all of his children and grandchildren together, ordered them to pack for a long absence, and set sail with them for Salvador. There, the baron took refuge in his large mansion on the Largo de Roma, where the family normally lived between harvests. But to his dismay, the mansion sat right on the road to the Bonfim Church, the patron saint of which was the subject of widespread devotion among Salvador's poor black population. From his balcony, he could see the enormous processions of poor people, including ex-slaves that wound their way to Bonfim Church to give thanks for the abolition of slavery. The baron found such expressions of popular joy intolerable and, irritated, brought everyone back to the plantation. He may have considered what he saw in Salvador even more terrifying than what was happening on his plantation. They say that the baron suffered a tremendous emotional shock at witnessing those events and died only a few months later. According to one of the tenants on the Cruz Plantation, the baron "died of rage" over what he had seen in the days after abolition.[34]

It is true that the Baron of Iguape died in September 1888, a few months after abolition, but we don't know to what degree the emotional impact of the end of slavery contributed to his death. Such stories about the death and suicide of ex–slave owners after abolition are common in the oral history of the Recôncavo. In some ways, they attest to the psychological impact of the Law of May 13 on the people who depended on enslaved labor.

The baron's death required the inventory and division of his property among his successors.[35] Inventory of the baron's property began the month after his death, under the direction of his son-in-law, Luís Rodrigues Dutra. The description of the property makes clear that we are discussing a very large estate: the baron owned 3,516 tarefas of land, 531 of which were for planting, while the others were pastures and forests. In his pastures grazed 360 head of oxen, 164 of which were employed on the plantation. On the other hand, the plantation house was not as ostentatious as most homes owned by the Recôncavo's great sugar planters. It was a two-story stone building with an arched roof, boasting three windows along the front and a terrace. The baron's family lived on the upper floor, which included a "parlor along the front," a dining room, a number of bedrooms, and a kitchen in back. Estate outbuildings included an infirmary, a residence for the manager, an aqueduct [to bring water] to the sugar mill's grinding wheel, a shed for holding bagasse (the detritus left by the cane grinding process), a stable, a blacksmith's shop, and sixty-three tile-covered senzalas (slave quarters), which, according to the executor of the estate were in a "state of ruin."[36] It doesn't appear in the inventory, but other sources indicate that the Cruz Plantation had a small chapel attached to the main house, where local priests said Mass, performed marriages, and baptized children who were born on the estate. A short way away from the sugar mill sat the plantation's Santo Antônio cemetery, the final resting place of slaves and free workers alike.

When Lúis Rodrigues Dutra was named executor of his father-in-law's estate, he also took over management of the plantation while the inventory and property divisions were carried out. As executor, he was required to keep a record of all estate income and expenses, until the property was divided among the baron's successors, which he did. Before the estate could be divided, all debts outstanding at the baron's death had to be paid. His careful notes about all of the property's income and expenses, including the costs of paying the workers, allow us to follow the day-to-day life of the plantation during his management, to know what life was like for the ex-slaves, and to see the kinds of relationships they developed with their ex-owners, six months after abolition.

The information contained in the postmortem inventory allows us to evaluate the impact that the loss of enslaved labor provoked in the plantation's management. During the first harvest after abolition, the plantation only produced 23.5 tons of sugar and thirteen barrels of molasses. Barickman calculated that this production probably represented "less than 10% of the 240 tons the Engenho [plantation] da Cruz had, in all likelihood, produced in a good year in the mid-1850s" and that the income produced would have been insufficient to cover the costs of the labor required to make it.[37] Aside from this, the harvest did not allow Rodrigues Dutra to meet the obligations of his father-in-law's contract with the Bahia Central Factories Limited, the British firm that owned the Iguape Central Sugar Mill, the industrial sugar mill that sat less than four miles from the plantation. The baron had agreed to furnish fifteen hundred tons of sugarcane to the central mill each year, but the disastrous harvest of 1888–1889 produced only 417 tons of sugar, less than one-third the amount contracted.[38]

Crossing data from the inventory with the baptismal register, as well as the civil registers of birth, deaths, and marriages, and the testimony of an elderly resident, made it possible to explore other aspects of the transformation that was taking place. The estate payroll records contained in the inventory do not label the plantation workers as ex-slaves, but the way workers were listed suggests that they were. During slavery, owners normally listed only slaves' first names in any record, and that was how the executor of the baron's estate entered the workers' names into the payroll record. The Iguape Parish registers confirm the supposition that many of the plantation workers had in fact been slaves of the deceased Baron of Iguape and indicate that most of them had been born on the Cruz Plantation.

The plantation clearly continued to operate with labor that had come out of slavery. Yet relationships had changed substantially since abolition. Most of the ex-slaves remained on the property, but in order to keep them working, Rodrigues Dutra had to pay them for each task that they performed. Actually, according to the local oral tradition, when the Baron of Iguape asked the captain of his schooner, a recently freed man, to take him to Salvador shortly after abolition, the ex-slave demanded to be paid for the service. Stunned, the baron retreated to the plantation house in wounded pride, where he died a few short months later.[39]

September was a month of intense activity on the Cruz Plantation. During that month, the property employed around 45 laborers, among which were only 14 women—4 of whom cut cane, 5 of whom worked grinding cane, and 5 of whom were "house people," in other words, domestic servants. The rest were men. In 1853, 127 slaves had worked on the property, among whom were 45 women. Clearly the second half of the nineteenth century had seen a significant reduction in the workforce, and particularly in the number of female laborers on the plantation. The size of the labor force may have dropped drastically with abolition, reflecting in part efforts by freed families to remove women from the cane fields.[40]

At Cruz that year, turning sugarcane into sugar involved seventeen skilled and semiskilled laborers. Among the skilled workers were the sugar master, the "overseer of cane grinding," the "kettleman," the fire tender, the clarifier, and the teache man, whose higher wages reflected their importance.[41] The kettleman, an African named Júlio, received Rs.3$600 for six days of work. For that amount of money, the highest paid domestic servant in the plantation house would have had to work for two weeks. The sugar master who supervised the sugar-making process earned even more than Júlio—Rs.4$200 for five days of work. A number of less-valued workers also labored in making sugar, including "cane suppliers" and "removers of baqasse," The five women (Eduvigem, Helena, Maria do Rosário, Esmerelda, and Adelaide) carried out these services. In October, other names were added to the list, including Antônia, Joana, Rosalina, and Maria dos Reis.[42]

During the second week of September, with the exception of Idelfonso and Roberto, most of the workers involved in making sugar worked six days a week. Altogether, however, they worked only ninety-six hours that week. In October, they worked even fewer hours each week. During the last week of October, the group was short a worker and only Valério, who oversaw the cane grinding, came to work all six days. The rest of the group worked four or five days, for a total of seventy hours, twenty fewer than in the second week of September. The carters followed the same trend. During the first week of October, with the exception of Justino and Firmo, everyone provided the plantation with six days of labor driving the carts that transported the cane. At the end of that same month, the workers only turned up for five days. It is possible that the crisis—especially the absence of credit and the decline of sugar prices—had reduced the activity on the plantation. On the other hand, perhaps Cruz Plantation was experiencing the same changes that were taking place on other Recôncavo properties where ex-slaves were systematically reducing the time that they dedicated to working on the plantation in order to dedicate more time to their own crops, or they were picking up jobs on plantations that offered better wages.

That same September, seventeen workers cut cane at Cruz Plantation. Among them were four women, Justina, Antônia, Leonarda, and Marcelina, who also peeled the leaves off the cut cane stalks. These workers earned according to the quantity of cane that they cut or cleaned, receiving 160 réis for each cart they filled with cane and 200 réis for each cart of cane that they cleaned of leaves. Among the cane cutters were two men, Idelfonso and Roberto, who were also involved in sugar making. They cut much less cane than the other men—only nine and six carts respectively rather than fifteen. They may have been putting in extra hours by cutting cane, and that may be why they cut so much less than the other workers that week. Perhaps they were cutting cane to supplement their earnings in the sugar mill.

The carters constituted another important group of agricultural workers. They transported the cut cane from the field to the mill, supplied firewood to the sugar mill and to the ovens in the manor house and, eventually, hauled the sugar to the city and returned with supplies. According to the payroll, the plantation employed nine drivers who received weekly wages, at 640 réis per day. In September, with the exception of Justino, all of the drivers worked six days a week. They were assisted by the "cart boys"—the boys who guided the oxen along the roads. The boy's positions as apprentices are clear, in that they appear in the registry as "Venceslau's boy," "Jacinto's boy," and so on. Their wages were also a bit lower, 500 réis each day.

"House people" constituted another important group of workers. These were the domestic servants and other "trusted" workers who served in the manor house, on its grounds, or in its pastures, stables, or barns. These numbered, all together, sixteen people, of whom five were women. Among the men were the cowhand Militão, Quintino "from the stable," the shepherd, the clerk, the gardener, and Dativo, the overseer. The shepherd, the gardener, and the stable hand worked only a few days. The others, however, worked the entire month and were paid monthly salaries. Those receiving the highest wages—Rs.15$000 per month—and were all men, including Militão the cowhand, Dativo the overseer, and the sugar crater. Among the women, certainly the people responsible for domestic service—Virginia, Leopoldina, and Etelvina—earned the most, receiving Rs.6$000 per month.

Workers also earned money for special assignments. In preparing the baron's funeral, the executor of the will paid several workers for extra trips to Cachoeira and the river landing at Calembá. On one of those trips, Justino, Cassiano, and Idelfonso brought back the baron's casket, for which they each were paid Rs.1$000.

Life on a plantation was a constant struggle. Caring for the cane fields and making sugar were complicated and time-consuming enough, but beyond that, the machines in the mill, as well as the carts and boats, had to be kept in good repair; the fences, roads, and bridges had to be maintained; the pastures cleaned, the horses, oxen, cattle, and other animals cared for; and the orchard and the kitchen garden tended. An infinite number of other tasks regularly came up. For that reason, some workers moved back and forth from one sector of the plantation to another. For example, Idelfonso spent two days grinding cane during the second week of September, for which he received Rs.1$400 each. That same week he cut nine carts of cane, receiving Rs.1$440, and he went to Cachoeira to pick up the casket in which his ex-master was buried, and as we already saw, in exchange he received Rs.1$000.

Comparing various documentary sources, including birth, baptism, marriage, and death registers, it was possible to determine an enslaved past for at least twenty-eight workers who appeared on the payroll of the Cruz Plantation. The mill workers constituted the largest number of formerly enslaved workers, twelve all together. Two of them, Júlio the kettleman, and Mateus, were Africans and probably among the oldest workers on the plantation at the time. Eduvigem, Helena, Esmeralda, Adelaide, and Adolfo were younger, but all about the same age, having been born between 1861 and 1868. In addition to them, we can identify the teache man Desidério, Idelfonso, Maria do Rosário, Maria dos Reis, and Valério as former slaves. Among the cane cutters who had been slaves and still lived on the plantation were Roberto, Justina, Antônia, and Leonarda. Among the "house people" were ex-slaves Virginia, Leopoldina, Etelvina, Dativo, and Quintino. Among the carters were ex-slaves Jecundo, Félix, Felipe, Justino, Antioco, and Felicíssimo. Ex-slave Policarpo performed odd jobs.

Checking the names of the children born and baptized on the Cruz Plantation between 1860 and 1871 revealed more information about several workers. Eduvigem, the daughter of the unmarried crioula slave Felismina, was born in 1860 and then baptized in the plantation chapel January 6, 1861, when she was two months old. That same day, Anísio, the six-month-old son of the enslaved African woman Felicidade also received the sacrament. On December 25, 1861, two more babies were baptized: five-month-old Adolfo, the son of the crioula slave Lourença and Policarpo, and the ten-month-old son of the parda slave Ursulina. On October 4, 1863, Maximiano, the twelve-month-old son of another enslaved woman, Etelvina, was baptized. She appeared on the 1888 plantation payroll as a domestic worker. On January 7, 1864, the enslaved woman Virginia's two-month-old criollo child Adelaide was baptized. Then on December 28, 1864, two more babies received the sacrament: enslaved woman Maria do Nascimento's five-month-old baby Helena, described as cabra, and the cabra enslaved woman Nascimenta's two-year-old parda daughter Esmeralda. On May 5, 1866, Quintino was baptized as the six-month-old pardo son of Leopoldina, described as an enslaved parda woman. Finally, on January 6, 1868, in the São João da Acutinga chapel, Felicíssimo, the son of Inácio Rodrigues Dutra's slave Justina, was baptized.[43]

The godparents of the children being baptized included a number of men and women listed on the 1888 plantation payroll. Among them were the parda ex-slave Leopoldina, godmother of the infant Adolfo do Natal in 1861. She appears on the 1888 "list of people in the house"; in other words, she was a domestic servant and, as we saw earlier, was the mother of Quintino, who was baptized in May 1866. Virginia, who worked in domestic service in 1888, was the mother of Adelaide, and godmother of the crioulo slave Ismael, baptized in February 1864. Dativo, the overseer in 1888, appears in the baptismal register as the godfather of a criollo named Gregório, the son of Generosa and baptized in January 1868.[44]

From the beginning of the nineteenth century, most baptisms occurred between Christmas and Epiphany, two days on which work seems to have been suspended. On those days, the pastor of the parish church in Iguape baptized in the plantation chapel all of the free and enslaved children who had been born over the course of the year.

The civil death registers instituted after the declaration of the republic in November 1889 reveal other names that appear in the 1888 list of payments. In March 1890, for example, Desidério Dutra, a single agricultural worker, sixty years of age, "whose ancestry was unknown," was buried in the Santo Antônio cemetery at the plantation. An African named Mateus who worked in the Cruz Plantation sugar mill died in June 1891 according to the register, and Júlio, the African kettleman at Cruz, in January 1896.[45]

Most of the ex-slaves identified had been born on the Cruz Plantation; many were also the children of slaves who had belonged to the plantation's owners since the middle of the nineteenth century. Of the twenty-eight ex-slaves whose families we can trace back several decades, only Anísio was the child of a woman brought directly from Africa. The rest were the children of pardas and crioulas, and thus the second or third generation of slaves. A list of slaves made in 1854, when the plantation belonged to Tomé Pereira de Araújo, the Baron of Iguape's father-in-law, includes the names of Policarpo's mother Urusulina; Virginia, a crioula and mother of Adelaide; and Maria do Nascimento, the crioula mother of Helena.[46] Tomé Pereira de Araújo acquired the plantation in 1826, and after his death in 1853, control of the plantation passed to his son-in-law, the Baron of Iguape. The fact that the property remained in a single family for most of the nineteenth century must have favored the formation and consolidation of extended families and solid community ties among the slaves.[47] When abolition took place in 1888, the mothers of Maximiano, Adelaide, Quintino, and Felicíssimo were alive and laboring on their master's property alongside their children. Leopoldina and her son Quintino worked together in domestic service: she was the cook and he was in the stables. One of her daughters, Maria do Rosário, worked in the sugar mill and was the common law wife of Militão the cowhand.

The ex-slaves identified above formed a community with extensive social networks, connecting various individuals and family groups. As elsewhere in Brazil, the ritual of baptism and networks of godparents played fundamental roles in the formation and strengthening of family and community ties. The godparentage system encouraged networks of fictive kinship, many of which dated from the period of enslavement. Ten of the forty-one baptisms between 1856 and 1871 involved enslaved godparents who lived on the plantation. These connections formed under slavery continued to be important to the ex-slaves thereafter.

Some of the ex-slaves mentioned above also appeared in the baptismal register for 1888 to 1902, and it is therefore possible to follow them from slavery to freedom. The surname and the location of the baptism served as guides in identifying the plantations' ex-slaves. On February 22, 1893, seven-month-old Benício was baptized. According to the priest he was the son of Eduvigem Dutra, mentioned above, and the ceremony took place in the Cruz Plantation chapel. The child's godmother was ex-slave Justina Dutra, who appeared on the 1888 payroll.[48] On September 25, 1893, one-year-old Maria, daughter of Gabriel Pereira Dutra and Maria Ferreira Dutra, was baptized. Her godfather was ex-slave Quintino Dutra.[49] A little more than four months previously, in a ceremony in the plantation chapel on May 13, 1893, the parish priest had baptized a newborn baby named Maria de São Pedro, daughter of ex-slave Esmeralda Dutra. Her godparents were ex-slaves Antioco Bernardo Dutra and Maria da Glória Dutra.[50] I doubt that the date was chosen by accident.

Children born between 1857 and 1870 became the nucleus of a community of freed people who lived and worked on the plantation after abolition. They were the parents of the first generation of the descendants of slaves born after abolition. The data demonstrates that many of the Cruz Plantation slaves took the surname of their former owner after abolition. This is not surprising: many ex-slaves did so in other areas with an enslaved past. Taking the surname Dutra may have been a survival strategy in a world in which personal relationships were essential for survival. In some situations, carrying the surname of a powerful family may have made a difference. Alternatively, sharing a surname may have strengthened group ties as well as identity. In that way, the families of ex-slaves who carried the owner's surname were developing a web of fictive kinship relationships on the basis of an enslaved past.[51]

As we saw earlier, from the middle of the nineteenth century on, baptisms usually occurred between Christmas and Epiphany and usually were celebrated in the plantation chapel. After abolition, however, baptisms began to take place throughout the year: as soon as the babies were a few months old, their parents brought them to the baptismal font. At the same time, baptismal ceremonies began to take place in the parish church in Iguape rather than in the plantation chapel. Perhaps the Dutra family was not granting access to the plantation chapel to people who were no longer under their control.

The Iguape civil marriage registries from 1888 to 1902 contain information about some of the ex-slaves. They indicate that Maria dos Reis, who worked as a "cane carrier," married José Fábio Dutra in the Iguape parish church in 1889. He was thirty-five, the son of Generosa, and she was twenty-eight, the daughter of Felismina, and therefore Eduvigem's sister.[52] That same year Fabiano dos Reis Dutra declared to the Iguape notary that he had a son, Cândido, with Maria dos Reis Dutra.[53] The difference in names between the two registrations could have been a mistake, but it could also mean that José Fábio, or Fabiano, was reluctant to openly declare himself a freed person.

The registers also contain information about other ex-slaves. Among them were Gabriel Dutra, son of the enslaved woman Leopoldina Dutra. He was twenty-five years old when he married Maria Leopoldina Gomes, who was twenty. On February 8, 1892, another person on the 1888 list of workers, Jecundo Dutra, married Ricardina Dutra, who was seriously ill. Jecundo was a carter on the plantation in 1888, but when he married Ricardina he was living on the Acutinga Plantation, about three kilometers from where he had been enslaved. Perhaps he moved after abolition.[54] On January 26, 1892, shortly after the São João celebrations, Etelvina and Valério Dutra were married in the plantation chapel. As indicated earlier, they had appeared on the 1888 list—Etelvina as a domestic servant and Valério as the "supervisor of the grinding wheel." Their witnesses were their ex-masters Luís Rodrigues Dutra and his wife Amélia Rodrigues Pereira Dutra, which suggests more than usually close personal ties between these ex-slaves and their ex-owners.[55]

The Iguape civil birth and death registers reveal other details of these ex-slaves' lives. On January 2, 1889, ex-slave Manoel Dutra appeared in the village of Iguape to report that the previous day, at two o'clock in the morning, on the Cruz Plantation, his common law wife, Adelaide Dutra, the daughter of Virginia Dutra, had given birth to a baby boy named Silvestre. On May 9, 1889, the birth of Felipa, the daughter of Valério Dutra and Helena Dutra, was registered. On June 20 of that same year, Silvano Dutra appeared to report that five days previously, his sister Esmeralda Dutra had given birth to a baby boy named Cristiano. She was single and, as already indicated, the daughter of Maria do Nascimento. On September 30, 1890, cowhand Militão da Silva, the common law wife of ex-slave Maria do Rosário, registered the birth of their twin daughters, Maria Felipa and Maria Paula.[56]

The death records provide other glimpses of these ex-slaves' lives. The few words that the clerks recorded could not hide the precarious nature of these lives. On December 28, 1889, Andrelina Bulcão (who sometimes signed herself as Andrelina Dutra), the wife of Máximo Damaceno, appeared at the

Iguape notary's office to report the death of her daughter, Maria das Virgens, from, she said, a case of worms. On May 8, 1890, Bráulia Dutra, the thirty-five-year-old daughter of Leonarda, died in childbirth. Both the deceased and her mother were ex-slaves. On July 20, 1897, the ex-slave Adelaide Dutra also notified the authorities of the death of a daughter, named Francisca, who had died from a dental infection.[57]

It was a difficult time, in which children and grandchildren buried the last of their relatives born in Africa, the last echo of the ties that they had with that continent. On June 5, 1891, freedman Policarpo Dutra declared that at three in the morning, the African Mateus Dutra, sixty-five years of age, and single, had died and been buried in the Santo Antônio cemetery.[58] In 1888, the Africans in question had still been working in the Cruz Plantation sugar mill according to the payroll.

All of this evidence indicates that some of the Cruz Plantation's slaves remained on the property for many years after the abolition of slavery. The same may have been the case on other plantations in the region. But we should not conclude that they stayed out of loyalty to their ex-masters. For some, remaining on the plantation represented the possibility of retaining access to the limited rights and the few bits of property that they had acquired over the course of a lifetime of struggle in slavery. Those who had special skills or better positions must have had better access to land as tenants on the plantations than as freed people without such connections. Oral tradition tells us that the crioulo Máximo became an overseer and everything suggests that he remained on the Cruz Plantation until he died. According to one elderly plantation morador, he was the only one of the workers who had come out of slavery to own an animal for riding. Idelfonso, on the other hand, "lived apart," growing crops on a roça on the plantation's land. "Living apart" was a description of those who managed to live without depending on or working for others, and it is possible that many of those who still lived in Iguape resided outside the control of their ex-owners.

Several conflicts arose when freed people tried to set limits on their relationships with the planters. On June 8, 1893, planter Luís Rodrigues Dutra complained to the police in Iguape that Firmino Bulcão, a morador on the nearby Acutinga Plantation, had insulted him and impugned his "honor." He said that he was in his doorway one day when he saw the accused passing by, with a gun in his belt and carrying a long machete. Luís Rodrigues ordered the man to put the weapons away, because he did not permit people to carry arms on his property. In response, from a distance, the accused began to insult him. A tenant heard the accused state that Luís Rodrigues did not have thc right to disarm him, had nothing to do with him, and threatened to pay the Rs.5$000 required to publish a complaint in the state capital newspapers. A worker in the brick kiln heard Firmino say that "he wasn't one of the poor moleques from the Cruz Plantation."[59]

This episode merits reflection. Given his surname, prior to abolition Firmino must have been a slave of the Bulcão family, owners of the Acutinga Plantation, which bordered the Cruz Plantation. Therefore, Dutra knew that he was talking to an ex-slave and expected to be obeyed. The incident is important, however, because of the way that Firmino defended his right to bear arms. Firmino Bulcão considered the reprimand that he received from the planter to be inappropriate, given his new condition as a free man and, therefore, threatened to complain about the ex-master to the newspapers. That threat reflected the experience of the last years of slavery, when slaves and abolitionists used complaints to the newspapers as a way of challenging the masters who punished or in some way threatened the freedom of their captives. The reference to "poor moleques" was a way of emphasizing the differences between his current condition and those of the people who had been slaves on the Dutra property.

After abolition, the community of ex-slaves on the Cruz Plantation was transformed. A survey of the seventeen plantation workers who appeared in criminal cases between 1889 and 1894 suggests that the composition of the working population on the property had undergone important changes. Of that number, only five appeared on the 1888 payroll list; the others had arrived after abolition. Most of the newcomers originated from areas near Iguape; they may have been ex-slaves. It is also possible that younger ex-slaves were moving around in search of work on the region's plantations and in its cities. As ex-slaves arrived at Cruz from neighboring plantations and Dutra hired migrant workers from the Bahian backlands known as *catingueiros*, social relations on the property changed. This movement intensified tensions and conflicts among the new arrivals and those who were well established.

These tensions could manifest themselves in family dramas. On the morning of April 5, 1889, the ex-slave Isabel Bulcão, together with other women, was washing clothes in a stream on the Cruz Plantation when she was stabbed by her former common law husband Possidônio Bulcão. She was taken to the Santa Casa da Misericórdia Hospital in Cachoeira, where she died four days later from her wounds. In the postmortem, the experts described Isabel as a woman whose color was parda and who appeared to be about twenty-two years of age. Some witnesses overheard Possidônio say that he had killed her because she had left him for a guy named Fortunato. Fortunato's name did not appear in the 1888 list of workers; perhaps he was an ex-slave who had migrated to the plantation after abolition.[60]

This criminal case allows further examination of the lives of this ex-slave couple. Isabel Bulcão had been a slave on the Calembá Plantation, belonging to the daughter of the Baron of Iguape, Maria Rodrigues Pereira Bulcão, after her parents' property was divided because of her mother's death in 1881. Isabel was the daughter of the African woman Claudiana and had a sister named Margarida. She was two months old when she was baptized on January 7, 1864, as the natural daughter of the slave Claudiana, property of, at that time, Lieutenant Colonel Inácio Rodrigues Dutra.[61] In other words, at birth, she belonged to the owners of the Cruz Plantation. Perhaps she returned to the Cruz Plantation after abolition to be close to her relatives there.

Research located no information about Possidônio Bulcão, aside from that in the criminal case: he was born on the Acutinga Plantation in Iguape to Leocádia, now deceased, and, at the time of the murder, was fifty-two years old and worked in agriculture. His surname, perhaps chosen after abolition, declared his past enslavement to the Bulcão family, owners of the Calembá Plantation, where he lived and worked his roça.

Possidônio Bulcão was tried in the Cachoeira courthouse and defended by the abolitionist attorney Antônio José Balieiro.[62] The defense that Balieiro prepared for his client is interesting, because it still carried the mark of the abolitionist debates. When the jury sentenced Possidônio to labor in the galleys in perpetuity, Balieiro declared that its members were moved by an "old hate" and for a "love of slavery, this vulture that should have disappeared from our midst a long time ago." According to the attorney, Possidônio received such a harsh sentence because the members of the jury opposed the law that had liberated him. Despite Balieiro's efforts, the sentence was confirmed by the superior court in 1891. Nevertheless, on May 11, 1892, almost ironically, two days before the fourth anniversary of abolition, ex-slave Possidônio died in prison in the state capital. His death certificate reads only that he was "preta," and that the cause of death had probably been the diabetes from which he had been suffering a long time.

Memories of the Post-Abolition Period

The testimony of an elderly plantation resident worker, Manoel Araújo Ferreira, better known as Manoelzinho, captures other aspects of the lives of the ex-slaves of the Cruz Plantation after abolition. He was born in 1904, in a Bahian backlands village called Tanquinho da Feira, the youngest of three

Ferreira children. When he was three, his father and an uncle moved the entire family to the Recôncavo; according to him, they were "fleeing the drought" and in search of work on the sugarcane plantations. At the time, the drought victims who migrated seasonally to the Recôncavo were called *catingueiros*. After abolition, in the face of what the planters called the "disorganization of agriculture," catingueiro labor was in high demand in the Recôncavo. But for that family, what had started as a short stay, as they waited for the rains to return to the northeastern backlands, turned into permanent residence. On the Cruz Plantation, Manoelzinho did "everything": he worked as a footman in the house; he took care of the china and silver, the kitchen and flower gardens, and served at meals. Later he was promoted to administrator.

His testimony is fundamental, not only because he had access to the family in the manor house, but also because he knew some of the plantation's elderly slaves. When he arrived on the Cruz Plantation in 1907, nineteen years after abolition, he had the opportunity to meet and develop relationships with people who, as he would say, "came from slavery," including several mentioned previously.

The past fascinated Manoelzinho; whenever he could, "discreetly," he talked to the workers who "had come out of slavery." Sometimes, when men came to get their pay or women came to the well for water, he found an opportunity to ask about their enslaved pasts. The pasts they transmitted carried classic images of plantation slavery: the slaves leaving early for the fields carrying a sack of food; labor in the fields from dawn to dusk; the overseer with a whip; plots to "take [a chicken or goat or two] from the master" when they wanted a change in diet. The day-to-day routine was broken only on holy days, especially Epiphany and the Feast of Saint Anthony, when they got together in the plantation yard to dance samba and practice capoeira.

Manoelzinho's memories of slavery differ distinctly from those of the ex-masters. He met Luís Rodrigues Dutra and his wife, "dona" Amélia, the Baron of Iguape's daughter. According to him, the two had the reputation of being "good" masters, but whenever they talked about slavery, they lamented the way that abolition took place and deplored its consequences. Their attitudes indicate that they were traumatized by the loss of control over their enslaved labor force and the memory stayed with them after abolition. Luís Rodrigues Dutra used to say, after abolition, " the masters stopped telling people what to do, and started being told what to do," an obvious exaggeration that translates the ex-master's lack of satisfaction with the social relations that were established after passage of the Law of May 13.

Many ex-slaves still lived on the plantation when Manoelzinho was a child. Among those he recalled were many who appeared on the 1888 payroll list, including the preta Andrelina and her husband, Máximo Damaceno; Cristiano the carter (according to Manoelzinho, the brother of Máximo); Policarpo (brother of Andrelina); Leonarda; Justino (nicknamed Pajoba); Tomás; Rodolfo; Esmeralda; Teodora; Valério the blacksmith; Fábio or Fabiano; Andreza; and Idelfonso. In other words, the documents confirm his testimony, and he was able to add some important information about family groups of ex-slaves who were living on the plantation. He said that Andrelina and Máximo lived in a house of wattle and daub, with a tile roof, near the manor house of their former owners. When he knew them, they were quite old and had three children: Francisco, nicknamed Chico de Máximo; Felipa; and Maria do Carmo.[63] Máximo was the "agricultural overseer" and, according to Manoelzinho, a quiet, "very serious," and elderly preto.

Manoel Ferreira also revealed details that help to define the roles that these ex-slaves played in the community. According to him, Andrelina periodically held a drumming circle or "batucagé"; she may have been a candomblé priestess. Adrelina's brother Policarpo had a common law wife and children, and they lived on a roça some distance from the sugar mill. He was "respected and sought out by all the moradores on the place," since he was knowledgeable about herbal medicine. He also led "prayers" on holy days, especially Epiphany and the Feast of Saint Anthony calling out the songs and praying.

According to Manoelzinho, everyone lived on their own, "in simple houses" (some of which were still called senzalas), planted crops behind their houses, and worked in the fields of the ex-masters. Many paid a "commission" to the Dutras to be allowed to process manioc in the plantation's manioc flour mill. For the privilege of planting their crops on their former masters' land, they gave a day of work to the plantation; they called this labor "paying the rent" and generally performed it on Mondays. On the other days, the planters had to pay wages for any labor they provided. But he observed that some masters used "trickery" and "mania" to get out of those obligations.

Clearly, for some freed people, remaining on the plantations meant maintaining their access to land for planting crops, preserving their values, and guaranteeing their community's survival. For Andrelina, it meant the ability to continue to honor her gods. For the freed people it was the chance to "live on their own," although ties of dependence still connected them to their former owners. Nevertheless, all ex-slaves did not remain on the properties permanently, as the Cruz Plantation documents demonstrate. From January to September 1888, Jacinto Dutra was a member of the plantation's "house pcople." In 1894, he was living on the Desterro Plantation, also in Iguape, when he was involved in a fight with another Desterro resident laborer.[64] The children of ex-slaves on the Cruz Plantation told Manoelzinho that many freed people left the plantation as soon as they became adults. They did not necessarily go very far away. One of Máximo and Andrelina's sons moved into the village of Iguape, and years later, their two girls moved to Cachoeira. Manoelzinho recalled that, in Cachoeira, Maria do Carmo found work as a domestic servant. Policarpo and Idelfonso's children migrated to Salvador.

The first generation of descendants of the people freed on May 13, 1888, may have migrated to other places. Many must have established themselves in other parts of the Recôncavo but close to the places they had been born and where their parents still lived. This generation came of age with expectations about survival that differed from those of their parents. But as the next chapter makes clear, they soon perceived that no matter where they went, defending freedom was a constant struggle.

EIGHT

COMMUNITY AND FAMILY LIFE
AMONG FREED PEOPLE

The previous chapter traced the post-emancipation trajectories of individuals and families who emerged from slavery, emphasizing their day-to-day interactions with their ex-masters. This chapter deepens the analysis of the changes that occurred within the rural communities of ex-slaves from the last years of the nineteenth century through 1910. My goal is to show how the end of captivity affected these individuals and groups and shaped freed people's participation in rural life. Exploring this dimension of the ex-slaves' experiences in the post-emancipation period shows that the options available to them and the decisions they made were influenced by community life and by the family ties maintained with great difficulty during slavery.

Detailed lists of the Pitinga Plantation slaves from 1871, 1883, and 1887 illuminate the experiences of the community of ex-slaves that remained on the property after abolition. Located in Santo Amaro, the plantation belonged to José Joaquim Pires de Carvalho e Albuquerque, the Baron of Pirajá. When his wife, the baroness, died in 1862, the couple's property was subject to a detailed inventory. For various reasons, that inventory did not begin until nine years later, in 1871, and was not completed until after the baron died in February 1888; consequently, the property, including the slaves, was described and evaluated on three different occasions. According to the list made in 1871, the couple owned 396 slaves and 18 ingênuos. Seventeen of those captives worked in the couple's Salvador mansion, but the others were distributed across six Santo Amaro plantations: São Miguel (41), Botelho (45), Our Lady of Desterro (59), Conde (106), and Pitinga (128).[1]

From 1871 to 1883, the baron's enslaved rural labor force shrank significantly. In 1871, the executors of the estate counted 379 rural slaves; twelve years later, that number had declined by 17.2 percent to 314. From 1883 to 1887, the number of captives on the baron's rural property dropped even more dramatically, reflecting the developing crisis of slavery. In 1887, only 196 rural slaves remained, reflecting a loss of 37.6 percent of the slaves in four years. But the labor force at Pitinga did not shrink so radically during those years—in 1887, there were still 93 captives on the estate. Perhaps the baron had transferred most of his remaining slaves there since it was his most profitable property.[2] Apparently, toward the end of the nineteenth century, Pitinga was the only one of the baron's properties with a sugar mill: the other plantations simply produced cane. Despite being the baron's best property at the time, Pitinga nonetheless showed clear signs of decline. Nothing had been modernized while the estate was in limbo and the sugar mill functioned with the old machines and grinders. The manor house was in no better condition: the evaluators described it as "very old," with a "floor in poor condition," "very basic" and without the kind of comfort that a well-to-do family required.

Table 8.1 shows the evolution of the enslaved property in the Baron of Pirajá's property in the last years of slavery. In 1871, all of the 127 slaves living on the Pitinga Plantation were Brazilian: of them, 101 were described as crioulos, 25 cabra colored, and 1 pardo. Most of them had been born on the property and belonged to the second or third generation to have lived there. Enslaved women (71) outnumbered enslaved men (56). In 1887, however, the number of men and women was almost equal, with the men having a slight edge—48 to 45. Perhaps the difference between the number of men and women had declined after 1871 because more women had been freed.

TABLE 8.1. Slaves Belonging to the Baron of Pirajá, 1871–1887

Plantations	1871	1883	1887
Pitinga	128	103	93
Conde	106	75	41
Desterro	59	53	—
São Miguel	41	48	31
Botelho	45	35	31
Total	379	314	196

Source: *IT*, 3/1206/1675/1 (1869–1887), APEB.

According to the lists, forty-six women with one or more children lived on the Pitanga Plantation. Other documents allow us to see that many of them were married, at least in their own eyes, if not in those of the state, to other Pitanga slaves. As on other large plantations, these families enjoyed a certain stability, which permitted most of them to remain together for more than two generations. Aside from parents and children, the documents identified grandparents, aunts, uncles, and cousins. Many of the couples formed part of extensive family networks, articulated through marriage and fictive kinship.

In 1871, forty-three slave cabins housed 128 slaves. The buildings were constructed with mud walls, wooden beams, and clay-tiled roofs and, according to the estate's executor, were in "ruins." By 1887, only twenty slave cabins remained to house ninety-three slaves. In sixteen years, the number of slave cabins had dropped by at least half. Perhaps the slave huts were so basic that the executor did not include them in the inventory. Or perhaps the slaves were living in houses that were no longer called slave quarters. Perhaps those who had obtained their freedom constructed homes far from the master's homes and brought their enslaved relatives to live with them.

The slave lists enabled us to follow a few families from 1871 to 1887. For example, table 8.2 shows that in the final years of the nineteenth century, members of the same family could have different experiences with slavery. Many of the slaves listed here only obtained their freedom after the passage of the Law of May 13. Of the seventy-nine individuals in the table, twenty-nine were still enslaved in 1887, twenty-three had been freed by the Law of the Free Womb and twenty were not listed and must have died or obtained their freedom earlier. Yet many of the people in the table witnessed or participated in family efforts to rescue a relative from slavery. Although in clear decline, slavery continued to mark the lives and define the opportunities available to these families.

TABLE 8.2. Selected Family Groups for the Pitinga Plantation, 1871–1887

Parents' names	Year of birth	Color	Profession	Children's names	Year of birth	Color
Silvéria	1826	Crioula	Field hand	Timóteo	1856	Crioula
Luís Gonzaga	—	—	—	Damásio	1858	Crioula
				Orminda	1860	Crioula
				Martinho	1861	Crioula
				Apolônia	1868	Crioula
				João	1870	Crioula
				Maria da Purificação	After 1871	—
Esperança	1841	Crioula	Field hand	Leonarda	1864	Crioula
				Aurelino	1870	
Serafina	1826	Crioula	Field hand	Cristina	1861	Crioula
Senhorinha	1823	Cabra	Field hand	Bonifácio	1861	Crioula
				Venância	1864	Cabra
				Paulo	1869	Crioula
Verecunda	1842	Crioula	Field hand	Emílio	1861	Crioula
				Olímpio	1865	Crioula
				Alexandrina	1868	Crioula
				Beatriz	1870	Crioula
				Eusébio	After 1871	—
				Cândida	After 1871	—
Henriqueta	1821	Crioula	Field hand	Delfina	1854	Cabra
				Joaquim	1865	Cabra
				Salustiana	1867	Cabra
Conegundes	1837	Crioula	Field hand	Tomé	1868	Cabra
				Esmeralda	1870	Cabra
				Mariano	1871	Cabra
				Dorotea	After 1871	—
Luciana	1822	Crioula	Field hand	Cecília	1857	Crioula
Hípio	1831	Crioula	Field hand	Josefina	1861	Crioula
				Valentina	1865	Crioula
				Rafaela	1867	Cabra
				Inês	After 1871	—

(continued)

TABLE 8.2. Continued

Parents' names	Year of birth	Color	Profession	Children's names	Year of birth	Color
Teodora	1841	Crioula	Field hand	Benigna	1862	Crioula
				Lúcia	After 1871	—
				Brígida	After 1871	—
Eusébia	1801	Crioula	—	Hipio	1831	Cabra
Cornélia	1817	Crioula	Field hand	Antero	1852	Preta
				Marciano	1853	Preta
Raimunda Pires	—	—	—	Esequiel	1849	Preta
				Olímpia	1851	Preta
				Constantino	1853	Preta
				Matildes	1853	Preta
Orminda	1860	Crioula	Field hand	Dalmácia	After 1871	—
				Diniz	After 1871	—
				Raimundo	After 1871	—
Delfina	1854		Field hand	Valentim	After 1871	
				Florência	After 1871	
				Placiana	After 1871	
Cristina	1861			Unnamed infant	After 1871	
Leonarda	1864			Abílio	After 1871	—
Cecília	1857			Eugênio	After 1871	
				Evaristo	After 1871	
				Unnamed infant	After 1871	
Olímpia	1851	Crioula	Field hand	Gregória	1870	Crioula
				Sofia	After 1871	
				Geminiana	After 1871	
				Herculano	After 1871	
				Onofre	After 1871	
Ludovina	—	—	—	Policarpo	1858	Crioula

Source: IT, 3/1206/1675/1 (1869–1887), APEB.

Post-1889 civil birth registers provide details on several of the families in table 8.2, and particularly three of them. In February 1889 and March 1892, Procópio Pires appeared in the notary's office in Santo Amaro: on his first visit, he reported the birth of twins, and on the second, the birth of a daughter named Henriqueta. The children's mother was Apolônia de Góes, and she and Procópio supported the family by farming the lands of the Pitinga Plantation. The Pitanga slave lists reveal that Procópio and Apolônia had belonged to the baron. In 1871, Procópio was listed as a twenty-four-year-old crioulo agricultural slave. He was the son of Davi and Felícia Pires, but they must have been enslaved on other properties because there are no references to the couple in the documents under discussion. In 1871, the evaluators noted that Davi was "lame in one leg" and valued him at Rs.300$000, a price well below what one would have normally paid for a slave of his age at the time. Eight years later, when he was thirty-two, his value had dropped by two-thirds, to Rs.100$000, and at that price, he may have been able to buy his freedom, because he does not appear on the 1887 list of slaves on the estate.[3]

In 1871, Apolônia de Góes was three years old when she and her five siblings were included in the baron's list. All of them were described as crioulos, including eight-month-old João; ten-year-old Martinho; eleven-year-old Orminda; Damásio who was more than twelve; and Timóteo, fifteen. The six children lived with their mother, Silvéria (who appears in table 8.2) a forty-five-year-old crioula agricultural slave, who was described as "sick." After 1871, Silvéria gave birth to a girl named Maria da Purificação, who was free by the Law of the Free Womb. By 1883, Apolônia's family had grown: her sister Orminda had given birth to three children—Dalmácia, Diniz, and Raimundo—all of whom were also free under the Law of the Free Womb. In 1887, Apolônia and three other siblings, Orminda, João, and Damásio, were still enslaved to the Baron of Pirajá, and all indications are that, for them, freedom came on May 13, 1888. Throughout those years, slavery divided Apolônia's family, all of whom were certainly involved in trying to obtain their freedom.[4]

After abolition, Apolônia's family continued growing. In June 1889, her sister Maria Orminda gave birth to twins, Antônio and Antônia. In June 1891, Orminda and her common law husband, Antero Ramos da Purificação, reported the birth of another child, Crescência.[5] By now, the couple had six children: three born under the Law of the Free Womb and three born after abolition.

Like his common law wife and her sister, Antero still lived on the Pitanga Plantation, where he had been born and raised. Like them, he had also been a slave of the Baron of Pirajá. In 1883, he was described as a crioulo slave of more than thirty years of age, who worked in agriculture. His father, Vicente da Purificação, appeared in the 1871 list simply as Vicente, a crioulo man of more than sixty years of age, "suffering from exhaustion." At the same time, the executor of the estate described his mother, Cornélia "so-and-so," as a crioula agricultural worker, fifty-four years of age, and ill.[6]

A second family group formed around another ex-slave couple, crioulos Rafaela de Jesus and Rodopiano dos Santos Soares, outlined in figure 8.1. Nearly a year after abolition, Rodopiano appeared in the Santo Amaro registry office to record the birth of their son Paulo, a few days previously. During that visit, he declared that he lived with Rafaela de Jesus and that they both worked in agriculture on the Pitinga Plantation. The slave lists reveal that Rafaela was the daughter of Hípio de Jesus and Luciana, born in 1831 and 1822 respectively, who were also Pitinga agricultural slaves. In 1871, Rafaela was four years old and described as cabra, suffering from epilepsy, and evaluated at Rs.100$000. She had three older sisters: fourteen-year-old Cecília; ten-year-old Josefina, and six-year-old Valentina. At that time her crioulo father, Hípio, was over forty and employed as the lead ox-cart driver. Clearly, he held a significant position in the Pitinga labor hierarchy. In the inventory, he was also described as "suffering from exhaustion" and evaluated at Rs.600$000.

In 1883, Rafaela, who suffered from epilepsy, was seventeen and had no children. Her owners evaluated her at Rs.100$000, a value much lower than those of other girls her age. At the time, her older sister Cecília was the mother of three ingênuo children: Eugênio, Evaristo, and "one who had not yet been baptized." Four years later, in 1887, Rafaela, Cecília, and Valentina remained enslaved to the Baron of Pirajá, but Josefina had either died or been freed. A year before abolition, Rodopiano was also on the list of slaves, and he and Rafaela probably only obtained their freedom after May 13.

Born in 1889, nearly a year after abolition, little Paulo joined a family who had suffered slavery for at least three generations. He grew up surrounded by grandparents, aunts, and uncles who had been enslaved. Some of his cousins had been born under the Law of the Free Womb. His great-grandmother, Eusébia, was a crioula slave born at the beginning of the century. She probably died a slave as well, since, in 1883, her name appears among the slaves on the property. At least eighty in 1883, she was no longer able to work and her owner considered her "without value." Paulo must certainly have heard stories about her, as well as about the family's struggles to stay together and the hopes that they had for the first children born after the Law of September 28, 1871.

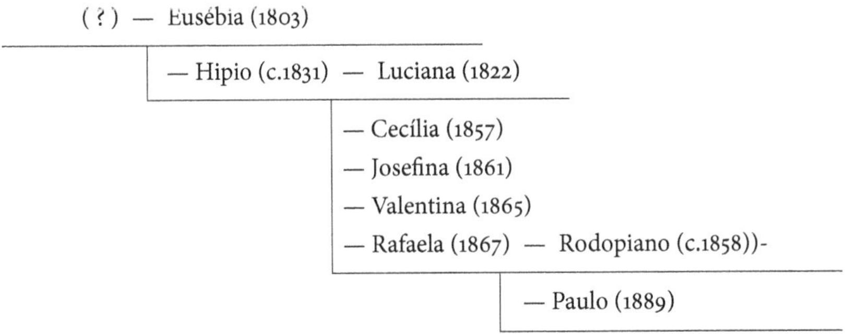

(?) — Eusébia (1803)

— Hipio (c.1831) — Luciana (1822)

— Cecília (1857)
— Josefina (1861)
— Valentina (1865)
— Rafaela (1867) — Rodopiano (c.1858))-

— Paulo (1889)

FIGURE 8.1. Family of Rafaela de Jesus and Rodopiano dos Santos Soares.

The third family group clearly had their efforts to stay together and free themselves from slavery inscribed in their trajectories. On August 15, 1890, Conegundes dos Anjos appeared at the registry office to report the birth of his granddaughter, Maria Estevão dos Anjos, the daughter of Esmeralda dos Anjos. Two months later, her mother appeared to report that little Maria Estevão had died of a "stomach sickness." The following year, Conegundes returned to the office to document that Esmeraldo had given birth to another child, this time a boy named Manoel do Rosário, described as preto. From the 1871 slave list, we know that Conegundes, a crioula, was the daughter of a woman named Felipa who had already died. She was also the mother of three children: Tomé described as cabra, age three (evaluated at Rs.200$000); Esmeralda, cabrinha, age one (evaluated at Rs.100$000); and a one-month-old infant, Mariano, also described as cabrinha (evaluated at Rs.50$000). Conegundes was lucky enough to raise her children herself, but as they grew up their evaluations increased rapidly, even though prices for slaves were falling. In 1883, Esmeralda was evaluated at Rs.400$000 and Tomé at Rs.500$000. Four years later, in 1887, Esmeralda's price had not changed, but her brother's had shot up to Rs.800$000. Their mother must have realized that she could never save enough money to free them. In 1887, Conegundas, Esmeralda, and Tomé were still enslaved and all indications are that they obtained their freedom on May 13.[7]

The evidence suggests that Conegundes and several members of her family remained on the plantation where they had been enslaved through the beginning of the twentieth century. On August 14, 1903, she appeared at the notary's office to record the birth of another granddaughter, a daughter of Esmeralda, named Maria do Carmo. Asked to explain why she had waited so long to report the baby's birth, she replied that "she was elderly and the child's mother was ill."[8]

Couples	Color	Profession	Children's names	Year of birth	Color
Apolônia de Góes (1)	—	Field hand*	Twins	1889	
Procópio Pires	—	Field hand	Henriqueta		
			Demétrio	1902	Preta
			José Paulo	1904	Cabra
Rafaela de Jesus (2)	Cabra	Field hand	Paulo	1889	
Rodopiano dos Santos Soares (3)	Crioula	Field hand			
Maria Benigna de S. Pedro (4)	Crioula	Field hand	Maria Rosa	1889	
			Arlinda	1890	Cabra
Claudemiro Neves da Conceição		Field hand	Marcelino	1902	Preta
Maria Orminda (1)		Field hand	Antônio e Antônia (twins)	1889	
Antero Ramos da Purificação (5)		Field hand	Crescência	1891	Preta
Leonarda Pires (6)	Preta	Roceira	Marcelino da Ressurreição	1890	Preta
Tobias de Santa Rosa (3)		Field hand	José de Santana	1891	Parda
Maria Delfina (7)			Maria das Mercês	1890	Cabra
Fortunato Calmon					
Esmeralda dos Anjos (8)	—	—	Maria Estevão dos Anjos	1890	Cabra
—			Manoel do Rosário	1891	Preta
			Maria do Carmo	1904	—
Cristina dos Reis (9)		Roceira	Gregória dos Reis	1890	Cabra
Maria Alexandrina (10)	Crioula	Field hand	Porfírio	1892	Parda
Policarpo de Góes (11)	Crioula	Field hand	Aniceto	1894	Parda
			Joana	1900	Parda

(continued)

TABLE 8.3. Continued

Couples	Color	Profession	Children's names	Year of birth	Color
Beatriz de Alcântara (10)	Crioula	Field hand	Eleutério	1892	Preta
Maria Lúcia (4)	Crioula	Field hand	Hermelino	1892	Parda
Esequiel dos Reis da Purificação (12)	Preta	Field hand	Auta	1893	Parda
Matildes dos Reis (12)	Preta	Field hand	Irineu de Góes		Parda
Demétrio de Góes (3)	Preta	Field hand			

* Literally lavoura.

Source: *Registro de Nascimento da freguesia do Rosário*, Santo Amaro, A-I and A-II (1889–1899), ASCMSA.

Explanatory notes: 1. Daughter of the slave woman Silvéria; 2. Daughter of enslaved couple Luciana and Hípio; 3. Ex-slave resident laborer on the plantation; 4. Daughter of Theodora; 5. Son of Cornélia; 6. Daughter of Esperança; 7. Daughter of Henriqueta; 8. Daughter of Conegundes; 9. Daughter of Serafina; 10. Daughter of Verecunda; 11. Son of Ludovina; 12. Son of Raimunda.

The civil birth registers provide the data for table 8.3, "Family Groups of Ex-Slaves Living on the Pitinga Plantation, 1889–1904." The table indicates the adults' names and those of the children born after abolition. Most important, it reveals the surnames that the slaves chose after emancipation.

Connecting these families to those in the baron's slave lists reveals the names of the grandparents of the children being registered and the fact that thirty-four ex-slaves remained on the Pitinga Plantation after emancipation. Taking the ninety-three captives on the property in 1887 as a base indicates that these thirty-four ex-slaves represented about a third of Pitinga's ex-slaves. Of the nineteen who declared their occupation, seventeen said they worked in agriculture, and only two said that they supported themselves from their subsistence plots. The reference to roceiros as opposed to agricultural workers certainly reflected the ways in which the members of the ex-slave community differentiated among themselves: it expressed the condition of people who supported themselves by farming their own plots rather than depending solely on work in plantation cane fields.

The civil birth registers for 1888 and 1899 contain information on twenty family groups. Only six of them appear to have been headed by women living without spouses, as indicated by their failure to report the names of their children's fathers to the clerk at the registry office. Married couples who lived together formed the other fourteen households. Eight of these couples had lived together on Pitinga in slavery, while at least one member of each of the other six couples had belonged to the baron and his wife. These family ties reinforced community cohesion and demonstrate that the freed people did not come out of slavery suffering from "social anomy."

Some marriages involved family groups that had lived on the Pitinga Plantation for at least two generations. Policarpo de Góes, a crioulo man born in 1858, and his common law wife, Maria Alexandrina, a crioula woman born in 1868, were both the children of Pitinga slaves. Policarpo's mother, Ludovina, seems to have died before 1871, but Maria Alexandrina's mother, Verecunda, remained enslaved until 1887. While a slave, she gave birth to six children, two of whom were ingênuos born under the Law of the Free Womb. Between 1892 and 1894, Policarpo de Góes registered the birth of two of his sons and her grandsons, Porfírio and Aniceto. The two boys were the descendants— on both their maternal and paternal sides—of at least three generations of Pitinga slaves. Verecunda herself went to Santo Amaro on June 12, 1892, to register the birth of another grandson, Eleutério, the son of her daughter Beatriz de Alcântara. In other words, years after abolition she struggled to care for her children and grandchildren. Verecunda and several members of her family seem to have remained on Pitinga at least through the end of the nineteenth century: On May 3, 1899, according to the register, her grandson Domingos, son of her daughter Cândida, was born on the estate.[9]

Another couple, Esequiel dos Reis do Espírito Santo and Maria Lúcia, was also descended from an extended family that had lived for many years on Pitinga. Esequiel had been born a captive, the son of the slave Raimunda, while his common law wife was an ingênuo born to the enslaved woman Teodora after the passage of the Law of the Free Womb. Esequiel had three siblings who were born as slaves—Constantino, Olímpia, and Matildes—and all of them were still enslaved in 1887. In 1883 Olímpia had three íngênuo children—Sofia, Geminiana, and Herculano. On August 22, 1893, Esequiel appeared at the notary's office in Santo Amaro to report the birth of his pardo son Hermelino a few days previously. The following year, he returned to register a daughter, baptized as Auta, whom he also described as parda.[10]

Figure 8.2 contains the details of three families formed by couples who lived with their children on the Pitinga Plantation from the middle of the nineteenth century to the beginning of the twentieth. As the evidence makes clear, the children born in the years immediately after abolition lived with grandparents, parents, aunts, uncles, and cousins who had been born in slavery.

The civil register also reveals married couples composed of ex-slaves from Pitinga and residents of other plantations. For example, on December 11,

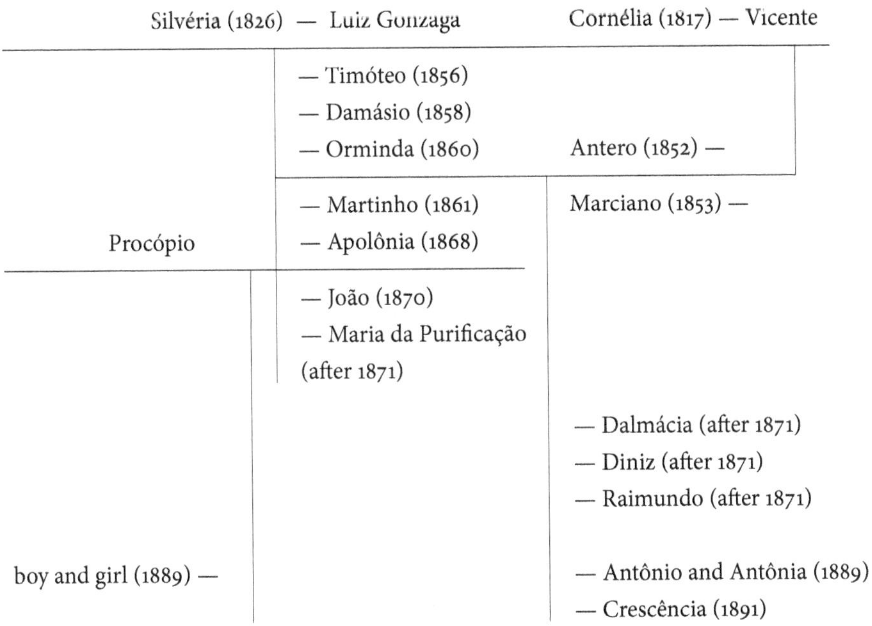

Silvéria (1826) — Luiz Gonzaga   Cornélia (1817) — Vicente

— Timóteo (1856)
— Damásio (1858)
— Orminda (1860)   Antero (1852) —

— Martinho (1861)   Marciano (1853) —
Procópio   — Apolônia (1868)

— João (1870)
— Maria da Purificação
(after 1871)

— Dalmácia (after 1871)
— Diniz (after 1871)
— Raimundo (after 1871)

boy and girl (1889) —   — Antônio and Antônia (1889)
— Crescência (1891)

FIGURE 8.2. Marriage alliances among selected Pitanga Plantation slaves.

1897, Adelina de Góes, the fifteen-year-old daughter of Matildes dos Reis, an ex-slave living on Pitinga, married nineteen-year-old João Lourenço de Anunciação, a morador and roceiro on the Santa Catarina Plantation.[11] Their marriage suggests that young people coming out of slavery had more options than their parents when choosing a partner, because they were able to look to other plantations for spouses. Perhaps emancipation allowed freed people to circulate more widely and encouraged the members of the Pitinga community to become involved with people living on other plantations.

The civil birth registers also help us to understand the logic with which ex-slaves chose their surnames.[12] Some adopted the surnames of the families of the ex-masters, Pires and Góes. For the most part, however, they chose surnames quite differently from the ex-slaves on the Cruz Plantation discussed in the previous chapter: nine took surnames referring to Christian devotion, while two used the surnames Silva and Alcântara. Five of them simply used compound names, as was the case with Leôncio José and Maria Elisa, an ex-slave couple who were agricultural workers on the plantation and baptized their preto son Paulino in June 1892.[13]

Those who adopted the surname Pires or Góes did not necessarily pass those names on to their children born after abolition. Ex-slave Leonarda

Pires (the daughter of Esperança Pires) registered her son, born in 1890, as Marcelino da Ressurreição. Perhaps the choice of names was a signal of the new times, in which parents felt freer to give whatever name they chose to their children.[14] Transmitting surnames to children and grandchildren was certainly a way of defining and strengthening the ties among the generations and may be evidence of a concern with connecting the newest family members to ancestors and maintaining family histories. It may explain why Maria Estevão dos Anjos, born in 1890, inherited the surname of her mother Esmeralda and her grandmother Conegundes.

Crossing data from various sources allows us to further examine the ex-slave communities formed around the old Recôncavo sugar plantations. The documents about Pitinga and other Recôncavo plantations show that the people coming out of slavery formed solid rural communities. Forged under slavery, these communities drew on family connections among the ex-slaves on the same plantations and nearby properties. They were fundamental to the ability of people who came out of slavery to reconstruct a community in freedom. In the post-abolition period, these communities were the basis on which the ex-slaves and their descendants sought new options for survival.

This was the context in which some communities of ex-slaves and their descendants managed to develop a degree of independence from ex-masters and their families. Although the freed villagers and their families lived on and farmed plantation land, they were no longer obliged to work for their former owners.[15] As the first decades of the twentieth century passed, ex-masters and their descendants found these villages inconvenient if they tried to modernize their old properties by installing an industrial central sugar mill or to cease sugar production altogether and convert their properties to cattle ranches.

The behavior of several individuals in these communities after abolition indicates that the ex-slaves continued to count on the aid and solidarity of their former partners in slavery.[16] This assistance included caring for the dead. For example, the crioulo Juvenal buried the African Salomão and then went to Santo Amaro to register his death. Ex-slave Policarpo Dutra, a morador on the Cruz Plantation, buried the African Mateus, who lived on the plantation where the two of them had served as slaves.[17]

Post-abolition conflicts demonstrate the persistence of mutual aid and solidarity among workers who lived near the large plantations. Truthfully, some conflicts only came to the authorities' attention if a member of the community violated local norms. Many times, the community got together to plant or harvest subsistence crops. They also organized large get-togethers, usually parties, or celebrations in which they sought to reinforce cooperative ties within the group. It was no accident, therefore, that conflicts involving the community erupted during those times.

On August 18, 1892, several "rural workers" went to Simplício's roça in Sumidouro, a village on the banks of the Pojuca River, "to dig up some tobacco plants." Roceiro Antônio José do Espírito Santo and his brother went in the afternoon and "managed to take out a few rows of plants, so the witness and his companions were invited to supper with Simplício that night, and that was how the fight started." Two guests had a disagreement, and in the subsequent fight, a roceiro named Tomás was mortally wounded.[18]

Fights broke out most frequently on Saturdays or holy days, in other words, when workers were excused from laboring in the cane. On the evening of the Feast of Saint John in 1899, Manoel Liberato do Nascimento, a thirty-eight-year-old man who "made his living from agriculture," was threatened in the doorway of his home by José Caetano, a morador on the Santana Plantation in Santo Amaro. Fuas Bandeira, a sixty-five-year-old African ex-slave later said that he heard Caetano ask for "São João" and then a fight broke out with Manoel Liberato.[19] On the night of July 20, 1901, after receiving his week's pay, José Jerônimo dos Santos, a "rural worker" at the Passagem Central Sugar Mill, went out to a samba near his home and "there had fun until 10:00 at night, when the fun ended." According to him, the fuss began when Antônio Francisco, a furnace tender from the same Passagem sugar mill, provoked everyone who was at the drumming circle. Other witnesses said that Antônio Fernandes and José Jerônimo had a misunderstanding over a tambourine.[20]

The references to "drumming circles" and sambas indicate that the religious faith and music forged from African heritages were significant parts of the ex-slaves' daily lives. Within these communities, ex-slaves could maintain and re-create religious traditions without interference from ex-masters.

The documents also point to social differentiation within the ex-slave communities. The freed people emerged from slavery in different situations. Access to the roças was an important factor differentiating among ex-slaves. The civil registers for the period nearly always distinguish between roceiros and lavradores. The term "lavrador," or living from agriculture (a lavoura), covered a wide variety of situations on the plantations, from rural worker to farmer, but "roceiro" always implied access to a plot of land. Roceiros enjoyed more options for survival than agricultural workers, even though roceiros were usually obliged to work their ex-masters' plantations in addition to their own farms. With their own plots they were able to grow a diverse group of crops and sell the surplus in local markets. We can see that the right to plant

FIGURE 8.3. Roceiros on the way to market, Cachoeira, 1930.
Arthur Wischral / Public Archive of the State of Bahia.

FIGURE 8.4. Roceiros at the market, Cachoeira, 1930.
Arthur Wischral / Public Archive of the State of Bahia.

pieces of land may have been a significant factor in the decision to remain on the plantation. Donato "so-and-so," for example, was a forty-five-year-old single man, born on the Mombaça Plantation, and a roceiro who did business at the market in Nazaré.[21]

Such distinctions between roceiros and other rural dwellers appear in other documents. Nearly 20 percent (19.5) of all the patients admitted to the Santo Amaro Santa Casa da Misericórdia (Charity Hospital) described themselves as roceiros. The others were registered as lavrador or indicated that they "lived from the lavoura." In some criminal cases, authorities described individuals as "rented," using the nickname for workers who migrated around the Recôncavo during the harvest and grinding season. Such a designation also included laborers labeled more formally as field hand (trabalhador da enxada) or agricultural worker (trabalhador agrícola). Some rural dwellers said that they lived from working in "other people's roças."

These people were temporary plantation workers, generally returning home at the end of the harvest. The majority of them had been born in parishes other than those in which they were working, as the example of two individuals who testified about a crime on the Cazumbá Plantation in Rio Fundo makes clear. They identified themselves as Porfírio Inácio de Oliveira, thirty-six years old, married, the son of Francisco de Pinho, born on the Sapucaia Plantation, "rural worker" on the Cazumbá Plantation; and Manoel Leocádio de Abreu, twenty-five years of age, single, the son of Cirilo Francisco de Abreu, born on the Brotas Plantation, and a "rural worker."[22]

The situation of these two men suggests that younger ex-slaves had less access to land than their elders and were therefore obliged to migrate seasonally to earn wages by "renting" their labor. That seems to have been the case with Josino Messias, a twenty-year-old single man who was accused of stealing cattle from the Brito Plantation in Santo Amaro in 1895. When arrested, this young man, whose age suggests that he may have been born an ingênuo under the Law of the Free Womb, said that "he worked on roças belonging to others" and "did not have a fixed address." He attributed the accusation of theft to the fact that "he did not want to work on the Brito Plantation for the very small salary that they are accustomed to paying there." Planters could use violence against rented workers, but such workers' refusal to accept conditions that they considered humiliating is also clear.[23]

In the criminal cases, generally the workers who said that they "lived from working other people's farms" had come from other parts of the Recôncavo. Given their ages, many of them came from plantations where they had probably been born as slaves. In 1901, the investigation of a crime at the Passagem

Central Sugar Mill involved two witnesses who described themselves as "rural workers" living and working on the Passagem Central Sugar Mill: José Justino da Silva, a twenty-year-old single man born on the Europa Plantation and Francisco Glicério dos Santos, a twenty-three-year-old single man who had been born on the Santa Cruz Plantation.[24]

The civil birth registers from the last decade of the twentieth century reveal a large number of women with children living in their parents' homes. This aspect of post-abolition daily life might indicate that the younger generations did not have the same access to land or a house on the plantation that their elders had. The case of Francisco Ambrósio, the descendant of the African Lucara da Costa Pinto, an ex-slave from the Europa Plantation, would suggest that was so. He said that he and his children worked his parents' and grandparents' roça until the middle of the twentieth century, but his siblings had been obliged to migrate to other areas well before that.[25] In the long run, it seems that the descendants of ex-slaves ceased to be moradores and became rented workers, without access to land.

The Integration of Freed People in Rural Communities

On the morning of November 24, 1889, on the Olhos d'Água Fazenda in the Oliveira Parish, something happened that drew the attention of everyone who lived in the surrounding area. Luísa, "a preta freedwoman" was found dead in her home that morning. What horrified local residents so much was the condition of the body: her face was covered in blood, one eye was swollen, and she had a deep cut on her left arm. Vitorina Alves, a twenty-year-old lavradora, the dead woman's cousin, said that she had been at home when her uncle, João Alves, arrived asking her to come and see Luísa, who was dead. When she arrived she saw her cousin's body on the ground near a jug of water. Shortly thereafter, she and another cousin, Francisca, the dead woman's sister, put the body on the plank on which she was accustomed to sleeping. They noted her bloody face and the bruises and cuts on her body.[26] Several women commented on the condition in which they found the body, including the dead woman's sister, eighteen-year-old, Francisca de Almeida, known as Chica, her cousins, twenty-eight-year-old Conceição Alves and twenty-five-year-old Jacinta Alves, and her aunt Joana Alves, who was fifty-five. All of them were lavradoras, born and raised on the Olhos d'Água Fazenda, where they were living. All of them thought the wounds on Luísa's face and body were odd and insisted that "herself" had not been sick. The news spread rather rapidly that she had been killed by her father, a "preta freedman" named João Alves.

Two weeks after the rumor mill began to point the finger of suspicion at the dead woman's father, the case finally came to the attention of the authorities. On December 3, sixty-year-old João Alves was arrested on the charge of having killed his daughter. Shortly thereafter, her body was exhumed, but it had suffered such decomposition that medical experts could not detect evidence of a crime. The investigation dragged on, however, and João Alves was only tried and found innocent on March 7, 1891, more than two years after his daughter's death.

Although the authorities never convicted anyone in Luísa's death, their investigation revealed details about the relationship between the ex-slaves and their ex-masters. Vitorina stated that the day before her death, her cousin Luísa had gone to the home of Herculano Alves de Freitas, where Mrs. Alves provided her with corn, manioc flour, and meat. The surname Alves, common to the couple and so many freed people in the case, may indicate that Luísa, her father, aunt, and the three cousins had once been slaves of Herculano and his wife. A possible former relationship between Luísa and Mrs. Alves also suggests that Luísa received the subsistence crops as compensation for work. Certainly, Luísa's sister, "Chica," continued working in the home of her "ex-mistress," "dona Teresa de Almeida," after abolition. Indeed, Chica had not been able to attend to her dead sister immediately because she had been taking care of the household chores for dona Teresa. Chica's surname suggests that she had been a slave of the Almeida family. She seems to have been the only member of her family who had not belonged to an Alves.[27]

This criminal case raises various issues about the post-emancipation lives of the people who were freed on May 13, 1888. It indicates how they were inserted into the communities in which they lived; it shows changes in the ways in which other rural social groups viewed ex-slaves in their new condition as freed people; and it reveals how the members of the freed community related to one another and the conflicts and adjustments within the communities as they struggled to survive after abolition. The complexities it raises require further reflection on the ways in which the ex-slaves were perceived or identified as members of the communities in which they lived.[28] Criminal cases in several parts of Bahia, including the Recôncavo, contain helpful information.

Escaping the past was difficult for the freed people who remained where they had served as slaves. In 1889, in defending himself from the charge of stealing cattle and crops in São Sebastião do Passé, Antônio Cecílio stated that his accuser, Zeferino dos Santos, "had never behaved when he belonged to Manoel dos Santos who, not being able to tolerate him, sold him to another master, who hadn't been able to make him behave either and so, let him go."[29] Planters themselves frequently referred to workers' enslaved pasts when they described the actions or behavior of their tenants. In May 1899, when he heard that one of his tenants had been killed, Luís Guilherme de Almeida Junqueira, owner of the Limoeiro Plantation in Nossa Senhora do Monte, accused Donato de Tal, whom he described as a "freedman" from the Mombaça Plantation, of the crime.[30]

Individuals living on the plantations continued to be identified by the connections that they had, or had once had, to the owners of the lands on which they lived. The African Nereo, an ex-slave of about sixty, who lived on the Tobá Fazenda, identified a guy named Marinho, "who had been a slave of the deceased Master Custódio, owner of the Maria Guarda Fazenda," as responsible for a series of thefts that had occurred in the area in May 1888. During the inquiry, Nereo himself revealed that he had been the slave of a planter in the region.[31] On August 17, 1888, the warden of the Casa de Correção da Bahia (Bahian House of Corrections) described the deceased prisoner Zeferino as "the ex-slave of the Baron of Cajaíba."[32] In July 1889 in the village of Itapicuru, Amâncio, accused of assault and battery, was identified as the "ex-slave of Jovino Garcia de Noronha."[33] Clearly, mentioning an enslaved past could be a way of criticizing behavior or putting individuals accused of crimes in their places.

Many times, the revelation of an enslaved past was quickly followed by some indication of the ties that the individual had, or had once had, to their former masters. On October 8, 1891, the Cachoeira public prosecutor accused Tranquilino "so and so," "ex-slave of Commander Albino José Milhazes," of having tried to shoot his common law wife, Maria Glicéria da Conceição, in a jealous rage on September 27 around three in the afternoon on Market Street. After the shooting, Tranquilino was pursued and captured by various plebeians, including the victim's sister. What is most surprising is that, when he was caught, his pursuers—poor people like himself—turned Tranquilino over to his ex-master, Albino José Milhazes.[34]

In some situations, the term "preto" meant ex-slave. Recall that the ex-slave João Alves accused of killing his daughter was identified as a "preto freedman." In a criminal case from Muritiba, one of the witnesses referred to the ex-slave Roque as the "preto Roque." In many cases, color appears as a distinctive mark of the past condition of the person in question. Here, previous enslavement and race became confused.

By the same token, ex-slaves frequently rejected socio-racial classifications that evoked an enslaved past, or belittled their condition as freed people. The day-to-day lives of the blacks who had emerged from slavery were marked by a permanent effort to distance themselves from the symbols and stigmas associated with their former condition. In 1889, the Condeúba public prosecutor accused the "ex-slave" Cesário of having shot Pedro José Soares in a bar on the afternoon of May 12, the day before the first anniversary of the Golden Law. The witnesses said that, that day, Soares entered the bar and greeted everyone present; everyone responded except the accused, so Soares went over to him and aggressively leaned against his knee. In reaction, the ex-slave shot and wounded the provocateur.[35]

Some of these episodes reveal that many freed people resisted being treated as slaves. On Sunday morning, September 28, 1890, on the Pegui Fazenda belonging to the widow Teodora Flores Venerote in the Colônia Leopoldina of southern Bahia, the workers—some of whom may have been ex-slaves—were waiting for the manager to finish the payroll so they could receive their week's pay. While they were waiting, the preta Macoléa, an ex-slave on the property, came out of the kitchen where she had been working, crossed the fazenda yard, and headed for the woods, smoking a pipe. As she did that, Sebastião, another ex-slave from the fazenda, followed her, and, when he caught up to her, began to whip her. Later when asked why he had done so, Sebastião told the subdelegado that he beat Macoléa out of jealousy. Those who witnessed his arrest saw how much he struggled when the authorities dragged him to the fazenda yard, tied him up, and then beat him. Sebastião seems to have viewed this treatment as a return to his former condition of enslavement.[36]

This case revealed how the local authorities identified ex-slaves. In the charge he prepared, the public prosecutor described Macólea as an "ex-slave" and a "preta." In court, the judge referred to the prisoner as an "ex-slave" and the phrase was stamped on the cover of the case, next to the defendant's name. By the same token, in their testimonies, freed people sometimes themselves pointed to an enslaved past, at times calling themselves "workers in the roça" and other times "day laborers." Macoléa identified herself an "employee" in the fazenda kitchen. The jury found Sebastião guilty of assault with a "demeaning weapon" and intent to injure. The evidence suggests that the members of the jury who decided Sebastião's fate believed that ex-slaves were not ready for freedom. According to the judge, nine months of jail time was a light sentence appropriate to Sebastião's inability to comprehend the "consequences of his actions."[37]

There were also conflicts in the ways in which the freed people defended their new free status. Many times, the tension grew out of disputes about the definition of the roles of the members of these rural communities. Many ex-slaves encountered people who continued to treat them as subordinates. Under such conditions, they had to reject the forms of treatment that they judged to be incompatible with their new condition as free people. Several incidents show the ways in which they struggled to distance themselves from any indication of their former enslavement.

Many of the conflicts in the countryside after abolition occurred because ex-slaves felt their freedom was being threatened. On January 21, 1889, the prosecutor from Geremboabo charged Tibúrcio Francisco, "who had been a slave of Francisco Joaquim de Carvalho," with beating Paulo Celestino de Santana on November 18, 1888, as he was returning from the market. Paulo Celestino, who was about eighteen years of age, single, and living on the Salgada Plantation, said that he went to the market in Coité with a load of raw brown sugar. On his way back, he came across his friend Tibúrcio and was shocked when Tibúrcio yelled at him and then hit him with a block of wood. Ludovina Maria, an ex-slave from the Lagoa Plantation, broke up the fight. When asked to describe the events in question, the witnesses identified Tibúrcio by his enslaved past. They knew his master, who probably lived in the area, but Tibúrcio no longer had a formal connection to the man, because he now lived and worked on another plantation, the Lagoa Salgada Plantation.

The testimony of Silvestre Barbosa de Sousa, an eighteen-year-old man who was traveling with Tibúrcio, allows us to see why the ex-slave exploded. He said that Tibúrcio had said, "Paulo got in a fight with his mother and she made me promise to come and beat him, and since I knew that he'd be coming this way, [when I saw him], I said you should get down off that burro so that we can decide the thing here." Shortly thereafter, the fight broke out. This testimony indicates that Tibúrcio expected a thrashing from Paulo, so to avoid being hit himself, he hit Paulo first.[38]

These identities may have been forged out of ideas about what freedom meant while slavery had still existed. For this reason, the ex-slaves identified themselves to the authorities as "moradores," "roceiros," or "lavradores," categories of free people living on the plantations prior to abolition. But these categories were also being redefined as ex-slaves struggled to distance themselves from their enslaved past.

NINE

OTHER POST-EMANCIPATION ITINERARIES

I'm going to Bahia
I'm going to see if there's money there
But nobody will die of hunger
If there's no money.

This chapter traces the trajectories of ex-slaves and their descendants who left the plantations for other parts of the Recôncavo after abolition. It sheds light on the way they experienced slavery and freedom, and shows how these experiences influenced freed people's decisions about migration and moving to the city. Following the freed people through time and space also reveals how they articulated their choices and their plans for freedom. The paths they took reveal the different strategies and arrangements that individuals and families made to survive and to live their lives after the end of captivity. The changes that freed people who migrated made in their personal trajectories—taking advantage of the professional experiences and the social ties constructed

during slavery or changing their surnames and learning a new profession—
reveal important aspects of the decisions they made and the paths they took
in the post-emancipation period.

Possibilities in a Post-abolition Bahia

In the days immediately following abolition, many men and women emerging from slavery left the plantations for other rural areas or the Recôncavo's towns and cities. In part, this movement was an extension of the slave
flight that had intensified in the late 1880s, as master-slave relations on the
plantations and in the surrounding area deteriorated. As I argued in chapter 1, slave flights—both individual and collective—intensified in the months
immediately preceding abolition. In chapter 5, I argued that immediately before and after May 13, 1888, many freed people moved to Maracangalha to
live or to reconnect with relatives. At the same time, other freed people were
moving on to the land of abandoned plantations in Monte Parish, possibly
hoping to establish roças away from their former masters' lands, but provoking complaints from the authorities.

With the official end of slavery, restrictions on the ex-slaves' movements
also ended and they no longer felt obliged to request "permission" from ex-
masters to leave the places where they had been enslaved. Thus, freed people
were no longer imprisoned in one place. Former owners saw freed people's
decisions to move as part of the "disorganization of labor" that the abolition
law of May 13 unleashed. One observed that the "freedmen have convinced
themselves of the agreeable impression that freedom means that practically
none of them should remain in the company of their ex-masters because that
seemed to them to be a continuation of captivity."[1] Without slavery, the freed
people refused to work in the cane fields and even left the plantations.

Prior to abolition in Bahia, as in other parts of Brazil, elites were terrified
at the thought of blacks abandoning the plantations for the towns and cities,
where they would fill the ranks of the unemployed and the poor. Indeed, the
image of a mass flight from the slave quarters was the projection of long-
standing seignorial fears, which intensified in the last decades of the nineteenth century. These fears did not dissipate after abolition, because, among
other reasons, they contributed to the elite argument for indemnification for
the loss of their enslaved property with abolition.

As slavery ended, the plantation owners used the fear of "black hordes"
occupying the towns and cities to demand that the imperial and provincial
governments take measures to repress vagrancy and vagabondage. Unsur-

prisingly, they defined vagrancy as the refusal to work in the cane fields and the departure from the plantations. A month after the Golden Law was declared, the Baron of Vila Viçosa wrote a long article calling for immediate repression of the insubordination and vagrancy that he argued were disrupting agriculture.[2] The following month, in July 1888, the Bahian Commercial Association expressed the same sentiments in a letter to Princess Isabel demanding imperial government action against what the BCA called the "vagabondage of the free and freed people."[3]

The police in the sugar districts responded to these demands in the months after abolition by targeting ex-slaves who left the plantations. When he arrested a freedman for vagrancy in August 1888, a Santo Amaro policeman recommended a severe punishment, to "send a message to his companions, especially now that the town is full of freedmen who have no employment, but are living solely from thievery.[4]

Although the repression of vagrancy did not resolve the problem of ex-slaves congregating in the towns and cities, the police in the Recôncavo continued to request assistance in controlling their movements. On April 4, 1889, in a letter to the provincial president of Bahia, the delegado of Alagoinhas detailed the difficulties he had in policing a city located at the convergence of three railroads, where, he wrote, a "foreign and unknown population" circulated. Among the causes of the mayhem, he complained, were "those who began to enjoy freedom because of the Law of May 13" and had abandoned the region's plantations and farms. According to the sheriff, "there are a great number of them, who came in search of work, and not finding any, gave themselves over to disorder." Accusing the freedmen of provoking disorder or giving themselves over to a life "without rules" was an argument designed to convince the provincial government of the need for increasing the city's police force.[5]

But to understand the movements of the freedmen and women we must go beyond elite fears and police repression and see things from the perspectives of those who were emerging from slavery. For many ex-slaves, migration meant distancing themselves from slavery. As Rebecca Scott observed, mobility was one element of what freed people defined as freedom.[6] In those days, many abandoned the plantations where they had been enslaved to return to the locales from which they had been taken by masters or to see relatives who lived on other plantations. As the ex-slave Argeu explained, on the day after abolition he left the plantation where he had been a captive: he had arrived on that property as part of his former owner's daughter's dowry.[7]

Many times, efforts to reunite families separated by slavery underlay the decision to migrate. On August 19, 1889, ex-slave José Pedro Calasans, a married man residing in the forests of Cachoeira de Itabuna in Ilhéus, wrote the provincial president requesting payment of his family's passage on the steamship that traveled from Salvador to Ilhéus. His appeal read:

> He has a small cacao farm and grows several subsistence crops, having gone in search of his descendants freed by the Golden Law of May 13, 1888—who were starving in the center of the province of Sergipe, and locating only three children, a widowed daughter-in-law and 8 grandchildren with whom—exhausted, broke, almost to the point of begging—he had to cross the backlands of that province; happily he was able to reach this capital, but, he was unable to reach his home because he had absolutely no way to pay the necessary ship passage to Ilhéus, he comes humbly and respectfully to beg your Excellency to have the generosity to order the Bahian Steamship Company, whose ship leaves for Ilhéus tomorrow morning, to give the supplicant and his family the necessary tickets, according to the attached list, because, Excellent Sir, with the exception of the supplicant, all of them are fleeing hunger, which they migrated to escape and, here in this hospitable Province, they are going to devote themselves to the day-to-day work in agriculture, following the example of their father and grandfather—develop a love of work and pure and healthy morality.[8]

The provincial president responded favorably, and the following day, the freedman and his family boarded a steamship for Ilhéus.

The effort to locate and reunite relatives did not always go so well. On May 21, 1888, freedwoman Isabel Pereira Teles, probably a resident at the imperial court in Rio de Janeiro, wrote to the minister of justice to request that her minor son, Eugênio, be returned to her. Around 1884 he had been taken as a servant to Salvador by a Dr. Afonso de Oliveira Marques Sobrinho. Unfortunately, however, there is no indication that Eugênio ever arrived there: his name does not appear in the records of individuals arriving through the port of Salvador between January 1884 and April 1888.[9]

Trying to move could place ex-slaves and their children in danger. On leaving her ex-master, ex-slave Maria Justina do Sacramento may have been trying to establish a home with her common law husband. On June 11, 1888, however, the delegado of São Felipe, José Leandro Gesteira, was called upon to investigate her disappearance, along with that of her four-year-old son.

Some suspected that they were being held in illegal captivity on the Coelho Plantation in Conceição de Almeida. A denunciation sent to the village authorities charged that the freedwoman might have been the victim of planter Manoel Francisco dos Prazeres, "who, abusing all of the power that the law gave him, resorts to all kinds of tyranny in his dealings with the poor and the miserable, ordering some to be assaulted, others to be raped, and all to finally be put in the stocks of his plantation, all for having committed the grave sin of not wanting to continue to work for him."[10]

At the time, Prazeres was the local subdelegado and the accusation seems to have originated with a political enemy. Many times, these political conflicts among planters were related to disputes over labor as slavery ended. Months later, on September 26, 1888, a planter in the area accused Manoel dos Prazeres of having placed "his rented worker," the freedman "Francisco Grosso," in the stocks after he had tried to leave Prazeres's property to work on the accuser's property.[11]

According to the case records, we know that Maria Justina had been a slave of Amâncio Soares dos Reis but she had been "rented out" to Captain Manoel dos Prazeres, from the "time of slavery." The freedwoman's common law husband informed the authorities that she lived on Prazeres's plantation because "she had been rented out [to the captain] when she was a slave" but that "shortly after she was freed she left the Captain for his company and [since then] she had been living with him." The ex-slave's decision to abandon the property on which she had been a captive to share a roof with her partner was a first step in exercising her freedom. That partner continued on to say that, days later, Maria Justina left home and, from what he could tell, wound up in a place called Bebedouro, on land belonging to Francisco Soares dos Reis, the brother of her ex-owner.

The couple's neighbors suggested other motives for the ex-slave woman's disappearance. Amâncio Soares dos Reis, Maria Justina's ex-master, said that the freedwoman appeared at his home with her four-year-old son and a young pardo boy on the night of June 1 and then left without saying where she was going.[12] A neighbor said that Amâncio beat Maria Justina and on one occasion heard her say, "Let me go, leave me alone or I'm going to tell the young master." The reference to the intervention of "the young master" may mean that Maria Justina intended to use the power of the ex-master to control her partner's violence. Having only recently come out of slavery, Maria Justina seems to have found her partner's tyranny unacceptable. Calling upon the protection of the ex-owner and treating him with deference did not mean that she preferred slavery. Rather, the freedwoman defended her freedom of movement and choice, because she left "the young master's" house without saying "where she was going."[13]

Manoel dos Prazeres was not the only planter to resist the departure of his former slaves. After abolition, the authorities received numerous complaints, often dictated to former abolitionists by ex-slaves, against ex-masters who physically punished ex-slaves or prohibited their departure from the plantations. On August 25, 1888, a letter published in the *Diário da Bahia* stated:

> The planters are trying various different ways to reestablish the authority that they lost with the Law of May 13. Now they are demanding that the authorities make them the guardians of the children born to the free womb, and in that way masking their interest in maintaining their lost power. Now they contract ex-slaves to work on the plantations and then fail to fulfill the promises they make or pay salaries, and when the exploited ones complain, instead of resolving the situation the planters try to compel them to work for free.[14]

According to the newspaper, the planters used their control over ingênuo children to keep parents on the plantations. On August 16, 1888, the ex-slave Eulália accused her ex-master, the owner of the Topá Plantation in Maragojipe, of holding her ingênuo children Teodora, Valentina, and Júlio against her will. She said that on the night of July 27, several individuals surrounded her house on the Sinunga Plantation, grabbed her children, and took them to the plantation where "they cannot get the necessary education and they are suffering the most horrible cruelty." She justified her right to the guardianship of her children by arguing that she was in a position to educate them.[15] The evidence suggests that taking the children was a way of forcing Eulália to return to the plantation where she had been enslaved.

Some planters used the Law of the Free Womb to sue for guardianship of their ex-slaves' ingênuo children. On October 8, 1888, Vitória, a freedwoman described as crioula and the mother of three children—twelve-year-old Vitorina, ten-year-old Porcina, and six-year-old Eutrópio—denounced her ex-master Marcos Leão Veloso, the owner of the Coité Plantation in Inhambupe, for refusing to release her children and keeping them in the cane fields "as though they were slaves, subject to punishment." The children's grandmother, an African Nagô named Felicidade, unsuccessfully attempted to convince Veloso to release them. The two women then enlisted the support of abolitionist Eduardo Carigé, who drew up a complaint accusing the ex-master of violating the Law of May 13 as well as Vitória's right to raise and educate her children "to be useful to the Nation."[16]

Antônio Calmon de Brito, the family court judge for Inhambupe, sided with the planter, arguing that the freedmen and women were ill prepared for a life of freedom. In his November 19, 1888, reply to the provincial president, he stated that a large number of freed people abandoned the plantations and farms after the passage of the Law of May 13. According to him, ex-slaves left Marcos Veloso's plantation on a large scale and many mothers "completely abandoned" their ingênuo children on the plantations "to throw themselves into prostitution" in neighboring villages. He accused Vitória of being one of them. The judge used arguments about morality to disqualify the ex-slaves as parents, labeling them as irresponsible and incapable of raising their own children. It appears that he managed to convince the provincial president, since the case went no further.[17]

On February 19, 1889, Adelina, an "ex-slave" labeled crioula in the documents, lodged a similar complaint with authorities. According to her, her former master, Dr. Porfírio Veloso, the owner of a plantation in Santo Amaro, sent men to assault her when she tried to leave his plantation to live in town. Adelina said that before the end of slavery, she, her son Belmiro (another crioulo), and "some partners" were transferred to the Jacu Plantation as part of the ex-master's daughter's dowry. After May 13, she decided to leave that plantation and take her son with her. On her way to Santo Amaro, she was surprised by four armed men who beat her and took her son along with the animals they were riding. Adelina managed to flee to town, but she accused the ex-master of chasing after her. She also claimed that her son was in the stocks on the Pinguela Plantation, near Jacu, and ended by requesting measures be taken to release her son and stop the ex-master's persecution. That same day, the chief of police ordered the family court judge in Santo Amaro to comply with her request.[18]

Despite the planters' predictions, there was no "mass" flight from the Recôncavo plantations. The evidence suggests that, as in other parts of Brazil, freedmen and women and their children gradually left the plantations over the course of several years.[19] Writing about the plantations of Pernambuco, Gilberto Freyre observed that the relative lack of mobility of the period prior to abolition was followed by an almost gypsy-like behavior by the 1920s, which the ex-slaves seem to have enjoyed. Boilers, cane grinders, farm hands "are now without any roots in this world. They wander from plantation to plantation." According to Freyre, stable relationships disappeared: between planters and workers; between planters and supporters; between planters, renters, and day laborers. Essentially, the "patriarchal cohesion" that had previously stabilized the region disappeared.[20]

In Freyre's view, the plantation workers' rootlessness grew out of the modernization of the sugar industry. Relationships on the central sugar mills in Brazil were impersonal rather than seignorial. Patriarchalism no longer enclosed and protected the workers under the tile roofs of the plantation manor houses. Freyre's nostalgic view obscured the reasons for the workers' mobility. Ex-slaves left the plantations for various reasons, including reestablishing affective ties broken under slavery and improving their ability to support themselves.

We must also think of the migrations in the context of the experiences that the freed people had in the post-emancipation period. Their decision to move away from the plantations could have been related to their hope of expanding the options for survival outside of the plantations or of distancing themselves from their former masters.

The civil registers contain information about some freedmen and women who left the plantations for the cities and towns. At the beginning of the twentieth century, Belarmino Balbino de Santana and Leolinda Isabel, two ex-slaves of the Passagem Plantation, were living on Sinimbu Street in Santo Amaro when their daughter Rita de Cássia was born. On November 25, 1903, laundrywoman Maria Domingas de Ramos registered the birth of her son Catarino da Cruz, a preta boy born in her home on the Beco da Inquisição in Santo Amaro. Maria had been born on the Macaco Plantation in São Francisco.[21] Constança Maria das Mercês, an ex-slave from the Cruz Plantation, registered her great-granddaughter in Cachoeira in December 1894. The girl, named Maria Valentina, was the child of Constança's granddaughter Saturnina Dutra.[22]

On June 2, 1902, lavrador Procópio Gomes de Sales, in a common law marriage with Apolônia de Góes, appeared at the notary's office in Santo Amaro to register the birth of their son Demétrio, described as preta. Prior to the birth of their first child, in 1889, the couple lived and worked on Pitinga, but in 1902, they moved to the Santa Catarina Plantation. Procópio revealed that, at the time, his common law wife was a domestic and had "lived in his company for many years." Thirteen years had passed between the registration of the two children, and in the interval, the couple's lives had changed in several ways. First, Procópio had dropped the surname Pires, which he had inherited from his former master, in favor of Gomes de Sales. By all accounts, Apolônia had ceased working in agriculture and was now a domestic.[23]

The patient records of Santo Amaro's Santa Casa da Misericórdia contain more information about the causes of and the meanings behind the ex-slaves' departures from the plantations between 1906 and 1917. Unfortunately, the

TABLE 9.1. Movement of Persons Born on the Plantations, 1906–1917

Destination	Number	Percent
Cities and towns	82	36
Other plantations	86	37.8
Central sugar mills (usinas)	29	12.6
Rural parishes	31	13.6
Total	228	100

Source: Livros de entrada de doentes no hospital, 1906–1917, ASCMSA.

earlier registers have been lost, but those that remain contain valuable information about the black and mestiço patients born on Recôncavo plantations. Aside from age, color, civil state, and profession, the administrator recorded the place of birth and the residence of the patient at the time he or she was admitted to the hospital. These references allow the reconstruction of the itinerary of some of the freedmen or their descendants who changed their place of residence during that period.

The data in the patient records of the Santa Casa is insufficient to define the profile of the entire ex-slave population and their descendants who left the plantations. Nevertheless, it does provide important insights into the alternatives available and the choices made by those who left the places where they had been born. The data indicates the directions that many people took after abolition and the migratory choices that individuals and families made, as well as the implications for their long-term trajectories.

Between 1906 and 1917, 228 people who had been born on the plantations lived elsewhere when they were admitted to the hospital as patients. Table 9.1 contains information about their place of birth and current address.

Freed people left the plantations for various locations—for other plantations, for the new industrialized cental sugar mills, for rural districts, towns, and cities. Among all patients, 64 percent had moved around within the Recôncavo's rural districts, and many of them continued to be involved in the sugar industry. More than half of the patients had moved to other plantations and central sugar mills; perhaps this proportion would have been larger if the sample only included those who indicated that they lived on other rural plantations.

The plantations attracted 58.9 percent of the migrants who remained in the rural area. On January 23, 1907, the hospital admitted Pedro de Nogueira, a forty-eight-year-old preta man who was living on the Brotas Plantation, but who had been born on the São Bento Plantation. On June 14, 1908, another preta man, twenty-three-year-old Ciriaco dos Santos, reported that he had been born on the Catacumba Plantation, but that he now lived on Traripe.[24] Unfortunately, it is impossible to tell how long these men had been at their new locations or when they left their place of birth. They may have been traveling from property to property according to the calendar of the cane, tobacco, and manioc harvests.

Large numbers of workers headed to the plantations for the cane harvest and then returned home when it was over. The register makes clear that many men and women worked only temporarily on the plantations. When he was admitted to the hospital on April 25, 1916, a sixty-six-year-old preta man, Marcolino Pires, born on the Jacu Plantation, reported that he worked on the Botelho Plantation as a "day laborer." In March 1917, a thirty-year-old preta woman, Umbelina de Jesus, born on the Fortuna Plantation, said that she worked as a "person paid by the day" on the Calolé Plantation.[25]

Moving to a plantation did not always mean working in the cane. Manioc and tobacco workers who rented land on the sugar plantations frequently worked in the cane harvest. But rural workers also moved from plantation to plantation to help out friends and relatives with roças.

Information about patients in the hospital indicates that the modernization of the sugar sector affected ex-slaves and their descendants in several different ways. Work accidents sent several central sugar-mill (usina) workers to the hospital. On August 31, 1915, thirteen-year-old preto Manoel Moreira, born on the Brito Plantation, found himself in the hospital because of an accident that occurred while he was working in the cane on the Itapetingui Plantation on November 25, 1916. Another young preta man, fifteen-year-old Félix dos Santos, appeared at the hospital for treatment of a problem that had developed while he cut cane on the Passagem Central Sugar Mill. He had been born on Camaçari.[26] Most workers appear to have gone to the new industrialized sugar mills to plant or cut cane. When he was admitted on July 13, 1908, Manoel Estevão, a forty-year-old worker born on the Botelho Plantation, declared that he lived on the São Carlos Plantation in Santo Amaro where he worked in the cane fields.[27] Felipe Bulcão, a seventy-three-year-old, single preto who had been born in Iguape also worked in the cane on the same property at the time.[28] To judge by the surname that he carried, Felipe had probably once been enslaved to the Bulcão family, owner of several plantations in Iguape.

Some plantation workers had clearly once been slaves. On August 3, 1910, preto Manoel Brás, a single man born on the Velho Plantation, was working at the São Carlos Central Sugar Mill. In 1887, he had been enslaved on the

TABLE 9.2. Occupations of Migrants to the Cities Checking into
Santo Amaro Hospital, 1906–1917

Occupation	Frequency	Occupation	Frequency
Agriculture	18	Stonemason	2
Roceiro	12	Watercarrier	2
Domestic	11	Wagoneer	1
Cook	1	Servant	1
Seamstress	5	Miner	1
Starcher	1	Street vendor	1
Servant	3	Cigar maker	1
Itinerant laborer	2	Salt worker	1
Day laborer	5	Oven worker	1
Carter	1	Sailor	1
Cabinetmaker	4	No information	3

Source: Livros de entrada de doentes no hospital, 1906–1917, ASCMSA.

Baron of Pirajá's Velho Plantation. The plantation's owners described him as a twenty-three-year-old single man, who was the son of the slave woman Eufrosina. The list of the plantation slaves also contained the names of his mother and his three sisters, Eufemia, Agostinha, and Dana. A year before the end of slavery, Manoel Brás and his entire family were still enslaved.[29]

Many hospital patients did not remain in the countryside. The data reveals that 36 percent of those patients born on plantations had moved to the towns or cities. As might be expected, most such hospital patients lived in Santo Amaro; even so, the data confirms that many ex-slaves left the plantations for urban centers. Table 9.2 lists the occupations of such people.

According to table 9.2, a large number of workers living in the city supported themselves from agriculture: 38.4 percent declared that they worked in agriculture or in a roça. The proximity of the town of Santo Amaro to the countryside made it possible for a person to live in the city and walk to the cane fields of some nearby central sugar mill or plantation. When she was admitted to the hospital, Cipriana Maria Pesote, a forty-four-year-old preta woman who had been born on the Tebaida Plantation, declared that she "lived from her roça" and resided on the Rua do Bonfim in Santo Amaro.[30] Ex-slave Antero Ramos da Purificação worked in agriculture and lived in town. When his daughter Crescência was born in June 1891, however, as noted in the previous chapter, he and his common law wife, Maria Orminda, were living on the Pitinga Plantation. By July 1918, he was living in Santo Amaro.[31]

FIGURE 9.1. Black women in the Dannemann cigar factory in São Félix, 1920.
Public Archive of the State of Bahia.

FIGURE 9.2. Black women and canoe paddlers on the dock at Cachoeira, 1930.
Arthur Wischral / Public Archive of the State of Bahia.

Some patients living in urban centers exercised professions that they had learned on the plantations. During that time, many trades practiced in the rural area fit the demands of the urban labor market quite well. Consequently, it is a mistake to suggest that rural ex-slaves were unprepared for life in the towns and cities. On March 16, 1916, Próspero dos Santos, described as a seventy-year-old single preta man who worked as a stonemason and in Santo Amaro said that he had been born on the Mombaça Plantation. The 1880 list of slaves for that plantation does include his name and his profession—stonemason. When he left the plantation for town, the ex-slave used the trade that he had learned on the plantation during slavery to his advantage.[32] Most ex-slaves, however, seem to have needed to learn new trades or professions in order to survive. Manoel Clemente, a seventy-year-old preta man born on the Tanque Plantation supported himself in Santo Amaro by hauling water. Manoel Cirilo da Hora, a twenty-eight-year-old single mulato man born on the Velho Plantation learned how to roll cigars to find work.[33]

Household labor absorbed a significant number of the workers leaving the plantations. Most of the women admitted to the hospital worked as domestics. They were the nannies, laundry women, and cooks in middle-class city households. Henriqueta Maria da Silva, a sixty-year-old preta woman born on the Brotas Plantation, was working as a domestic servant in Santo Amaro when she was admitted to the hospital in October 1906, diagnosed with anemia. But women were not the only domestic servants. On October 15, 1916, Dionísio dos Santos, a sixteen-year-old parda man born on the São Bento Plantation well after abolition, declared that he worked as a servant in Santo Amaro.[34]

Street vending does not seem to have been a significant source of income for ex-slaves leaving the plantations. At least one female patient at the Santa Casa born on a plantation worked as a street vendor: she was Delfina Ribeiro, a sixty-eight-year-old preta woman, born on the Pericoara Plantation and admitted on February 16, 1916.[35] But her experience seems to have been rare. Perhaps becoming a street vendor was extremely competitive for women and therefore difficult for those who left the plantations.

As in the countryside, life in the city was difficult for those who had emerged from slavery. It is not surprising, therefore, that some turned to begging. When Venância "so-and-so," a sixty-eight-year-old single mulata woman born on the Pitinga Plantation was admitted to the hospital on November 5, 1920, she had been living in Santo Amaro as a "beggar." The 1887 list of Pitinga slaves reveals her presence on the plantation as the thirty-six-year-old single daughter of Patria. Her mother was probably the woman of that name enslaved on the Conde Plantation, which belonged to the same owner in 1871.[36]

The hospital data describes only those ex-slaves or their descendants who were moved around within the Recôncavo, many of whom continued to be linked to the sugar industry. In the years after abolition, freedmen and women also moved quietly to rural parishes that lay farther from the cane fields, especially to the coastal or frontier regions. They may also have migrated to southern Bahia toward the end of the nineteenth century, drawn by the developing cacao sector there.[37] Aside from the hope of growing cacao themselves, agricultural wages on the cacao plantations and farms were more attractive than those paid in cane. According to a study carried out by the Ministry of Agriculture in 1912, the average wage of a cacao worker was Rs.2$000, in comparison to Rs.1$500 in the sugar districts. The same study showed that the cacao harvest attracted rural workers from many other areas in search of better salaries.[38]

Coastal villages and towns may also have attracted freedmen and women who had been born in the rural parishes of the Recôncavo. Future studies about communities near the mangroves around the Bay of All Saints and the Atlantic coastal region known as the *baixo sul*, just to the south of the bay, may turn up evidence of people who deserted the cane fields after slavery ended.

Some ex-slaves attempted to return to Africa. In her research on ships' passengers departing Brazil for Africa, Kim Butler identified a noticeable increase in the number of Africans and crioulos traveling to Lagos, the West African port city that today sits in Nigeria. Two weeks after May 13, fifty-four passengers embarked for that city. The following year, large numbers of Africans and their descendants were still leaving for the ports of Africa.[39] At abolition, most surviving Africans in Brazil had obtained their freedom, but many may have decided to wait to return to Africa until their children and grandchildren were also freed from slavery by the Law of May 13. It may have been for this reason that, on May 9, 1888, the same day that the newspapers reported the news that the abolition bill had passed, businessmen in Salvador advertised the availability of passage to the coast of Africa on the Brazilian ship *Cecília*. Another advertisement promised that within the month another ship, this one called *Bonfim*, would leave for Lagos.[40]

The Recôncavo in Motion

Unfortunately, the population censuses for 1872 and 1890 do not provide any specific information about the movements of the Recôncavo's black population in the last two decades of the nineteenth century. Nevertheless, it is possible to use the census to reconstruct some of those movements. We know that in the last years of that century some Recôncavo urban centers—chiefly Salvador, Santo Amaro, São Félix, and Cachoeira—attracted many free and freed people. The 1872 census counted 8,146 inhabitants in the urban parish of Our Lady of the Rosary of the Port of Cachoeira: 79.6 percent of those people were blacks and mestiços. By 1890, the city's population had jumped to 12,607 persons. Individuals whom the census takers described as preta composed 20.1 percent of that total. Including caboclos and mestiços in that number reveals that the nonwhite population of the city reached a bit more than 72 percent.[41]

Between the two censuses, we also can see an increase in the population of the neighboring town of São Félix. In 1872, 2,857 people lived in the parish of the Child Jesus of São Félix: among them, 14.5 percent were preta. In 1890, the year that São Félix became a city, the population had risen to 4,358 inhabitants, of whom 21.8 percent were preta. Only 36.6% percent were white. In the first years of the twentieth century, the population of this interior river port town continued to grow. It should be underscored that the populations of both São Félix and Cachoeira fluctuated daily as men and women who lived in the nearby rural parishes arrived each morning to work in the cigar factories and went home at the end of the day.

The towns of São Félix and Cachoeira had always attracted people because they were centers of regional commerce and, especially, of riverine shipping. By abolition, however, they were also attracting workers because of their new position as centers of the cigar industry. Between 1880 and 1890, cigar factories there experienced impressive growth in exports to Europe. Employment in associated activities also grew. There is some evidence of the growth in the labor force in the largest cigar factories in the region between the end of the nineteenth century and the beginning of the twentieth. The Dannemann factory, founded in São Félix by two German immigrants, employed between three hundred and four hundred workers in 1877; in 1921, they counted on twelve hundred workers. In 1887, Costa Ferreira and Penna, also in São Félix, but with a branch in Muritiba, employed seventy workers; in 1921, that number had grown to about one thousand. The Suerdieck Company, based in Cachoeira, employed about four hundred workers in 1916; in 1921, that number had jumped to nine hundred.[42]

In addition to being centers of the tobacco industry, the two towns constituted important points of contact between Salvador and more distant parts of the northeastern interior, generically referred to as the backlands. Throughout the nineteenth century, mule trains had loaded supplies brought by the boats from Salvador and carried them deep into the backlands, returning animals, hides, and other goods. Construction of the railroads at the end of the nineteenth century increased the towns' role as commercial entrepôts, and railroad construction jobs attracted large numbers of freedmen and women, as well as fugitive slaves, in the last years of slavery. The increased circulation of people and merchandise allowed the expansion of the labor market for street vendors, carters, muleteers, boatmen, canoe paddlers, stevedores, and sailors, all professions traditionally exercised by blacks and mestiços.

In contrast to what was happening in the towns, the population of Iguape, Cachoeira County's largest nineteenth-century sugar district, fell. In 1872, 7,159 people lived in the Santiago do Iguape Parish, of whom 43.5 percent were preta. By 1890, the district's population had risen to 9,741 inhabitants, a smaller number of which (34.8 percent) were preta, but only 10.6 percent were white. When slavery ended, blacks and people of mixed race (mestiços) made up almost 90 percent of the population. Over the next three decades, however, the Iguape Parish suffered a significant drop in population, reflecting the crisis in the sugar industry following abolition. In 1912, the parish priest stated that the parish was in a state of decline and "without hope for the future." He estimated that the parish's population had fallen to five thousand inhabitants. The 1920 census found only 6,487 persons living in Iguape.[43]

The evidence suggests that many people left the rural districts of the Recôncavo for Salvador in the last years of the nineteenth century. In 1872, 129,109 people lived in the Bahian provincial capital, according to the census. In 1890, that number had jumped to 171,412. At that time, pretos made up 26.9 percent of the population. Combining the categories of pretos with mestiços, we see that nonwhites composed 67.4 percent of the population.[44] In the 1880s, Salvador was the principal destination of people fleeing slavery in the Recôncavo; it appears that Salvador continued to be an important destination after slavery ended.

Some rural migrants entered the urban labor market in professions traditionally held by the free and freed population. Data about itinerant labor and domestic service, two important sectors of the urban labor market, suggests the degree to which the movement of slaves and freedmen and women affected the composition of the city's labor force.

In his study of the ganhadores (TR: literally "earners," here translated as "itinerant laborers"), who provided a multitude of services for hire in the streets of Salvador, historian João Reis found that 11.6 percent of the 1,703 who registered with the city between 1887 and 1893 had been born in the sugar areas, including the counties of Santo Amaro, São Sebastião do Passé, Cachoeira, and São Francisco do Conde. Many of them were ex-slaves. If we include the itinerant laborers born in other parts of the Recôncavo, the percentage rises to

17.5 percent. In other words, many of Salvador's itinerant laborers had abandoned the cane fields in the last years of slavery, or the first years of freedom.[45]

A few of the registered itinerant laborers who left the plantations told the authorities something about where they had originated or the names of their former masters. Manoel João, a fifty-two-year-old caboclo from Santo Amaro stated that "he had been the slave of the deceased Baron of Pirajá." Manoel Panfilo, a twenty-six-year-old fula man from the Monte Parish declared that he was "the servant of Joaquim Alves da Cruz Rios," owner of a plantation in São Francisco do Conde. José Antônio de Oliveira, a forty-six-year-old preta man, also from Santo Amaro, had been "the slave of the Baron of Alagoinhas." Some reported that they had been freed by the Law of May 13. Several men who had been freed by the Golden Law labored together in one of the work groups based in Salvador's Lower City Commercial District. They included Manoel Longuinho, a twenty-seven-year-old fula man from Santo Amaro, the ex-slave of Senator Junqueira; Anacleto Teixeira Magno de Nazaré, a preta man; and Julião Maurício Wanderley, a fula man born in the Matoim Parish, formerly enslaved to Cotegipe.[46]

In Salvador, ex-slaves from the same parishes joined the same work groups. Ângelo Veríssimo da Purificação and Paulo Narciso das Chagas Viana, black men from the Monte Parish in São Francisco do Conde, both belonged to the group based in the Rua da Louça. Some group members even came from the same property. José Antero, a twenty-eight-year-old fula man, and Pedro Celestino, a twenty-six-year-old cabra man, had been born in Passé Parish and had belonged to the same owner. They were both part of the group based in Carne Seca alley. Eighteen-year-old Pedro Francisco de Sousa and his brother, nineteen-year-old Nilo Manoel de Sousa, pretos born in Paripe where they had belonged to the same owner, worked together and lived together, on Laranjeiras Street. These freed people, as well as free people living in the city, seemed to be reestablishing the affective ties and friendships built on the plantations.[47]

Seventeen of the fifty-eight itinerant workers from the parishes where the largest sugar plantations were located—Nossa Senhora do Monte, Socorro, Rio Fundo, Bom Jardim, Iguape, Matoim, Paramirim, and São Sebastião do Passé—practiced a profession that they had probably learned in their places of origin. Among the trades they exercised were tanner, blacksmith, cabinetmaker, carpenter, builder, shoemaker, barber, footman, farmer, and muleteer. The presence of these skilled slaves in Salvador suggests that the departure of workers from the plantations did not involve only those who labored in agriculture.

The men and women who left the plantations after abolition confronted a growing effort on the part of the provincial and municipal authorities to regulate the professions traditionally practiced by blacks. From the end of the nineteenth century on, as slavery declined in the cities and towns, Bahian authorities began adopting measures to discipline urban laborers, most of whom were blacks newly emerged from slavery. One of these new policies required itinerant laborers to register with the authorities.

The city authorities also began to regulate other employment sectors that attracted freed workers, including wagon drivers and water haulers. According to a sample of the registrations carried out prior to July 1893, 2,452 workers labored in the streets of Salvador, among whom were 1,721 itinerant laborers, 473 wagon drivers, and 248 water haulers. On July 24, 1893, the *Jornal de Notícias* reported that the period of open registration would end on August 6, 1893, and that thereafter any unregistered person engaged in those activities would face a fine of Rs.10$000, or four days in prison. Thereafter, approved individuals were obliged to wear a hat and an arm patch that indicated their registry number.[48]

As slavery was ending, the authorities also began to try to regulate domestic service. On December 30, 1886, in response to the demands of the chief of police and the "complaints of the public," the Salvador City Council developed regulations to govern dealings between employers and domestic servants in the city. The measures attempted to establish rules for hiring domestic labor and guidelines for interactions between servant and employer. The councilmen announced that they were dealing with a thorny issue, since "the class that dedicates itself to domestic service" was not accustomed to rules.[49] Actually, however, the new rules reflected concerns in the 1880s about the rapid decline of slavery in Salvador. The city council was also responding to "Bahian families" and their anxiety about the supply of free and freed domestic labor and, especially, about how to control domestic servants now that slavery had ended.[50]

The city council developed a twenty-seven-article domestic labor code. The code established minimum standards of hygiene for domestic workers, required workers to comply with contracts, and, in general, placed household servants under the control of the police. Article 1 stated that the police department would maintain a register of free and freed people experienced as cooks, footmen, laundrywomen, nannies or wet nurses, valets, coachmen, gardeners, hotel clerks, stable boys, or boardinghouse workers—in other words, a register of all domestic servants. Article 3 forbade anyone with a contagious disease or whose looks might offend an employer to register. Also forbidden to register were individuals with criminal records, minors without parental consent, and married women without their husband's permission.

The council was attempting to place female domestic servants under patriarchal control. When she registered, the servant received a booklet, furnished by the city council and authenticated by the police department, which she was required to present to employers. The booklet contained blank pages on which the delegado or the chief of police might record observations about her behavior. The first notebook was free, but thereafter, the servant was required to pay Rs.1$000 for each one. The servant was also required to appear at the police headquarters with the notebook each year.[51]

The domestic labor code also defined rights and responsibilities of employers and servants. Article 9 stated that servants who left their employer prior to the date stipulated in the contract would be fined Rs.20$000 or spend four days in prison. In compensation, Article 10 granted the servant the right to leave his or her employer if wages were not promptly paid or for other "just causes." The code also stated that employers could fire servants for illness, drunkenness, incompetence, as well as "offenses and lack of respect" toward the employer or a member of his family.[52]

Article 15 governed wet nurses. A physician selected by the city council or a representative of the police would establish the parameters of each breastfeeding contract, and the wet nurse was obliged to comply with them. Wet nurses were required to take medical exams and those who hid illnesses or who were unable to breastfeed the employer's child would be fined Rs.20$000 or spend four days in jail. Wet nurses who abandoned the child they were feeding prior to the end of the period for which they had been contracted (in other words, the period during which the child was to be breastfed) would be fined Rs.40$000 or the equivalent of eight days' salary. The wet nurse retained the right to refuse to work for an employer who, among other things, failed to pay wages, maltreated her, or obliged her to provide services that had not previously been arranged.[53]

Salvador's Domestic Labor Code was subject to the approval of the Bahian legislature, but on January 4, 1887, the provincial president ordered that it be implemented in advance of a formal vote. The immediate creation of a register for female domestic servants was one of the consequences of the provincial president's decision. Following the requirements established by the city council, the book contains the name, place of birth, civil state, age, profession, "characteristics," and nationality of the registrant. The Public Archive of

Occupation	Women	Percent	Men	Percent	Total	Percent
Cook	265	47.6	25	11.1	290	37.1
Servant	77	13.8	58	25.8	135	17.3
Nanny	64	11.5	—	—	64	8.2
Wet nurse	20	3.6	—	—	20	2.6
Starcher	69	12.5	—	—	69	8.8
Seamstress	12	2.2	—	—	12	1.6
Laundress	20	3.6	—	—	20	2.6
Housekeeper/ butler	20	3.6	84	37.3	104	13.3
Domestic service	9	1.6	1	0.4	10	1.3
Gardener	—	—	23	10.3	23	2.9
Coachman	—	—	15	6.6	15	1.9
Other Services	—	—	19	8.5	19	2.4
Total	556	71.5	225	28.5	781	100

Source: Livro de matrícula das criadas domésticas, 1887–1893, APEB.

Bahia holds part of the *Livro de matrículas de criadas domésticas* (Register of domestic servants) covering the period from 1887 to 1893, although entries for 1893 are incomplete.[54]

The register contains extensive information about this important urban labor sector. All together, 791 people appear in its pages: 556 women and 225 men. In other words, 71.5 percent of the people employed in domestic service were women. The authorities recorded a trade for all but ten of the domestic servants they registered. That data is contained in table 9.3.

The table makes clear that a gender division of labor functioned within the servants' quarters of the middle- and upper-class homes of Salvador. For obvious reasons, all of the wet nurses were female, but so were the nannies. Women also made, repaired, and otherwise cared for clothing, doing all the washing, ironing, and sewing. To a certain degree, the predominance of women in these roles reflected the preferences of the employers. But men and women both disputed control of the kitchens and pantries of the city's well-to-do. Women did most of the cooking, but the *copa*, or pantry, was primarily men's responsibility, meaning that men supervised the larder, the family china and silver, the serving of meals, and the admission of visitors to the home. In other words, men worked as butlers in well-to-do Bahian

TABLE 9.4. Domestic Servants by Color

Color	Frequency	Percent
Preta	337	43.6
Parda	273	35.3
Cabra	101	13.0
Cabocla	15	1.9
White or "almost white"	48	6.2
Total	774	100

Source: Livro de matrícula das criadas domésticas, 1887–1893, APEB.

homes. Men also held most of the positions in the gardens and stables, caring for flowers, vegetables, and herbs, as well as animals.

As in the *Livro de matrícula dos ganhadores* (Itinerant laborers registry), the police used multiple terms to describe the color of domestic servants' skin. They labeled black women preta, crioula, or fula. They described mixed-race women (mestiças) along a continuum of shades of brown from *parda-clara* (light brown) to *parda-escura* (dark brown). White domestic servants were described as either "pale whites" or "almost whites." Table 9.4 summarizes the perceived skin color of Salvador's domestic servants based on the primary categories of the period.[55]

The table demonstrates that people described as black or mixed dominated the domestic service sector. Together, these two categories represented 93.8 percent of the people who cooked, cleaned, and cared for the children and homes of Salvador's middle and upper classes. Only eight maids were African women. White male or female servants were also rare, and their number would be even smaller if we removed those classified as "almost white." But we cannot conclude that the significant number of black servants meant that poor whites refused to work in the homes of wealthy whites. Employment ads from the period demonstrate many employers' preference for black servants.

Of all the domestic servants, 205, or 25.9 percent came from the rural and urban parishes of the Recôncavo. One hundred and ten servants, or 13.9 percent of the total, came from the centers of the sugar industry (Santo Amaro, São Francisco, Cachoeira, and São Sebastião do Passé). Among the servants born in those parishes were some who clearly came from the plantations. Among them was Laurentina Dutra, who, when she registered in 1887, told the police that she was the daughter of Joana Dutra (now deceased), forty-two years of age, single, a cook, and "rented" in the home of her ex-master Luís Rodrigues Dutra in Salvador's prestigious Vitória Parish.

Laurentina had been a slave on the Cruz Plantation and, from all appearances, continued to be connected to her ex-master in the capital. Simoa Dutra was another domestic servant in Salvador who was born on a Recôncavo sugar plantation: she told the authorities that she was a cabra-colored maid, the forty-year-old daughter of Manoel Luís and Simoa, that she also came from the Cruz Plantation, and that she was rented out in the well-to-do Graça district.

Two other Cruz Plantation ex-slaves registered as domestic servants in 1893. Maria Serafina Dutra, a thirty-five-year-old single cook, was born in Iguape as the daughter of the ex-slave Generosa Dutra and rented out in a Rio Vermelho home. Orminda Pereira, a thirty-five-year-old single parda maid, was also born in Iguape, the daughter of our friend Etelvina Dutra, and had been rented out in the home of Francisco Teixeira de Carvalho since 1883.[56] At that time, Orminda's mother and her brother Maximiano were still living and working on the Cruz Plantation. Moreover, Orminda still had relatives in the places where she had been enslaved, and the register suggests that, despite the distance, she still had connections to them.

It is possible that some of the people who left the plantations when slavery ended found work in independent urban professions. The evidence seems to suggest that, after abolition, this labor sector grew, especially the number of street vendors who sold lottery tickets, fruit, sweets and other delicacies, and shined shoes. After the Brazilian Empire collapsed in 1889, subsequent republican governments established rigid financial and police controls over the city's street vendors. At the end of the century, the street vendors were required to purchase a license from the city council before they could sell their wares. Successive municipal governments and the local press launched campaigns to remove street vendors from the city center, arguing that doing so would improve public health and traffic circulation in the city. On March 18, 1895, the *Jornal de Notícias* appealed to the municipal authorities to remove the "busy women vendors" from the intersection of Duarte, Cabeça, Vigário Ally, and São Pedro streets. According to the editorial, in the evenings the market there interrupted public transit.[57]

All through the end of the nineteenth century and the beginning of the twentieth, Salvador's authorities tried to push street vendors out of the Baixa dos Sapateiros district. On February 24, 1899, the *Jornal de Notícias* approved city hall's decision to renew the prohibition against street vendors—male and female—occupying the sidewalks. On May 2, 1899, the authorities expelled the vegetable vendors and "and other salespeople" who occupied the market square in the Baixa dos Sapateiros, alleging that they tied up traffic and dirtied the streets with "all sorts of filth that they managed to gather together in baskets and jugs." Another newspaper approved the operation and recommended that the same measures be taken on the city's docks, Castro Alves Square, and other places "where a great many street vendors remained, day and night, with boards, jugs and trays of sweets, in clear violation of city regulations."[58]

Fifteen months later, in September 1900, the *Jornal de Notícias* complained about commerce involving trays, boards, and jugs in Castro Alves Square. "And, aside from the shoe shiners, you see a busy market selling bread, sweets, fruit, etc, even medicinal plants." According to the newspaper, people trying to walk through the area could not use the sidewalks, because the "vagrants" blocked the way with their legs stuck out, with boxes of boot black, straw baskets and trays of candies.[59] In August 1904, the *Diário de Notícias* celebrated the city's decision to remove all baskets, jugs, and trays of vegetables and beans messing up the streets in the Baixa dos Sapateiros.[60]

Ex-slaves from the plantations certainly were trying to break the ties that bound them to slavery by moving to the city. Earlier we saw itinerant laborers from the sugar parishes working together in the same gang and, at times, living on the same street. In 1901, when the neighbors called the police because she was beating her grandson, the difficult lives of Maria Luísa Dutra Bulcão, a crioula laundrywoman and ex-slave from the Cruz Plantation, and her family were documented in the pages of a police report. Maria Luísa reported that she did not live with her daughter, Maria do Espírito Santo, but she was always at her home. For her part, Maria do Espírito Santo said she could not sleep at home every night because she was "rented out" as a cook. She also said that she did not report her mother to the police for beating her son because she did not want to see the older woman suffer.[61] She had probably decided that reporting her mother would condemn her to another round of captivity.

The incorporation of ex-slaves into urban communities was permeated with conflict. Sometimes, in the middle of an argument, freed people would remember their enslaved past. On February 20, 1892, several young men and women from Cachoeira—some of whom were itinerant laborers—were going from house to house, visiting friends to dance samba. Among those they visited was a man known as Nicolau Muniz, a day laborer, born on the Vitória Plantation. After the group left, Nicolau and his common law wife noticed that some of their belongings had disappeared and decided to get them back. When they caught up with the group, Nicolau asked two of their number, Fuão, known as the "Crioulo," and the "itinerant laborer Aprígio" to return the stolen items. A fight broke out and Nicolau took off running, with the group chasing him shouting, "Kill the Black [Negro] guy." Negro here had more than just a racial meaning—in this case it also referred to his former position as a slave. Certainly the group that threatened Nicolau knew that they were talking to an ex-slave. The list of slaves on the Vitória Plantation made in 1871 records the presence there of Nicolau, crioulo, forty years of age, "crippled in his left hand," sailor.[62]

According to Manoel Querino, there were people in Salvador called the "collectors of traditions," elderly people who knew what had gone on in the neighborhood. Some of them kept scrapbooks about the important people and events in the neighborhood. Recognition by the collectors as "socially important" became something of a competition among neighborhood families, but anyone who wanted to know about their rivals' "weaknesses" only had to look for the "man with the archive." Among the factors that could damage the reputation of these contenders for prominence was an enslaved past. To embarrass a family, it was enough to say that "so-and-so was born at such-and-such a time, his parents were so-and-so and so-and-so, his grandmother was a slave and was sometimes beaten." Or, alternatively, "So-and-so, who acts like he's as good as anyone else, is the son of a slave woman who fled the plantation as a young girl; she came here, she had a great deal of luck, and the children were already well settled when the master showed up [to reclaim her]. They fought to keep it [their past in slavery] all a secret and they succeeded, because of their wealth and their connections."[63]

Ex-slaves and their descendants, whether in the city or the countryside, rejected descriptions that evoked their former condition as slaves, especially if such references were aimed at devaluing their new condition as freed people. On the morning of March 2, 1906, in Preguiça Street, Maria Secundina da Conceição, whom the police clerk described as a preta-colored twenty-seven-year-old laundrywoman, felt insulted at being called "little black girl" by a fisherman named Fábio. As a result, there was quite a vociferous argument, ending with Fábio beating Maria Secundina quite seriously.[64] The reference to slavery could be made in other ways. On the night of March 15, 1891, in Cachoeira, Laudelino Ferreira da Silva was assaulted after threatening to whip Pompeu "so-and-so," a worker at the Dannemann cigar factory in São Félix.[65] Whipping someone meant to reduce them to the condition of a slave, and Laudelino paid dearly for the offense.

Beyond these differences, the movement of escaping slaves and freed people after abolition put men and women who experienced rural slavery in contact with those who had lived in the towns and cities. The streets of Salvador became a site for the exchange of their experiences as laborers from the city and the countryside labored together in the same work gangs. All of these ex-slaves became free citizens on May 13, 1888, and began to develop

FIGURE 9.3. Black family, Cachoeira, 1911. Their posture and clothing indicate that they sought to demonstrate that they had achieved a degree of upward social mobility.

new ways of interacting, no longer based on the differences between the free, the freed, and the enslaved. Perhaps that is why, as João Reis argues, during this period urban workers began to try to act as a class.[66] It is not surprising, then, that thirty-one strikes broke out in Salvador and the Recôncavo between 1888 and 1896.[67]

The possibility that urban workers were beginning to form a class requires deepening research into the connections between the experience of slavery and the post-emancipation Bahian workers' movement. The ways in which workers made their demands, including the repeated direct or metaphorical references to slavery, offer one avenue for doing so. When they protested the dismissal of fellow workers in 1889, cigar makers in the Dannemann factory in São Félix stated that slavery was over. In October 1909, workers, machinists, and firemen of the Viação Férrea (Railway) accused the company of trying to turn them into "humiliated slaves" by denying overtime, instituting fines, and transferring them from place to place.[68]

On this basis, slavery could be evoked as the experience of a social class. On May 12, 1902, when calling upon the "Bahian people" not to forget "our emancipation," in a letter published in a city newspaper, the labor leader and ex-abolitionist Ismael Ribeiro spoke out in the name of "my ancestors."[69]

Epilogue

IN THE CENTURIES TO COME: PROJECTIONS OF SLAVERY AND FREEDOM

Today, these memories (of abolition)
leave a sadness and an inexpressible melancholy. . . .
So many dreams! [. . .] So many illusions! . . .
We thought that when the slaves were free,
Our Brazil would enter a period of peace, happiness,
and boundless progress;—The "Golden Age" that the
humanitarians always suggested would arrive but that,
is still a long way, a very long way, off, in the centuries to come.

—ANDRÉ REBOUÇAS, *Diário e notas autobiográficas*

Abolition occurred in the context of intense social agitation: unrest on the plantations, individual and collective flight, popular hostility to slavery, and the radicalization of the abolitionist movement. The Bahian authorities feared that the end of slavery would unleash a broader process of social change with unforeseen consequences. These fears were not groundless. In other slave societies, abolition had awoken new and old aspirations and demands, and the results did not always favor the ex-masters. Ex-slave owners in Bahia feared that the end of slavery would mean more than substituting one labor regime for another. They feared losing control of the abolition process, in the face of the initiatives of the ex-slaves.

Slavery was extinguished at the high point of a mass movement in Brazil. Through their struggle against slavery, ex-slaves in Bahia defined their hopes, dreams, and plans in ways that went well beyond the end of slavery. For ex-slaves, freedom meant access to land and the right to choose their place of work, to move about without asking anyone's permission, to be free from police harassment, to worship African gods, or to venerate Catholic saints as they chose. In other words, they did not want to be treated like captives and, above all, they wanted to have citizenship rights.

It is not surprising, then, that the question of the social "place" that the freedmen and women would occupy in what was then termed the "Brazilian Communion" took center stage in political debates after May 13. This discussion began in the early nineteenth century when Brazilian elites realized that slavery would eventually give way to free labor. Ex-masters and their representatives maintained that the social and racial hierarchies developed over the course of three centuries of slavery should be maintained when ex-slaves became free men and women.

Official pronouncements by the Bahian authorities provide avenues through which to explore contemporary elite thinking about the introduction of ex-slaves to freedom. Opposing those who insisted that abolition would bring only idleness and vagrancy, and possibly trying to calm its readers, the editors of the *Diário da Bahia* wrote on May 13, 1888:

> The race being freed will know how to show itself worthy of the freedom that, in part, is being given to them and, in part, they conquered themselves. Once the nightmare of labor in the fields is no more, they will labor to win their place in the Brazilian Communion. The energy of these people exiled from their native lands, formerly isolated by slavery, will increase our national capacity significantly. The free man will now be able to fertilize with his sweat, the soil that he previously stained with his blood! . . . The freedmen will not be uncontrolled idlers, scavenging and committing crimes as dangerous vagabonds. Instead we can count on them to contribute to prosperity. When they leave the slave quarters, those freed will leave behind the debasing habits they contracted in slavery; and once they finish celebrating, they will begin the life of free men, to which they are entitled.[1]

The editorialists took a position different from those of most ex-masters. They argued that slavery had debased its victims and that ex-slaves' bad habits were a product of the slave system. They also denied that the ex-slaves were unprepared for freedom and maintained that they would not become vagrants. Rather, they stated that the freedmen would use their labor to join the so-called Brazilian Communion. Or better yet, they would continue to contribute to the wealth and prosperity of others. For that reason, they should abandon the "habits" that, supposedly, they had acquired in captivity.

In a notice published shortly after abolition, the Salvador City Council declared:

> The new citizens, whose dignity abolition reinstated, like us, have the responsibility to protect our national rights, the progress of our common nation, and improve our birthplaces vis-à-vis world civilization. And now that they will demand the rights that inequitable laws denied their race for centuries, they should find in work, in family and in peace a way to generously recognize the social status that has been guaranteed them by the power of the State.[2]

The city council was concerned about maintaining order. That is why the council members sought to connect ex-slaves to the national project of civilization and progress. Interestingly, the council anticipated that the freedmen and women would demand their rights, but made clear that they should do so in an orderly fashion. Once again, labor appeared to be a guarantee of progress and national peace.

In both of these documents the writers used the term "race" to define the freed people's new social condition. With the end of slavery, Bahian elites fell back on the idea of race to classify the new citizens. Although equal from the perspective of civil rights, the people were differentiated (or should be considered unequal) on the basis of their racial classification. This conception of race was perfect for those who were trying to maintain and reinforce the old hierarchies. On this basis they could justify new policies of control over the entire population of African descent, not just those who had recently emerged from slavery. New policies of racial exclusion were beginning to be defined.[3]

The debate around defining the place that former slaves would occupy in society aimed at controlling the entire black population, not only those who had recently emerged from slavery. Regulations adopted by provincial and municipal authorities pointed to a growing effort to control the black population's day-to-day lives. As discussed in the previous chapter, Bahian authorities adopted measures to control urban workers, especially several meant to clean up the streets and register those workers.

Even so, this study demonstrates that freedmen and women reacted to the policies of exclusion and formulated their own projects for social engagement in freedom. Specifically, they developed strategies for survival that attempted to counteract ex-masters' plans to maintain them in subaltern positions. On Recôncavo plantations, ex-slaves struggled with ex-masters to establish rights to land, to reshape day-to-day social relations, to limit ex-masters' interference in their personal and family lives, and to demand treatment compatible with their condition as free persons. Ex-masters feared that these initiatives posed a serious threat to the social order and tried to undermine them. That is why ex-masters characterized such behavior as "drunkenness" or "deliriousness."

Fear that the freedmen and women would upend the social order explains why the celebrations of May 13 distressed ex-masters and the authorities so much. As I argued, the presence of over three thousand pretos in the streets of Salvador worried Aristides Novis. During the celebrations of May 13 in Caravelas, liberal and conservative politicians organized separate parades celebrating abolition, and ex-slaves participated in both. On May 19, a confrontation took place between the two political factions, and two freedmen were mortally wounded. Those who were trying to restrict freedmen to the world of work did not see the ex-slaves' presence in both political associations as a good sign.

These social tensions and clashes over the popular classes' plans for freedom continued in the years after abolition. The social movements that developed were impregnated with the feelings and expectations forged in the struggles against slavery. Unfortunately, this aspect of the history of the era has still not been the object of systematic study. Ex-slaves' participation in the social struggles of the period was silenced. It was as if the slaves' efforts to free themselves lost their meaning after May 13, 1888, and belonged to a past that ex-masters tried to erase.

Abolitionist efforts (or at least the efforts of certain sectors of the abolitionist movement) did not end on May 13, 1888. In the following years, former abolitionists pushed to amplify the social space available to the black population and became involved in several related conflicts. Abolitionist lawyers continued to provide legal assistance to ex-slaves, including defending them in the courts. Some continued to use the press to criticize the treatment of ex-slaves on the plantations and to denounce police violence against persons of color.[4]

Abolitionist Luís Tarquínio, an upwardly mobile parda man, wrote several newspaper articles protesting prejudice against ex-slaves. In an article on April 2, 1889, he challenged those who believed that European immigrants should replace ex-slaves in the Bahian labor force and defended the "national laborer" against those who argued that Bahia's "native sons" were inferior to

Europeans, incapable and unprepared for a life in freedom. He wrote that the "label of lazy and indolent thrown at our people is a vile lie." He criticized the mentality of the Bahian elite and declared that only a change in attitude on the part of the owners and administrators in Bahia would improve labor relations. He argued that the owner, the boss, the housewife, and the managers had to rid themselves of their "habits acquired during slavery" and begin to treat the worker as "their equal," paying him for his work, before they could criticize "our people."[5]

For many years after emancipation, abolitionist and teacher Cincinatos França maintained a night school in Cachoeira for freedmen and women. In 1889, Professor Cincinatos had more than fifty students, among whom were day laborers and canoe men who had migrated from the cane districts. Throughout 1888 and 1889, Eduardo Carigé circulated petitions and testified in court in defense of men and women persecuted by ex-masters who refused to release ingênuo children, pay wages, or refrain from corporal punishment. In April 1889, he was at the forefront of protests against the high prices of manioc flour.

During the same period, freedmen and women, as well as their descendants, also sought to improve their situations as free citizens. Ex-slaves and other poor people, most of whom were black, led the most important street protests that took place in the first decades of the republican era. In the year after abolition, conflict between supporters and opponents of the Brazilian monarchy, including popular groups, wracked Salvador. The Bahian elite was terrorized by the involvement of people who had recently emerged from slavery events in defense of the monarchy. These events were linked to the political conflicts taking place in Rio de Janeiro as 1888 came to an end, especially after the organization of the Black Guard (Guarda Negra). According to Flávio Gomes, the creation of this militia sparked a debate about the political position of the freedmen. At the imperial court, this debate led to armed conflict between freedmen and republicans—something that would also take place in Bahia.[6]

These confrontations reached their highest point on June 15, 1889, when militant republican Silva Jardim landed in Bahia. On that day, there were bloody street conflicts between the militant republicans and popular groups who supported the monarchy. Historian Brás do Amaral, an eyewitness, described the events in language that expressed his prejudice against the street protesters. According to him, the crowd was made up of "filthy people, wearing rough clothing, covered in dirt and mud, who appeared to be laborers who had come to the city for the day from the outlying slums." One of them, whom he described as "a preto," using a term that referred explicitly to slaves prior to abolition, pulled the republican flag down from the Republican Club shortly after Silva Jardim disembarked from the *Companhia Bahiana* ship. He went on to express anxieties common to slave owners before abolition: "Without the fear of the police, the disgusting impulses of the ferocious nearly savage plebeians, like the African and the Indian, will erupt and soon overcome the instruction that they had been given [under slavery]."[7]

The protests were most violent around the docks but they extended inland as far as the working-class neighborhoods of Taboão and Baixa dos Sapateiros. At the Bahian Medical College in the Terreiro de Jesus, there was a tremendous confrontation between the "popular groups" and medical students. The crowd hurled stones at the college, which was the center of support for a republican form of government. According to Amaral, that day, "a crowd of people in tatters" stood outside the medical college and "periodically threw rocks" at it, offending the honor of both the school and the students. According to Amaral, the crowd became more agitated after rumors circulated that boatmen had joined the protest. The crowd's response to the participation of the seamen may reflect the important role that they had played in the antislavery movement in the decade before abolition.[8] In those years, the boatmen had been at the forefront of efforts to rescue slaves being sold to the Brazilian South. The day after the demonstration, the Bahian press announced that the Black Guard, led by the "celebrated" Macaco Beleza, was active in Bahia.

According to Brás do Amaral, the poor responded negatively to propaganda advocating the creation of a Brazilian Republic. After June 15, 1889, he wrote, it was not unusual to hear the "masses" ridicule or even vilify supporters of the republic. On November 15 that same year, when the news arrived in Salvador that the monarchy had been overthrown and a republic established, elites feared that a riot along the lines of the one that occurred on June 15 would recur. Indeed, once the republic was formalized, members of popular groups began to insult and sometimes throw rocks at the supporters of the new regime. The problem was generalized throughout the city. According to Amaral, "in the middle of the crowd was "a degenerate alcoholic with a horrible nickname, who probably intensified his frenzy with doses of intoxicants and developed through this excess a bloody and vehement eloquence; he was the one who united the unemployed sectors of the infamous plebian classes and led the anti-republican demonstrations after June 15."[9] Still emotionally caught up in the conflict, Amaral failed to register the name of the "alcoholic degenerate" in his text. Other sources indicate, however, that he was describing Manoel Benício do Passos, nicknamed Macaco Beleza, the freedman and abolitionist activist who had been involved in antislavery street demonstrations in the 1880s.

Teodoro Sampaio believed that the declaration of the republic and the exile of Emperor Pedro II in November 1889 brought Macaco Beleza back to the streets. When Beleza heard the news, he broke with his former abolitionist partners and came out in defense of the monarchy. He was involved in antirepublican street protests and riots in 1892. When he spoke, he never missed an opportunity to jab at the republic and its supporters by referring to Emperor Pedro II as the president of Brazil or cheering Princess Isabel whom he called "the mother of the captives." Eventually, according to Sampaio, the Bahian authorities arrested him and shipped him out of the state, but not until several years later.[10]

One particular passage in Amaral's text reveals that antislavery sentiments continued to inspire the political behavior of the popular classes. He reported that the "enemies of republicanism" were inciting hatred among the people by spreading a rumor that the leaders of the republic was planning to revoke the Law of May 13, re-enslave those who had been freed, and prohibit "men of color" from exercising responsible positions in public administration or the military, as was happening in the United States of America.[11] Clearly, therefore, popular groups understood that they were not only fighting slavery but also a system that aimed at excluding them from power on the basis of the color of their skin.

The old seignorial arrogance flowed freely from Amaral's pen. In his view, plebeians could not act on their own, much less reflect politically on what was happening around them. He preferred to believe that the "masses" were incited and guided by the "enemies" of the republic, just as in the past, they had supposedly been led by abolitionists.

The city's popular classes, especially the ex-slaves, had good reasons for their lack of confidence in the supporters of the republic. When they came to power, they implemented energetic measures of police control to discipline the day laborers, the carters, and the domestic servants, most of whom were blacks or mestiços. In the cities, many gathering points for the black population were destroyed and there was harsh police repression against candomblé, batuque, samba, capoeira, and any other demonstration of what the authorities called "Africanisms." At the end of the century, these anti-African measures, strongly inspired by scientific racism, had serious implications for the black population, since they reinforced the racial barriers that made access to better living conditions and an expansion of the rights of citizenship more difficult.

This may explain why governors of the republican period tried to remove all meaning from the celebrations of May 13, at least in any official program. By the end of the 1890s, the celebration had lost much of the excitement of the early years. There were political reasons to encourage the public to forget the date and the events that had led up to the end of slavery. To a certain extent, the authorities did not want to highlight the role of the monarchy—now in exile—in such a significant event. Perhaps more important, they hoped to quiet conflict and bury the hope born in the struggles against slavery and for citizenship.

Notes

ABBREVIATIONS

ACS	Arquivo do Conde de Subaé, Private
ACMS	Arquivo da Cúria Metropolitana de Salvador
AJFAP	Arquivo de João Ferreira de Araújo Pinho Júnior, Private
AMS	Arquivo Municipal de Salvador
AMSA	Arquivo Municipal de Santo Amaro
APCSE	Arquivo da Província Carmelitana de Santo Elias (Belo Horizonte)
APEB	Arquivo Público do Estado da Bahia
ARC	Arquivo Regional de Cachoeira
ASCMSA	Arquivo da Santa Casa de Misericórdia de Santo Amaro
BACB	Biblioteca da Associação Comercial da Bahia
BN	Biblioteca Nacional (Rio de Janeiro)
BPEBa	Biblioteca Pública do Estado da Bahia
CBC	*Coleção Barão de Cotegipe*, IHGB
CCS	Coleção Conde de Subaé, IHGB
CRCC	Cartório de Registro Civil de Cachoeira
CRCI	Cartório de Registro Civil de Santiago do Iguape
CRCRF	Cartório de Registro Civil de Rio Fundo
CRCS	Cartório de Registro Civil de São Sebastião do Passé
CRCSA	Cartório de Registro Civil de Santo Amaro
CRCSF	Cartório de Registro Civil de São Félix
CRCSL	Cartório de Registro Civil de Santana do Lustosa
HAHR	*Hispanic American Historical Review*
IGHB	Instituto Geográfico e Histórico da Bahia
IHGB	Instituto Histórico e Geográfico do Brasil (Rio de Janeiro)
IT	*Inventário*
JLAS	*Journal of Latin American Studies*
LED	*Livro de Entrada de Doentes*
LICC	*Livro de Inventários do Convento do Carmo*
LRB	*Livro de Registro de Batismos*

LRC	Livro de Registro de Casamentos
LRN	Livro de registro de nascimentos
LRO	Livro de registro de óbitos
PC	Processo crime
PCi	Processo civil
UFBA	Universidade Federal da Bahia

TRANSLATOR'S INTRODUCTION

1. On the first and last ships to land slaves in Brazil see www.slavevoyages.org. The slave trade was officially outlawed in 1831, but a clandestine trade continued strongly until 1850, after which it rapidly petered out. See, in English, Bethel, *Abolition of the Brazilian Slave Trade*.

2. Barickman, "Persistence and Decline," pp. 590, 596.

3. A full discussion of the historiography of Brazilian slavery is beyond the scope of this text. For further information, see Schwartz, "Historiography of Early Modern Brazil"; Reis and Klein, "Slavery in Brazil"; and Weinstein, "Postcolonial Brazil." For an overview of the history of Brazilian slavery, see Klein and Luna, *Slavery in Brazil*.

4. Lara, *Campos da violência*, pp. 19–21; Schwartz, "Historiography of Early Modern Brazil" pp. 100, 120; and Reis and Klein, "Slavery in Brazil," p. 182.

5. For a provocative critique of this literature, see Weinstein, "Decline of the Progressive Planter," p. 82. See also Reis and Klein, "Slavery in Brazil," p. 182.

6. See, for example, Prado Júnior, *História econômica do Brasil*; and Fernandes, *Negro in Brazilian Society*.

7. Eisenberg, *Sugar Industry in Pernambuco*.

8. See, for example, Mahony, "Past to Do Justice to the Present."

9. For an overview of his shift specific to the early modern period, but applicable to the historiography of slavery and freedom in the postcolonial period as well, see Schwartz, "Historiography of Early Modern Brazil," pp. 100–102, 105–114. On the critique of the "thingafication" of slaves, see, for example, Chalhoub, *Visões da liberdade*. For the critique that the "new" social and cultural history of slavery gave insufficient attention to violence and repression see Gorender, *A escravidão reabilitada*. For a summary of the issues see, Reis and Klein, "Slavery in Brazil," p. 183.

10. For the benefits that oral history can bring, see Rios and Castro, *Memórias do cativeiro*.

11. See, for example, Chalhoub, *Visões da liberdade*; and Graham, *Caetana Says No*.

12. See, for example, Ginzburg, *Cheese and the Worms*.

13. Schwartz, "Resistance and Accommodation in Eighteenth-Century Brazil." See, for example, Stein, *Vassouras*, 70 and chapter 6; and Schwartz, "'Mocambo,'" pp. 316–317.

14. Reis, *Slave Rebellion in Brazil*.

15. Schwartz, "'Mocambo'"; Reis and Silva, *Negociação e conflito*.

16. Lara, *Campos da Violência*, p. 342.

17. Barickman, "'Bit of Land Which They Call a Roça,'" p. 658. The introduction to Barickman's article remains an excellent overview of the literature on slave provision grounds in the sugar-plantation regions of the Americas.

18. Barickman, "'Bit of Land Which They Call a Roça,'" p. 680.

19. Barickman, *Bahian Counterpoint*, especially pp. 57–63.

20. On the enslaved family, see among others, Slenes, "Black Homes, White Homilies," pp. 126–130; On the early history of the enslaved family, see Graham, "Slave Families on a Rural Estate in Colonial Brazil"; Schwartz, *Slaves, Peasants and Rebels*, chapter 5; and Matosso, *To Be a Slave in Brazil*, pp. 109–113. For more recent treatments, see Slenes, *Na senzala, uma flor*; Mahony, "Creativity under Constraint"; Reis, *Histórias de vida familiar e afetiva de escravos na Bahia do século XIX*; and Libby and Frank, "Naming Practices in Eighteenth- and Nineteenth-Century Brazil," pp. 71–79.

21. On the historiography of abolition in English, see Weinstein, "Decline of the Progressive Planter"; and Needell, "Brazilian Abolitionism, Its Historiography and the Uses of Political History."

22. Important studies in this area include Chalhoub, *Visões da liberdade*; Machado, *O plano e o pânico*; Mattos, *Das cores do silêncio*; and Grinberg, *Liberata*.

23. Important contributions in this regard, in English, include Andrews, *Blacks and Whites in São Paulo*; Scott, *Abolition of Slavery and the Aftermath of Emancipation in Brazil*; Cruz, "Puzzling Out Slave Origins in Rio de Janeiro Port Unionism"; and Graden, *From Slavery to Freedom in Brazil*. In Portuguese, see Gomes and da Cunha, *Quase-cidadão*.

24. Butler, *Freedoms Given; Freedoms Won*; Graden, "From Slavery to Freedom in Bahia, 1791–1900"; Graden, *From Slavery to Freedom in Brazil*; Brito, "A abolição na Bahia"; Brito, *A abolição na Bahia*.

25. On cacao, see Mahony, "The World Cacao Made"; and Garcez and de Freitas, *Bahia cacaueira*. On tobacco, see Baud and Koonings, "A lavoura dos pobres."

26. Among others, see Klein and Engerman, "Transition from Slave to Free Labor"; Tomich, "Contested Terrains"; Litwak, *Been in the Storm So Long*; and Scott, *Degrees of Freedom*, among others.

27. Lara, "Escravidão, cidadania e história do trabalho no Brasil"; Weinstein, "Erecting and Erasing Boundaries."

28. The classic study of racial ideology in Brazil, in English, is Skidmore, *Black into White*. For additional references, see Butler and Helg, "Race in Postabolition Afro-Latin America." For a fascinating study of the way that notions about race and color changed with abolition, see Castro, *Das cores do silêncio*.

29. Schwartz, *Sugar Plantations in the Formation of Brazilian Society, Bahia: 1550–1835*, pp. 510n96, 24–25, 434.

30. Scott, "Defining the Boundaries of Freedom in the World of Cane," p. 92.

31. For an insightful discussion of the issues related to translating text from Portuguese to English, and specifically the word "lavoura," see Sotelino, "Notes on the Translation of *Lavoura Arcaica* by Raduan Nassar," pp. 524–525.

32. On the legal history of marriage, family, and inheritance law, see Lewin, *Surprise Heirs*, vol. 2, especially pp. 101, 234, 271.

FOREWORD

1. The foreword has been translated by its author from the first Brazilian edition, with minor additions and clarifications.

2. "God is in the particular" (or "in the detail") is an expression used by the art historian Aby Warburg. Carlo Ginzburg, one of the leading practitioners of microhistory, uses it as the epigraph of his methodological essay "Sinais: Raízes de um paradigma indiciário," in Ginzburg, *Mitos, emblemas, sinais: morfologia e história* (São Paulo: Companhia das Letras, 1989 [originally published in 1986]), p. 143.

3. Robert Darnton, "Os trabalhadores se revoltam: o grande massacre dos gatos na rua Saint-Severin," in Darnton, *O grande massacre de gatos*.

4. See, among others, the studies cited in the bibliography by Célia Maria Marinho Azevedo, Hebe Maria Mattos de Castro, Sidney Chalhoub, and Maria Helena Machado; also Mendonça, *Entre a mão e os anéis*; and Pena, *O jogo da face*. On the crisis in the slave market, see Mello, "Expectations of Abolition and Sanguinity of Coffee Planters in Brazil, 1871–1881"; and Slenes, "Brazilian Internal Slave Trade, 1850–1888."

5. On this, see also the article by Bert Barickman, "Até a véspera," cited in the bibliography.

6. See Scott, "Defining the Boundaries of Freedom in the World of Cane."

7. As an example, see the studies by Rebecca Scott, listed in the bibliography.

8. See Fraga's master's thesis, supervised by João José Reis and published with the title *Mendigos, moleques e vadios na Bahia do século XIX*.

INTRODUCTION

1. See Prado Júnior, *História econômica do Brasil*, pp. 169–170.

2. Among others see Ianni, *Raças e classes sociais no Brasil*; and Martins, *O cativeiro da terra*.

3. See Reis and Silva, *Negociação e conflito*; Chalhoub, *Visões da liberdade*; and Lara, *Campos da violência*.

4. See Reis, *Rebelião escrava no Brasil*; Oliveira, *O liberto*; and Slenes, *Na senzala, uma flor*.

5. See Scott, *Abolition of Slavery and the Aftermath of Emancipation in Brazil*. For a pioneering discussion about the meaning of abolition and abolitionist militancy in Brazil, see R. Graham, *Escravidão, reforma e imperialismo*.

6. See Andrews, *Negros e brancos em São Paulo (1888–1988)*.

7. See Castro, *Das cores do silêncio*; see also Machado, *O plano e o pânico*.

8. Butler, *Freedoms Given, Freedoms Won*; Graden, *From Slavery to Freedom in Brazil*.

9. See Xavier, *A conquista da liberdade*; see also Rios and Castro, *Memórias do cativeiro*.

10. See Schwarcz, *O espetáculo das raças*; and Albuquerque, *O jogo da dissimulação*.

11. The focus on trajectories has generated a creative and challenging literature. See, for example, Levi, *Le pouvoir au village*; and Gribaudi, *Itineraires ouvriers*. For a

pioneering life history of a cane cutter in Puerto Rico, examining behaviors, attitudes, and survival strategies, see Mintz, *Worker in the Cane.*

12. For a critique of the literature on the "transition" to free labor, see Lara, "Escravidão, cidadania e história"; and Chalhoub, *Visões da liberdade*, pp. 19–20.

13. Among studies of blacks in post-emancipation Bahia, see Wimberly, "African Liberto and the Bahian Lower Class"; Butler, *Freedoms Given, Freedoms Won*; Bacelar, *A hierarquia das raças*; and Braga, *Na gamela do feitiço.* On abolition and its consequences in Bahia, see Dale Graden's pioneering 1991 PhD dissertation published as Graden, *From Slavery to Freedom in Brazil.* On the impact of abolition in the southern Bahian cacao region, see Mahony, "World Cacao Made," especially chapters 9 and 11.

14. See among others, Mintz, *Caribbean Transformations*; Foner, *Nothing but Freedom*; Fields, *Slavery and Freedom on the Middle Ground*; Berlin, *Freedom: A Documentary History*; Litwack, *Been in the Storm So Long*; Saville, *Work of Reconstruction*; Scott, *Abolition of Slavery*; Scott, *Degrees of Freedom*; Turner, *From Chattel Slaves to Wage Slaves*; O'Donovan, *Becoming Free in the Cotton South*; and Figueroa, *Sugar, Slavery and Freedom.*

15. For a discussion of "crossing data," see Slenes, *Na senzala, uma flor*, p. 14. This methodology allowed Slenes to reconstruct the post-emancipation trajectories of ex-slaves in a rural São Paulo town. See Slenes, "Histórias do Cafundó," pp. 37–102. On using names to track individuals, their ancestries, and their social networks, see Ginzburg, *A micro-história*, pp. 175–176.

16. *Livro de registro de óbitos* (hereafter LRO), C-1 (1889–1892), 29v, Cártorio de Registro Civil de Santo Amaro (hereafter CRCSA).

17. *Livro de registro de nascimentos* (hereafter LRN) (1889–1897), f109, Cartório de Registro Civil de São Félix (hereafter CRCSF).

18. LRN (1889–1906), p. 21, Arquivo da Cúria Metropolitana de Salvador (hereafter ACMS). On Mombaça Plantation, see *Inventário* (hereafter IT), 7/3148/14 (1875–1895), Ana de Jesus Muniz Vianna Bandeira, pp. 167–173, Arquivo Público do Estado da Bahia (hereafter APEB).

19. LRN (1889–1906), ACMS, p. 42; *Livro de inventários do convento do Carmo* (hereafter LICC) (1796–1935), pp. 125–127v, ACMS.

20. LRN, p. 12, Cartório de Registro Civil de Rio Fundo (hereafter CRCRF). For the list of slaves who fled Paranaguá Plantation, see *Echo Santamarense*, June 1, 1882, p. 4, Biblioteca Pública do Estado da Bahia (hereafter BPEBa).

1. SLAVES AND MASTERS ON SUGAR
PLANTATIONS IN THE LAST DECADES OF SLAVERY

1. Schwartz, *Segredos internos*, pp. 68–73.

2. Barickman, *Um contraponto baiano*, p. 40.

3. Mattoso, *Bahia*, pp. 40–41.

4. Barickman's meticulous research demonstrates that the Recôncavo's society and economy were not simply dedicated to export agriculture. Alongside and even within

sugar plantation-based export agriculture, farmers grew a large variety of subsistence crops to be sold in local markets. Barickman, *Um contraponto baiano.*

5. On the collapse of the Bahian sugar economy, see Mattoso, *Bahia: a cidade do Salvador,* pp. 239–376; Pang, *O engenho Central do Bom Jardim,* pp. 21–78; and Barickman, "Até a véspera," pp. 209–227.

6. On the province's enslaved population, see Conrad, *Os últimos anos da escravatura,* pp. 345–362.

7. On November 8, 1831, the Brazilian imperial government approved a law prohibiting the importation of enslaved laborers from Africa. The law was never enforced and became known as a "law for the English to see." Nearly nineteen years later, on October 4, 1850, the government finally abolished the trade with the passage of the Eusébio de Queirós Law. The law was passed in the context of intense British pressure to end the trade, a large supply of newly imported slaves in Brazil, and significant planter fear of slave revolts. Nevertheless, slave traders continued to try to clandestinely land new groups of Africans through 1857.

8. For this data, see Schwartz, *Escravos, roceiros e rebeldes,* p. 92.

9. Studies of the enslaved family are now quite numerous. See, for example, Slenes, "Escravidão e família." A more detailed discussion is Slenes, *Na senzala, uma flor.* See also Metcalf, "A vida familiar dos escravos em São Paulo no século dezoito," pp. 232–235. On Bahia see Reis, *Histórias de vida familiar e afetiva dos escravos;* Oliveira, *O liberto;* and Mahony, "Creativity under Constraint."

10. Gudeman and Schwartz, "Purgando o pecado original," pp. 56–58.

11. According to Luís Anselmo Fonseca, agriculture and commerce were the two economic sectors most resistant to the end of slavery in Brazil. Fonseca, *A escravidão, o clero e o abolicionismo,* p. 637. TR: Recôncavo sugar planters could express their opposition to the end of slavery through powerful Bahian political representatives. The Baron of Vila Viçosa (1841–1915), owner of a plantation in Santo Amaro, was a member of the Brazilian Chamber of Deputies from 1891 to 1893. Over the course of his career, José Antônio Saraiva (1823–1895) was a senator, cabinet minister, special envoy, and finally prime minister (March 1880–January 1882; May 1885–August 1885). The Baron of Cotegipe (1815–1889) was one of the most influential politicians of the Brazilian Empire. He was a senator from 1855 to 1889 and held several cabinet appointments in the 1870s and 1880s, culminating with that of prime minister from August 1885 to March 1888, when the Princess Regent fired him. The Baron of Moniz Aragão (1841–1898) was educated in Germany and pursued a diplomatic career before returning to Brazil to administer his sugar estates and take a position as a member of the city council of Salvador and president of the town council in Santo Amaro. He maintained an active correspondence with Cotegipe. For further discussion in English of the imperial politics of Brazil in this period see Graham, *Patronage and Politics in Nineteenth-Century Brazil;* Pang, *In Pursuit of Honor and Power;* Barman, *Citizen Emperor;* Barman, *Princess Isabel of Brazil;* Needell, *Party of Order;* and Needell, "Brazilian Abolitionism, Its Historiography and the Uses of Political History."

12. *IT, caixa* 4 (1882–1902), Arquimedes Pires de Carvalho, pp. 308–309, Arquivo Municipal de Santo Amaro (hereafter, AMSA).

13. Barickman, "Até a véspera," p. 227.

14. *Relatório do Imperial Instituto Bahiano de Agricultura feito por seu presidente, barão de Sergimirim, em 10 de fevereiro de 1871*, APEB. Sergimirim reported Bahia's enslaved population to be 179,561, of whom about 100,000 worked in agriculture and herding. But reducing the total by removing the 50,000 children, elderly and ill, whom the planters considered "parasites" in the heart of the plantations, leaves a total productive agricultural population—the more important statistic—of a little more than 40,000 workers.

15. The Portuguese spelling of this and other documents cited in this book has been modernized. Coleção Conde de Subaé (hereafter CCS), *lata* 550, *pasta* 25, *Livro de contas (serviço agrícola) de Francisco Moreira de Carvalho, 1863–1887*, Instituto Histórico e Geográfico do Brasil (hereafter IHGB).

16. *IT, caixa* 4 (1882–1902), Arquimedes Pires de Carvalho, AMSA. According to Stuart Schwartz, the use of monetary rewards or other incentives in dealing with slaves seems to have been quite common on sugar plantations in Bahia during the colonial period. Schwartz, *Segredos internos*, p. 140.

17. Slenes, *Na senzala, uma flor*, p. 197.

18. *IT, caixa* 4 (1882–1902), Arquimedes Pires de Carvalho, pp. 284–288, AMSA. According to the bookkeeper, the cane farmers received 652 of the 3,473 loaves of sugar, each of which weighed about 5 arrobas.

19. Several studies emphasize the importance of subsistence plots to slaves in plantation areas. Mintz found the cultivation and sale of subsistence crops constituted an economic alternative for slaves who lived on the plantations and that subsistence plots allowed slaves to resist the conditions imposed upon them by planters. He saw slaves with subsistence plots as a proto-peasantry. Dale Tomich suggested that, in Martinique, the development of independent cultivation and commercial activities by slaves was the focal point of slave struggles with masters over working conditions and material life on the plantations. Mintz, *Caribbean Transformations*, pp. 225–250; Tomich, "Houses, Provision Grounds and the Reconstitution of Labour," pp. 260–261; Cardoso, *Escravo ou camponês*. For a detailed study specific to Bahia's Recôncavo, see Barickman, "'Bit of Land Which They Call a Roça.'"

20. Investigation of attack on slave Daniel, *Processo crime* (hereafter PC), 9/310/11 (1875), APEB.

21. Interrogation of crioulos Joaquim Inácio Piranduba and Petronila Gouveia, June 18, 1864, *Delegados, maço* 6218 (1881–1882), APEB.

22. Interrogation of Piranduba and Gouveia, June 18, 1864, *Delegados, maço* 6218 (1881–1882), APEB.

23. CCS, *lata* 550, *pasta* 25, *Livro de contas FMC, 1863–1887*, IHGB.

24. Vilhena, *A Bahia no século XVIII*, 1:185–187.

25. Calmon Du Pin e Almeida, *Ensaio sobre o fabrico do açúcar*, p. 60.

26. Mintz, *Caribbean Transformations*, pp. 225–250; Tomich, "Houses, Provision Grounds and the Reconstitution of Labour," pp. 260–261; Cardoso, *Escravo ou camponês*. For a discussion of these debates in Brazil, see Barickman, "'Bit of Land Which They Call a Roça,'" pp. 649–653.

27. Flávio Gomes calls attention to the conflicts between masters and slaves in Rio de Janeiro about the "right" to cultivate roças. Gomes, *Histórias de quilombolas*, pp. 244–245.

28. Investigation into the beating of Júlia, africana, March 26, 1885, p. 16, *PC* 6225 (1885), APEB.

29. Investigation into the beating of Júlia, africana, pp. 12–13, *PC* 6225 (1885), APEB.

30. "O drama do cativeiro," in *O Escudo Social*, São Felipe, Bahia, October 14, 1933, p. 2. My thanks to Edinelia Maria Oliveira de Souza for allowing me to consult this document.

31. Feitor-mor Francisco to the Conde de Subaé, June 30, 1879, *Correspondências* (1879), Arquivo do Conde de Subaé (hereafter ACS). TR: This is a collection of the count's papers held by his descendants and not the collection in the IHGB.

32. *PC*, 23/794/5 (1883), Anastácio, André, and Miguel. See also Delegado of Santo Amaro to the Chefe de Polícia, June 8, 1882, *Delegados, maço* 6219, APEB.

33. Subdelegado of the parish of Rua do Paço, Felipe Rodrigues Monteiro, to the Chefe de Polícia, March 29, 1877, *Subdelegados, maço* 6245 (1877), APEB.

34. Juiz Municipal of the Vila do Conde, Severino dos Santos Vieira, to the Chefe de Polícia, March 21, 1879, *Juízes, maço* 6391 (1879), APEB.

35. Chalhoub saw similar actions by slaves in Rio de Janeiro as a reflection of their perceptions of and positions on the institutional changes under way in Brazil at this time. Chalhoub, *Visões da liberdade*, pp. 180–181.

36. TR: On Brazilian abolitionist laws, see Conrad, *Destruction of Brazilian Slavery*.

37. Chalhoub, *Visões da liberdade*, p. 160.

38. Um Lavrador Bahiano, *A emancipação*, pp. 1–11, 29.

39. Silva, "Os escravos vão à Justiça." On other Brazilian regions, see Grinberg, *Liberata*.

40. Juiz da Vara Civil of Salvador, Antônio Luís Afonso de Carvalho, to the Chefe de Polícia, August 26, 1879, *Juízes, maço* 6391, (1879), APEB.

41. Juiz da Vara Civil of Salvador, Antônio Luís Afonso de Carvalho, to the Chefe de Polícia, September 21, 1880, *Juízes, maço* 6392 (1883), APEB.

42. Subdelegado of the Santana Parish, Salvador Aires de Almeida Leite, to the Chefe de Polícia, November 2, 1875, with enclosure; petition by Raimundo Bitencourt written at his request by José Eduardo Reges, October 1875, *Subdelegados, maço* 6243 (1874–1875), APEB.

43. Brito, *A abolição na Bahia*, pp. 26–31.

44. Chefe de Polícia to the Delegado of Santo Amaro, October 19, 1881, *Polícia, correspondências expedidas, maço* 5844 (1880–1881), p. 354, APEB.

45. Chefe de Polícia to the Delegado of Mata de São João, February 12, 1881, *Polícia, correspondências expedidas, maço* 5844 (1880–1881), p. 11, APEB.

46. Chefe de Polícia to the Delegado of São Francisco, May 19, 1881, *Polícia, correspondências expedida, maço* 5844 (1880–1881), p. 115v, APEB.

47. Chefe de Polícia to the Delegado of Abrantes, October 30, 1879, *Polícia, correspondências expedida, maço* 5638 (1870–1880), p. 147v, APEB.

48. Chefe de Polícia to the Delegado of Abrantes, October 30, 1879, *Polícia, correspondências expedida, maço* 5638 (1870–1880), pp. 146–150, APEB.

49. Chefe de Polícia to the Delegado of Nazaré, February 24, 1881, *Polícia, correspondências expedidas, maço* 5844 (1880–1881), p. 22v, APEB.

50. Joaquim Rodrigues Ferreira, Subdelegado of the parish of Santana to the Chefe de Polícia, March 3, 1881, *Subdelegados, maço* 6248 (1882–1883), APEB.

51. *O Asteróide,* "Abolicionismo," September 30, 1887, p. 4, Biblioteca Nacional (hereafter BN).

52. Brito argues that Bahian abolitionists provided refuge to fugitive slaves in the same way as the "Caifazes" abolitionist group of São Paulo that encouraged captives to flee to *quilombos.* Brito, *A abolição,* p. 170, On the spaces in which escaped slaves were hidden in Salvador, see also Graden, *From Slavery to Freedom,* pp. 142–152. TR: For further discussion of the Caifazes in São Paulo in English, see Machado, "Slavery and Social Movements in Nineteenth-Century Brazil," pp. 169–70; Conrad, *The Destruction of Brazilian Slavery,* pp. 242–245.

53. On the question of escapes and their political impact on the Bahian abolitionist movement, see Brito, *A abolição,* pp. 26–30.

54. Francisco Félix Bahia, Subdelegado of the Pilar Parish to the Chefe de Polícia, February 17, 1876, *Subdelegados, maço,* 6244 (1876), APEB.

55. Chefe de Polícia to the Delegado of São Félix, November 2, *Subdelegados, maço,* 6504 (1884), slave of Auta Elisa de Figueredo, APEB.

56. Chefe de Polícia to the Delegado of São Félix, *Polícia, correspondências expedidas, maço* 5857 (1882–1884), p. 45, APEB.

57. A decree on April 7, 1883 forbade the company that won the contract to build the branch linking Alagoinhas to the town of Timbó from owning or employing slaves. It is possible that the contracts for earlier construction projects carried similar prohibitions. On this decree see Secretaria da Cultura da Bahia, *Documentação jurídica sobre o negro no Brasil,* p. 78.

58. *Echo Santamarense,* February 16, 1882, p. 4, BPEBa.

59. *Echo Santamarense,* January 21, 1882, p. 3; see also June 1, 1882, p. 3, BPEBa.

60. *Echo Santamarense,* June 1, 1882, p. 4, BPEBa.

61. Baronesa de Monte Santo to Francisco Moreira de Carvalho, Conde de Subaé, May 19, 1882, *Correspondências* (1882), ACS.

2. TENSION AND CONFLICT ON A RECÔNCAVO SUGAR PLANTATION

1. Campos, *Tempo antigo, crônicas d'antanho,* p. 377.

2. Campos, *Tradições bahianas,* pp. 377–378. Campos is probably the source for Gilberto Freyre's remark in *Casa-grande e senzala* that the Carmelite Friars stood out for treating their slaves well. Freyre mentions a Carmelite who was cut up into little pieces by his slaves. Freyre, *Casa-grande e senzala,* p. 440. See also Ott, *Povoamento do Recôncavo,* 2:58.

3. Oliveira, *São Sebastião do Passé,* pp. 16–18.

4. *PC,* 22/757/01, 1884, APEB.

5. Campos in *Tradições bahianas*, and Ott in *Povoamento do Recôncavo* were the only two authors to address this event. Fonseca discussed the clergy's involvement in slavery, but he did not mention Friar João Lucas. Fonseca, *A escravidão, o clero e o abolicionismo*.

6. According to Stuart Schwartz, weeding the cane field was a year-round task, and when the slaves completed other projects, they were sent back to weed again. The harvest began in August or September and lasted until May. For the tasks involved in growing and making sugar, see Schwartz, *Segredos internos*, pp. 100–103. See also Pinho, *História de um engenho*, pp. 357–369.

7. *PC*, 22/757/01, 1884, p. 54, APEB.

8. *PC*, 22/757/01, 1884, p. 33, APEB.

9. *PC*, 22/757/01, 1884, p. 49, APEB. TR: The Portuguese word *parceiros* might best be translated in this case as "partner" or "mate" and certainly implies friendship. There is some debate as to whether this term was used by the enslaved themselves or introduced by notaries and others in the process of recording events involving multiple slaves working together. Nevertheless, Fraga believes that, in this case, the term may have been used by the enslaved themselves because it appears frequently in the record. Walter Fraga, personal communication, February 2011.

10. *PC*, 22/757/01, 1884, p. 26, APEB.

11. *PC*, 22/757/01, 1884, p. 58, APEB.

12. *PC*, 22/757/01, 1884, p. 49, APEB.

13. *PC*, 22/757/01, 1884, p. 42, APEB. For baptisms the priest celebrated, see *Livro de registros de batismos da freguesia de São Sebastião das Cabeceiras do Passé*, book 7 (1862–1875), ACMS.

14. *PC*, 22/757/01, 1884, p. 4–43v, APEB.

15. *PC*, 22/757/01, 1884, p. 5v, APEB.

16. *PC*, 22/757/01, 1884, p. 45v, APEB.

17. The Order of Nossa Senhora do Monte do Carmo was among the oldest in Brazil. According to Vilhena, it was established in Salvador in the 1580s. The monastery was built on Salvador's Monte Calvário (Calvary Hill), which later came to be called Carmo, and around which the parish of Santo Antônio Além do Carmo grew up. At the end of the eighteenth century, Carmelite property also included a monastery in Cachoeira, sugar plantations and fazendas, managed by sixteen members of the order. Altogether there were 183 Carmelites in Bahia, but according to Vilhena, "today the number of religious has dropped a great deal because of internal conflicts that have plagued the group for years, as a result of which many left the order and few have entered." Vilhena, *A Bahia no século XVIII*, 2:444–445. On the Bahian Carmelite order see also Accioli, *Memórias históricas e políticas da Bahia*, pp. 198–213, and Alves, *Convento e ordem 3a. do Carmo*.

18. There were another seven sugar plantations with mills in that parish in addition to Terra Nova: Laranjeiras, Pojuca, Retiro, Agua Boa, Pimentel, Laranjeiras Novas, and Papassú. Vigário Felipe Barbosa da Cunha, *Notícias sobre a Freguesia de S. Sebastião das Cabeceiras de Passé*, cited in Accioli, *Memórias*, 5:404–405.

19. Ott called Terra Nova one of the oldest sugar plantations in the São Sebastião do Passé Parish. It is important not to confuse the Carmelite's Terra Nova Plantation with

another of the same name belonging to the Visconde de Bom Jardim, located in Rio Fundo Parish, in the town of Santo Amaro. Ott, *Povoamento do Recôncavo*, 2:58–59. The Carmo Plantation entry in the registry of sugar plantations dated 1807 reads: "Sugar plantation located in the Passé Parish, 8 leagues from the port, belonging to the Religious Order of Carmo." *Livro de Matrícula de engenhos*, p. 8v, APEB.

20. Friar Francisco Rogério das Dores Mello to the Presidente da Província, January 27, 1835, *Conventos maço* 5273 (1824–76), APEB. Nascimento found that the Carmelites and the Benedictines were the religious orders with the most landed property in nineteenth-century Bahia. Nascimento, *Patriarcado e religião*, p. 286.

21. Muller, *Memória histórica sobre a religião na Bahia*, p. 96.

22. Schwartz examines the involvement of religious orders in sugar production in detail. Schwartz, *Segredos internos*, pp. 92–93.

23. Accioli, *Memórias históricas e políticas da Bahia*, pp. 462–463.

24. Tomás Aquino Ribeiro, Provincial, to the Presidente da Província, January 26, 1848, *Conventos, maço* 5273, APEB. The income reported from the houses was Rs.3:800$440; from the rental properties, Rs.408$430; from the Pilar Hospital, Rs.324$000; and from the 1847 harvest, prior to expenses, Rs.9:824$242. Altogether, this represented just over 14 contos (Rs.14:357$112), but according to Ribeiro, the debts came to 50 contos (Rs.50:000$000). He also reported that some of the debts had been forgiven by "our correspondent," Manoel José de Almeida, and that was how they were able to avoid foreclosure.

25. Muller, *Memória histórica sobre a religião na Bahia*, p. 96.

26. Tomás Aquino Ribeiro, Provincial, to the Presidente da Província, January 26, 1848, *Conventos, maço* 5273, APEB. According to Ribeiro in 1848–1849 the religious belonged to the Carmelite Order of Bahia, of whom twenty-eight were in the capital and the rest spread between Cachoeira and various other provinces.

27. Campos noted that Friar Alexandrino José do Rosário Figueiroa returned to Salvador horrified after spending a night with Friar João Lucas at the Carmo Plantation because the manager was "stingy and so full of rage." Campos, *Tradições bahianas*, p. 378.

28. *Livro e Inventários do Convento do Carmo da Bahia, 1796–1935*, pp. 125–127v, Arquivo da Província Carmelitana de Santo Elias (Belo Horizonte) (hereafter APCSE).

29. Schwartz, *Segredos internos*, p. 127.

30. Machado, *Crime e escravidão*, pp. 88–90.

31. *PC*, 22/757/01, 1884, p. 33v, APEB.

32. *PC*, 22/757/01, 1884, p. 15, APEB.

33. *PC*, 22/757/01, 1884, pp. 15, 23, APEB.

34. *PC*, 22/757/01, 1884, p. 13, APEB.

35. *PC*, 22/757/01, 1884, pp. 31 and 37v, APEB.

36. *PC*, 22/757/01, 1884, p. 27, APEB.

37. Campos reproduced a letter from one of his readers who stated that he had known about conflicts Friar Lucas had at the Carmelite Monastery. The correspondent said: "I knew Friar Lucas, the subject of your story, 'A encelada do Carmo.' In 1881, or in early 1882, for a few days while I was in school, I lived at the Carmelite Monastery. Friar Lucas was the superior in charge of 3 or 4 other religious. I remember

the names of two of them: Friar Inocêncio and Friar João. He was constantly arguing with the latter in ways that scandalized the students living at the monastery." Campos, *Tradições bahianas*, 378.

38. On September 19, 1882, Alfredo Devoto sent the chief of police a copy of the questions directed to the eleven slaves involved in the death of Friar João Lucas. The delegado of Vila de São Francisco also received a copy of this document. *Delegados, maço* 6219, APEB.

39. *PC*, 22/757/01, 1884, pp. 44–45v, APEB.

40. *PC*, 22/757/01, 1884, p. 33v, APEB.

41. Ott, *Povoamento do Recôncavo*, 2:58.

42. *PC*, 22/757/01, 1884, p. 52, APEB.

43. *PC*, 22/757/01, 1884, pp. 51–51v, APEB.

44. *PC*, 22/757/01, 1884, p. 47v, APEB.

45. *PC*, 22/757/01, 1884, p.50v, APEB.

46. *PC*, 22/757/01, 1884, pp. 55v–56v, APEB.

47. On punishments on Bahian sugar plantations, see Schwartz, *Segredos internos*, pp. 123–27; see also Mattoso, *Ser escravo no Brasil*, pp. 98–121. On the relationship between punishments and seignorial power, see Lara, *Campos da violência*, pp. 29–96.

48. For an in depth discussion about the internal economy of slavery, see Machado, *Crime e escravidão*, pp. 103–112. Machado argues that the misappropriation of agricultural produce allowed the enslaved, among other things, to forge autonomous spaces within slavery. For the Recôncavo, see Barickman, *Um contraponto baiano*, pp. 107–116.

49. *PC*, 22/757/01, 1884, p. 52v, APEB.

50. Augusto de Araújo Santos, delegado to the Chefe de Polícia, *Delegados, maço* 6214, APEB. The upper part of the document is too damaged to identify its date.

51. Campos, *Tradições bahianas*, pp. 378–379. Campos based his statements on the testimony of a student who boarded at the Carmo Monastery while he studied at the Bahian Medical College. He also cited "a serious and trustworthy" ex-slave as confirming the story. He believed that the events in question occurred between 1876 and 1879.

52. On nutritional deficiencies among the enslaved population of Rio de Janeiro, see Karasch, *A vida dos escravos*, pp. 253–254.

53. TR: According to João Reis, the Malê revolt was the "most effective urban slave revolt ever to occur on the American continent. Hundreds of Africans took part. Nearly seventy were killed, and more than five hundred, according to a conservative estimate, were sentenced to death, prison, whipping or deportation. If an uprising of equal proportions were to happen today [in 1993] in a Salvador with over 1.5 million inhabitants, it would entail the sentencing of over twelve thousand people." Reis, *Slave Rebellion in Brazil*, xiii.

54. On the Malê revolt, see Reis, *Rebelião escrava*, chapter 16. Machado, *Crime e escravidão*, pp. 35–36, analyzes the Law of June 10, 1835.

55. *Gazeta da Tarde*, April 26, 1884, p. 1, BPEBa. In this issue of the paper, a member of the jury accused of abolitionist sympathies defended himself.

56. On the death penalty for slaves in the nineteenth century, see Pirola, "A Lei de 10 de Junho de 1835," pp. 140–142.

57. Campos, *Tradições bahianas*, p. 378.

58. Among other sources on this topic, see Mattoso, *Ser escravo no Brasil*; Chalhoub, *Visões da liberdade*; Castro, *Das cores do silêncio*; Machado, *O plano e o pânico*; Azevedo, *Onda negra*; and Wissenbach, *Sonhos africanos, vivências ladinas*, particularly chapter 1.

59. Manoel Félix da Cunha, delegado of Alagoinhas, to the Chefe de Polícia, *Delegados, maço* 6214, APEB.

60. Reis and Silva argue that this form of flight intensified after 1870. Reis and Silva, *Negociação e conflito*, pp. 71–72.

61. On abolition and abolitionists in Bahia from a political perspective, see Brito, *A abolição na Bahia*, especially chapter 3.

62. On the Benedictines, see Slenes, "Senhores e subalternos no Oeste Paulista," in Alencastro, *História da vida privada no Brasil*, p. 268. On the Benedictines and the Carmelites in the province of Rio de Janeiro, see Secretária da Bahia, *Documentação jurídica*, pp. 157–158.

63. *PC*, 22/757/01, 1884, p. 213, APEB. See also Campos, *Tradições bahianas*, p. 378.

64. Machado, *Crime e escravidão*, pp. 65–66.

65. "Graves crimes impunes," *Echo Santamarense*, October 20, 1882, p. 1, editorial, BPEBa.

3. CROSSROADS OF SLAVERY AND FREEDOM, 1880–1888

1. For an early discussion of popular participation in the abolitionist movement, see Costa, *Da senzala à colônia*. Machado broke new ground in our understanding of popular participation in abolitionism in the Brazilian Southeast. See Machado, *O plano e o pânico*, especially chapter 4. Brito outlined the political impact of popular involvement in the Bahian abolition movement in *A abolição na Bahia*, especially chapter 3; Graden, *From Slavery to Freedom in Bahia*, especially part 3, addresses the same issue. By the latter, see also "Voices from Under."

2. See Pinho, *História de um engenho*, p. 510. TR: Carigé was "one of the few members of the Bahian bourgeoisie to demand immediate abolition from the late 1860s." He was a controversial figure, who helped to establish one of Salvador's abolitionist societies. His activities focused largely on Salvador, but he also had followers in the towns and rural districts of the Recôncavo. He was well known for his public speaking and, after abolition, became a journalist. Graden, *From Slavery to Freedom*, p. 164.

3. The conditions that led slaves to flee from slavery were not limited to Salvador. Machado, *O plano e o pânico*, p. 156, documented the same situation in São Paulo. For Rio de Janeiro, see Chalhoub, *Visões da liberdade*, pp. 212–248.

4. Subdelegado of Mares, Herculano Lopes, to the Chefe de Polícia, January 19, 1884, *Subdelegados, maço* 6249 (1884–1885), ABEP.

5. Delegado of Cachoeira, Manoel José Fortunato, to the Chefe de Polícia, May 9, 1876, *Delegados, maço* 6213 (1876–1877), APEB. Fortunato later admitted that he had denounced a neighbor who stole his crops as a fugitive slave. Gouveia admitted that he used the gun found in his house for hunting.

6. On the imprisonment of Eleutério, see Subdelegado of the parish of Santo Antônio, Antônio Teodoro Coelho, to the Chefe de Polícia, February 8, 1877. On João da Silva, see, in the same packet, Subdelegado of Rio Vermelho district to the Chefe de Polícia, April 25, 1877, *Subdelegados, maço* 6245 (1877), APEB.

7. Subdelegado of Pirajá Parish, José Leôncio Ribeiro Sanches, to the Chefe de Polícia, October 23, 1877, *Subdelegados, maço* 6245 (1877), APEB.

8. Chefe de Polícia to the Delegado of Santo Amaro, Francisco Antônio de Carvalhal, April 13, 1882, *Polícia, Correspondências expedidas, maço* 2852 (1881–1882), p. 217v, APEB.

9. Subdelegado of Santana Parish, Salvador Aires de Almeida Ferreira, to the Presidente da Província, May 4, 1874, *Subdelegado, maço* 6243 (1874–1875), APEB.

10. Subdelegado of Pilar Parish, José Cândido Pereira, to the Chefe de Polícia, April 21, 1875, *Subdelegados, maço* 6243 (1874–1875), APEB.

11. José Augusto da Veiga Ornelas to the Chefe de Polícia, May 1, 1877, *Polícia-assuntos diversos, maço* 6499 (1876–1877), APEB.

12. Manoel Pereira Marinho to the Chefe de Polícia, January 3, 1877, *Subdelegados, maço* 6245 (1877), APEB.

13. "Atentado contra a propriedade legal," *Echo Santamarense*, April 14, 1883, p. 1.

14. Sampaio, "O abolicionismo," p. 22.

15. Eduardo Carigé to the Chefe de Polícia, March 16, 1886, *Polícia, maço* 6505 (1886), APEB.

16. Sampaio, "O abolicionismo," pp. 10–15.

17. Subdelegado of Conceição da Praia Parish, Manoel Joaquim de Andrade, to the Chefe de Polícia, July 8, 1887, *Subdelegados, maço* 6252 (1887), APEB.

18. Subdelegado of Cachoeira, José S. de Araújo, to the Chefe de Polícia, September 22, 1887, *Delegados, maço* 6226 (1887–1888), APEB.

19. Subdelegado of Pirajá Parish, Francisco Paraassu Cachoeira, to the Chefe de Polícia, March 26, 1888, *Subdelegados, maço* 6253 (1888–1889), APEB.

20. Sampaio, "O abolicionismo," pp. 27–28.

21. The Alípio barbershop on Palácio Street (today the Rua Chile) was mentioned by name. Sampaio, "O abolicionismo," pp. 6–7.

22. Sampaio, "O abolicionismo," p. 7.

23. *Diário da Bahia*, January 4, 1889, p. 2.

24. Sampaio, "O abolicionismo," p. 2.

25. "O Sr. Eduardo Carigé aos seus concidadãos (IV)," *Diário da Bahia*, January 4, 1889, p. 2. On the locations of the wage earning slaves' work groups, see Reis, "De olho no canto," pp. 209–216.

26. Sampaio, "O abolicionismo," p. 24.

27. Machado, *O plano e o pânico* (especially chapter 4), shows that in southeastern Brazil, the abolitionist movement sheltered the demands and aspirations of several different popular groups.

28. On the participation of Ismael Ribeiro in the abolitionist movement, see Brito, *A abolição na Bahia*, pp. 68–69.

29. Vila Viçosa, "A Lei de 13 de Maio e o seu complemento," *Diário da Bahia*, July 1, 1888, p. 2.

30. "Atentado contra a propriedade legal," *Echo Santamarense*, April 14, 1883, p. 1.

31. Letter from Alfredo Devoto, Delegado of Salvador's first district, to the Chefe de Polícia, May 14, 1883. *Delegados, maço* 6220 (1882–1883), APEB.

32. *Echo Santamarense*, October 26, 1882, "O estado da província," p. 1.

33. *Echo Santamarense*, January 25, 1883, p. 1.

34. *O Guarany*, August 10, 1884, p. 1.

35. Brito, *A abolição na Bahia*, pp. 204–223, discusses the founding of the two Recôncavo antiabolitionist societies.

36. "Transcript of an article from the *Jornal de Notícias*," *O Guarany*, March 25, 1885, p. 1, BN. On March 31, the same newspaper announced the measures taken by the União Agrícola "against the deranged abolitionist propaganda." In a statement sent to the imperial government, the group protested the abuses and crimes being committed by "speculating abolitionists."

37. "Verdadeira Philantropia," *O Guarany*, November 29, 1884, p. 2, BN.

38. Abaixo-assinado content setenta e sete assinaturas de "lavradores e comerciantes" of the parish of Muritiba to the Presidente da Província, March 11, 1885, *Escravos-assuntos, maço* 2897 (1873–1887), APEB.

39. PC 4321–15, 1887, versus Cesário Ribeiro Mendes, ARC. Among the witnesses that Bulcão mentioned were eight major slave owners: Francisco Prisco Paraíso, Francisco Maria de Almeida, Manoel Adeodato de Sousa, Temístocles da Rocha Passos, Durval de Sousa Lopes, Henrique Pereira Teixeira, Joaquim Marinho Aragão, and Amâncio da Rocha Passos.

40. Delegado of Cachoeira, Joaquim Inácio Albernaz, to the Chefe de Polícia, July 24, 1887, *Delegados, maço* 6226 (1887–1889), APEB. See also the letter from the same delegado on September 2, 1887.

41. At the time, Joaquim Inácio Albernaz, from Sento Sé, was a forty-four-year-old businessman living in Cachoeira. He probably obtained his position through the local Conservative Party.

42. Delegado of Cachoeira, Joaquim Inácio Albernaz, to the Chefe de Polícia on September 13, 1887, *Chefes de polícia, maço* 2987 (1880–1889), APEB. Albernaz denied that a planter had beaten a slave to death. He also refuted the charge that the slave Luís had been illegally punished, insisting that he had been placed in the stocks but not punished in any other way.

43. On the accusations against Delegado Albernaz, see "O princípio do fim," *O Asteróide*, September 27, 1887, p. 1, BN; see also in the same newspaper, "Ataque à imprensa," September 30, 1887, p. 2.

44. This brief report is based on the depositions of witnesses in the investigation of such incidents. See vol. 1 (1888), *Judiciário, caixa* 1973, Arquivo Regional de Cachoeira (hereafter ARC).

45. Chefe de Polícia, Domingos Rodrigues Guimarães, to the Presidente da Província, September 10, 1887. See also the letter of September 22, 1887, *Chefes de polícia, maço* 2897 (1880–1889), APEB.

46. Alves, *Matas do sertão de baixo*, pp. 50, 53.

47. Chefe de Polícia to the Delegado of Nazaré, *Polícia, correspondências expedidas*, January 25, 1883, *maço* 5856 (1882–1883), ff. 255v–256, APEB.

48. Aristides Novis to Cotegipe, Bahia, July 11, 1888, *Coleção Barão de Cotegipe* (hereafter CBC), *lata* 918, *pasta* 27, IHGB.

49. TR: One should not overestimate planter isolation, as Cotegipe was prime minister of Brazil from August 1885 to March 1888. According to Jeffrey Needell, however, Cotegipe's administration was largely responsible for the radicalization of the abolition movement after 1885. His government followed the "moderate reformism" of the Dantas and Saraiva cabinets, which had unsuccessfully attempted to bring an abolition law through Parliament. Cotegipe was particularly hostile to abolition, especially if it did not include indemnification to planters who would lose their human property. Once appointed, he moved actively to repress the abolitionist movement. In response, abolitionists and slaves moved to direct action, including encouraging mass escapes and challenging planters directly. Needell, "Brazilian Abolitionism, Its Historiography and the Uses of Political History," 247–260.

50. Inocêncio Teixeira Barbosa, owner of the Engenho Cachoeirinha, to the Chefe de Polícia, February 12, 1885, *Polícia-escravos, maço* 6347 (1881–1885), APEB.

51. Francisco Ribeiro Lopes to the Chefe de Polícia on March 19, 1885, *Polícia, maço* 6504 (1885), APEB.

52. Rodrigo Antônio Falcão, owner of Palma Plantation, to the Chefe de Polícia, January 22, 1888, with attached power of attorney authorizing Francisco Correia Tavares to take control of the escaped slaves in the House of Corrections, June 21, 1887, *Polícia-escravos, maço* 6348 (1886–1889), APEB.

53. *Livro de Contas, lata* 550, *pasta* 25 (1863–1887), document without page numbers, notation of March 3, 1887, CCS, IHGB.

54. See Dean on this attitude among Paulista slave owners. Dean, *Rio Claro*, p. 146.

55. Alves, *Matas do sertão*, p. 54.

56. Aristides Novis to Cotegipe, Bahia, July 11, 1888, CBC, *lata* 918, *pasta* 27, IHGB.

57. Pinho, *História de um engenho*, p. 511.

58. Brito argues that it was probably Cesário Mendes's group that distributed the pamphlets on the Recôncavo sugar plantations. Brito, *A abolição na Bahia*, p. 154.

59. "Cruel expectativa," *O Tempo*, April 14, 1888, p. 1.

60. "Carta de Outeiro Redondo," *Gazeta da Tarde*, April 17, 1888, p. 1.

61. "A questão atual," *O Tempo*, April 18, 1888, p. 1.

62. "A questão atual," *O Tempo*, April 18, 1888, p. 2.

63. "A questão atual," *O Tempo*, April 18, 1888, p. 2.

64. "A questão atual," *O Tempo*, April 18, 1888, p. 1.

65. "A questão atual," *O Tempo*, April 18, 1888, p. 1.

66. *Diário da Bahia*, May 2, 1888, p. 1. On the Baron of São Francisco see the May 4, 1888, edition of the same newspaper.

67. *Diário da Bahia*; see also May 5, 1888, p. 1.

68. Vila Viçosa, "A Lei de 13 de Maio e o seu complemento," *Diário da Bahia*, July 1, 1888, p. 2.

4. MAY 13, 1888, AND ITS IMMEDIATE AFTERMATH

1. On the repercussions of the news of abolition within the enslaved population in the town of Santo Antônio, see Alves, *Matas do sertão*, p. 257. According to him, the slaves "heard the great news at Vargem Grande where the telegraph came in from the road," Graham calls attention to the meanings of abolition as a jumping-off point for our understanding of the end of slavery. Graham, *Escravidão, reforma e imperialismo*, p. 10.

2. *Diário de Notícias*, May 9, 1888, p. 1, BPEBa.

3. Delegado of the Vila of São Francisco, Luís de Oliveira Mendes, to the Chefe de Polícia, June 16, 1888, *Delegados, maço* 6227 (1885–1889), APEB.

4. "Ultimas palavras," *O Tempo*, May 19, 1888, p. 1; "Festejos abolicionistas," *O Tempo*, May 23, 1888, p.1, Instituto Geográfico e Histórico da Bahia (hereafter IGHB).

5. Reis and Silva show that during the struggles for Brazilian independence, African and crioulo slaves alike were thinking about the abolition of slavery. Reis and Silva, *Negociação e conflito*, pp. 93–98. Kraay analyzed the important role of black officers in the political independence process. Kraay, "Politics of Race in Independence— Era Bahia," in Kraay, *Afro-Brazilian Culture and Politics*, pp. 30–56. Kraay has also written on the Dois de Julho celebrations. See Kraay, "Between Brazil and Bahia." On the various meanings of the celebrations of political independence in post-abolition Bahia, see Albuquerque, *Algazarra nas ruas*. On the abolition celebrations, see Brito, *A abolicão na Bahia*, pp. 265–269. Abolition celebrations took place in other Brazilian regions as well. See Stein, *Vassouras*, p. 302.

6. Speech of legislative representative A. Bahia on May 14, 1888, *Anais da assembléia legislativa provincial da Bahia*, vol. 1, p. 68, BPEBa.

7. Sampaio, "O abolicionismo," p. 28.

8. *Diário da Bahia*, May 19 1888, p.1, BPEBa. Albuquerque, *O jogo da dissimulação*, pp. 126–129.

9. President of the town council of Santa Rita do Rio Preto, Salviano de Souza Milhomens, to Presidente da Província, June 7, 1888, *Escravos-assuntos, maço* 2900 (1880–1889), APEB.

10. *Jornal de Notícias*, January 22, 1889, p. 1, BPEBa

11. *Diário da Bahia*, May 15, 1888, p. 1, BPEBa. On the celebrations of May 13 in Salvador, see Graden, *From Slavery to Freedom*, pp. 194–195. See also Brito, *A abolição na Bahia*, pp. 142–143.

12. Session of May 14, 1888, *Anais da assembléia legislativa*, 1:68, BPEBa.

13. Novis's discourse cannot be separated from the context of the political disputes between the Liberal and Conservative parties for leadership in the passage of the law that abolished slavery. Both parties claimed credit.

14. Aristides Novis to the Barão de Cotegipe, May 16, 1888. CBC, *lata* 918, *pasta* 23, IHGB.

15. Novis to Cotegipe, May 16, 1888. CBC, *lata* 918, *pasta* 23, IHGB.

16. Prince Pedro of Bragança declared Brazilian political independence from Portugal on September 7, 1822. For the most part, the process was peaceful, but the Portuguese resisted in several parts of their former colony, including in Bahia, from

which Portuguese troops were not expelled until July 2, 1823, after significant fighting. During the nineteenth-century, the Second of July was the most important civic festival in Salvador, "overshadowing Brazilian Independence Day and other imperial holidays." It involved significant popular participation, including carnival-like parades headed by two floats, one of an indigenous man and the other of an indigenous woman. For more on the Second of July celebrations and their meanings, see Kraay, "Between Brazil and Bahia."

17. *LRN*, no. 2 (1893–1897), p. 1, Cartório de Registro Civil de Cachoeira (hereafter CRCC).

18. Foner argues that in the U.S. South, ex-slaves tried various strategies to free themselves from the "marks of slavery," one of which was destroying the authority that the ex-masters could exercise over their lives. Foner, "O significado da liberdade," p. 12. On the meaning of abolition see Graham, *Escravidão, reforma e imperialismo*, p. 10.

19. "O drama do cativeiro," interview with ex-slave Argeu in *O Escudo Social*, October 14, 1933, p. 2.

20. Interview with ex-slave Argeu, October 14, 1933, p. 2.

21. Alves, *Matas do sertão*, pp. 257–258.

22. Alves, *Matas do sertão*, p. 258.

23. G., *Regeneração agrícola do estado da Bahia*, p. 5.

24. Alves, *Matas do sertão*, p. 54.

25. Alves, *Matas do sertão*, p. 54; "Suicídio," *Diário do Povo*, February 26, 1889, p. 1.

26. TR: Vila Viçosa was also a representative Chamber of Deputies from 1891 to 1893.

27. "A lavoura de cana de açúcar, as causas de sua decadência nesta província e o seu estado depois da Lei de 13 de Maio," *Diário da Bahia*, February 24, 1889, p. 2, BPEBa.

28. *Diário da Bahia*, p. 2, BPEBa.

29. *Diário da Bahia*, p. 2, BPEBa.

30. G., *Regeneração agrícola*, pp. 5–6.

31. G., *Regeneração agricola*, p. 2.

32. Bittencourt, *Letícia*, pp. 68–69.

33. Bittencourt, *Letícia*, p. 69.

34. Bittencourt, *Letícia*, p. 94.

35. Bittencourt, *Letícia*, p. 95.

36. Bittencourt, *Letícia*, pp. 83–84.

37. Campos, *Tempo antigo, crônicas d'antanho, marcas do passado, histórias do Recôncavo*, pp. 159–160.

38. This seignorial resentment manifested itself in other regions of Brazil during slavery. On the coffee region of the province of São Paulo, see Costa, *Da senzala à colônia*, pp. 442–443.

39. Marques, *As voltas da estrada*, p. 185.

40. Barão de Moniz Aragão assinada também pelo vice, Capitão Francisco Norberto de Menezes to the Presidente da Província, May 19, 1888. *Câmara*, maço 1436 (1881–1889), APEB.

41. Barão de Moniz Aragão and Captain Francisco Norberto de Menezes to the Presidente da Província, May 19, 1888. *Câmara*, maço 1436 (1881–1889), APEB.

42. The attitudes of the ex-slaves approximate what James Scott calls a hidden transcript, in other words, a "hidden discourse" invented by subalterns unable to openly criticize their superiors, through which they questioned those superiors without exposing themselves to repercussions. Scott, *Domination and the Arts of Resistance*, pp. 1–5.

43. This piece of the letter shows the ideological slant of Moniz Aragão's discourse, in insisting that the "moral force" of the planters had guaranteed that the ex-slaves would not fall into crime.

44. Barão de Moniz Aragão, president of the town council of São Francisco, to the Presidente da Província, July 10, 1888, *Câmara, maço* 1436 (1881–1889), APEB.

45. Moniz Aragão, president of the town council of São Francisco, to the Presidente da Província, Confidential, July 10, 1888, *Câmara, maço* 1436, (1881–1889), APEB.

46. Moniz Aragão to the Presidente da Província, July 10, 1888, *Câmara, maço* 1436, (1881–1889), APEB.

47. Interview with Mrs. Faustina dos Santos, August 27, 2000. The informant lives on the Apí Fazenda in São Sebastião do Passé. The day abolition took place continues to occupy a privileged position in the memories of the descendants of slaves in the Recôncavo. Many children and grandchildren of slaves still remember their impressions and their parents' and grandparents' feelings about that day. The rumor that abolition would be followed by land distribution circulated in a number of Brazilian regions. See, for example, Stein, *Vassouras*, p. 304. According to Richard Graham, the ex-masters feared that abolition would bring with it agrarian reform. Graham, *Escravidão, reforma e imperialismo*, pp. 183–184.

48. According to Afrânio Garcia, in the sugarcane districts of the northeastern Brazilian province of Pernambuco, the word "man" referred only to owners of large sugarcane farms and sugar plantations and this is the way Faustina used the word in her memories of her grandfather. Garcia, *O Sul*, p. 49.

49. Subdelegado of Palame to the Chefe de Polícia, July 7, 1888. *Subdelegados, maço* 6252 (1887–1888), APEB.

50. Subdelegado of Palame to the Chefe de Polícia, July 7, 1888. *Subdelegados, maço* 6252 (1887–1888), APEB.

51. Delegado of Inhambupe, Justiano Pinto de Meireles, to the Chefe de Polícia, May 28, 1888. *Delegados, maço* 3003 (1887–1889). On the town of Campo Largo see the letter from the Delegado to the Chefe de Polícia, July 4, 1888, *Delegados, maço* 6226 (1887–1888). On Vila Viçosa, see Delegado Juvenal Lourenço de Jesus to the Chefe de Polícia, July 5, 1889, *Delegados, maço* 6223 (1887–1889), APEB.

52. Barão de Vila Viçosa, *Diário da Bahia*, August 14, 1888, p. f2, BPEBa.

53. *Diário da Bahia*, February 26, 1889, p. 2, BPEBa. This article, the third in a series, was written on January 25.

54. *Diário da Bahia*, February 26, 1889, p. 2, BPEBa.

55. *Diário da Bahia*, February 26, 1889, p. 2, BPEBa.

56. "Vila de São Francisco," *Diário da Bahia*, January 6, 1889, p. 1, BPEBa.

57. Aristides Novis to Cotegipe, Bahia, January 11, 1889, CBC, *lata* 918, *pasta* 30, IHGB.

58. I was unable to locate the *Diário de Notícias* from January 31 to February 6, 1889, but the material about São Francisco was transcribed in a book by Pedro Tomás Pedreira. See Pedreira, *Memória histórico-geográfica de São Francisco do Conde,* pp. 113–115.

59. Barickman, "Até a véspera," pp. 186–187.

60. Antônio Lourenço de Araújo, Delegado of Santo Amaro, to the Chefe de Polícia, May 12, 1889, *Delegados, maço* 3003 (1887–1889), APEB.

61. Juiz de orfões of the Vila of São of São Francisco, João Rodrigues Teixeira, to the Presidente da Província, September 20, 1889. *Câmara,* 1436 (1881–1889), APEB. The provincial president informed the judge that the town council was authorized to employ the poor in public works that would benefit the town.

62. "Vila de São Francisco," October 26, 1889, *Diário do Povo,* p. 1, BPEBa.

63. Delegado of Cachoeira, Rosalvo Meneses Fraga, to the Chefe de Polícia, July 16, 1889, *Delegados, maço* 6227 (1885–1889), APEB.

64. Relatório do inspetor especial de terras públicas, Dionísio Gonçalves Martins, to the Presidente da Província, October 9, 1889, *Terras Públicas, maço* 4850 (1876–1891), APEB. The report was prepared on the basis of a questionnaire created by engineer Ramos de Queirós containing twelve questions about the availability of Brazilian-born workers, their nature and their attitude toward work, available jobs, and public policies to integrate them productively into society.

65. Bello, *Memórias,* p. 12. Bello's observations refer to what happened on the Tentugal Plantation in Pernambuco's Zona da Matta, but it is an important indicator of what took place on the Bahian plantations.

66. Barão de Cotegipe to Araújo Pinho, Rio de Janeiro, November 20, 1888, *Coleção Araújo Pinho, lata* 548, *pasta* 84, IHGB.

67. *Diário de Notícias,* December 4, 1888, p. 2, APEB.

68. *Diário de Notícias,* December 4, 1888, p. 2, APEB.

69. *Diário de Notícias,* December 4, 1888, p. 2, APEB.

70. Delegado of São Francisco, Luís de Oliveira Mendes, to the Chefe de Polícia, December 16, 1888, confidential, *Polícia-delegados, maço* 6227 (1885–1889), APEB.

71. "Vila de São Francisco," *Diário da Bahia,* January 6, 1889, p. 1, BPEBa.

72. *Diário da Bahia,* January 14, 1889, p. 1, BPEBa.

73. Public Prosecutor of Santo Amaro, João José de Oliveira Junqueira, to the Presidente da Província, December 17, 1888, *Promotores, maço* 2772 (1887–1889), APEB.

74. José Bruno Ferreira, Subdelegado of the Parish of Rio Fundo, December 12, 1888, *Delegados, maço* 6227 (1885–1889), APEB.

75. Delegado of Santo Amaro, António Lourenço de Araújo, to the Chefe de Polícia, December 11, 1888, *Polícia-delegados, maço* 6227 (1885–1889), APEB.

76. Delegado of Santo Amaro, António Lourenço de Araújo, to the Chefe de Polícia, October 25, 1888, *Delegados, maço* 6227 (1885–1889), APEB.

77. Delegado of Santo Amaro to the Chefe de Polícia, November 18, 1888, *Delegados, maço* 6227 (1885–1889), APEB.

78. Delegado of São Francisco, Luís de Oliveira Mendes, November 27, 1888, *Delegados, maço* 6227 (1885–1889), APEB.

79. Delegado of São Francisco, Luís Oliveira Mendes, December 18, 1888, *Delegados, maço* 6227 (1885–1889), APEB. Olímpio was returned to the delegado but he was over thirty five years of age and could no longer be drafted into the army.

80. Delegado of Curralinho, José de Queirós Vieira, to the Chefe de Polícia, January 25, 1889, *Delegados, maço* 6227 (1885–1889), APEB. On Santarém, see Delegado José Joaquim P. Gondim to the Chefe de Polícia, November 28, 1889 in the same packet.

81. Iniciativas para a criação das Companhias de Guardas do Corpo de Polícia, December 1889, *Polícia-assuntos, maço* 6507 (1888–1889), APEB.

82. Projetos para a segurança pública do governador Manoel Vitorino, February 21, 1890, *Secretária de Governo, maço* 1753 (1890), p. 14, APEB. TR: Between May 13, 1888, and the date of this proposal, February 21, 1890, the Brazilian monarchy with its associated highly centralized state fell to a military coup and was replaced by a federal republic. Among other changes, provinces became states and appointed provincial presidents were replaced by elected governors.

83. "Código rural," *Jornal de Notícias*, October 11, 1890, p. 1, BPEBa. In Puerto Rico, sugar planters also complained that the freedmen only worked two or three days a week. Mattei, "El liberto en el régimen de trabajo azucarero de Puerto Rico, 1870–1880," p. 117.

5. HEADS SPINNING WITH FREEDOM

Epigraph: Lyrics of a samba sung by the residents of the Cinco Rios Usina (the central sugar mill that was formerly the Maracangalha Plantation), recorded by Valdevino Neves Paiva, in *Maracangalha*, pp. 71–72. Valdevino Neves worked at the *usina* during the 1950s and began to record the lyrics of sambas sung by the resident workers.

1. On custom as a field of confrontation and change, see Thompson, *Costumes em comum*, pp. 16–17. Confrontations between masters and ex-slaves after emancipation have been detected in other parts of the Americas. See Tomich, "Houses, Provisions Grounds and the Reconstitution of Labour," p. 241.

2. *PC*, 29/1032/04 (1888), pp. 4–8v, APEB.

3. *PC*, 29/1032/04 (1888), p. 7v, APEB.

4. *PC*, 29/1032/04 (1888), pp. 9–10, APEB.

5. *PC*, 29/1032/04 (1888), pp. 10v–12v, APEB.

6. *PC*, 29/1032/04 (1888), pp. 12v–13, APEB.

7. Subdelegado of São Francisco, Ernesto Alves Rigaud, to the Chefe de Polícia, June 30, 1888, *maço* 2987 (1880–1889), APEB.

8. *PC*, 29/1032/04 (1888), p. 74, APEB.

9. Telegram from the Delegado of São Francisco to the Chefe de Polícia, July 6, 1888, *maço* 2987 (1880–1889); *PC*, 29/1032/04 (1888), pp. 24v–25, APEB.

10. *PC*, 29/1032/04 (1888), pp. 24v–25v, APEB.

11. *PC*, 29/1032/04 (1888), p. 32v.

12. Actually, the cause of the conflict was not new, because, according to Stuart Schwartz, fencing cane fields and other farm fields was uncommon on Recôncavo plantations. The proximity of the properties continually provoked altercations among the planters. Schwartz, *Segredos internos*, p. 103.

13. Vilhena *A Bahia no século XVIII*, 1:185–187.

14. *PC*, 29/1032/04 (1888), p. 31v, APEB.

15. *PC*, 29/1032/04 (1888), pp. 25–26, APEB.

16. *PC*, 29/1032/04 (1888), pp. 30–36, APEB.

17. Hebe Mattos discusses ex-slaves' expectations of access to land after abolition. Hebe Mattos, *Das cores do silêncio*, especially chapters 17 and 18. Silvia Lara notes that for many slaves, freedom meant maintaining access to land acquired during slavery. As noted earlier, the planting of subsistence crops as a goal of ex-slaves was not limited to Brazil. Lara, "Escravidão, cidadania e história," p. 28. On ex-slaves and subsistence crops elsewhere, see, for example, Saville, *Work of Reconstruction*, pp. 118–119.

18. As Carolyn Fick has observed, the desire to own land formed an essential part of the ex-slave's vision of freedom. That was because, without land, which provided the possibility of working for themselves and their family, freedom was nothing more than a judicial abstraction. Fick, "Camponeses e soldados negros na Revolução de Saint-Domingue," p. 225.

19. *PC*, 29/1032/04 (1888), p. 32, APEB.

20. *PC*, 29/1032/04 (1888), p. 25, APEB.

21. For a list of the slaves at the Maracangalha Plantation in 1872, see *IT*, 1/95/137/1 (1871–1877), pp. 403–408, APEB.

22. *PC*, 29/1032/04 (1888), p. 89v, APEB.

23. Shortly after the death of the Baron of Passé, Cruz Rios had been about to acquire Maracangalha, but failed to do so, because of the machinations of Moniz Aragão and his allies.

24. *Registro de terras da freguesia do Monte (São Francisco do Conde)*, 4748 (1857–1862), pp. 17–17v, APEB.

25. *IT*, 1/95/137/1 (1871–1877), APEB. The Viscount of Passé died owning Rs.605:377$330 to merchants and banks in the provincial capital; among his creditors were the Baron of Pereira Marinho, a rich merchant from Salvador and source of capital to many Recôncavo planters.

26. For a biography of the Count of Passé, see Bulcão Sobrinho, "Titulares baianos," pp. 137–138. Passé was born in São Francisco do Conde in 1793, and was a central figure in the principal political events in Bahia throughout the nineteenth century, including the War of Independence, the suppression of the Sabinada, and the organization of combatants for the Paraguayan War. See also Pinho, *História de um engenho do Recôncavo*, pp. 509–510; this author tells a story about the last years of life of the Count of Passé.

27. *IT*, 1/95/137/1 (1871–1877), p. 17, APEB.

28. On the Baron of Moniz Aragão and other Bahian planters see Bulcão Sobrinho, "Titulares baianos," p. 25. According to Rheingantz, Moniz Aragão became a baron on August 14, 1877. Rheingantz, *Titulares do Império*, p. 56.

29. On the strategies for family alliances of the Bahian planters, see Mattoso, *Família e sociedade*, pp. 139–158. See also Schwartz, *Segredos internos*, p. 229. According to the latter author the Argolo, Moniz Barreto, Aragão, Bulcão, Rocha Pita, and Vilas Boas families were linked through a complex network of endogamous ties, principally

of marriages among cousins over various generations and secondary relationships sealed with baptisms and marriages.

30. The Baron of Cotegipe owned the Cabochi, Freguesia, Quibaca, and Sapucaia Plantations. Maracangalha, Cassarangongo, and Mataripe belonged to Moniz Aragão.

31. Moniz Aragão to Cotegipe, November 26, 1878, *CBC*, *lata* 873 A, *pasta* 142, IHGB.

32. Moniz Aragão to Cotegipe, Cassarangongo, November 27, 1878, *CBC*, *pasta* 144, IHGB.

33. Moniz Aragão to Cotegipe, November 27, 1878, *CBC*, *pasta* 144, IHGB.

34. Moniz Aragão to Cotegipe, November 27, 1878, *CBC*, *pasta* 144, IHGB.

35. Moniz Aragão to Cotegipe, Bahia, May 19, 1879, *CBC*, *pasta* 144, IHGB.

36. Moniz Aragão to Cotegipe, August 4, 1880, *CBC*, *lata* 873, *pasta* 147; see also Moniz Aragão to Cotegipe, April 2, 1881, *lata* 873 A, *pasta* 149, IHGB.

37. Moniz Aragão to Cotegipe, July 17, 1882, *CBC*, *lata* 873 A, *pasta* 152, IHGB.

38. This strategy was not new. Schwartz observed that as early as the eighteenth century, Bahian plantations were using slaves in supervisory positions and that, over time, the tendency to employ slaves in that way increased. Schwartz, *Segredos internos*, p. 134.

39. Moniz Aragão to Cotegipe, Engenho Cassarangongo, October 23, 1883, *CBC*, *lata* 873 A, *pasta* 169, IHGB.

40. Moniz Aragão to Cotegipe, November 7, 1883, *CBC*, *lata* 873 A, *pasta* 170, IHGB.

41. Moniz Aragão to Cotegipe, October 3, 1887, *CBC*, *lata* 873 A, *pasta* 199, IHGB. TR: Pagode is an Afro-Brazilian music and dance.

42. See chapter 4 of this book in which I analyze letters that the Baron of Moniz Aragão, in his role as president of the town council of São Francisco, sent to the provincial president of Bahia.

43. *PC*, 29/1032/04 (1888), p. 56v, APEB.

44. In Saint Domingue, the abolition of slavery encouraged many freedmen to expand the areas on which they were farming subsistence crops, especially on properties abandoned by the ex-masters. See Fick, "Camponeses e soldados negros na Revolução de Saint-Domingue," p. 218.

45. *PC*, 29/1032/04 (1888), pp. 71–71v, APEB.

46. *PC*, 15/538/7 (1889), p. 2, APEB.

47. *PC*, 18/646/05 (1888), p. 2, APEB.

48. Felipe Álvares da Paixão, subdelegado of Boa Vista, Canavieiras, to the Chefe de Polícia, May 31, 1888, *maço* 3003 (1887–1888), APEB.

49. Litwack, *Been in the Storm So Long*, p. 142, emphasizes this question in the U.S. South.

50. *PC*, 32/1152/14 (1889), pp. 1–38v, APEB.

51. On the importance of cattle on the plantations, see Freyre, *Nordeste*, pp. 73–79. According to Freyre, the slave and the ox formed the "foundation of sugar civilization" in the Northeast. On the Maracangalha Plantation, the "tame" oxen, in other words, those that were employed in labor on the plantations, carried curious names, many of which referred to historical personalities, nationalities, or indications of the animal's personality. They included Crybaby, Nobleman, Little Love, Sovereign, Brazilian,

French, Sailor, Kiss the Girls, Boyfriend, Adjutant, Stuck-up, Turtle, Bonaparte, and Labatut. *IT*, 1/93A/133/1 (1877–1878), p. 72, APEB.

52. *PC*, 15/538/2 (1889), p. 6, APEB.

53. *PC*, 15/538/2 (1889), pp. 17v–19v, APEB.

54. *PC*, 15/539/2 (1889), p. 18, APEB.

55. *PC*, 15/538/2 (1889), p. 21v, APEB.

56. Subdelegado of the Passé Parish, João Leôncio Ribeiro Sanches, to Chefe de Polícia, March, 20, 1889, *maço* 6253 (1888–1889); *PC* 15/538/2 (1889), pp. 25v–26, APEB.

57. *PC*, 15/538/2 (1889), p. 21v, APEB.

58. *PC*, 15/538/2 (1889), p. 24, APEB.

59. *PC*, 15/538/2 (1889), pp. 24–24v, APEB.

60. *PC*, 15/538/2 (1889), pp. 25v–26, APEB.

61. *PC*, 15/538/2 (1889), pp. 20v–28, APEB.

62. The symbolic burial of political objects aimed at making fun at superiors in the social hierarchy was a significant part of the traditions of popular struggles in nineteenth-century Bahia. On this see Reis, *A morte é uma festa*, pp. 165–167.

63. Wounding or killing animals considered to be powerful was a way of demonstrating dissatisfaction or taking revenge for some injustice suffered by popular groups in various times and places. For an example of such behavior in France, see Darnton, *O grande massacre de gatos*, pp. 131–132. See also Thompson, *Senhores e caçadores*, on the clandestine slaughtering of pigs on royal English properties in the eighteenth century. In the world of the plantations, sabotaging production included slaughtering or wounding cattle, especially animals utilized in agricultural service. See also Tomich, *Slavery in the Circuit of Sugar*, p. 252.

64. A complete version of the samba cited at the beginning of the chapter can be found in Paiva, *Maracangalha*, p. 72.

65. *PC*, 15/538/2 (1889), p. 27v, APEB.

66. *PC*, 15/538/2 (1889), pp. 27v–28, APEB.

67. See *Livro de registro de batizados da freguesia do Monte* (1879–1888), pp. 5 and 14, ACMS.

68. *PC*, 15/538/2 (1889), p. 17v, APEB.

69. *PC*, 15/538/2 (1889), p. 29v, APEB.

70. *PC*, 15/538/2 (1889), p. 25v, APEB.

71. *PC*, 15/538/2 (1889), p. 26, APEB.

72. The lyrics of Dorival Caymmi's song read: "Eu vou prá Maracangalha; eu vou!; Eu vou de liforme branco; Eu vou!; Eu vou de chapeu de palha; Eu vou!; Eu vou convidar Anália; Eu vou!; Se Anália não quiser ir; Eu vou só!; Eu vou só!; Eu vou só!; Se Anália não quiser ir; Eu vou só!; Eu vou só!; Eu vou só sem Anália; Mas eu vou!" [I'm going to Maracangalha, I'm going! I'm going in a white suit, I'm going! I'm going in a straw hat, I'm going! I'm going to invite Anália to go with me, I'm going; And if Anália doesn't want to go, I'll go alone, I'll go alone; I'll go alone without Anália; but I'll go!]

73. Minister of Agriculture to the Presidente da Provincia of Bahia, June 15, 1888, and attachment of telegram from the Juiz Comissário of Ilhéus, Teodoro Augusto

Cardoso, to the Minister of Agriculture, May 24, 1888, *Avisos Recebidos do Ministério da Agricultura*, 783 (1888), p. 89, APEB.

74. Interim special inspector of public lands to the Presidente da Província da Bahia, January 21, 1889, *maço* 4847–1 (1840–1889), APEB.

75. *PC*, 25/885/7, APEB.

76. Delegado of the Town of São Francisco, Luís de Oliveira Mendes, to the Chefe de Polícia, June 16, 1888, *maço* 3003 (1887–1889), APEB.

77. TR: The incident took place on Saturday, March 16, but delays in publication meant that two Saturdays had passed by the time the story actually appeared in the *Diário da Bahia*.

78. "Assalto à propriedade," *Diário da Bahia*, March 28, 1889, p. 1, BPEBa.

79. "Um crime monstruoso," *Diário da Bahia*, April 6, 1889, p. 2, BPEBa.

80. "Um crime monstruoso," *Diário da Bahia*, April 6, 1889, p. 2, BPEBa. The complainant considered that event as a threat to freedom and the right to private property. He also insisted that the local authorities should not investigate the crime, since the subdelegado had ordered the crime committed and the delegado was related to the people who ordered the crime.

81. "Falla do Presidente da Província" (1889), p. 151. According to the provincial president's report to the legislature, the owners of Maracangalha received Rs.400:000$000 in a loan to establish the Maracangalha Central Sugar Mill, which had the capacity to grind three hundred tons of cane daily. On January 18, 1889, the *Jornal de Notícias* reported that the Baron of Moniz Aragão sent examples of the cane contracts that Maracangalha Central Sugar Mill would be signing with cane farmers interesting in participating in the venture. The paper reported that the new sugar mill had received 400,000 réis available for the expansion, and that interested planters and farmers would only have to invest 10 percent themselves. Half of the funds were designated for the construction of twenty kilometers of new railroad to Catú. The sugar produced would be consigned to Manoel José Lopes Lisboa e Sobrinho, a merchant in Salvador.

82. See Tomich, *Slavery in the Circuit*, p. 262.

6. AFTER ABOLITION

1. Barickman, "Até a véspera," pp. 209–227.

2. Sampaio, "Meu avô paterno, Tertuliano Coelho Sampaio," p. 2.

3. "Manifestação de apreço," *O Tempo*, May 23, 1888, p. 2, IGHB.

4. *Diário da Bahia*, July 17, 1888, p. 1, BPEBa.

5. Men and women who hired themselves out as casual laborers in Brazil's cities were known as *ganhadores* or *ganhadoras*—literally earners—at this time. Men carried merchandise in the ports, or found work as masons and carpenters. In Salvador for much of the nineteenth century, they carried people up the steep hill between the commercial lower city neighborhoods by the bay and the well-to-do residential neighborhoods or religious and government institutions on the bluff above. Women sold food and snacks on commercial street corners and in well-to-do neighborhoods alike. Reis, "De olho no canto."

6. "Consequências da lei de 13 de maio," *O Tempo*, July 25, 1888, p. 1, IGHB.

7. Pinho, *História de um engenho*, p. 512.

8. Aristides Novis to the Barão de Cotegipe, March 1, 1888, CBC, *lata* 918, *pasta* 21, IHGB.

9. Aristides Novis to the Barão de Cotegipe, May 16, 1888, CBC, *lata* 918, *pasta* 23, IHGB.

10. Aristides Novis to the Barão de Cotegipe, May 18, 1888, CBC, *lata* 918, *pasta* 24, IHGB.

11. Aristides Novis to the Barão de Cotegipe, Salvador, May 30, 1888, CBC, *lata* 918, *pasta* 25, IHGB.

12. Schwartz, *Sugar Plantations*, p. 138.

13. On subsistence among sugar-plantation slaves, see Schwartz, *Segredos internos*, p. 127. In his view, the daily rations on Bahian sugar plantations during the colonial period were both scarce and of poor quality, as a result of which the slaves preferred to grow their own food.

14. Robert Slenes argues that avoiding dependence on food provided by the master would have also implied the possibility of improving the food "quality." Slenes, *Na senzala, uma flor*, pp. 190–191.

15. Daily rations were a source of conflict between ex-masters and ex-slaves in other parts of the post-abolition Americas. In Puerto Rico, after emancipation, ex-slaves on plantations demanded daily rations in addition to wages. Mattei, "El liberto en el régimen de trabajo," pp. 107–108.

16. Aristides Novis to the Barão de Cotegipe, May 18, 1888, CBC, *lata* 918, *pasta* 23, IHGB.

17. Dale Graden offers a different interpretation of this letter from the Freguesia Plantation manager. See Graden, "Voices from Under," p. 155.

18. Aristides Novis to the Barão de Cotegipe. July 11, 1888, CBC, *lata* 918, *pasta* 27, IHGB.

19. Aristides Novis to the Barão de Cotegipe, Bahia, July 11, 1888, CBC, *lata* 918, *pasta* 27, IHGB.

20. For a discussion of these questions, see Tomich, *Slavery in the Circuit of Sugar*, p. 255.

21. Slenes argues that this was a constant struggle in slave societies. Slenes, *Na senzala, uma flor*, p. 111.

22. Aristides Novis to Cotegipe, August 25, 1888, CBC, *lata* 918, *pasta* 28, IHGB.

23. On weeding, see Schwartz, *Segredos internos*, p. 128.

24. Schwartz, *Segredos internos*, pp. 96–98.

25. On the schedule for planting and harvesting tobacco, see Ministério de Agricultura, Indústria e Comércio, *Aspectos da economia rural Brasileira* (Rio de Janeiro, 1992), pp. 430–431.

26. Aristides Novis to the Barão de Cotegipe, October 6, 1888; CBC, *lata* 918, *pasta* 29, IHGB.

27. Aristides Novis to the Barão de Cotegipe, October 6, 1888; CBC, *lata* 918, *pasta* 29, IHGB.

28. Aristides Novis to the Barão de Cotegipe, October 6, 1888; CBC, *lata* 918, *pasta* 29, IHGB.

29. "A crise atual," *O Tempo*, August 1, 1888, p. 1, IGHB.

30. "A crise atual," *O Tempo*, August 1, 1888, p. 1, IGHB.

31. "Sediciosos," *O Tempo*, December 19, 1888, p. 1, IGHB.

32. Wanderley Pinho argued that this account book "provided a snapshot of the manager's anguish." Pinho, *História de um engenho*, pp. 512–517.

33. See the text of the May 30, 1888, letter from Novis to Cotegipe quoted in the first part of this chapter.

34. TR: The original uses *saveiro*, but following Richard Graham, I am translating the term to boat. Graham, *Feeding the City*, p. 82.

35. TR: For a discussion of the terms for black, see the introduction to the English-language edition in this volume.

36. *Livro de contas dos engenhos* (1889–1898), Araújo Pinho Collection, IHGB.

37. On such payments to free laborers see Barickman, "Até a véspera," pp. 206–207.

38. I compared the names on the Benfica payroll with the 1882 Matrícula register for the Count of Subaé. Matrícula de escravos do conde de Subaé, 1886, ACS; Lista de pagamento dos trabalhadores do Engenho Benfica, February 1913, Arquivo de João Ferreira de Araújo Pinho Júnior (hereafter AJFAP).

39. According to Lamberg, this system had many good points, "since it made use of those workers who did not want to be employed by the day, as well as those who grew less lucrative crops." The poor results grew out of the shortage of animals to haul the cane, as well as the old machinery that could only extract minimum amounts of juice from the cut cane. He concluded that the pretos mistrusted the owners, "formerly their owners and masters," and only a few of them became sharecroppers. Faithful to his racist convictions, he observed that the blacks' "invincible indolence" contributed to the system's failure. He also remarked that the system had been successfully adopted on the Novo Plantation, belonging to Mr. Cruz Rios, and that many tenant farmers, the majority of which had been enslaved until recently, were earning relatively large profits each year on the basis of small crops. On the other hand, the tenant farmers had a number of head of cattle and could cultivate cereals and fruit for their own subsistence. Lamberg, *O Brazil*, pp. 199–200.

40. Lamberg, *O Brazil*, pp. 81 and 199.

41. The announcement indicated that those interested should go to the plantation or to 11 Julião Street, demonstrating that they hoped to attract farm workers who were living in the city, presumably ex-slaves who had migrated there after abolition. *Jornal de Notícias*, January 15, 1895, p. 2, BPEBa.

42. TR: *Pagando a renda* literally means "paying for the income." The freedmen used this ironic term to indicate that they had to pay landowners for the privilege to earn money.

43. Research by Edinélia Maria Oliveira Souza, "Cruzando memórias e espaços de cultura," shows that between 1930 and 1960, around the town of dom Macedo Costa, in the southern Recôncavo, it was fairly common to find the descendants of slaves renting land from plantation owners.

44. Caderneta de receitas e despesas (1911–1912) anotações de João Ferreira de Araújo Pinho Júnior, AJFAP.

45. *IT*, 05/2184/2653 (1999), Francisco Moreira de Carvalho, Conde de Subaé, APEB.

46. João Ferreira de Araújo Pinho to Pinho Júnior, June 4, 1893, AJFAP. It is important to note that free and freed workers were paid in these ways when slavery still existed. The plantation accounts distinguished between the free workers "paid by the day" from those who were paid "by the task." The slaves could be paid in both forms when they worked on Sundays. The postmortem inventory of the owner of the Lagoa Plantation in Santo Amaro distinguished between the various ways of paying free workers and slaves. See *IT*, *lata* 4 (1901–1902), Arquimedes Pires de Carvalho, pp. 300–309, AMSA.

47. Administrator to João Ferreira de Araújo Pinho Júnior, July, 12, 1927, and Administrator to João Ferreira de Araújo Pinho Júnior, August 19, 1927, AJFAP.

48. Rebecca Scott observed that the collective action among sugar workers increased their bargaining power and inhibited the exercise of force on the sugar plantations of Louisiana after abolition. Scott, "Stubborn and Disposed to Stand Their Ground," pp. 106–107.

49. This phenomenon occurred in other parts of the Americas after abolition. Eiss, "Share in the Land," pp. 61–63.

50. According to the Brazilian Agriculture Ministry, most tobacco growers in this period were "lavradores without resources." On the schedule for planting and harvesting tobacco, see Ministério da Agricultura, Indústria e Comércio, *Aspectos da economia rural brasileira*, pp. 430–431.

51. Administrator of Benfica to João Ferreira de Araújo Pinho Júnior, July 15, 1930, ACS.

52. José Antônio de Santana, administrator of the Benfica Plantation, to João Ferreira de Araújo Pinho Júnior, July 29, 1930; August 5, 1930, ACS.

53. Administrator Santana to João Ferreira de Araújo Pinho Júnior, Benfica, January 17, 1928; January 24, 1928; and February 1, 1928, AJFAP.

54. Rebecca Scott argued that in Louisiana, ex-masters' fears that ex-slaves would quit their plantations increased the latter's negotiating power. Scott, "Stubborn and Disposed to Stand Their Ground," p. 107.

55. Silvia Lara suggested the term "divided week." Personal communication, September 2, 2003.

56. Interview with Francisco Ambrósio, July 21, 2003.

57. Sampaio, *Feira de Santana*, pp. 76–81. At the beginning of the 1920s, Gastão Sampaio found that the owners of cattle ranches allowed farmers to plant roças on their land in exchange for clearing pastureland.

58. Eul-Soo Pang recognized the powerful change in Recôncavo work habits created by the modernization of the sugar industry there after abolition. According to him, most freedmen worked only four days for their previous owners and three for themselves. Pang, *O engenho Central*, pp. 55–56.

59. Eric Foner observed that in the Caribbean the labor shortage empowered freedmen in their struggles with former owners. The difficulties owners faced in obtaining

labor helped freedmen to determine their and their families' working conditions and the rhythm of labor, as well as compensation for it. Foner, *Nada além da liberdade*, p. 70.

60. Interview with Mariana da Costa Pinto Victória Filha, daughter of the owner of Carapiá Plantation in Santo Amaro, October 19, 2001.

61. Litwack, *Been in the Storm So Long*, p. 227.

7. TRAJECTORIES OF SLAVES AND FREED PEOPLE ON RECÔNCAVO SUGAR PLANTATIONS

1. Calmon, *Memórias*, p. 40.

2. Alves, *Matas do sertão*, p. 46.

3. Studies of the post-emancipation experience in parts of the Americas indicate that some ex-slaves remained in the areas when they had been enslaved. See Fields, *Slavery and Freedom*, p. 190; and Litwack, *Been in the Storm*, p. 243.

4. To re-create life stories of ex-slaves who remained on the plantations on which they had been enslaved, I employed the same methods used by several historians of Brazilian slavery who have recently produced biographies and studies of enslaved trajectories. See, for example, Graham, *Caetana diz não*; and Reis, *Domingos Sodré*.

5. This chapter was inspired, in large part, by Scott, "Exploring the Meaning of Freedom," pp. 19–21. Without ignoring the oppression that followed abolition, Scott proposed that historians should seek to understand that the initiatives and choices of the ex-slaves were central to the relationships established in the post-abolition period throughout the Americas.

6. Litwack, *Been in the Storm*, p. 228.

7. *Livro de entrada de doentes da Santa Casa*, 1906–1913, Arquivo da Santa Casa de Misericórdia de Santo Amaro (hereafter ASCMSA).

8. *IT*, 8/3444/4 (1887–1891), Barão de Pirajá, "Lista de escravos do Engenho Pouco Ponto, em 1887," p. 548, APEB; *Livro de entrada de doentes* (1906–1911), p.n.p., ASCMSA.

9. *Livro de entrada de doentes* (1911–1913), p.n.p.; ASCMSA; *IT*, 3/1206/1675/1 (1869–1887), Baronesa of Pirajá, p. 73, APEB.

10. *Livro de entrada de doentes*, 1906–1913, ASCMSA.

11. The statistics on Rio Fundo were drawn from *LRN*, no. 1 (1889–1919), CRCRF; the data on Santana de Lustosa was collected from *LRN*, no. 1 (1889–1900), Cartório de Registro Civil de Santana do Lustosa (hereafter, CRCSL).

12. Interview with Francisco Ambrósio, July 21, 2003.

13. *O Tempo*, January 1, 1889, p. 2. The sentence comes from a complaint that on Christmas night 1888 kids had been riding horses they did not own into the village of Belém.

14. Hebe Mattos called attention to the importance of family and social ties for the integration of the freedmen into the rural world of southeastern Brazil. These ties weighed heavily in the decision to remain on the plantations. Castro, *Das cores do silêncio*, p. 355.

15. TR: Wimberly, "Expansion of Afro-Bahian," pp. 82–83.

16. For the story of Anacleto Urbano da Natividade, see *IT*, 02/591/1044/14, Joana Maria da Natividade Tosta (1856–1857), APEB; Wimberly, "African Liberto," pp. 190–191.

Wimberly based her arguments on interviews with Yeda Bahia dos Santos, one of Anacleto's descendants.

17. Through his study of Martinique, Dale Tomich calls attention to the ways in which the freedmen who remained on the sugar properties there after emancipation tried to change their working conditions. See Tomich, "Contested Terrains," pp. 241–254.

18. *Livro de Registro de Casamentos* (hereafter *LRC*), Freguesia do Iguape (1857–1902), pp. 161v–69, ACMS.

19. Caderneta de receitas e despesas (1911–1912), notes by Pinho Júnior, AJFAP.

20. For the interview with the ex-slave Argeu, see *O Escudo Social*, October 14, 1933, p. 2.

21. *PC, lata* 1 (1903), pp. 1–11, AMSA.

22. Marques, *As voltas da estrada*, p. 198. Ex-slave Nasário Ribeiro used this sentence to explain his upward social and political mobility in Amparo.

23. Lamberg, *O Brazil*, p. 197.

24. Sampaio, *Feira de Santana e o vale do Jacuipe*, p. 119. Manoel Araújo Ferreira referred to the moradores of Baixa Grande on the Cruz Plantation during an interview on December 7, 2002.

25. *PC*, 9/310/19 (1891), pp. 2–53v, APEB. The *juiz de direito* in the town of São Francisco, Benigno Dantas de Brito, threw out the case on a technicality, in an apparent attempt to protect the plantation owner.

26. *PC*, 32/1152/8 (1892), pp. 1–14v, APEB. The case was heard in the São Félix Court House on March 24, 1892. Despite his protests of innocence, Pedro was convicted and sentenced to the maximum penalty under Article 302 of the Criminal Code—four years in prison.

27. *PC*, 32/1143/5 (1896), pp. 2–9, APEB.

28. *PC*, 26/915/7 (1893), pp. 2–10v, APEB. Assis accused the plantation owner of trying to rape his sister—a minor—and of persecuting his entire family for stopping him. The investigation never led to a trial, since the judge—clearly trying to protect Bitencourt—decided that the damage done to the victim consisted of "minor wounds," with no long-term consequences.

29. Interview with freedman Argeu, *Escudo Social*, October 14, 1933, p. 2.

30. Rego, *Meus verdes anos*, p. 205. Lins do Rego, one of Brazil's most prominent novelists, was born in 1901 and spent a large part of his childhood on his maternal grandfather's Corredor Plantation in Paraiba state.

31. Rego, *Meus verdes anos*, pp. 61–62.

32. Rego, *Menino de engenho*. This novel, originally published in 1932, is largely based on the author's experiences on his grandfather's plantation.

33. Silva, "Notas e impressões sobre o districto de S. Thiago do Iguape," pp. 418–419. Celestino da Silva's observations date from 1917.

34. The discussion of this event is based on an interview with José Luís Barbosa Dutra, the great-grandson of the Baron of Iguape, on February 18, 2002. He received the information from his father who was an adolescent when abolition took place and observed the events in question. The former manager of the plantation, Manoel

Araújo Ferreira, known as Manoelzinho, told me a very similar story in an interview on December 7, 2002.

35. TR: Brazilian inheritance law was and is quite different from Anglo-American inheritance law. At the time, it contained very strict provisions for the distribution of property and significantly limited the ability of property owners to will their property to heirs. The law was based on the presumption of community property in marriage and equal partible inheritance among successors, rather than heirs, so until the twentieth century, "no more than a third of a decedent's estate could devolve by legacy." Lewin, "Natural and Spurious Children," p. 357. While the inventory and division process was under way, management of estates fell to the executor, under the supervision of the courts. The best summary of Brazilian inheritance law and its implications for history is Lewin, "Natural and Spurious Children," p. 357. For a detailed and nuanced discussion of the issues, see Lewin's two-volume study *Surprise Heirs*.

36. *IT*, 2/519/964/17 (1888–1892), Barão de Iguape, pp. 8–15, APEB.

37. Barickman, "Persistence and Decline," p. 583.

38. Barickman, "Até a véspera," pp. 178–179.

39. Interview with Manoel Araújo Ferreira, December 7, 2002.

40. *IT*, unnumbered *lata*, Tomé Pereira de Araújo, (1853) pp. 8–15, ARC.

41. TR: For discussions of the tasks involved in sugar making, see Schwartz, *Sugar Plantations*, pp. 142–145. For a comparison with sugar making in the British Caribbean, see Dunn, *Sugar and Slavery*, chapter 6.

42. According to Stuart Schwartz, the slaves employed in the sugar mills had generally been born in Brazil and had begun to learn their trade at a very young age. In the boiling house, the manipulation of the temperatures in the furnaces and in the cauldrons of boiling cane required great skill and many years of experience. Schwartz, *Segredos internos*, p. 132.

43. *Livro de registro de batismos da freguesia do Iguape* (1856–1871), fls 113, 160, 201, 230v, 274v, 345, ACMS.

44. *Livro de Registro de Batismos* (hereafter *LRB*), *Freguesia do Iguape* (1856–1871), p. 306v, ACMS.

45. *LRO*, *Distrito do Iguape*, n.p. (1889–1900), pp. 57, 85, 145, Cartório de Registro Civil de Santiago do Iguape (hereafter CRCI).

46. *IT*, unnumbered *lata*, Tomé Pereira de Araújo (1853), ARC.

47. *Livro de notas do tabelionato de Cachoeira*, no. 90, p. 40; bill of sale for the Cruz Plantation by Manoel Pereira de Macedo Aragão to Tomé Pereira de Araújo, September 27, 1826, APEB.

48. *LRB*, *Freguesia do Iguape* (1893–1902), p. 6, ACMS.

49. *LRB*, *Freguesia do Iguape* (1893–1902), p. 5, ACMS.

50. *LRB*, *Rreguesia do Iguape* (1893–1902), p. 50v, ACMS.

51. On the relationship between adoption of names and identity formation in the city of Campinas, São Paulo, see Xavier, *A conquista da liberdade*, pp. 114–115.

52. *LRC*, *Freguesia do Iguape* (1857–1902), p. 201, ACMS. For this project, I only examined marriages registered between 1888 and 1902.

53. *LRN*, *Distrito do Iguape*, no. 1 (1888–1897), p. 61v, ACMS.

54. *LRC, Freguesia do Iguape*, no. 1 (1857–1902), p. 160, ACMS.

55. *LRC, Freguesia do Iguape*, no. 1 (1857–1902), p. 161v, ACMS.

56. *LRN, Distrito do Iguape*, no. 1 (1889–1897), pp. 1, 21, 62v, and 69, ACMS.

57. *LRO, Distrito do Iguape*, n.p. (1889–1900), pp. 46, 65v, CRCI.

58. *LRO, Freguesia do Iguape*, pp. 56v, 85v, 145.

59. *PC*, 15/309/12 (1893), pp. 2–10, APEB.

60. *PC*, 4432 (1891), summary of the charges against Possidônio Bulcão by the Cachoeira public prosecutor in 1899, APEB.

61. *LRB, Freguesia do Iguape* (1856–1871), p. 210v, ACMS.

62. Antônio José Balieiro was an attorney and a member of the abolitionist movement in Cachoeira. He primarily represented slaves who sued their masters for freedom.

63. *LRN, Freguesia do Iguape*, no. 1 (1889–1897), n.p., CRCI. The register records the birth of a daughter named Maria do Carmo to Andrelina and Máximo. Andrelina and Máximo Damaceno were married on November 23, 1896, in the Iguape Parish church but prior to that they had lived together as man and wife, with children. *LRC, Freguesia do Iguape*, no. 1 (1857–1902), pp. 160, 161v, and 176v, ACMS.

64. *PC*, 12/419/10 (1894), pp. 11–13, APEB. Severiano Pinto died in the Misericórdia Hospital in Cachoeira the day after the crime. Jacinto fled and in November 1894 still had not been located.

8. COMMUNITY AND FAMILY LIFE AMONG FREED PEOPLE

1. *IT*, 3/328/1797/13 (1898), José Joaquim Pires de Carvalho e Albuquerque, Barão de Pirajá, APEB. In his will dated September 15, 1869, the baron declared that he was the son of the Viscount of Pirajá, "Grandee" of the empire. He was married to Aguida Maria Zeferina da Silva, who died the same year and with whom he had no children

2. *IT*, 3/1206/1675/1 (1869–1887), Aguida Maria Zeferina da Silva, Baronesa of Pirajá, APEB. The document contains property evaluations carried out in 1871, 1883, and 1887.

3. *LRN*, A-1 (1889–1893), p. 157v, CRCSA. See also *IT*, 3/1206/1675/1 (1869–1887), APEB.

4. The baroness's postmortem inventory includes the slave lists. For the births of the twins born to Procópio Pires and Apolônia de Góes, see *LRN*, A-1 (1889–1893), p. 5, CRCSA.

5. *LRN*, A-1 (1889–1893), p. 170, CRCSA.

6. *IT*, 3/1206/1675/1 (1869–1887), p. 17, APEB.

7. *IT*, 3/1206/1675/1 (1869–1887), fls 23–32; *LRN*, 3 (1900–1905), pp. 77 and 141v; *LRO*, O-1, p. 105, CRCSA.

8. *LRN*, 3 (1900–1905), p. 174, CRCSA.

9. *LRN*, 2-A (1893–1900), p. 3 and 12v, CRCSA; *IT*, 3/1206/1675/1 (1869–1887), pp. 154–156, APEB.

10. *LRN*, 2-A (1893–1900), p. 3, APEB.

11. *LRN*, B-1 (1889–1898), p. 130v, CRCSA.

12. Names provide important historical evidence of personal experiences, important events, world views, ideas, and cultural values. Gutman, *Black Family in Slavery*

and Freedom, pp. 185–186. On naming practices on large slave properties in Brazil, see Florentino and Machado, "Famílias e mercado," pp. 62–63. Regina Xavier revealed important elements of the way that freed people constructed their names in Campinas, São Paulo, toward the end of the nineteenth century. Xavier, *A conquista da liberdade*, pp. 114–115. For a pioneering study on the adoption of names and surnames in Bahia, see Azevedo, "Sobrenomes no Nordeste," pp. 103–116.

13. *LRN*, A-1 (1889–1893), p. 165v, CRCSA. On the basis of death certificates recorded between 1890 and 1899 in Salvador, Azevedo argued that 32 percent of pretos had no surname. Azevedo, "Sobrenomes do Nordeste," p. 116.

14. For an analysis of the issue, see Gutman, *Black Family*, especially chapter 6.

15. Doris Rinaldi Meyer offers important perspectives for thinking about the ways in which communities of ex-slaves tried to create their own spaces in which to escape from the control of their former owners. The author studied the efforts of rural workers in Pernambuco's sugar region to establish spaces independent from the power of the planters and distinguish between the "plantation world" and what they called the "world of the saints," a space occupied and blessed by the moradores. Meyer, *A terra do santo*.

16. Exploring the life stories of ex-slaves in Campinas, São Paulo, Xavier demonstrated how ties of solidarity among people who suffered slavery together were preserved after abolition. Xavier, *A conquista da liberdade*, pp. 135–152.

17. *LRO*, (1889–90), p. 85v, CRCI. João Reis observed that the preparation and burial of deceased friends and relatives by the living was one of the most important elements of a good death in both Portuguese and African cultures. Reis, *A morte é uma festa*, pp. 89–103.

18. *PC*, 11/396/19 (1892), pp. 5–9v, APEB.

19. *PC*, 33/1153/21 (1899), pp. 2–14; See *PC*, 33/1154/11 (1901), pp. 2–12, APEB.

20. *PC*, 33/1154/11 (1901), pp. 2–8, APEB.

21. *PC*, 18/648/17 (1899), APEB.

22. *PC*, 15/538/2 (1889), APEB.

23. On Josino Messias see *PC*, 38/1344/1 (1895), APEB.

24. *PC*, 33/1154/11 (1901), APEB.

25. Interview with Francisco Ambrósio, former morador of the Europa Plantation, July 21, 2003.

26. *PC*, 15/538/8 (1890), pp. 2–5v, APEB.

27. *PC*, 15/538/8 (1890), pp. 7–8, APEB.

28. This discussion grows out of Clifford Geertz's ideas about notions of personhood in Balinese society. See Geertz, *A interpretação das culturas*, pp. 225–236.

29. *PC*, 9/210/16 (1889), pp. 10–11, APEB.

30. *PC*, 18/648/17 (1899), pp. 8–36, APEB.

31. *PC*, 18/646/5 (1888), p. 7v, APEB.

32. Justiano Rabelo Santos, administrator of the Bahian House of Corrections to the Chefe de Polícia, August 17, 1888, *Polícia-cadeias*, 6282 (1887–1889), APEB.

33. *PC*, 8/284/10 (1889), APEB.

34. *PC*, 4432 (1892), APEB.

35. *PC*, 3/433/6 (1889), APEB.

36. *PC*, 20/695/18 (1890), APEB.

37. *PC*, 20/695/18 (1890), APEB.

38. *PC*, 8/274/11 (1889), pp. 1–9v, APEB.

9. OTHER POST-EMANCIPATION ITINERARIES

Epigraph: Excerpt from a *samba-de-roda* (circle samba) called "I'm Going to Bahia" collected by Gastão Sampaio at the beginning of the twentieth century and published in *Feira de Santana e o vale do Jacuipe*, p. 235.

1. Oliveira, *A indemnização*, pp. 35–36. Planters abandoned their properties in a number of different regions. A descendant of Pernambuco sugar-plantation owners recalled: "With abolition, the slaves of the Tentugal [Plantation], like those on the other plantations, abandoned the lands belonging to their owners, moving to nearby villages or small cities, and sometimes, even to Recife. In their primitive minds, abolition meant freedom from the hoe and gang labor, [and the ability] to wander around, hungry and drunk on cachaça. A little while later, most of them came back; misery forced them to seek out the protective shade of the plantations . . . but their return could not make up for the economic crisis that the Golden Law provoked. Bello, *Memórias*, p. 12. The author was born on a northeastern sugar plantation in 1885.

2. *Diário da Bahia*, August 14, 1888, p. 2, BPEBa.

3. "Representação da Comissão de Lavoura e Comércio da Associação Comercial enviada ao governo imperial," July 11, 1888, Biblioteca da Associação Comercial da Bahia (hereafter BACB).

4. *Diário da Bahia*, July 1, 1888, p.1, BPEBa; *Relatório da Junta Diretora da Associação Comercial da Bahia, 15 de fevereiro de 1889*, p. 13, BACB. On the imprisonment of the freedman, see Antônio Lourenço de Araújo, Delegado of Santo Amaro to the Chefe de Polícia, August 28, 1888, *Polícia*, 6506, APEB.

5. Anísio Pinto Cardoso, Delegado of Alagoinhas to the Chefe de Polícia, April 4, 1889, *Delegados*, 6221 (1883–1889), APEB.

6. Scott, "Exploring the Meaning of Freedom," p. 11.

7. "O drama do cativeiro," *Escudo Social*, October 14, 1933, p. 2.

8. José Pedro Calasans to the Presidente da Província, August 19, 1889, *Companhia de Navegação Bahiana*, 5025 (1888–1889), APEB. The list of family members includes José Pedro de Calasans, children Henrique, Antônio, and Florinda; the daughter-in-law Josefa; and grandchildren José (11), Isaias (9), Altino (7), José Antônio (3), Joviniana (6), Lúcia (13), and two other small children. In the attached note, the provincial president granted José Pedro and his family thirteen passages on the *Visconde Marinho* steamship that would leave Salvador for Ilhéus the following day. As Julie Saville argues, family reconstruction was the precondition for establishing an independent domestic economy. Saville, "Grassroots Reconstruction," p. 178.

9. Chefe de Polícia to the Presidente da Província, May 21, 1888, *Chefes de polícia*, 2987 (1880–1889), APEB.

10. *PC*, 10/363/5 (1888), pp. 2–8, APEB.

11. *PC*, 9/663/2 (1888), pp. 2–4, APEB.

12. *PC*, 9/663/2 (1888), pp. 9–12, APEB.

13. *PC*, 9/663/2 (1888), pp. 22–23, APEB. The subdelegado of Almeida Parish concluded that the ex-slave's disappearance had not been proven, much less that she had met with violence.

14. "Escravidão de Libertos," *Diário da Bahia*, August 25, 1888, p. 1. BPEBa. The editorial had an abolitionist tone since it encouraged ex-slaves to use the print media to complain, just as their ex-owners were doing. It also claimed that some ex-masters were sending old and otherwise "useless" ex-slaves to the authorities in the capital, so as not to have to support them.

15. Ex-slave Eulália to the Presidente da Província, August 16, 1888, *Judiciário-assuntos*, 2751 (1887–1889), APEB. Antônio de Freitas Mello, probably a relative of the ex-master, wrote the letter on her behalf. Freitas Mello closed his petition by evoking the provincial president's abolitionist sympathies by reminding him that he was a founder of the abolitionist 13th of May Society and the representative of "her serene royal highness the princess regent who extinguished slavery on Brazilian soil on May 13th of the current year." In his reply, the president ordered the Maragojipe family court to take appropriate action.

16. Vitória (at the request of abolitionist Eduardo Carigé) to the Presidente da Província, October 8, 1888. *Escravos-assuntos*, 2901 (1883–1889), APEB.

17. Antônio Calmon de Brito to the Presidente da Província, November 19, 1888, *Juízes*, 2416 (1882–1889), APEB.

18. *Processo cível* (hereafter *PCi*), 40/1430/16 (1889), p. 2, APEB. The petition was copied over by Manoel Antônio da Silva. On February 26, officials notified the court that the minor, Adelina, had been handed over.

19. On the mobility of ex-slaves in the cities of São Paulo, see Naro, "Revision and Persistence," p. 77.

20. Freyre, *Região e tradição*, pp. 113–115.

21. *LRN*, 3 (1900–1905), pp. 66–72 and 132, CRCSA. The entry for Rita de Cássia, the daughter of Belarmino and Leolinda Isabel, is dated May 23, 1902.

22. *LRN*, 2 (1893–1897), p. 77v, CRCC.

23. *LRN*, 3 (1900–1905), pp. 62v–63, CRCSA.

24. *Livro de Entrada de Doentes* (hereafter *LED*) (1906–1911), n.p., ASCMSA. Pedro was diagnosed with cirrhosis and admitted on January 23, 1907. Ciriaco dos Santos was admitted with a gunshot wound on June 14, 1908.

25. *LED* (1913–1918), ASCMSA. Marcolino Pires was admitted on April 25, 1916. The same book records the admittance of Umbelina de Jesus on March 1, 1917.

26. *LED* (1906–1911), n.p., ASCMSA. The admission is dated November 25, 1911. For Félix dos Santos see *Livro de entrada de doentes* (1913–1918), admitted on November 25, 1916, ASCMSA.

27. *LED* (1906–1911), n.p., ASCMSA. Manoel Estevão was diagnosed with syphilis and admitted on July 13, 1908.

28. On these two patients see *LED* (1906–1911), n.p., ASCMSA.

29. *LED* (1906–1911), n.p., ASCMSA; On Manoel Brás, see *IT*, 8/344/4 (1887–1891), pp. 233–234, APEB.

30. *LED* (1906–1911), n.p., ASCMSA. Entry for Cipriana Maria Pesote, May 29, 1907.

31. *LED* (1918–1921), ASCMSA. Admission made July 14, 1918.

32. On the ex-slave Próspero dos Santos, see *LED* (1913–1914), n.p., ASCMSA. On the slaves from the Mombaça Plantation see *IT*, 7/3148/14 (1875–1895), Ana de Jesus Muniz Viana Bandeira, APEB. The plantation was located in the Monte Parish and possessed 123 slaves.

33. *LED* (1911–1918), ASCMSA. Manoel Clementino was admitted on October 25, 1915, for the treatment of bronchitis. For Manoel Cirilo da Hora, see *LED* (1913–1918), ASCMSA, admitted on June 6, 1916.

34. *LED* (1906–1911), ASCMSA. The patient was admitted on February 21, 2906. On Dionísio dos Santos, see *LED* (1913–1918), admission made on October 15, 1916.

35. *LRN* (1906–1911), ASCMSA. The itinerant laborer Delfina Ribeiro was admitted to treat her rheumatism.

36. On the ex-slave Venância, see *LED* (1918–1921), ASCMSA. Admitted to the hospital on November 5, 1920 to, according to the doctor, treat "vermin"; on November 20, the ex-slave died. On Venância's earlier history, see *IT*, 3/1206/1675/1 (1869–1887), pp. 112v–114, Baronesa of Pirajá; see also *IT*, 8/3444/4 (1887–1891), 2:227, APEB.

37. Mary Ann Mahony has studied Afro-Brazilians in the cacao sector. See Mahony, "Afro-Brazilians, Land Reform, and the Question of Social Mobility," pp. 59–79.

38. Ministério da Agricultura, Indústria e Commércio, *Aspectos da economia rural brasileira*, pp. 471–472.

39. Butler, *Freedoms Given, Freedoms Won*, p. 143.

40. *Diário de Notícias*, May 9, 1888, p. 2, BPEBa.

41. Diretoria Geral de Estatísticas, *Recenseamento da População do Brasil a que se procedeu no dia 1º de agosto de 1872*, Brasil, p. 73, 85; Ministério da Indústria, Viação e Obras Públicas, Diretoria Geral de Estatística, *Recenseamento de 1890 (31 de dezembro)*, p. 12.

42. Ministério da Agricultura, Indústria e Comércio, *Aspectos da economia rural brasileira*, pp. 432–434. On the impact of the tobacco industry on the economies of São Félix and Cachoeira, see Wimberly, "African Liberto," pp. 87–93.

43. *Freguesias-limites*, caixa 430 (1912), ACMS. For the 1920 Iguape population, see Ministério da Agricultura, Indústria e Comércio, Diretoria Geral de Estatística, *Recenseamento do Brasil realizado em 10. de setembro de 1920*, p. 347. Pedro Celestino da Silva's population estimate for Iguape of 9,114 inhabitants seems exaggerated. Silva, "Notas e impressões," p. 403.

44. Mattoso, *Bahia Século XIX*, pp. 91–124, analyzed the population of Salvador and the Recôncavo. On migration to Salvador, see Santos, *A República do povo*, p. 15.

45. Reis, "De olho no canto," pp. 199–242.

46. *Polícia, Livro de Matrícula dos cantos*, maço 7116, APEB. For the itinerant laborers mentioned see pp. 2, 29, 48, and 62. Mattos also analyzes the numbers from the register of itinerant laborers. Mattos, "Negros contra a ordem," pp. 74–96.

47. *Polícia, Livro de Matrícula dos cantos*, maço 7116, APEB. pp. 5, 95, and 144.

48. *Jornal de Notícias*, July 24, 1893, p. 2, "Matrículas," BPEBa.

49. *Papéis avulsos (1886)*, Arquivo Municipal de Salvador (hereafter AMS). The labor codes were presented to the Provincial Assembly on December 30, 1886.

50. Other Brazilian cities implemented measures to control domestic servants. On Rio de Janeiro, see Graham, *Proteção e obediência*.

51. *Papéis avulsos (1886)*, Parts 1–8, AMS.

52. *Papéis avulsos (1886)*, Parts 9–10, AMS.

53. *Papéis avulsos (1886)*, Part 15, AMS.

54. *Livro de Matrículas das criadas domésticas*, n.p. (1887–1893), APEB.

55. Here I follow the same classification system as João Reis did in describing the racial profile of the itinerant laborers. Reis, "De olho no canto," p. 234.

56. *Livro de matrícula das criadas domésticas*, números de registros 141, 309, 572, 577, APEB.

57. *Jornal de Notícias*, March 18, 1895, p. 1, BPEBa. For the confrontations between the women street vendors and the municipal authorities, see Soares, "As ganhadeiras," pp. 57–71.

58. "Pelas Ruas," *Jornal de Notícias*, February 24, 1889, p. 2; "Pelas Ruas," May 4, 1889, p. 1. BPEBa.

59. "Pelas Ruas," *Jornal de Notícias*, September 15, 1900, p. 1, BPEBa.

60. "Quitandas ao ar livre," *Diário de Notícias*, August 1, 1904, p. 3, BPEBa.

61. On the ex-slave Maria Luísa Dutra Bulcão, see PC, 215/1/6 (1901), pp. 2–10, APEB.

62. *IT, caixa* 158 (1871–1900), Egas Moniz Barreto de Aragão, p. 12; *Lesões corporais* (1892–1893), case against Domingos Ramos Sacramento, ARC.

63. Querino, *A Bahia de outrora*, pp. 224–225.

64. PC, 215/20/4 (1906), pp. 6–11, APEB. Fábio Teixeira de Sousa was arrested for the beating of Maria Secundina.

65. *Lesões corporais* (1891–1893), Inquiry into Pompeu "so-and-so" (de tal), pp. 9–11, ARC. Actually, Joana "so-and-so," a resident in Sabão Street, threatened to beat Pompeu when she learned that he had insulted her daughter.

66. Reis, "De olho no canto," pp. 239–241.

67. Fontes, "Manifestações operárias na Bahia," p. 56. See also Souza, *Tudo pelo trabalho livre!*

68. J. Fontes, "Manifestações operárias na Bahia," p. 56, p. 110. Interestingly, as recently as the 1970s in Pernambuco, very long work days were called "slavery." See Lopes, *O vapor do diabo*, pp. 58–59.

69. *Jornal de Notícias*, May 12, 1902, p. 1, BPEBa.

EPILOGUE

1. *Diário da Bahia*, May 13, 1888, p. 1, BPEBa.

2. *Diário da Bahia*, May 15, 1888, p. 1, BPEBa.

3. On the debate about race and citizenship in Bahia after abolition, see Albuquerque, *O jogo da dissimulação*. For a more thorough debate about intellectuals and the racial question, see Schwarcz, *O espetáculo das raças*; and Skidmore, *Preto no branco*. See also Hasenbalg, *Discriminação e desigualdades raciais*.

4. After abolition, the abolitionists continued to insist on including agrarian reform among the package of reforms that they recommended to end slavery. See also Graham, *Escravidão, reforma e imperialismo*, p. 184.

5. *Jornal de Notícias*, April 2, 1889, p. 1. The articled, titled "Trabalho" (Labor), is signed L. T., the initials of Luís Tarquínio. See the discussion about race in the last years of the nineteenth century, especially chapters 2 and 6.

6. See Fávio Gomes on the street confrontations that occurred at the imperial court and the debate over political participation on the part of ex-slaves. Gomes, "No meio das águas turvas," pp. 75–96.

7. Amaral, "Memória histórica," pp. 15–16.

8. Amaral, "Memória histórica," p. 17.

9. Amaral, "Memória histórica," p. 32.

10. Sampaio, "O abolicionismo," p. 28; unpublished manuscript, n.d., pasta Teodoro Sampaio, p. 22, IGHB.

11. Amaral, "Memória histórica," p. 31.

Glossary

ARROBA: unit of weight, usually approximately 32 pounds or 14.746 kilograms

BAGAÇO: bagasse, stalks of sugarcane after pressing; often used as fodder and/or fuel; Bagaceira: shed where the bagasse was stored

BRAÇA: unit of measure corresponding to 2.2 meters or approximately 6 feet

CABRA: man or woman with one black parent and one mulato(a) or pardo(a) parent

CAIFAZ: literally Caiaphas, nickname for the members of a radical abolitionist group formed in 1886 in São Paulo, who assisted thousands of slaves in abandoning the plantations where they were enslaved

CANA DO REGO: literally, trench cane; local term for newly planted sugarcane

CARTÓRIO: local registry office; town or city clerk's office

COMADRE: co-mother; godmother or kinswoman (fictive)

CRIOULO(A): Brazilian-born African man or woman

DELEGADO/SUBDELEGADO: police delegate or subdelegate; police inspectors

ENGENHO: sugar plantation including extensive lands and slaves as well as a mill for processing sugarcane into sugar

FARINHA: flour, in Bahia usually manioc flour

FAZENDA: rural property, usually farm or ranch

FEITOR, FEITOR-MOR: overseer, general overseer

FULA: light-skinned person of mixed African and European ancestry

INGENÛO: child born to an enslaved woman after the institution of the Law of the Free Womb in 1871

LIBERTO(A): freed slave

MEL: in Brazilian sugar-making terminology, the sugarcane syrup from which could be made cachaça or sugar, but not rum; not molasses

MESTIÇO(A): a generic term for a man or woman of mixed ancestry; mixed-race person

MORADOR: resident worker; free and freed people who lived and worked on the plantations and ranches. In the documents on which this book is based, morador and *trabalhador*, or "resident and worker," seem to have referred to the same group of workers

MORENO(A): literally brown, person of mixed ancestry

MULATO(A): a man or woman of mixed African and European descent

NEGRO(A): one of two terms for black (see also Preto[a]), usually used for Brazilian-born free black person

PARDO(A): man or woman of mixed African and European descent; literally means "brown," usually modified by light or dark

PRETO(A): pejorative term for black, usually applied by elites to enslaved Africans prior to abolition and, afterward, to individuals presumed to have recently been enslaved

REAL (PL. RÉIS): unit of currency; conto de réis: unit of currency equivalent to 1,000 réis

ROÇA: in the Recôncavo, a subsistence plot on plantation land on which slaves were allowed to grow crops for their own use

ROCEIRO: in the Recôncavo, a person who farms a subsistence plot

TAREFA: task or daily quota; in the late nineteenth-century Recôncavo, the area of 30 braças by 30 braças or 4,356 square meters

USINA: fully industrialized central sugar mill that produced sugar on the basis of cane grown by many planters and farmers in the area; not a cane farm

Bibliography

PUBLIC ARCHIVES AND LIBRARIES

Arquivo da Cúria Metropolitana de Salvador
Arquivo da Província Carmelitana de Santo Elias (Belo Horizonte)
Arquivo da Santa Casa de Misericórdia da Bahia
Arquivo da Santa Casa de Misericórdia de Cachoeira
Arquivo da Santa Casa de Misericórdia de Santo Amaro
Arquivo Municipal de Salvador
Arquivo Municipal de Santo Amaro
Arquivo Público do Estado da Bahia
Arquivo Regional de Cachoeira
Biblioteca da Associação Comercial da Bahia
Biblioteca Nacional (Rio de Janeiro)
Biblioteca Pública do Estado da Bahia
Cartório de Registro Civil de Cachoeira
Cartório de Registro Civil de Rio Fundo
Cartório de Registro Civil de Santana do Lustosa
Cartório de Registro Civil de Santiago do Iguape
Cartório de Registro Civil de Santo Amaro
Cartório de Registro Civil de São Félix
Cartório de Registro Civil de São Sebastião do Passé
Instituto Geográfico e Histórico da Bahia
Instituto Histórico e Geográfico do Brasil (Rio de Janeiro)

PRIVATE COLLECTIONS

Arquivo de João Ferreira de Araújo Pinho Junior
Arquivo do Conde de Subaé

NEWSPAPERS

Diário da Bahia
Echo Santamarense
Gazeta da Bahia
O Guarany
O Tempo

ORAL SOURCES

Faustina dos Santos, September 20, 2000.
Francisco Ambrósio, July 21, 2003.
Luís Barbosa Dutra, February 18, 2002.
Manoel de Araújo Ferreira, December 7, 2002.
Mariana da Costa Pinto Victória Filha, October 19, 2001.

PUBLISHED PRIMARY SOURCES

Accioli, Inácio. *Memórias históricas e políticas da Bahia* [Historical and political memories of Bahia]. Anotada por [Annotated by] Braz do Amaral. Salvador: Imprensa Oficial do Estado, 1937.

Amaral, Brás H. Do. "Memória histórica sobre a Proclamação da República na Bahia" [History of the proclammation of the republic in Bahia]. Salvador: *Revista do Instituto Geográfico e Histórico da Bahia* 30 (1904): pp. 3–52.

Bittencourt, Anna Ribeiro de Góes. *Letícia*. Bahia: Tipografia Reis, 1908.

Brazil, Diretoria Geral de Estatísticas. *Recenseamento da População do Brasil a que se procedeu no dia 1º de agosto de 1872* [Census of 1872]. 21 vols. Rio de Janeiro: Leuzinger and Filhos, 1873–1876.

Brazil, Ministério da Agricultura, Indústria e Comércio. *Aspectos da economia rural brasileira* [Aspects of the Brazilian rural economy]. Rio de Janeiro: Oficinas Gráficas Villas Boas, 1922.

Brazil, Ministério da Agricultura, Indústria e Comércio. Diretoria Geral de Estatística. *Recenseamento de 1º de setembro de 1920* [Census of September 1, 1920]. 5 vols in 17. Rio de Janeiro: Tipografia da Estatística, 1928.

Brazil, Ministério da Indústria, Viação e Obras Públicas. Diretoria Geral de Estatística. *Recenseamento de 1890 (31 de dezembro)* [Census of December 31, 1890]. Rio de Janeiro: Oficina da Estatística, 1898.

Calmon Du Pin e Almeida, Miguel. *Ensaio sobre o fabrico do açúcar* [Essay on the production of sugar]. Salvador: FIEB, 2002. Facsimile of the 1834 edition.

Cincinnatus, pseudonym of Luíz Tarquínio. *O elemento escravo e as questões econômicas do Brazil* [Slave labor and economic questions]. Bahia: Tipografia dos Dois Mundos, 1885.

Fonseca, Luís Anselmo. *A escravidão, o clero e o abolicionismo* [Slavery, the clergy and abolitionism]. Recife: Editora Massangana, 1988. Facsimile of the 1887 edition.

G., J. C. *Regeneração agrícola do estado da Bahia* [Agricultural recovery in the state of Bahia]. Bahia: Litografia V. Oliveira, 1892.

Lamberg, Maurício. *O Brazil.* Rio de Janeiro: Tipografia Nunes, 1896.

Lima, Bertolino Pereira. *Biografia* (unpublished manuscript), 1930.

Oliveira, Miguel Ribeiro de. *A indemnização* [Indemnification]. Bahia: Tipografia de João Gonçalves Tourinho, 1888.

Sampaio, Teodoro. "O abolicionismo" [Abolitionism], (unpublished manuscript), n.d. pasta Teodoro Sampaio, IGHB.

Secretaria Da Cultura Da Bahia. *Documentação jurídica sobre o negro no Brasil: 1800–1888 (índice analítico)* [Legal documentation on blacks in Brazil: 1800–1888 (Analytical Index)]. Salvador: DEPAB, 1989.

Tarquínio, Luíz. *Preceitos moraes e cívicos* [Moral and civic precepts]. Bahia: [?], 1901.

Um Lavrador Bahiano. *A emancipação: Breves considerações* [Emancipation: Brief considerations]. Bahia: Tipografia Constitucional, 1871.

BOOKS, THESES, AND ARTICLES

Albuquerque, Wlamyra R. *Algazarra nas ruas: Comemorações da Independência na Bahia (1889–1923)* [Clamor in the streets: Commemorating independence in Bahia]. Campinas: Editora da UNICAMP, 1999.

———. *O jogo da dissimulação: Abolição e cidadania negra no Brasil* [The Game of disimulation: Abolition and black citizenship in Brazil]. São Paulo: Companhia das Letras, 2009.

Alencastro, Luís Felipe de, ed. *História da vida privada no Brasil: A corte e a modernidade nacional* [A history of private life in Brazil: The court and national modernity]. São Paulo: Companhia das Letras, 1999.

Alves, Isaías. *Matas do sertão de baixo* [Forests of the southern backlands], Bahia. Rio de Janeiro: Refer Ed., 1967.

Alves, Marieta. *Convento e ordem 3a. do Carmo* [The monastery and the third order of Carmelites]. Salvador: Publicação da Prefeitura do Salvador, 1949.

Andrews, George Reid. *Blacks and Whites in São Paulo (1888–1988).* Wisconsin: University of Wisconsin Press, 1991.

———. *Negros e brancos em São Paulo (1888–1988).* Translated by Magda Lopes. Technical revision and presentation by Maria Ligia Coelho Prado. São Paulo: EDUSC, 1991.

Azevedo, Célia Maria Marinho. *Onda negra, medo branco: O negro no imaginário das elites, século XIX* [Black wave, white fear: Blacks in the elite imagination in the nineteenth century]. Rio de Janeiro: Paz e Terra, 1987.

Azevedo, Eliane. "Sobrenomes no Nordeste e suas relações com a heterogeneidade étnica" [Surnames in the Northeast and their relationship to ethnic heterogeneity]. Campinas, *Estudos Econômicos* 13:1 (Jan/April 1983): 103–116.

Bacelar, Jeferson. *A hierarquia das raças: Negros e brancos em Salvador* [Racial hierarchy: Blacks and whites in Salvador]. Rio de Janeiro: Pallas, 2001.

Barickman, B. J. "Até a véspera: O trabalho escravo e a produção de açúcar nos engenhos do Recôncavo baiano (1850–1881)" [Up until the last minute: Slave labor and sugar production of the sugar plantations of the Bahian Recôncavo]. *Afro-Ásia* 21–22 (1998–1999).

———. *A Bahian Counterpoint: Sugar, Tobacco, Cassava and Slavery in the Recôncavo, 1780–1860.* Stanford, CA: Stanford University Press, 1998.

———. "'A Bit of Land Which They Call a Roça': Slave Provision Grounds in the Bahian Recôncavo, 1780–1870." *HAHR* 74, no. 4 (November 1994): 649–687.

———. "Persistence and Decline: Slave Labour and Sugar Production in the Bahian Recôncavo, 1850–1888," *JLAS*, 28:3 (October 1996): 581–633.

———. *Um contraponto baiano: Açúcar, fumo, mandioca e escravidão no Recôncavo, 1780–1860* [A Bahian counterpoint: Sugar, tobacco, manioc and slavery in the Reconcavo, 1780–1860]. Translated by Maria Luisa X. do A. Borges with a general revision of the translation by the author. Rio de Janeiro: Civilização Brasileira, 2003. Expanded Brazilian edition of *A Bahian Counterpoint*.

Barman, Rodrick J. *Citizen Emperor: Pedro II and the Making of Brazil, 1825–91.* Stanford, CA: Stanford University Press, 1999.

———. *Princess Isabel of Brazil, Gender and Power in the Nineteenth Century.* Wilmington, DE: Scholarly Resources, 2001.

Baud, Michiel, and Kees Koonings, "A lavoura dos pobres [The crop of the poor]: Tobacco Farming and the Development of Commercial Agriculture in Bahia, 1870–1930." *JLAS* 31, no. 2 (May 1999): 287–329.

Bello, José Maria. *Memórias* [Memoirs]. Rio de Janeiro: José Olympio, 1958.

Berlin, Ira, ed. *Freedom: A Documentary History of Emancipation, 1861–1867.* New York: Cambridge University Press, 1982.

Bethel, Leslie. *The Abolition of the Brazilian Slave Trade.* Cambridge: Cambridge University Press, 1970.

Blassingame, John W. *The Slave Community, Plantation Life in the Antebellum South.* New York: Oxford University Press, 1972.

Braga, Júlio. *Na gamela do feitiço—Repressão e resistência nos candomblés da Bahia* [In sorcery's bowl: Repression and resistance in Bahian Candomblé]. Salvador: Edufba, 1995.

Brito, Jailton Lima. "A abolição na Bahia: Uma história política, 1870–1888" [Abolition in Bahia: A political history, 1870–1888]. Master's thesis, UFBA, 1996.

———. *A abolição na Bahia: 1870–1888.* Salvador: Centro de Estudos Baianos, 2003.

Bulcão Sobrinho, Antônio de Araújo Aragão. "Titulares baianos" [Bahian title holders] (unpublished manuscript in the Arquivo Público do Estado da Bahia).

Butler, Kim D. *Freedoms Given, Freedoms Won: Afro-Brazilians in Post-Emancipation São Paulo and Salvador.* New Brunswick, NJ: Rutgers University Press, 1998.

Butler, Kim D., and Aline Helg. "Race in Postabolition Afro-Latin America." In *The Oxford Handbook of Latin American History*, edited by José C. Moya, pp. 257–280. New York: Oxford University Press, 2011.

Calmon, Pedro. *Memórias* [Memoirs]. Rio de Janeiro: Nova Fronteira, 1995.

Campos, João da Silva. *Tempo antigo, crônicas d'antanho, marcos do passado, histórias do Recôncavo* [Past times, stories of yesteryear, landmarks of the past, and stories from the Recôncavo]. Bahia: Secretária de Educação e Saúde, 1942.

———. *Tradições bahianas* [Bahian traditions] (Revista do Instituto Geográfico e Histórico da Bahia). Bahia: Gráfica da Escola de Aprendizes Artífices, 1930.

Cardoso, Ciro F. S. *Escravo ou camponês* [Slave or peasant]. São Paulo: Editora Brasiliense, 1987.

Castro, Hebe Maria Mattos de. *Das cores do silêncio: Os significados da liberdade no Sudeste escravista—Brasil, século XIX*. [Of the colors of silence: The meanings of freedom in the slaveholding southeast—Brazil in the nineteenth century]. Rio de Janeiro: Arquivo Nacional, 1995.

———. *Memórias do cativeiro família, trabalho e cidadania no pós-abolião* [Memories of Captivity: Family, work and citizenship after abolition]. Rio de Janeiro: Civilização Brasileira, 2005.

Chalhoub, Sidney. *Visões da liberdade: Uma história das últimas décadas da escravidão na Corte* [Visions of freedom: A history of the last decades of slavery in the Court]. São Paulo: Companhia das Letras, 1990.

Costa, Emilia Viotti da. *Da senzala à colônia* [From the slave quarters to the homes of sharecroppers]. São Paulo: Livraria Ciências Humanas, 1982.

Conrad, Robert. *The Destruction of Brazilian Slavery, 1850–1888*. Berkeley: University of California Press, 1972.

———. *Os últimos anos da escravatura no Brasil* [The last years of slavery in Brazil]. Translated by Fernando de Castro Ferro. Rio de Janeiro: Civilização Brasileira, 1978.

Cruz, Maria Cecília Velasco e. "Puzzling Out Slave Origins in Rio de Janeiro Port Unionism: The 1906 Strike and the Sociedade de Resistência dos Trabalhadores em Trapiche e Café." *HAHR* 86: 2 (2006): pp. 205–245.

Darnton, Robert. *O grande massacre de gatos e outros episódios da história cultural francesa*. Translated by Sonia Coutinho with a technical revision by Ciro Flamiron Cardoso. Rio de Janeiro: Graal, 1986. Portuguese translation of *The Great Cat Massacre and Other Episodes in French Cultural History*. New York: Basic Books, 1984.

Davis, Shelton H., ed. *Antropologia do direito: Estudo comparativo de categorias de dívida e contrato* [The anthropology of law: A comparative study of debt and contracts]. Rio de Janeiro: Zahar Editores, 1973.

Dean, Warren. *Rio Claro: A Brazilian Plantation System, 1820–1920*. Stanford, CA: Stanford University Press, 1976.

Dunn, Richard S. *Sugar and Slavery: The Rise of the Planter Class in the English West Indies, 1624–1713*. Chapel Hill: University of North Carolina Press, 1972.

Eisenberg, Peter L. *Modernização sem mudança: A indústria açucareira em Pernambuco, 1840–1910* [Modernization without change: The sugar industry in Pernambuco]. Translated by João Maia. Rio de Janeiro: Paz e Terra, 1977.

———. *The Sugar Industry in Pernambuco: Modernization without Change, 1840–1910*. Berkeley: University of California Press, 1974.

Eiss, Paul K. "A Share in the Land: Freedpeople and the Government of Labour in Southern Louisiana, 1862–65." *Slavery and Abolition* 19, no. 1 (April 1998): 46–89.

Fernandes, Florestan. *A integração do negro na sociedade de classes* [Integrating the black into a class society]. 2 vols. São Paulo: Ática, 1978.

———. *The Negro in Brazilian Society*. Translated by Jacqueline D. Skiles, A. Brunel, and Arthur Rothwell. Edited by Phyllis B. Eveleth. New York: Columbia University Press, 1969.

Fick, Carolyn. "Camponeses e soldados negros na Revolução de Saint-Domingue: Reações iniciais à liberdade na província do sul (1793–1794)" [Peasants and black soldiers in the revolution of Saint-Domingue: Initial reactions to freedom in the southern province]. In *A outra história: Ideologia e protesto popular nos séculos XVII a XIX* [The other history: Ideology and popular protest in the eighteenth and nineteenth century], edited by Frederick Krantz, translated by Ruy Jungmann, pp. 211–226. Rio de Janeiro: Editora Jorge Zahar, 1990.

Fields, Barbara Jeanne. *Slavery and Freedom on the Middle Ground: Maryland during the Nineteenth Century*. New Haven, CT: Yale University Press, 1985.

Figueroa, Luis A. *Sugar, Slavery and Freedom in Nineteenth-Century Puerto Rico*. Chapel Hill: University of North Carolina Press, 2005.

Florentino, Manolo, and José Roberto Góes. *A paz das senzalas: Famílias escravas e tráfico Atlântico* [Peace in the slave quarters: Slave families and the Atlantic slave trade]. Rio de Janeiro: Civilização Brasileira, 1997.

Florentino, Manolo, and Cacilda Machado. "Famílias e mercado: Tipologias parentais de acordo ao grau de afastamento do mercado de cativos (século XIX)" [Families and the market: Typologies of kinship according to the degree of distance from the slave markets]. *Afro-Ásia* 24 (2000): 51–70.

Foner, Eric. *Nada além da liberdade: A emancipação e seu legado* [Nothing but freedom: Emancipation and its legacy]. Translated by Luís Paulo Rouanet with a technical revision by John M. Monteiro. Rio de Janeiro: Paz e Terra, 1988.

———. *Nothing but Freedom: Emancipation and Its Legacy*. Baton Rouge: Louisiana State University Press, 1983.

———. "O significado da liberdade" [The meaning of freedom]. Translated by Luís Paulo Rouanet. *Revista Brasileira de História* (*São Paulo*) [Journal of Brazilian History] 8, no. 16 (1988): 9–36.

Fontes, José Raimundo. "Manifestações operárias na Bahia: O movimento grevista, 1888–1930" [Factory workers' demonstrations in Bahia: The strike movement, 1888–1930]. Master's thesis, UFBA, 1982.

Fraga, Walter. *Mendigos, moleques e vadios na Bahia do século XIX* [Beggars, black boys and vagrants in nineteenth-century Bahia]. São Paulo: HUCITEC, 1996.

Freyre, Gilberto. *Casa-grande e senzala: Formação da família brasileira sob o regime da economia patriarcal* [Mansions and shanties: The formation of the Brazilian family under the patriarchal economic regime]. Rio de Janeiro: José Olympio, 1987.

———. *Masters and Slaves: A Study in the Development of Brazilian Civilization*. Translated by Samuel Putnam. New York: Alfred A. Knopf, 1946.

———. *Nordeste: Aspectos da influência da cana sobre a vida e a paisagem do Nordeste do Brasil* [Northeast: Aspects of the influence of sugar cane on the life and landscape]. Rio de Janeiro: José Olympio Editora, 1985.

———. *Região e tradição* [Region and tradition]. Rio de Janeiro: José Olympio Editora, 1941.

Garcez, Angelina Nobre Rolim, and Antônio Fernando Guerreiro de Freitas. *Bahia cacaueira: Um estudo da história recente* [The Bahia of cacao: A study in recent history]. Centro de Estudos Baianos, 1979.

Garcia, Afrânio Raul, Jr. *O Sul: Caminho do roçado: Estratégias de reprodução camponesa e transformação social* [The south: The way of the small farmer; Stategies of peasant reproduction and social transformation]. Brasília: Marco Zero, 1990.

Geertz, Clifford. *A interpretação das culturas.* Rio de Janeiro: Guanabara, 1989 (Portuguese translation of *The Interpretation of Cultures: Selected Essays.* New York: Basic Books, 1973.)

Genovese, Eugene D. *From Rebellion to Revolution: Afro-American Slave Revolts in the Making of the Modern World.* Baton Rouge: Louisiana State University Press, 1992.

Ginzburg, Carlo, et al. *The Cheese and the Worms: The Cosmos of a Sixteenth-Century Miller.* Baltimore: Johns Hopkins University Press, 1980.

———. *A micro-história e outros ensaios* [Microhistory and other essays]. Translated by Antônio Narino. Lisboa: Difel, 1989.

Gomes, Flávio dos Santos. *Histórias de quilombolas: Mocambos e comunidades de senzalas no Rio de Janeiro—século XIX* [Histories of escaped slaves: Escaped slave communities and communities in the slave quarters in nineteenth-century Rio de Janeiro]. Rio de Janeiro: Arquivo Nacional, 1995.

———. "No meio das águas turvas: Racismo e cidadania no alvorecer da República; A Guarda Negra na Corte—1888–1889" [In turbulent waters: Racism and citizenship at the dawn of the Republic, The Black Guard at the Imperial Court—1888–1889]. *Estudos Afro-Asiáticos* 21 (1991): 75–96.

Gomes, Flávio dos Santos, and Olívia Maria Gomes da Cunha, eds. *Quase-cidadão: Histórias e antropologias da pós-emancipação no Brasil* [Quasi-citizen: Histories and anthropologies of the postemancipation period]. Rio de Janeiro: Editora Fundação Getúlio Vargas, 2006.

Gorender, Jacob. *A escravidão reabilitada* [Slavery rehabilitated]. São Paulo: Ed. Atica, 1990.

Graden, Dale Torston. "From Slavery to Freedom in Bahia, 1791–1900." PhD dissertation, University of Connecticut, 1991.

———. *From Slavery to Freedom in Brazil: Bahia, 1835–1900.* Albuquerque: University of New Mexico Press, 2006.

———. "Voices from Under: The End of Slavery in Bahia, Brazil." *Review of Latin American Studies* 3, no. 2 (1991): 145–161.

Graham, Richard. *Escravidão, reforma e imperialismo* [Slavery, reform and imperialism]. Translated by Luís João Caio. São Paulo: Editora Perspectiva, 1979.

———. *Feeding the City: From Street Market to Liberal Reform in Salvador, Brazil, 1780–1860.* Austin: University of Texas Press, 2010.

———. *Patronage and Politics in Nineteenth-Century Brazil.* Stanford, CA: Stanford University Press, 1994.

———. "Slave Families on a Rural Estate in Colonial Brazil." *Journal of Social History* 9, no. 3 (1976): 382–402.

Graham, Sandra Lauderdale. *Caetana diz não: Histórias de mulheres da sociedade escravista brasileira [Caetana Says No: Women's Stories from a Brazilian Slave Society]*. Translated by Pedro Maia Soares. São Paulo: Companhia das Letras, 2005.

———. *Caetana Says No: Women's Stories from a Brazilian Slave Society*. Cambridge: Cambridge University Press, 2002.

———. *Proteção e obediência: Criadas e seus patrões no Rio de Janeiro, 1860–1910*. Translated by Viviana Bosi. São Paulo: Companhia das Letras, 1992. Portuguese translation of *House and Street: The Domestic World of Servants and Masters in Nineteenth-Century Rio de Janeiro*. Cambridge: Cambridge University Press, 1988.

Gribaudi. Maurizio. *Itineraires ouvriers: Espaces et groupes sociaux à Turin au début du XXe siècle*. Paris: École dês Hautes Études em Sciences Sociales, 1987.

Grinberg, Keila, *Liberata: A lei da ambiguidade* [Liberata: The law of ambiguity]. Rio de Janeiro: Relume Dumará, 1994.

Gudeman, Stephen, and Stuart Schwartz. "Purgando o pecado original: Compadrio e batismo de escravos na Bahia no século XVIII" [Purging original sin: Godparentage and slave baptisms in eighteenth-century Bahia]. In *Escravidão e invenção da liberdade: Estudos sobre o negro no Brasil* [Slavery and the invention of freedom: Studies of blacks in Brazil], edited by João José Reis, pp. 33–58. São Paulo: Brasiliense, 1988.

Gutman, Herbert G. *The Black Family in Slavery and Freedom, 1750–1925*. New York: Pantheon Books, 1976.

Hasenbalg, Carlos Alfredo. *Discriminação e desigualdades raciais no Brasil*. Rio de Janeiro: Graal, 1979.

Hebred, Jean. "Slavery in Brazil: Brazilian Scholars in the Key Interpretive Debates." In *Translating the Americas* 1 (2013): 47–95.

Ianni, Octávio. *Raças e classes sociais no Brasil* [Races and social classes in Brazil]. São Paulo: Brasiliense, 1987.

Karasch, Mary C. *A vida dos escravos no Rio de Janeiro, 1808–1850*. Translated by Pedro Maia Soares. São Paulo: Companhia das Letras, 2000. Portuguese translation of *Slave Life in Rio de Janeiro, 1808–1850*. Princeton, NJ: Princeton University Press, 1987.

Klein, Herbert S., and Stanley Engerman. "The Transition from Slave to Free Labor: Notes on a Comparative Economic Model." In *Between Slavery and Free Labor: The Spanish-Speaking Caribbean in the Nineteenth Century*, edited by Manuel Moreno Fraginals, Frank Moya Pons, and Stanley L. Engerman, pp. 255–269. Baltimore: Johns Hopkins University Press, 1985.

Klein, Herbert S., and Francisco Vidal Luna. *Slavery in Brazil*. Cambridge: Cambridge University Press, 2009.

Kraay, Hendrik. "Between Brazil and Bahia: Celebrating Dois de Julho in Nineteenth-Century Salvador." *Journal Latin America Studies* 31 (1999): 255–286.

———. "The Politics of Race in Independence-Era Bahia: The Black Militia Officers of Salvador, 1790–1840." In *Afro-Brazilian Culture and Politics: Bahia, 1790s to 1990s* edited by Hendrik Kraay, pp. 30–56. New York: M. E. Sharpe, 1998.

Krantz, Frederick, ed. *A outra história: Ideologia e protesto popular nos séculos XVII a XIX* [The other history: Ideology and popular protest in from the seventeenth to the nineteenth centuries]. Translated by Ruy Jungmann. Rio de Janeiro: Jorge Zahar Editor, 1990.

Lara, Silvia Hunold. *Campos da violência: Escravos e senhores na capitânia do Rio de Janeiro, 1750–1808* [Fields of violence: Slaves and masters in the captaincy of Rio de Janeiro, 1750–1808]. Rio de Janeiro: Paz e Terra, 1988.

———. "Escravidão, cidadania e história do trabalho no Brasil" [Slavery, citizenship and the history of work in Brazil]. São Paulo: *Projeto História* 16 (1998): 25–38.

Levi, Giovanni. *Le pouvoir au village: Histoire d'une exorciste dans le Piémont du XVIIe siècle* [Power in the village: History of an exorcist in the seventeenth-century piedmont]. Torino: Gallimard, 1985.

Lewin, Linda. "Natural and Spurious Children in Brazilian Inheritance Law from Colony to Empire: A Metholdological Essay." *The Americas* 48 (1992): 351–396.

———. *Surprise Heirs*. Vol. 1, *Illegitimacy, Patrimonial Rights and Legal Nationalism in Luso-Brazilian Inheritance, 1750–1821*. Stanford, CA: Stanford University Press, 2003.

———. *Surprise Heirs*. Vol. 2, *Illegitimacy, Inheritance Rights, and Public Power in the Formation of Imperial Brazil, 1822–1889*. Stanford, CA: Stanford University Press, 2003.

Libby, Douglas Cole, and Zephyr Frank. "Naming Practices in Eighteenth- and Nineteenth-Century Brazil: Names, Namesakes, and Families in the Parish of São José, Minas Gerais." *Journal of Family History* 40, no. 1 (2015): 64–91.

Litwack, Leon F. *Been in the Storm So Long: The Aftermath of Slavery*. New York: Vintage Books, 1980.

Lopes, José Sérgio Leite. *O vapor do diabo: O trabalho dos operários do açúcar* [The devil's steam: Labor and sugar workers]. Rio de Janeiro: Paz e Terra, 1978.

Machado, Maria Helena. *Crime e escravidão: Lavradores pobres na crise do trabalho escravo, 1830–1888* [Crime and slavery: Poor farmers in the crises of slave labor, 1830–1888]. São Paulo: Brasiliense, 1987.

———. *O plano e o pânico: Os movimentos sociais na década da abolição* [The plan and the panic: Social movements in the decade of abolition.]. Rio de Janeiro: UFRJ/EDUSP, 1994.

———. "Slavery and Social Movements in Nineteenth-Century Brazil: Slave Strategies and Abolition in São Paulo." *Review* (Fernand Braudel Center), Rethinking the Plantation: Histories, Anthropologies and Archaeologies 34, nos: 1/2 (2011): 163–191.

Mahony, Mary Ann. "Afro-Brazilians, Land Reform, and the Question of Social Mobility in Southern Bahia, 1880–1920." *Luso-Brazilian Review* 34, no. 2 (winter 1997): 59–79.

———. "Creativity under Constraint: Enslaved Afro-Brazilian Families in Brazil's Cacao Area, 1870–1890." *Journal of Social History* 41, no. 3 (spring 2008): 633–666.

———. "A Past to Do Justice to the Present: Historical Representation, Collective Memory and Elite Rule in Twentieth-Century Southern Bahia, Brazil." In *Reestablishing the Political in Latin American History: A View from the North*, edited by Gilbert Joseph, pp. 102–137. Durham, NC: Duke University Press, 2001.

———. "The World Cacao Made: Society, Politics, and History in Southern Bahia, Brazil, 1822–1919." PhD dissertation, Yale University, 1996.

Marques, Xavier. *As voltas da estrada* [The curves in the road]. Salvador: Secretaria da Cultura e Turismo / Conselho Estadual de Cultura, Academia de Letras da Bahia, 1998.

Martins, José de Souza, *O cativeiro da terra* [Captive on the land]. São Paulo: Ciências Humanas, 1979.

Mattei, Andres Ramos, ed. *Azúcar y esclavitud* [Sugar and slavery]. San Juan: Universidad de Puerto Rico, 1982.

———. "El liberto en el régimen de trabajo azucarero de Puerto Rico, 1870–1880" [The freedman in the sugar labor regime of Puerto Rico, 1870–1880]. In *Azúcar y esclavitud*, edited by Mattei, pp. 107–123. San Juan: Universidad de Puerto Rico, 1982.

Mattos, Wilson Roberto de. "Negros contra a ordem: Resistências e práticas negras de territorialização cultural no espaço da exclusão social—Salvador-Ba (1850–1888)" [Disorderly blacks: Resistences and black practices in cultural territorializing in the space of social exclusion]. PhD dissertation, PUC-SP, São Paulo, 2000.

Mattoso, Kátia M. de Queirós. *Bahia: A cidade do Salvador e seu mercado no século XIX* [The city of Salvador and its market in the nineteenth century]. São Paulo: HUCITEC, 1978.

———. *Bahia Século XIX: Uma província no império* [Nineteenth-century Bahia: A province in the empire]. Rio de Janeiro: Nova Fronteira, 1992.

———. *Família e sociedade na Bahia do século XIX* [Family and society in nineteenth-century Bahia]. Bahia: Corrupio, 1988.

———. *Ser escravo no Brasil*. São Paulo: Brasiliense, 1988.

———. *To Be a Slave in Brazil, 1550–1888*. Translated by Arthur Goldhammer, with a foreword by Stuart B. Schwartz. New Brunswick, NJ: Rutgers University Press, 1986.

Mello, Pedro Carvalho de. "Expectations of Abolition and Sanguinity of Coffee Planters in Brazil, 1871–1881." In *Without Consent or Contract: The Rise and Fall of American Slavery: Conditions of Slave Life and the Transition to Freedom. Technical Papers.* Vol. 2, edited by Robert William Fogel and Stanley L. Engerman, pp. 629–646. New York: W. W. Norton, 1992.

Mendonça, Joseli Maria Nunes. *Entre a mão e os aneis: A Lei dos Sexagenários e os caminhos da Abolição no Brasil* [Between the hand and the rings: The sexagenarian law and the paths to abolition in Brazil]. Campinas: Editora da NICAMP, 1999.

Metcalf, Alida. "A vida familiar dos escravos em São Paulo no século dezoito: O caso de Santana de Parnaíba" [Family life of São Paulo slaves in the eighteenth century: The case of Santana de Parnaíba]. *Estudos Econômicos* 17 (1987): 229–243.

Meyer, Doris Rinaldi. *A terra do santo e o mundo dos engenhos: Estudo de uma comunidade rural nordestina* [The land of the saints and the world of the sugar plantations: A study of a rural northeastern community]. Rio de Janeiro: Paz e Terra, 1979.

Mintz, Sidney W. *Caribbean Transformations*. Baltimore: John Hopkins University Press, 1984.

———. *Worker in the Cane: A Puerto Rican Life History*. New Haven, CT: Yale University Press, 1964.

Muller, Christiano. *Memória histórica sobre a religião na Bahia (1823–1923)* [Historical memoir about religion in Bahia]. Bahia: Imprensa Oficial do Estado, 1923.

Naeher, Julius. *Land und Leute in der brasilianische Provinz Bahia* [Land and people of the Brazilian province of Bahia]. Leipzig, 1881.

Naro, Nancy Priscilla Smith. "Revision and Persistence: Recent Historiography on the Transition from Slave to Free Labour in Rural Brazil." *Slavery and Abolition* 13, no. 2 (August 1992): 68–85.

Nascimento, Anna Amélia Vieira. *Patriarcado e religião: As enclausuradas Clarissas do convento do desterro da Bahia, 1677–1890* [Patriarchy and religion: The cloistered Clarissas of Bahia's desterro convent]. Bahia: Conselho de Cultura, 1994.

Needell, Jeffrey D. "Brazilian Abolitionism, Its Historiography and the Uses of Political History." *JLAS* 42 (2010): 231–261.

———. *The Party of Order: The Conservatives, the State and Slavery in the Brazilian Monarchy, 1831–1871*. Stanford, CA: Stanford University Press, 2006.

O'Donovan, Susan Eva. *Becoming Free in the Cotton South* (Cambridge, MA: Harvard University Press, 2007).

Oliveira, Jardilina de Santana. *São Sebastião do Passé: 278 anos de história* [278 years of history in Saint Sebastian of Passé]. Bahia: Gráfica Santa Helena, 1997.

Oliveira, Maria Inês Cortes. *O liberto: O seu mundo e os outros, Salvador, 1790–1890* [The freedman and his world: Salvador, 1790–1890]. São Paulo: Corrupio, 1988.

Ott, Carlos. *Povoamento do Recôncavo pelos engenhos, 1535–1888* [Settlement of the Recônvavo through the sugar plantations, 1535–1888]. 2 vols. Bahia: Editora Bigraf, 1996.

Paiva, Valdevino Neves. *Maracangalha: Torrão de açúcar, talhão de massapê* [Maracangalha: Soil for sugar, soil of massapé]. Bahia: Gráfica Santa Helena, 1996.

Pang, Eul-Soo. *In Pursuit of Honor and Power: Noblemen of the Southern Cross in Nineteenth-Century Brazil*. Tuscaloosa: University of Alabama Press, 1988.

———. *O Engenho Central do Bom Jardim na economia baiana: Alguns aspectos de sua história, 1875–1891* [The industrial sugar mill of Bom Jardim in the Bahian economy: Some aspects of its history, 1875–1891]. Translated by Nivalda Gueiros Leitão. Rio de Janeiro: Arquivo Nacional, IHGB, 1979.

Pedreira, Pedro Tomás. *Memória histórico-geográfica de São Francisco do Conde.* [Historical and geographical memoir of São Francisco do Conde]. Brasília: Centro Gráfico do Senado, 1977.

Pena, Eduardo Spiller. *O jogo da face: A astúcia escrava frente aos senhores e à lei na Curitiba provincial* [The face game: Slave cunning before masters and the law in provincial Curitiba]. Curitiba: Aos Quatro Ventos, 1999.

Pinho, Wanderley. *História de um engenho do Recôncavo: Matoim, Novo Caboto, Freguesia: 1552–1944* [History of a Recôncavo sugar plantation: Matoim, New Caboto, Parish: 1552–1994]. São Paulo: Editora Nacional, 1982.

Pirola, Ricardo Figueiredo. "A Lei de 10 de Junho de 1835: Justiça, escravidão e pena de morte" [The Law of June 10, 1835: Justice, slavery and the death penalty]. PhD dissertation, UNICAMP, 2012.

Porto Alegre, Sylvia. "Fome de braços—Questão nacional: Notas sobre o trabalho livre no Nordeste do século XIX" [Hunger for labor—a national question: Notes on free labor in the nineteenth-century Northeast]. *Cadernos do CERU* 2 (1986): 67–91.

Prado Júnior, Caio. *História econômica do Brasil*. 3rd ed. [Economic history of Brazil]. São Paulo: Brasiliense, 1961.

Querino, Manoel. *A Bahia de outrora* [The Bahia of yesteryear]. Bahia: Progresso Editora, 1946. First edition published 1916.

Rebouças, André. *Diário e notas autobiográficas* [Diary and autobiographical notes]. Rio de Janeiro: José Olympio, 1938.

Rego, José Lins do. *Menino de engenho* [Plantation boy]. Rio de Janeiro: José Olympio Editora, 1974. First edition published 1932.

———. *Meus verdes anos (Memórias)* [My green years (memoirs)]. Rio de Janeiro: José Olympio, 1956.

Reis, Isabel Cristina Ferreira dos. "A família negra no tempo da escravidão: Bahia, 1850–1888." [The black family in time of slavery]. PhD dissertation, Campinas, SP: Unicamp, 2007.

———. *Histórias de vida familiar e afetiva de escravos na Bahia do século XIX*. Salvador: UFBA, 1998.

Reis, João José, ed. *A escravidão e a invenção da liberdade: Estudos sobre o negro no Brasil* [Slavery and the invention of freedom: Studies about blacks in Brazil]. São Paulo: Brasiliense, 1988.

———. *A morte é uma festa: Ritos fúnebre e revolta popular no Brasil do século XIX* [Death is a festival: Funeral rituals and popular protest in nineteenth-century Brazil]. São Paulo: Companhia das Letras, 1991.

———. "De olho no canto: Trabalho de rua na Bahia na véspera da abolição." *Afro-Ásia* 24 (2000): 199–242.

———. *Domingos Sodré, um sacerdote africano: Escravidão, liberdade e candomblé na Bahia do século XIX* [Domingos Sodré, an African priest: Slavery, freedom and candomblé in nineteenth-century Bahia]. São Paulo: Companhia das Letras, 2008.

———. *Rebelião escrava no Brasil: A história do levante dos malês, 1835* [Slave rebellion in Brazil: The history of the Malês uprising, 1835]. São Paulo: Brasiliense, 1986.

———. *Slave Rebellion in Brazil: The Muslim Uprising of 1835 in Bahia*. Translated by Arthur Brakel. Baltimore: Johns Hopkins University Press, 1993.

Reis, João José, and Herbert S. Klein. "Slavery in Brazil." In *The Oxford Handbook of Latin American History*, edited by José C. Moya, pp. 180–211. New York: Oxford University Press, 2011.

Reis, João José, and Eduardo Silva. *Negociação e conflito: A resistência negra no Brasil escravista*. São Paulo: Companhia das Letras, 1989.

Rheingantz, Carlos G. *Titulares do Império* [Titled men of the empire]. Rio de Janeiro: Ministério da Justiça / Arquivo Nacional, 1960.

Rios, Ana Maria Lugão Rios, and Hebe Maria Mattos de Castro. *Memórias do cativeiro: Família, trabalho e cidadania no pós-abolição* [Memories of captivity: Family, work and citizenship in the post-emancipation period]. Rio de Janeiro: Civilização Brasileira, 2005.

Russell-Wood, A. J. R. "Brazilian Archives and Recent Historiography on Colonial Brazil." *Latin American Research Review* 36, no. 1 (2001): 75–105.

Sampaio, Gastão. *Feira de Santana e o vale do Jacuípe* [The city of Feira de Santana and the Valley of the Jacuipe River]. Salvador: Bureau Gráfica e Editora, 1982.

———. "Meu avô paterno, Tertuliano Coelho Sampaio" [My paternal grandfather, Tertuliano Coelho Sampaio] (unpublished manuscript), 1980.

———. *Nazaré das Farinhas* [The city of Nazareth of the manioc flour]. Bahia: Empresa Gráfica da Bahia, 1974.

Santos, Jocelio Telles dos. "A Mixed-Race Nation: Afro-Brazilians and Cultural Policy in Bahia, 1970–1990." In *Afro-Brazilian Culture and Politics: Bahia, 1790s to 1990s,* edited by Hendrik Kraay, pp. 117–133. New York: M. E. Sharpe, 1998.

Santos, Mario Augusto da Silva. *A República do povo: Sobrevivência e tensão— Salvador, (1890–1930)* [Republic of the people: Survival and tension, Salvador, 1890–1930]. Salvador: EDUFBA, 2001.

Saville, Julie. "Grassroots Reconstruction: Agricultural Laborers and Collective Action in South Carolina, 1860–1868." *Slavery and Abolition* 12, no. 3 (December 1991): 173–182.

———. *The Work of Reconstruction: From Slave to Wage Laborer in South Carolina, 1860–1870.* Cambridge: Cambridge University Press, 1996.

Schwarcz, Lilia Moritz. *O espetáculo das raças: Cientistas, instituições e questão racial no Brasil, 1870–1930* [The spectacle of the races: Scientists, institutions and the racial question in Brazil, 1870–1930]. São Paulo: Companhia das Letras, 1995.

Schwartz, Stuart. *Escravos, roceiros e rebeldes* [Slaves, peasants and rebels]. Translated by Jussara Simões. Bauru: EDUSC, 2001.

———. "The Historiography of Early Modern Brazil." In *The Oxford Handbook of Latin American History,* edited by José C. Moya, pp. 98–131. New York: Oxford University Press, 2011.

———. "The 'Mocambo': Slave Resistance in Colonial Bahia." *Journal of Social History* 3, no. 4 (summer 1970): 313–333.

———. "Resistance and Accommodation in Eighteenth-Century Brazil: The Slaves' View of Slavery." *HAHR* 57, no. 1 (1977): 69–81.

———. *Segredos internos: Engenhos e escravos na sociedade colonial, 1550–1835.* São Paulo: Companhia das Letras, 1988. Portuguese translation of *Sugar Plantations in the Formation of Brazilian Society.*

———. *Slaves, Peasants and Rebels: Reconsidering Brazilian Slavery.* Translated by Laura Teixeira Motta. Champaign: University of Illinois Press, 1995.

———. *Sugar Plantations in the Formation of Brazilian Society: Bahia, 1550–1835.* Cambridge: Cambridge University Press, 1985.

Scott. James C. *Domination and the Arts of Resistance: Hidden Transcripts.* New Haven, CT: Yale University Press, 1990.

Scott, Rebecca J., ed. *The Abolition of Slavery and the Aftermath of Emancipation in Brazil.* Durham, NC: Duke University Press, 1988.

———. "Defining the Boundaries of Freedom in the World of Cane: Cuba, Brazil and Louisiana after Emancipation." *American Historical Review* 99, no. 1 (February 1994): 70–102.

———. *Degrees of Freedom: Louisiana and Cuba after Slavery.* Cambridge, MA: Harvard University Press, 2005.

———. "Exploring the Meaning of Freedom: Postemancipation Societies in Comparative Perspective." In *The Abolition of Slavery and the Aftermath of Emancipation in Brazil*, edited by Rebecca J. Scott, pp. 1–22. Durham, NC: Duke University Press, 1988.

———. "Stubborn and Disposed to Stand their Ground: Black Militia, Sugar Workers and the Dynamics of Collective Action in the Louisiana Sugar Bowl, 1863–87." *Slavery and Abolition* 20, no. 1 (April 1999): 103–126.

Skidmore, Thomas. *Black into White: Race and Nationality in Brazilian Thought*. New York: Oxford University Press, 1974.

———. *Preto no branco: Raça e nacionalidade no pensamento Brasileiro*. Translated by Rúl de Sá Barbosa. Rio de Janeiro: Paz e Terra, 1976.

Silva, Pedro Celestino da. "Notas e impressões sobre o districto de S. Thiago do Iguape" [Notes and impressions about the Saint Thiago do Iguape district]. *Anais do Arquivo Público da Bahia* 26 (1938): 391–424.

Silva, Ricardo Tadeu Caíres. "Os escravos vão à Justiça: A resistência escrava através das ações de liberdade, Bahia, século XIX" [The slaves go to court: Slave resistance as seen in freedom lawsuits, Bahia, nineteenth century]. Master's thesis, UFBA, 2000.

Slenes, Robert W. "Black Homes, While Homilies: Perceptions of the Slave Family and of Slave Women in Nineteenth-Century Brazil." In *More Than Chattel: Black Women and Slavery in the Americas*, edited by David Bary Gaspar and Darlene Clark Hine, pp. 126–146. Bloomington: Indiana University Press, 1996.

———. "The Brazilian Internal Slave Trade, 1850–1888: Regional Economies, Slave Experience, and the Politics of a Peculiar Market." In *The Chattel Principle: Internal Slave Trades in the Americas*, edited by Walter Johnson, pp. 325–370. New Haven, CT: Yale University Press, 2004.

———. "Escravidão e família: Padrões de casamento e estabilidade familiar numa comunidade escrava (Campinas, século XIX)" [Slavery and family: Marriage and family stability in a slave community (Campinas, nineteenth century)]. *Estudos Econômicos* 17 (1987): 217–227.

———. "Histórias do Cafundó." In *Cafundó: A África no Brasil: Linguagem e sociedade*, edited by Carlos Vogt, Peter Fry, and Robert W. Slenes, pp. 37–102. São Paulo: Companhia das Letras, 1996.

———. *Na senzala, uma flor: Esperanças e recordações na formação da família escrava, Brasil Sudeste, século XIX* [A flower in the slave quarters: Hopes and memories in the formation of the slave family, nineteenth century]. Rio de Janeiro: Nova Fronteira, 1999.

———. "Senhores e subalternos no Oeste Paulista" [Elites and subalterns in the Paulista West]. In *História da vida privada no Brasil: A corte e a modernidade nacional*, edited by Luís Felipe de Alencastro, 2:233–290. São Paulo: Companhia das Letras, 1997.

Soares, Cecília Moreira. "As ganhadeiras: Mulher e resistência negra em Salvador no século XIX" [Female slaves for hire: Women and black resistance in Salvador in the nineteenth century]. *Afro-Ásia* 17 (1996): 57–71.

Sotelino, Karen Catherine Sherwood. "Notes on the Translation of *Lavoura Archaica* by Raduan Nassar." *Hispania* 83, no. 3 (Special Portuguese issue, September 2002): 524–533.

Souza, Edinélia Maria Oliveira. "Cruzando memórias e espaços de cultura: Dom Macedo Costa—Bahia (1930–1960)" [Bringing together memories and cultural spaces: Dom Macedo Costa—Bahia (1930–1960)]. *Projeto História* (São Paulo) 18 (May 1999): 361–379.

Souza, Robério S. *Tudo pelo trabalho livre! Trabalhadores e conflitos na pós abolição (Bahia 1892–1909)* [Everything for free labor! Workers and conflicts in post-abolition Bahia, 1892–1909]. Salvador: EDUFBA, 2011.

Stein, Stanley. *Vassouras: A Brazilian Coffee County, 1850–1890; The Roles of Planter and Slave in a Changing Plantation Society.* Cambridge, MA: Harvard University Press, 1957.

———. *Vassouras: Um Município Brasileiro do Café, 1850–1900* [Vassouras: A Brazilian coffee municipality, 1850–1900]. Translated by Vera Block Wrobel. Rio de Janeiro: Nova Fronteira, 1990.

Stuckey, Sterling. *Slave Culture: Nationalist Theory and the Foundations of Black America.* New York: Oxford University Press, 1987.

Thompson, E. P. *Costumes em comum: Estudos sobre a cultura popular tradicional.* Translated by Rosaura Eichemberg with a technical revision by Antônio Negro, Christina Meneguello and Paulo Fontes. São Paulo: Companhia das Letras, 1998. Portuguese translation of *Customs in Common: Studies in Traditional Popular Culture.* London: Merlin Press, 1991.

———. *Senhores e caçadores: A origem da Lei Negra.* Translated by Denise Bottmann. Rio de Janeiro: Paz e Terra, 1987. Portuguese translation of *Whigs and Hunters: The Origin of the Black Act.* London: Allen Lane, 1975.

Tomich, Dale W. "Contested Terrains: Houses, Provisions Grounds and the Reconstitution of Labour in Post Emancipation Martinique." In *From Chattel Slaves to Wage Slave: The Dynamics of Labour Bargaining in the Americas,* edited by Mary Turner, pp. 241–260. Bloomington: Indiana University Press, 1995.

———. "Houses, Provision Grounds and the Reconstitution of Labour in Post Emancipation Martinique." In *From Chattel Slaves to Wage Slaves: The Dynamics of Labour Bargaining in the Americas,* edited by Mary Turner, pp. 260–261. Bloomington: Indiana University Press, 1995.

———. *Slavery in the Circuit of Sugar: Martinique and the World Economy, 1830–1848.* Baltimore: Johns Hopkins University Press, 1990.

Turner, Mary, ed. *From Chattel Slaves to Wage Slaves: The Dynamics of Labour Bargaining in the Americas.* Bloomington: Indiana University Press, 1995.

Vilhena, Luís dos Santos. *A Bahia no século XVIII* [Bahia in the eighteenth century]. 3 vols. Salvador: Editora Itapuã, 1969.

Vogt, Carlos, Peter Fry, and Robert Slenes, eds. *Cafundó: A África no Brasil; Linguagem e Sociedade* [Cafundó: Africa in Brazil; Language and society]. São Paulo: Companhia das Letras, 1996.

Weinstein, Barbara. "The Decline of the Progressive Planter and the Rise of Subaltern Agency: Shifting Narratives of Slave Emancipation in Brazil." In *Reclaiming the Political in Latin American History,* edited by Gilbert M. Joseph, pp. 81–101. Durham, NC: Duke University Press, 2001.

———. "Erecting and Erasing Boundaries: Can We Combine the 'Indo' and the 'Afro' in Latin American Studies?" *Estudios Interdisciplinários de América Latina e el Caribe* 19, no. 1 (2008): 129–144.

———. "Postcolonial Brazil." In *The Oxford Handbook of Latin American History*, edited by José C. Moya, pp. 212–256. New York: Oxford University Press, 2011.

Wimberly, Fayette Darcel. "The African Liberto and the Bahian Lower Class: Social Integration in Nineteenth-Century Bahia, Brazil, 1870–1900." PhD dissertation, University of California, Berkeley, 1988.

———. "The Expansion of Afro-Bahian Religious Practices." In *Afro-Brazilian Culture and Politics: Bahia 1790s to 1990s*, edited by Hendrik Kraay, pp. 74–89. Armonk, NY: M. E. Sharpe, 1998.

Wissenbach, Maria Cristina Cortez. *Sonhos africanos, vivências ladinas: Escravos e forros em São Paulo (1850–1880)* [African dreams, ladino lives: Slaves and freed people in São Paulo (1850–1880)]. São Paulo, HUCITEC, 1998.

Xavier, Regina Célia Lima. *A conquista da liberdade: Libertos em Campinas na segunda metade do século XIX* [The conquest of liberty: Freed people in Campinas in the second half of the nineteenth century]. Campinas: CMU-UNICAMP, 1996.

Index

São João da Acutinga, 180
São Paulo, xii, xvi, xxv, 253n52
São Paulo province, 71, 249n15, 277n12, 277n16
São Pedro, Maria de, 6, 182
São Roque Parish, 136
São Sebastião, 6, 30, 31, 61, 231
São Sebastião das Cabeceiras do Passé Parish, 37
São Sebastião do Passé Parish, 91, 173, 207, 226, 227,
  254n19
Saturnino, 32, 39, 40, 42, 49
Sauípe, Baron of, 65, 151
Schwartz, Stuart, xiv, xv, xix, 12, 146, 251n16, 254n6,
  265n12, 267n38, 275n42
Scott, Rebecca, xx, xxvii, 213, 272n48, 272n54, 273n5
seignorial authority, 143, 151, 167, 242, 262n38
Sento Sé, 259n41
senzalas (slave quarters), 114, 176
Sergimirim River, 10, 251n14
Sergipe, 37, 214
sharecroppers (*colonos*), 16, 71, 155–56, 161, 271n39
Silva, Pedro Celestino da, 174, 280n43
Silva, Roberto Moreira da, 125, 129, 131
Silva Campos, João da, 30, 36, 48, 50, 53, 85–86, 129
Silvestre, 32, 33, 34, 39, 42, 46, 49
slave-master relationship, 55; conflict and tensions in,
  50, 53, 68, 117–18; devastation of, 71; documentation of, 31; emancipatory laws and, 22; post-
  abolition hierarchy of, 79; increased intervention
  of authorities in, 24, 51, 53; unraveling of, 44, 70
slavocrats, 49, 55, 66
slave owners, 113–14: abolition and, xvii, 65–68;
  customary prerogatives of, 52, 53; fears of, 71, 117;
  grant freedom, 66, 69–70, 74, 88; harshness of,
  xvi; murdered by slaves, xxiii–xxiv, 29–31, 42; organization by, 65–66; rituals of power of, 116; sell
  slaves, 60; slave lists kept by, xiii, xv, xxiv; slaves
  appeal to, 21; violence against slaves by, 29
slave revolts and rebellion, xxv, 20, 21, 35, 48, 57,
  115–16; against Carmelites, 37; of 1830s, 18; fears of,
  250n7; urban, xiv, 256n53
slavery, Brazilian: abolition and, xvi, 1; crisis of
  legitimacy of, xxiv, xxv, 28, 33, 50, 53, 66, 191;
  damage of, xiv, 237; final days of, 56, 68–73;
  historiography of, xii–xvii; internal economy of,
  xv, 17, 47; as moral constraint, 82; nature of, xii,
  xiv, xv; political support for, 250n11; radical dissociation between freedom and, xxiii; transition
  from, xii, 2, 3–4
slaves: as active participants in abolition, xvi, 28,
  260n49; baptisms of, 13, 32, 180–82, 186, 196;
  clothing for, 15–16, 115, 118; as collateral, 93; demographics of, 11–12, 13, 251n14; descendants of, 160–62,
  165; elderly, 24; food and rations for, 15, 20, 36,
  47, 48, 50, 146, 270nn13–15; as foremen, 40–41;
  gender ratio of, 12; as house servants, 57, 80, 82,

179; housing for, 114, 159, 176, 192; humanity of,
  xii; imprisonment of, 49; independence of, 18–20;
  indigenous people as, 10; lists of, xiii, 6, 12, 191;
  livestock raised by, 16; on Maracangalha, 114,
  115–23; mobility of, 20; names of, 177; news and,
  57; as personal servants, 116; at Pitinga, 191–202;
  plan for freedom, 87; promotions and rewards
  for, 16, 119, 251n16, 267n38; protests by, xii; rental
  of, 215; rights of, 22, 23; sales of, 60, 116, 117, 118,
  195, 208, 241; skilled in navigation, 57, 60, 63,
  110; as small farmers, 16, 18; surveillance of, xiv;
  survival strategies of, 6; terms for, xviii; violence
  by owners against, xiv, 29, 30; wages paid to, 14,
  62; work slowdowns and stoppages by, xvi, 74, 145.
  See also families, slave; fugitive slaves; resistance
  by slaves
slave trade, xi, 10, 11, 39, 250n7, 246n1
Slenes, Robert W., xxii, xxvii, 16, 146, 249n15, 270n14
social order, 85; abolition and, 79, 90; breakdown
  of social control and, 78, 187; hierarchy and, 82,
  109–10, 142, 237; patriarchalism and, 218; threats
  to, 86, 93, 106; traditional forms of, 142–43
social history, xii, xiv
Sociedade do Comércio, 118
Socorro Parish, 227
sources: account books, 15, 271n32; archival, xiii;
  birth records, 5, 163, 165, 177, 179, 201, 206; census
  records, 224–25; church records, xxi, 177, 182;
  civil records, xxi, 181, 183, 195, 199, 200, 201, 203,
  206; correspondence, 77, 87, 89, 90, 93, 94–95,
  97, 115–16, 116–18, 119–20, 143–44, 167–68; court
  and criminal records, 31, 39, 49, 207; depositions,
  106–7, 108–9, 127; documentary, 5; folklore, 30,
  31, 85–86; hospital records, 163, 218–19; itinerant
  laborers registry, 231; land registers, 113; legal records, xxiii, xxiv; novels, 83–87, 169, 173–74; plantation records, 153, 163, 177; police records, 68–69,
  104, 233; postmortem estate inventories, 5–6, 12,
  113, 114, 175–77, 191; probate records, xxiv; register
  of domestic servants, 230; slave lists, xiii, 6, 12, 191.
  See also newspapers; oral history and tradition
Subaé, Francisco Moreira de Carvalho, Count of,
  15–16, 17, 20, 21, 28, 69, 155, 156, 157
Subaé river, 10
subalterns, xiii, xxiii, 239, 263n42
subdelegados, 215, 269n80, 279n13, 283; of Conceição
  da Praia Parish, 61; of Mares Parish, 58; of Palame,
  92; of Passé Parish, 44; of Pilar Parish, 26, 60; of
  Pirajá Parish, 61; of Santana Parish, 25, 59; of São
  Francisco do Conde, 17, 104, 106, 122
subsistence plots. See *roças*
Suerdieck Company, 225
sugarcane, 16, 37, 119, 191; beets vs., 11; cutters of,
  15, *164*, 178, 180; drought and, 93, 94; harvest of,
  14–15, 19, 20, 31, 94, 178, 220, 254n6; grinding of,
  15, 20, 37, 82, 84, 94, 149–50, 153, 178; schedule of,

sugarcane (*continued*)

220; soils for, 114; weeding of, 15, 20, 31, 32, 149, 153, 254n6. See also *mel*

sugar culture and sugar industry: in Bahian Recôncavo, xvi, 1, 9–10, 11; brown, 210; Caribbean competition to, 93; cattle and, 267n51; crises of, 86, 90, 93–97, 140, 155, 156; declining prices of, 11, 93, 94–95, 144, 145; declining production of, 15–16, 95, 169; exports and exporters of, 95, 143–44; jeopardized, 122; modernization of, 218, 220, 272n58; molasses and, 90, 95, 176; output of, 176, 251n18; in Pernambuco's Zona da Mata, xxv; sacks for, 154; sale of, 119; sector of, 93; skilled workers in, 177, 179, 181, 275n42. See also sugarcane; sugar mills; sugar plantations

sugar mills, xix, 15, 20, 37, 82, 84, 93, 149–50, 159; accidents in, 220; cattle-powered, 125, 271n39; central (industrial), 94, 160, 165, 202, 219, 220; closing of, 152; at Cruz, 176, 179, 181, 183; at Maracangalha, 114, 116, 119, 133, 137; number of, 254n18; at Pitinga, 191; skilled labor in, 275n42; at Vila de São Francisco do Conde, 153. See also *usinas*

sugar plantations, xi, xix, 4, 250n4; abandoned, 212; abolition and, xvi, 63–64, 81, 85; administrative hierarchy of, 40; on Bay of All Saints, 57; cane field fires on, 97–101; of Carmelites, 37, 40; cemeteries on, 181; conflict and tension on, 18, 29–55, 93, 170, 172–73; converted to cattle ranches, 202; credit and capital on, 93–94, 118, 144, 147–48; daily work on, 179–80; economy of, xv, 93–94; *engenho*, xv, xix, 283; establishment of, 10; ex-slaves remain on, 163, 165–66, 169–70, 205; family ties on, 6; fences on, 93, 94, 97–99, 107–9, 122, 155, 157, 173, 179, 265n12; harvest on, 31, 140, 149; labor crisis on, 140; as locus of black communities, 166; main houses of, 151, 175–76, 191; management of, 18, 144–52; moral economy of, xvi; output of, xi; proximity of, 13; in Puerto Rico, 265n83; religion on, 176; restoration of order on, 88; slavery and, 7. *See also* families, planter; plantations; planters; *and under names of individual plantations*

suicide, 81, 174, 175

Sumidouro, 203

Sunday, as customary nonwork day, 14, 15, 18, 21, 45–46, 47, 50, 51, 53, 54, 146

survival strategies, 6; of ex-slaves, xvi, 104, 162, 166

Taboão, 241

Tanquinho da Feira, 186

Tapas (Nupes), 10

Tarquínio, Luís , 239, 282n5

telegraph, 74, 261n1

Teodora (Cruz Plantation), 188, 200

Terreiro de Jesus, 241

theft: of cattle, 99, 123, 124–33; by freedmen, 123–24; by slaves, 17, 256n48

Tibúrcio, 32, 34, 35, 39, 42, 50, 53

tobacco, 11, 37, 140, 143, 150, 155, 156, 203, 220, 272n50; cigar factories and, 140, 222, 225, 234, 235; industry of, 157–58; price of, 157; rolling cigars, 223

Tomich, Dale, 138, 251n19, 274n17

Torquato, Pedro, 32, 33–34, 39, 42, 43, 50

Tosta family, 167

trabalhador agrícola (agricultural worker), 205

trabalhador da enxada (field hand), 205

tradition, abolition and, 80, 84

transition from slavery to free labor, xvi, 143; controlled by landowners, 66, 72; at Maracangalha Plantation, 113–23; studies of, xii, 138, 140

Travassos, 83, 84, 85

Tupinambá Indians, 10

Umburanas, 170

Uncle Tom's Cabin (Stowe), 83

unemployment, 95, 96; of freedmen, 165

União Agrícola, 259n36

United States: African-Americans in, 4; "black" as term in, xviii–xix; ex-slaves in, xiii, xvii, 262n18; prohibitions against free blacks in, 242; research on slavery in, xv, xvi, 2–3; transition to freedom in, 22, 160

Universidade Estadual de Campinas (Unicamp), xxvi

Ursulina, 180, 181

usinas (industrialized central sugar mills), xix, 4, 160, 165, 202, 220, 265, 284

vagrancy, 99, 100, 102, 122, 140, 158, 213, 237

Valério, 168, 178, 180, 188

Veloso, Marcos Leão, 216, 217

Venância, 223, 280n36

Viação Férrea (Railway), 235

Vicente, 110, 112, 130, 131

Vila do São Francisco, 44, 60, 98, 101, 136, 153

Vila Viçosa, 92–93

Vila Viçosa, Antônio Joaquim Pires de Carvalho e Albuquerque, Baron of, 63, 65, 81–82, 83, 90, 93–94, 213, 250n11, 262n26

Vilhena, Luís dos Santos, 17–18, 108, 254n17

violence: against ex-slaves, 170, 173; by ex-slaves, 104–5; as form of control, xii, xiv; amongst freemen, 203, 209, 210, 233; by police, 239; against slaves, xiv, 29; against women, 185, 206–7, 208, 209, 215, 217, 234

Virginia (Cruz Plantation), 180, 181

Visconde Marinho (ship), 278n8

Vitória, 216, 217

Vitória Parish, 231

wage labor, wages, 71, 147, 151–52; demands for, 158; just, 151; plantation payrolls and, 153–55; transition from slavery and, 2, 140

Wanderley, Firmino, 104–5, 132
Weinstein, Barbara, xvii
West-Central Africa, 10
women, 222; from Africa, 181; as beggars, 223; as cane workers, 178, 180; cattle theft and, 131; as domestics, 163, 173, 177, 179, 180, 183, 189, 209, 218, 232; as factory workers, 222; as fugitive slaves, 24, 25, 60, 69; gender ratio of male slaves and, 12, 114, 191; as head of families, 199; pregnancy of, 60; as slave owners, 25, 113; as slaves, 35, 47–48, 80, 110–11, 114; as street vendors, 223, 269n5; violence against, 185, 206–9, 215, 217, 234, 274n28; as wet nurses, 229

Yorubas, 10. *See also* Nagôs